Speaking Management

Stephen Keith McGrath

Speaking Management

How to Spot Language Traps and Resolve Contested Management Terms

Springer

Stephen Keith McGrath
Business, Education, Law and Arts
University of Southern Queensland
Springfield, QLD, Australia

ISBN 978-981-16-2212-0 ISBN 978-981-16-2213-7 (eBook)
https://doi.org/10.1007/978-981-16-2213-7

This Springer imprint is published by the registered company Springer Nature Singapore Pte Ltd.
The registered company address is: 152 Beach Road, #21-01/04 Gateway East, Singapore 189721, Singapore

Preface

This book is about regaining control over the human tool we call language.

Its genesis was an investigation of governance that identified disagreement on a wide range of management terminology. This prompted questions as to how and why this type of problem could be occurring in so many different areas. Investigation led to identification of ten recurring language usage habits or patterns that cause confusion in word usage. These unfortunate habits have caused us to lose control over our own language relating to concepts where meaning is difficult to verify. The origins of some of these linguistic mistakes were traced back to ancient times. These mistakes or traps have had an impact well beyond the field of management and have bedevilled human communication ever since, inhibiting productivity across many fields.

This book provides a practical guide giving simple steps that enable 'fake' conflict to be avoided. In doing this, it challenges the philosophical foundation of much previous philosophical work. For example, it presents a linguistic solution to the problem of universals; it deconstructs deconstructionism; it proposes a resolution to the conflict between Popper and Wittgenstein (by identifying difficulties with Wittgenstein's 'family resemblance' concept, as well as, with Popper's views of definition and Russell's theory of descriptions); it challenges conventional religious thinking by separating the terms spiritual and ethereal.

By going back to such elementary basics, the book moves forward with surprising conclusions that challenge conventional wisdom in many fields.

Springfield, QLD, Australia — Stephen Keith McGrath

Acknowledgements

I wish to acknowledge my good friend and PhD supervisor Jon Whitty for his insightful reviews of my academic writing over many years.

Contents

1 **Introduction** 1

Part I Confusion in Language Usage

2 **The Ten Linguistic Traps** 9
References 10

3 **Key Difficulties of Language Usage** 11
3.1 Dichotomies 11
3.2 The Whole or the Sum of Parts – The Missing Couplings 12
3.3 Language Development 12
3.4 Classification Systems 13
3.5 Rushing Past Definition 14
References 14

4 **Defining Key Initial Terms** 17
4.1 Summary of Derived Definitions 17
4.2 Concept 18
4.3 Definition 18
4.4 Essence 19
4.5 Meaning 20
4.6 Normative 20
4.7 Purpose 21
4.8 Soul 22
References 22

5 **Defining Meaning and Truth** 23
5.1 Define 'Meaning' 23
5.2 Essentialism 32
5.3 Existentialism 32
5.4 Defining True and Truth 34
5.5 Relativism 37
5.6 Nominalism 38

5.7 Nihilism 38
5.8 Observation 39
References 39

6 Philosophical Examination of the Ten Linguistic Traps/Issues 41
6.1 Issue 1 Fact v Opinion (Attitudes) 41
6.2 Issue 2 Meaning v Representation 44
6.3 Issue 3 Word v Phrase Meanings 46
6.4 Issue 4 Dogma v Human Framework 48
6.5 Issue 5 Secular Essence v Ethereal Essence (Beliefs) 49
6.6 Issue 6 Intension v Extension 56
6.7 Issue 7 Objects v Concepts 57
6.8 Issue 8 Detail v Overview 61
6.9 Issue 9 Process v Content 66
6.10 Issue 10 Set v Sub-Set 68
6.11 Consequent Philosophical Problems 69
References 70

7 Resolution of Consequent Philosophical Problems 73
7.1 Wittgenstein's Family Resemblance Concept 73
7.2 Popper v Wittgenstein 78
7.3 Popper's Philosophy 80
7.3.1 Diarrhesis Versus Definition 80
7.3.2 Empiricism v Rationalism 82
7.3.3 Nominalism Versus Essentialism 84
7.3.4 Overall Evaluation 86
7.4 Derrida's Philosophy 88
7.4.1 Impact of the Mangle on Derrida's Philosophy 89
7.5 Summary Evaluation of All Considered Philosophers' Positions . . 90
7.6 Observations on Philosopher Positions 90
7.7 The Trend Away from Definitions 91
References 92

8 Development of a Theory of Meaning for Conceptual Terms 95
8.1 Clarity over Ambiguity 95
8.2 Qualia 96
8.3 Mathematics and the Definition of Conceptual Terms – Omitted Variables (OVB), Autoregression and Endogeneity 98
8.4 Generic Applicability 100
8.5 Definitional Position 101
8.6 Application 103
8.7 Features of the Mangle 103
References 104

9 **Implications of This Theory** ... 105
9.1 The Converse of Diarrhesis ... 105
9.2 The Problem of Universals ... 106
9.3 Essentially Contested Concepts ... 107
9.4 The Relationship Between Language and Mathematics ... 107
9.5 Support for the Mangle ... 107
9.6 Observations on the Axioms and Rules ... 109
9.7 Robustness of the Language Tool ... 110
References ... 111

Part II Resolving Terminology Confusion in Management and Project Management

10 **Governance** ... 115
10.1 The Definitional Method ... 116
10.1.1 Group Rules Pre-definition ... 116
10.1.2 Steps to Determine a Connotative (Intensional) Conventional Definition of Each Term ... 117
10.1.3 Group Rules Post-definition ... 118
10.2 Application of the Method ... 118
10.2.1 Key Definitional Issues ... 118
10.2.2 Summary of Definitions ... 119
10.2.3 Framework for Governing an Organisational Entity ... 119
10.3 Observations and Conclusions ... 120
References ... 121

11 **Power Defined (Part 1): Power and Its Exercise** ... 123
11.1 Introduction ... 123
11.2 Definitional Confusion Regarding Power Terminology ... 124
11.3 Is Power Really an Essentially Contested Concept? ... 124
11.4 Why Is Definition of the Word Power Important? ... 125
11.5 The Ontology of Definition ... 126
11.6 Approach ... 127
11.7 Method ... 129
11.8 Group Rules Post Definition ... 130
11.9 Group Rules Pre Definition ... 130
11.10 Define 'Authority' ... 131
11.11 Define 'Legitimate' and 'Legitimacy' ... 135
11.12 Define 'Power' ... 138
11.13 Define 'Influence' ... 149
11.14 Summary of Definitions ... 151
11.15 Analysis and Conclusion ... 152
Appendix ... 152
References ... 166

12 Power Defined (Part 2): Enablers, Mechanisms, Tools and Channels of Power 169
12.1 Introduction 169
12.2 Define 'Direct' 170
12.3 Define 'Control' 172
12.4 Define 'Regulate' 173
12.5 Define 'Regulation' 174
12.6 Group Rules Post Definition 175
12.7 Summary of Definitions 176
12.8 Building the Machinery of Power 176
12.9 Testing the Machinery of Power 179
12.9.1 Government 179
12.9.2 General Management 181
12.9.3 Project Management 181
12.10 Driving the Machinery of Power 181
12.11 Analysis and Conclusion 184
Appendix 185
References 196

13 Ethics, Morality, Values, Principles and Beliefs 197
13.1 Introduction 197
13.2 Literature Review of Ethics and Definitional Confusion 198
13.3 Approach 200
13.4 Method 201
13.5 Group Rules Pre-definition 201
13.6 Define Principles 203
13.7 Define Values 204
13.8 Define Ethics 210
13.9 Define Beliefs 216
13.10 Define Morals 222
13.11 Group Rules Post Definition 225
13.12 Summary of Definitions 226
13.13 Observations on the Refining Method and Its Application 227
13.13.1 On the Refining Method 227
13.13.2 On the Application of the Refining Method 227
13.13.3 Implications 227
13.14 Conclusions 228
Appendix 229
References 243

14 Who Are 'Good' Morals/Ethics Good for? 245
14.1 Introduction 245
14.2 Ethics Chapter Definitions 245
14.3 Literature Review 246
14.3.1 Collaboration Models 247
14.3.2 Interaction Models 249
14.3.3 Communications Models 249

14.4 Approach 250
14.4.1 Definitional Space 251
14.4.2 Group Allegiances 251
14.4.3 Individual Communication Process 253
14.5 Method 254
14.6 The Ethical Models 255
14.6.1 Ethical Cycle – A Map of Terminology 255
14.6.2 Ethical Eye – A Map of Allegiances 256
14.6.3 Communication Process 257
14.7 Observations 261
14.7.1 User Requirements 261
14.7.2 Adherence to Principles 261
14.7.3 Universal Morality 262
14.7.4 Standard of Proof 262
14.7.5 Normativity and Religion 262
14.7.6 Religious Texts 263
14.7.7 Reification 263
14.7.8 Proscriptive Rules 263
14.7.9 Truth in Language 263
14.7.10 Happiness Versus Reality 264
14.8 Implications for Ethical Schools of Thought 264
14.9 Conclusions 265
References 266

15 Leadership and Strategic Management 267
15.1 Introduction 267
15.2 Definitional Confusion Regarding Leadership, Strategy and Management Terminology 268
15.2.1 Strategy 268
15.2.2 Leadership and Management 268
15.2.3 Strategic Management 269
15.3 Approach 269
15.4 Method 269
15.5 Group Rules Pre-definition 271
15.5.1 Group Pre-definition Rule 1 – Select the Group of Terms to Be Defined 271
15.5.2 Group Pre-definition Rule 2 – Determine the Order of Definition 272
15.5.3 Group Pre-definition Rule 3 – Definitional Terms Requiring Prior Definition 272
15.6 Define 'Leadership' 273
15.7 Define 'Strategy' 276
15.8 Define 'Management' 281
15.9 Define 'Strategic Management' 284

15.10 Group Rules Post Definition 285
15.11 Summary of Definitions 285
15.12 Observations and Refinements on the Method and Its Application 286
15.12.1 On the Method 286
15.12.2 On the Application of the Method 286
15.12.3 Implications 286
15.13 Conclusions 287
Appendix 288
References 291

16 Accountability and Responsibility 293
16.1 Application of the Definitional Refining Method 293
16.2 Practitioner Usage Issues/Considerations 294
16.3 Summary of Definitions 295
16.4 Implications of these Definitions 295
16.5 Sources of Liability/Accountability 295
16.6 Responsibility Assignment Matrices (RAMs) and Position Descriptions (PDs) 296
16.7 A RAM Is a Responsibility, Not an Accountability Assignment Matrix 296
16.8 RAM Coding Conventions and Task Specification 297
16.9 Blurring of Boundaries 298
16.10 Observations and Conclusions 299
References 300

17 Stakeholders 301
17.1 Application of the Definitional Refining Method 302
17.2 Key Definitional Considerations 302
17.3 Summary of Definitions 302
17.3.1 Impact on and Relationship with Previous Stakeholder Categorisations 303
17.4 The Stakeholder Locus of Interest 303
17.5 New Stakeholder Category Definitions 304
17.6 Interpretation and Relationship to Previous Classifications 305
17.7 Primary, Secondary & Tertiary Stakeholders 306
17.8 Stakeholder Theory – A Company or an Activity Base? 308
17.9 What Type of Stakeholders Are Customers? 309
17.10 Rationale for Customer Labelling 310
17.11 Customer Terminology 311
17.12 Veracity Check 311
17.13 Summary of all Definitions 312
17.14 Observations 313
17.15 Conclusions 314
References 315

Part III How to Speak Management and Know What We Are All Talking About

18 How to Speak Management 319
18.1 Context 319
18.2 Re-ordering of Rule Numbers 320
18.3 Accountability and Responsibility 321
18.4 Governance 323
18.5 Power 325
18.6 Stakeholders and Customers 326
18.7 Leadership 328
18.8 Ethics 330
18.9 Meaning, Soul, Essence and Truth 331
18.10 Avoiding the Disaster Cycle 333
References 334

19 Observations and Conclusions 335
19.1 Observations 335
19.2 Conclusion 336
Reference 337

Appendix – Lexicon of Contested and Associated Terms 339
References 342

List of Figures

Fig. 6.1 **Popper's table of ideas.** (Sourced from Popper (2002)) 62

Fig. 10.1 Framework for governing an organisational entity 120

Fig. 12.1 The machinery of power 176

Fig. 14.1 Ethical cycle – a map of terminology 256

Fig. 14.2 The ethical eye – a map of allegiances 257

Fig. 14.3 Communication process model 258

Fig. 14.4 Haidt's Social Intuitionist Model 260

Fig. 17.1 Stakeholder Locus of Interest 303

List of Tables

Table 2.1 Linguistic traps causing definitional confusion ... 10

Table 4.1 Derived refined definitions of philosophical terms ... 18

Table 5.1 Definitions of 'mean' ... 24
Table 5.2 Definitions of 'meaning' ... 28

Table 11.1 Definitions of 'authority' ... 152
Table 11.2a Definitions of 'legitimate' ... 153
Table 11.2b Definitions of 'legitimacy' ... 156
Table 11.3 Definitions of 'power' ... 157
Table 11.4 Definitions of 'influence' ... 162

Table 12.1 Definitions of 'direct' ... 185
Table 12.2 Definitions of 'control' ... 188
Table 12.3 Definitions of 'regulate' ... 190
Table 12.4 Definitions of 'regulation' ... 192
Table 12.5 Mechanisms, tools and channels of power ... 193

Table 13.1a Definitions of 'principle' (n) ... 229
Table 13.1b Definitions of 'principles' (n)(pl) ... 232
Table 13.2a Definitions of 'value' (n) ... 232
Table 13.2b Definitions of 'values' (n)(pl) ... 236
Table 13.3 Definitions of 'ethics' (n)(pl) ... 236
Table 13.4a Definitions of 'belief' (n) ... 238
Table 13.4b Definitions of 'beliefs' (n)(pl) ... 239
Table 13.5a Definitions of 'moral' (a) ... 240
Table 13.5b Definitions of 'morals' ... 242

Table 15.1a Definitions of 'lead' (vt) ... 288
Table 15.1b Definitions of 'leader' ... 289
Table 15.1c Definitions of 'leadership' ... 289

Table 15.2 Definitions of 'strategy' 290
Table 15.3a Definitions of 'manage' 290
Table 15.3b Definitions of 'management' 291

Table 18.1 Traps and rule numbering 321
Table 18.2 Key features of accountability and responsibility 322
Table 18.3 Key features of governance terms 324
Table 18.4 Key features of power terms 325
Table 18.5 Key features of stakeholder terms 327
Table 18.6 Key features of leadership terms 329
Table 18.7 Key features of ethics terms 330
Table 18.8 Key features of Meaning, soul, essence and truth 332

Table A.1 Definitions from Parts I and II 339
Table A.2 Project management definitions 342

Chapter 1
Introduction

Have ever found yourself confidently saying something you thought anyone in ear-shot would agree with, only to find yourself being rejected, ostracised or subjected to ridicule, harassment or worse? If so, read on; this book explores how such unintended outcomes can be accidentally generated by the way we use language and it also gives tools for taking positive action to avoid them.

Of course, these distressing outcomes can also be generated by other things such as lack of knowledge, experience, cunning, guile or awareness of different ethnic, organisational or personal background circumstances, experiences, or culture. They can also be generated by desire to get something from the other person/ people without adequately considering what their needs might be. However, there is another hidden set of factors that has recently been discovered through the research described in this book. These are underlying structural patterns in the way we habitually use language. These can accidentally generate unsatisfactory outcomes in areas of life ranging from personal relationships to world peace.

Language evolved for attracting attention and describing objects. Until these tasks could be accomplished, there was no hope of conducting more esoteric activities, like discussions of concepts that cannot be seen. The unsatisfactory outcomes mentioned above are really about concepts that exist in the mind, notwithstanding the physical injury that can result. As we develop technologically, an increasing number of new concepts that have no visible physical existence become necessary. Consider, for example, ultrasound, X-rays and radiation, along with computer programs and mental concepts such as governance, resilience and sustainability - terms that were not used in earlier centuries.

This increase in linguistic load upon a tool not 'designed' to handle it magnifies the impact of any difficulty we have in reaching a common understanding of what the new words we invent actually mean, or rather, represent. It is hardly surprising that a tool developed for primitive uses may have some difficulty in accommodating more advanced uses. However the analysis described in this book found that that the tool we call language can accommodate the new conceptual use it is now being put

S. K. McGrath, *Speaking Management*,
https://doi.org/10.1007/978-981-16-2213-7_1

to, but only if something is substituted for the physical verification process that is readily present for attracting attention or describing objects – namely associating particular sounds with sight and touch.

This is not surprising when viewed from an evolutionary perspective, but it is not one we would normally consider, even though it is somewhat obvious in other areas of life. For example, we don't expect a reciprocating engine to move, unless we develop the concept of locomotion and support it with wheels in a device that we have come to call a locomotive or a car. Similarly, we don't expect a reciprocating engine to fly, unless we combine it with locomotion, develop the concept of flight and support it with something we have come to call an aeroplane. It is therefore not inconsistent with our other developmental experiences to consider that the tool we call language may need something else to support its application in transitioning from objects to concepts. Of course, that is just illustration by analogy, which is not the same as proof of existence, but it suffices to demonstrate the point. The rigour of proof is contained in more substantial investigations that are documented in this book.

The verification process identified in this book as being necessary for concepts, is the process of reaching explicit agreement on what the words denoting concepts actually mean. This sounds simple and obvious in theory and there are many concepts that are not contested and where dictionary definition is quite adequate. But for contested concepts, this theoretical simplicity can have practical difficulty akin to herding cats. With contested concepts, peoples' egos, reputations and consequently, belief systems, consultancies, incomes and even religions can get built around the various understandings (or misunderstandings) of them. This can make reaching agreement on meaning an almost intractable problem. Furthermore, previous lack of recognition of these problematic language usage patterns has led to development of beliefs that have become accepted 'truth' and these beliefs can be difficult to abandon. Adherence to belief requires conflict resolution, ranging from negotiation through to war. Recognising and dealing with these linguistic traps is therefore an important issue for achieving relationship happiness and world peace. The question is how to do it.

Fortunately, while the existence of these language usage traps was a difficult realisation to come to, and the mechanisms contributing to them were quite difficult to discover, once pointed out, they are relatively easy to understand, as are the ways of avoiding them. The problem is that knowledge of all the various interpretations of the meaning of a particular conceptual word is spread across multiple individuals, who may resist accepting any interpretation other than their own. This is a circumstance where neither democratic nor totalitarian processes can produce satisfactory resolution (agreement on meaning) without someone's sense of logic and rightness being violated. Avoiding that outcome requires some individual to research all the meanings, do the difficult and time-consuming work of determining the key essence of all those meanings, and transparently documenting their reasoning. Once that is done, it cannot be logically challenged on the basis of predisposition, preference, bias or opinion. It can only be so challenged by identifying any issue it may have missed or by challenging some logic in its analysis. Furthermore, for such challenge to be useful, it would have to propose an adjusted meaning that accommodates all the previously documented considerations as well as the new issue identified. It is unlikely that a practitioner could devote the time that would be necessary to do this, let alone with the rigour to withstand critical academic scrutiny. So, it is more likely to be done by a scholar.

The purpose of writing 16 papers for my PhD, when a handful would have sufficed to just get the piece of paper, was to develop a comprehensive set of rigorous resolutions of contested terms across the field of management. This was done to comprehensively demonstrate the need to do so through documenting the existing confusion and providing a substantial body of knowledge with the capacity to generate agreement. That agreement is not something that can be reached by either vote or mandate. Different people can have different understandings of the same term which may be equally valid, as no one person's view is necessarily better than anyone else's; that is until the necessary work has been done to determine the essence of meaning of the contested term. This requires major effort from an informed, independent individual to have any chance of succeeding, otherwise efforts descend into attempts to influence in favour of one competing opinion or ideology, and the outcome ceases to depend upon truth or logic.

This book contains such work for contested terms across the field of management. It is the agreement with and any modifications to the terms listed in the lexicon in the Appendix of this book that then become important. This book cannot alone bring about agreement, but it proposes the basis upon which it can be reached.

There are many different understandings of various concepts and being able to reconcile these is an important but easily overlooked communication skill. Techniques for reconciling meanings are practical skills that can be incorporated into our emotional quotient (EQ) as a mechanical process; something that can be learned as well as taught.

This book will be useful for people who find themselves in any governance or leadership role. The techniques in this book are not obvious; they are hidden, like culture and personal experience. Unless we adequately define and agree the meanings of our concepts, we can easily understand them differently to others without knowing it. This is a key realisation and skill for managing relationships.

As soon as we start talking about concepts, we need a metaphorical stick to spring the traps hidden in the leaves on the forest floor, so we don't step in them and get caught.

The ten linguistic rules in this book can be applied to problems where a stalemate has been reached, or where people are talking at cross purposes, or where it is difficult to grasp what the problem really is. They can be applied when you have been talking about some topic where you had the feeling the other person didn't have a clue what it was they were talking about, or where you realised long afterwards that they had a completely different understanding of that concept to what you did. These are the tell-tale signs of falling into linguistic traps. Looking through the list of the ten traps and the rules for avoiding them is the means of identifying them. Seeking the essential meaning of competing usages is the key to addressing them.

Life is replete with such linguistic circumstances that can lead to conflict breaking out. Multiple such instances were documented in the papers of my PhD, some of which are included as chapters in this book. So it is worthwhile removing the linguistic contribution to any conflict before starting to fight about it, whether it is between individuals or countries; it makes little sense for conflict to continue over what may just turn out to be a misunderstanding of the meaning of a word.

The source material for this book came from the fields of organisational management and organisational project management. While it is potentially dangerous to generalise, the lessons learned here were linguistic. Language is used in every area of life. So the fields studied simply presented a microcosm of the experience of managing life in general. The work identified linguistic traps, so it is not field-specific conclusions that are being generalised here. Rather, it is the fact that problems with a general tool (language) have been identified and it is most unlikely that those problems would be restricted to just the area in which they were first noticed.

To make sense of the findings of the case studies that were conducted, the philosophical underpinnings of these linguistic problems were investigated. This required sense to be made of some areas of contest between science and religion. It became evident that some of the hidden, conflict-generating traps in common language usage date back to Aristotle and Plato. This led to the realisation that there are structural traps that have occurred in the evolution of our language, and that these have produced linguistic difficulty that has profoundly affected the fields of philosophy, religion and spirituality.

A key realization enabling identification of these difficulties was that words are just noises humans make, which can be agreed upon to mean anything. But once agreement has been reached within a particular language group, then the meaning can be fixed. It is not until that point has been reached that we can actually know what anyone else is talking about in relation to those concepts. This renders futile any conflict occurring prior to this point.

This book deals with use of the language mechanism for sharing power between groups of people to satisfy everybody's need-to-know and to be productive. It arose from PhD research into the governance relationship between projects and their parent organisations. That research kept running up against roadblocks relating to confusion over definitions. It soon became apparent that no progress would be made until that issue was addressed. That became a substantial task, demonstrating that lack of adequate definition was itself a key issue. A method for resolving definitional confusion in groups of related terms was then developed and applied to many areas of management. Analysis of these definitional exercises indicated there were ten separate definitional errors or linguistic traps that were commonly occurring. These are outlined in this book, which is in four parts, three formal Parts and an Appendix, as outlined below.

Part I identifies the ten commonly occurring linguistic traps that lead to disagreement and conflict. It explains what can be done about them in practical terms that practitioners can relate to. It then examines their philosophical origins, leading to proposal of a resolution that has academic rigour. It identifies how ambivalence and even opposition to definition has become accepted in some areas of philosophy, contributing greatly to conceptual confusion. This is traced this back to the family resemblance concept developed by Ludwig Wittgenstein in his deterministic, modernist attempt to codify the relationship between words, mathematics and meaning. This failed, and produced the famous stalemate between Wittgenstein and Popper, as described in the book Wittgenstein's Poker. The issues surrounding this stalemate can be removed by removing the contributing definitional errors of both philosophers.

Part II contains case studies that develop a definitional refining method and then test it in repeated applications to various areas of management. Its chapters first demonstrate that such unnecessary conflict exists, before applying the method to them, producing clear non-overlapping definitions of the various concepts. This provides a transparent means for avoiding linguistic confusion and for reaching agreement on meaning. The chapters deal with management terms where disagreement and conflict commonly occurs, namely power, governance, ethics, leadership and management. Where possible, the definitional space is mapped, providing useful visual representations, some of which enable the range of previous theories to be located within them. Some of these representations are further developed into various mechanisms and models that are also susbsequently tested.

Part III is a summarised version of Parts I and II, containing tips on how to speak management and know what you are talking about, akin to an 'idiots' or 'dummies' guide.

The Appendix contains a lexicon of all 70 contested management and general terms defined in this book, developed from applying the new principles and rules. It also contains definitions of a further 18 contested but more specialised project management terms sourced from other published applications of these new principles and rules.

For the book to present a comprehensive, complete argument, it was necessary to include both the scholarly reasoning and the practical outcomes. Consequently, the table of contents is quite detailed so that practitioners, scholars and general readers alike can skip the sections of lesser interest to them while still being able to find sufficient of the argument to satisfy their need for explanation and to use the tools presented.

Practitioners as well as casual and non-academic readers may wish to start at Part III and then select other sections that may interest them.

Part I
Confusion in Language Usage

Chapter 2
The Ten Linguistic Traps

Table 2.1 below lists all ten traps (or issues as they were referred to in the research (McGrath 2019)) that Part I of this book finds are causing definitional confusion. Each issue has been assigned a shorthand label that highlights its underlying dichotomy.

The rest of Part I investigates the philosophical issues surrounding these traps. To put this in context, the nature of dichotomies, their relevance to governance (which was where this work started), the origins of language and the advantages and disadvantages of classification systems are first briefly reviewed.

S. K. McGrath, *Speaking Management*,
https://doi.org/10.1007/978-981-16-2213-7_2

Table 2.1 Linguistic traps causing definitional confusion

#	Shorthand label	Definitional issue
1	Fact v opinion (attitudes)[a]	Normativity resulting from unwarranted inclusion of attitudes.
2	Meaning v representation	Seeking meaning in the words themselves rather than in what they denote or signify
3	Word v phrase meanings	Failing to identify silent or assumed qualifiers resulting in unwarranted inclusion of items.
4	Dogma v human framework	Regarding frameworks as dogma or truth rather than as only a human representation of it, producing a 'blinkered' approach.
5	Secular v ethereal essence (beliefs)[a]	Normativity from inclusion of beliefs arising from not defining in terms of secular essence, allowing definition to stray outside the 4 dimensions we have physical access to.
6	Intension v extension	Defining terms by extension resulting in key omissions.
7	Objects v concepts	Applying linguistic realisations/ principles appropriate only for concepts as if they were also applicable to objects.
8	Detail v overview	Using precision/ detailed methods for understanding the internal workings of an entity, leading to infinite regress in circumstances where only sufficient detail for communication clarity is needed.
9	Process v content	Content being inappropriately included in process and processes appropriate to particular content being applied to another content area where it was inappropriate.
10	Set v sub-set	Drawing a conclusion about a set from a sub-set when the conclusion is not applicable to wider application.

[a]The distinction between attitudes and beliefs comes from Copi and Cohen (1990) who use these categories to separate genuine disputes from those that are merely verbal. In this book, belief is equated to dogma and attitude is equated to preference

References

Copi, I. M., & Cohen, C. (1990). *Introduction to logic*. Macmillan.

McGrath, S. K. (2019). *What is project governance? Disclosing the source of confusion and revealing the essence of governance*. PhD Thesis, University of Southern Queensland.

Chapter 3
Key Difficulties of Language Usage

There are several features of language usage outlined here that can lead us into accidentally setting these linguistic traps for ourselves.

3.1 Dichotomies

The Oxford dictionary defines dichotomy as "a division or contrast between two things that are or are represented as being opposed or entirely different". This means that there are things that are mutually exclusive. For example, Descartes rationalised the mind/ body dichotomy (Descartes & Cottingham, 1996) which then introduced for him the problem of how they are connected, as he was talking about human beings. Descartes' dichotomy had both scientific and religious motivation according to Skirry (2018), who also noted that his religious motivation was to show that "mind or soul *can* exist without the body", but he stopped short of being able to demonstrate that the soul is immortal.

Any such distinction regarding the internal workings of any living entity has to be imagined or exist only in our minds, as the entity itself exists and functions; and so in the natural state, all things within an entity are inextricably connected together, and no such distinction can actually physically exist. So it is the existence in our minds of concepts that can be mutually exclusive that require dealing with. Dichotomies can be secular or ethereal and Descartes focused on one that contained both aspects.

S. K. McGrath, *Speaking Management*,
https://doi.org/10.1007/978-981-16-2213-7_3

3.2 The Whole or the Sum of Parts – The Missing Couplings

The research described in this book initially focused on governance and settled on the matter that the word governance is a sign to a meaning that things (some parts of the entity) need to be coupled (connected) together in such a way that this coupling brings about the capability to direct and control the entity. Governance is the gestalt, the 'besides' in Aristotle's "the whole is something *besides* the parts" (Cohen, 2016, S13) of the entity that enables it to be directed and controlled. It is an emergent quality, formed from the relationship the parts have with each other.

There are many things that have been coupled together in our thinking about these subjects that present difficulties. Many dichotomies were detected from the analytical and empirical work reported in this book and these are listed in the ten traps in Table 2.1.

The metaphor of the blind men appraising an elephant can be used to demonstrate the difficulties of appraising governance; everyone conceptualizes it from the perspective of their own experience of it. However, this metaphor breaks down insofar as the elephant is concerned as it is actually an entity that does exist, whereas the concept of governance exists only in our minds and in the instantiations of its various artefacts. Nevertheless, the analogy of blindness in the observers is useful as they cannot see what it is that exists nor realize that it actually exists across all of the parts surveyed.

Therefore, to get to the essence of governance, it was necessary to look across its various representations/instantiations/particulars/frameworks, remove unwarranted inclusions and determine things that are common across all instantiations of it, without ignoring the connections between all its elements.

3.3 Language Development

Pinker and Bloom (2011) consider that language has evolved and been shaped by natural selection. Carstairs-McCarthy (2015) note that the earliest direct evidence of written language is no more than about 5000 years old while the origins of spoken language go back much earlier than that. They note "there are no uncontroversial counterparts in the fossil record for specific stages in linguistic evolution" (Carstairs-McCarthy, 2015). Lewis et al. (2017) list over 7000 languages spoken in the world, however Carstairs-McCarthy (2015) note that language appears to have evolved only once (unlike the eye which has evolved quite differently in octopuses, mammals and insects). They therefore reason that the acquisition of speech must have happened before the contemporary human group became separated by the breakup of Gondwanaland 40 to 60,000 years ago and after our ancestors became bipedal, producing the L-shaped vocal tract. They note it also seems likely that it occurred after 200,000 years ago from both archaeological evidence and statistical calculations based upon DNA.

Carstairs-McCarthy (2015) note that apes (whose vocal tracts are not suitable for speech sounds and whose brains have not co-evolved to be able to process speech) were successfully taught sign language in the 1970s and he considered that:

> One effect of the ape language experiments was to give new life to the old idea that language in humans may have originated in gesture, and only later been transferred to the vocal channel (Armstrong et al., 1995). One of the attractions of this proposal has always been that it seems to provide a solution to the problem of how humans originally learned to handle the arbitrary relationship between words and meaning… (but this) rubicon … was almost certainly crossed by our primate ancestors long before the appearance of hominoids.

This view that the relationship between words and meaning is arbitrary implies that words cannot be said to constitute meaning; they can only convey it – in over 7000 different ways/sound groups. Words are therefore a 'sign to' something rather than being something of themselves.

3.4 Classification Systems

Eppler et al. (2011) outline the advantages and pitfalls of typologies, listing advantages as to "make sense… by distinguishing items or phenomena based on their similarity… reduce complexity, provide a systematic overview, facilitate detailed comparisons, enable a change of perspectives, and help in structuring observations or imagining new solutions". They also note that the goals of any classification are the minimization of within-group variance and maximization of between-group variance, i.e. they seek within-group homogeneity. They note that "segmentation, according to most scholars in the field, has to exhibit the following traits… consistent, unique classificatory principles… the categories are mutually exclusive (non-overlapping); the system is complete (all items can be placed in a group)". (Eppler et al., 2011).

They list the potential disadvantages/risks associated with classifications as:

> their tendency to render concrete those items, that are in short-term flux, long-term evolution, or poorly understood; and to reify items that are not so neat and tidy in the first place… (and they may) have an inertia that marginalizes alternative viewpoints and under-emphasize important attributes… (such as) the loss of information due to generalization inherent in classifications… framing effects… (which) limit creativity and the ability to "think outside of the box"… (and) may lead to stereotypical thinking and false dichotomies taking things apart that naturally belong together. (Eppler et al., 2011).

They also commented on the relevance of typologies, noting there is a need to sort and arrange things to achieve successful outcomes and that "Convenience, economy and efficiency are the bases of classification." (Eppler et al., 2011).

This gives a clue as to the need for and limitations of any conceptual framework that is developed to explain anything. A framework is basically a classification system that can be both a gift and a curse from the experienced insightful practitioner; it can be very useful in most cases while also being false and misleading at the margins. Reification of any framework can then lead to marginalisation of people at those margins. Words describing concepts are simply classifications of things and so run the risks associated with classification.

3.5 Rushing Past Definition

The importance of definition has been recognized for a very long time. Smith (2014) notes that "The definition was an important matter for Plato", "Concern with answering the question "What is so-and-so?" are at the centre of the majority of Plato's dialogues" and "Aristotle himself traces the quest for definitions back to Socrates". Thomas Hobbes (1588–1679) said:

> When a man's discourse beginneth not at definitions, it beginneth either at some other contemplation of his own, and then it is still called opinion; or it beginneth at some saying of another, of whose ability to know the truth, and of whose honesty in not deceiving, he doubteth not; and then the discourse is not so much concerning the thing than the person; and the resolution is called Belief and Faith." Hobbes (1996).

John Locke (1632–1704) asked:

> whether the greatest part of the disputes in the world are not merely verbal, and … if the terms they are made in were defined, and reduced in their signification (as they must be where they signify anything) to determined collections of the simple ideas they do or should stand for, those disputes would not end of themselves, and immediately vanish" Locke (1690).

John Stuart Mill (1806–1873) said

> It would, however, be a complete misunderstanding … to think that because a name has not at present an ascertained connotation, it is competent to anyone to give it such a connotation at his own choice. The meaning of a term actually in use is not an arbitrary quantity to be fixed, but an unknown quantity to be sought (Mill, 1874).

Before proceeding to the ten issues identified as causing definitional confusion in management terms, there are several key terms which require prior definition. This is done below by applying a cut-down version of the process described in Chap. 10, known as the full Mangle and referred to here as 'the mini-Mangle', which accepts the Oxford dictionary without surveying other dictionaries, reduces its definition to an essential definition, and ranges across the issues identified in the Mangle without writing to its formal structure.

References

Armstrong, D. F., Stokoe, W. C. & Wilcox, S. E. (1995). *Gesture and the nature of language*. Cambridge: Cambridge University Press.

Carstairs-McCarthy, A. (2015). Origins of language. In M. Aronoff & J. Rees-Miller (Eds.), *The handbook of lingusitics*. Wiley.

Cohen, S. M. (2016). Aristotle's metaphysics. In Zalta, E. N. (Ed.), *The Stanford encyclopedia of philosophy* (Winter 2016 Edition)

Descartes, R., & Cottingham, J. (1996). *Meditations on first philosophy: With selections from the objections and replies*. Cambridge University Press.

Eppler, M. J., Hoffmann, F. & Pfister, R. (2011). Rigor and relevance in management typologies: Assessing the quality of qualitative classifications, *mcm institute working paper,* Vol. 1 No. July 2011, University of St. Gallen.

Hobbes, T. (1996). *Leviathan*. Oxford University Press.

Lewis, M. P., Simons, F. G., Fennig, D. C., & Summer Institute of Linguistics. (2017). *Ethnologue®: Languages of Africa and Europe*. SIL International.

Locke, J. (1690). An essay concerning human understanding. In J. Manis (Ed.), *Electronics classics series*. Hazleton.

Mill, J. S. (1874). *A system of logic, ratiocinative and inductive*. Harper & Brothers.

Pinker, S., & Bloom, P. (2011). Natural language and natural selection. *Behavioral and Brain Sciences, 13*(4), 707–727.

Skirry, J. (2018). *Rene descartes: The mind-body distinction* [Online], Internet encyclopedia of philosophy.. Available: http://www.iep.utm.edu/descmind/.. Accessed 17 July 2018.

Smith, R. (2014). Aristotle's logic. In Zalta, E. N. (Ed.) *The Stanford encyclopedia of philosophy* (Spring 2014 Edition).

Chapter 4
Defining Key Initial Terms

In analysing the ten traps, the key terms identified as requiring prior definition were: definition, meaning, essence and soul. In defining meaning, it was necessary to first define truth. The term 'concept', which is pivotal to the argument presented here, is included below for completeness, as is the term 'normative' which is used throughout. The term 'purpose' is also used in resolving some of these definitions and so has also been included.

As many of the terms have independent application across many fields, the order of definition is unimportant and so they are presented alphabetically, with the exception of 'meaning' which is presented as a separate chapter below due to its length.

The definitional method ranges from simply accepting the Oxford dictionary definition, through a mini-Mangle approach, to full formal application of the Mangle (for the term "meaning") as appropriate to the term being defined. Resolution of within-group consistency issues is done within each term and cross-referenced to the other terms where necessary.

4.1 Summary of Derived Definitions

The definitions derived below are presented in Table 4.1.

S. K. McGrath, *Speaking Management*,
https://doi.org/10.1007/978-981-16-2213-7_4

Table 4.1 Derived refined definitions of philosophical terms

Term	Definition
Concept	*An abstract idea*
Define	*To state what is signified by a term*
Definition	*A statement of what is signified by a term*
Essence	*A property or group of properties of something without which it would not be what it is*
Essential definition	A *definition in terms of essence only*
Mean	*Intend to convey*
Meaning	*What is intended to be conveyed*
Meaning of life	*Nil*. The purpose of life is a separate question that does make sense.
Normative	*Including an opinion*
Purpose	*The reason for which something is done or created or for which something exists*
Soul	*Life-force*
Truth	*The quality of being in accordance with the facts*

4.2 Concept

The word 'concept' is not one that is colloquially confused or contested, and so the default position of using the Oxford Dictionary and reducing it to its essential content can be adopted.

The Oxford Dictionary definition of concept is an abstract idea. This is already an essential definition and so can be accepted. This will be used in discussing Issue 7 below.

The word 'concept' will therefore be defined here as *an abstract idea*.

4.3 Definition

The term 'definition' is not one whose everyday usage is uncertain or prone to causing contention and so the default position of using the Oxford dictionary and reducing it to its essential content can be adopted.

The Oxford Dictionary (accessed on 28/1/2017) defines 'define' (verb) as:

1. State or describe exactly the nature, scope, or meaning of.
   - 1.1. Give the meaning of (a word or phrase), especially in a dictionary.
   - 1.2. Make up or establish the character or essence of.
2. Mark out the boundary or limits of.
   - 2.1. Make clear the outline of; delineate.

Origin: Late Middle English (also in the sense 'bring to an end'): from Old French definer, from a variant of Latin definire, from de- (expressing completion) + finire 'finish' (from finis 'end').

It also defines 'definition' (noun) as:

1. A statement of the exact meaning of a word, especially in a dictionary.
   1.1. An exact statement or description of the nature, scope, or meaning of something.
   1.2. *Mass noun* The action or process of defining something.
2. *Mass noun* The degree of distinctness in outline of an object, image, or sound.
   2.2. The capacity of a device to make images distinct in outline.

The essence of these can be expressed as define = *to give the meaning of a word* and definition = *a statement of the meaning of a word*. However, this tempts what (Mill, 1874) calls vulgar definition (his full quotation appears in the discussion of Issue 2 below) and will therefore be amended to *a statement of what is signified by a term*. This is applicable to both physical objects and concepts. It also accommodates all the above Oxford Dictionary definitions. The definition of define therefore becomes *to state what is signified by a term*.

'Essential definition' can then be defined as *definition in terms of essence only*. This will be used in discussing Issue 2 below.

4.4 Essence

The term 'essence' may have had varying interpretations, including ethereal and physical, put upon it historically, but it is not one whose everyday usage is uncertain. The default position of using the Oxford dictionary and reducing it to its essential content can therefore be adopted.

The Oxford Dictionary defines essence as:

1. intrinsic nature or indispensable quality of something, especially something abstract, which determines its character.
   1.1. *Philosophy count noun* A property or group of properties of something without which it would not exist or be what it is.
2. An extract or concentrate obtained from a plant or other matter and used for flavouring or scent.

The sense of these definitions is of something that is purely what it is, with nothing else added, specifying the bare minimum to be able to identify it. A food essence is a thing that can be pointed at and chemically analysed for purity and is a physical instantiation of the abstract concept. It is the abstract concept itself that will be defined here. Definition 1 above contains examples and is vague. Definition 1.1 will therefore be worked on. Although inanimate objects exist, using the word existence can introduce belief systems and so will be excluded it to keep the definition purely secular. This avoids the metaphysical or ethereal/ religious question of whether or not it is the intrinsic nature of a human being to have a soul and whether a soul therefore constitutes essence. Including values or beliefs in definitions can only lead to unresolvable debate and lack of agreement and we simply seek to uniquely identify what it is we are actually talking about, free from any unnecessary connotations. Omitting existence from our definition can have absolutely no impact upon whether a soul exists or not. Furthermore, if we can recognise things from their presence or actions then we do not need to venture into another dimension of comprehension, such as an ethereal one, to describe them; and if we cannot agree on what our words represent in the three physical dimensions plus time that we know we have access to, then we have little chance of resolving anything in dimensions beyond that anyway.

Essence is therefore defined as *A property or group of properties of something without which it would not be what it is*.

Note that this does not exclude soul from being an essence, but it does exclude soul from being a required part of essence.

4.5 Meaning

Defining meaning requires application of the full Mangle process and consideration of various 'isms'. Because of its length, it is presented separately below in Chap. 5. It first defines truth then in defining mean and meaning, considers the impact upon these of essentialism, existentialism, relativism (which required definition of truth), nominalism and nihilism. It challenges the logic of the phrase 'meaning of life', suggesting use of the phrase 'purpose of life' instead. It produces definitions of truth as *the quality of being in accordance with the facts*, mean (v) as *intend to convey*, and meaning as *what is intended to be conveyed*.

4.6 Normative

The word 'normative' is not one that is colloquially confused or contested, and so the default position of using the Oxford Dictionary and reducing it to its essential content can be adopted.

The Oxford dictionary defines 'norm' as "something that is usual, typical, or standard" and normative as "establishing, relating to, or deriving from a standard or norm, especially of behaviour".

The words 'typical' and 'standard' can both be described as 'usual'. Furthermore, the word 'norm' is not used in relation to engineering or project management standards, which give requirements rather than norms, and the term 'normal practice' is used rather than the single term. The Oxford definition of 'norm' can therefore be reduced to an essential definition as *something that is usual.* This can refer to physical objects, behaviour or concepts, and concepts include opinions, which in turn includes attitudes, beliefs and value judgements.

The term 'normative' has a more restricted scope than the term 'norm' but refers to more than just behaviour and "establishing, relating to, or deriving from" can be expressed more succinctly and generically as 'including', producing an essential definition as *including a norm.* However, this does not convey the full sense in which the word is normally used, which is referring to something that is based upon opinion rather than fact. The word 'norm' will therefore be replaced with 'opinion' producing a definition as *including an opinion*. This could be expressed more succinctly as *opinionated* however the Oxford definition of that term is "*characterized by conceited assertiveness and dogmatism*". Opinions are generally included in definitions by accident rather than by design and while it is appealing to just substitute that word, it contains connotations beyond what is intended and so will not be used.

Normativity causes difficulties when included in definition as what is a norm for one person or group may not be for others and it is not the business of definition to impose norms; it is just to adequately describe things.

This produces a definition of normative as *including an opinion*.

4.7 Purpose

The word 'purpose' is not one that is colloquially confused or contested, and so the default position of using the Oxford Dictionary and reducing it to its essential content can be adopted.

The Oxford Dictionary defines purpose as *the reason for which something is done or created or for which something exists*. This is already an essential definition and so can be accepted.

The word 'purpose' will therefore be defined here as *the reason for which something is done or created or for which some-thing exists*.

4.8 Soul

While there may not be universal agreement on the existence of a human soul, the term is not one whose everyday usage is uncertain and so the default position of using the Oxford dictionary and reducing it to essential content can be adopted.

The Oxford Dictionary defines soul as:

1. The ethereal or immaterial part of a human being or animal regarded as immortal.

- a person's moral or emotional nature or sense of identity.

synonyms: spirit · psyche · (inner) self · innermost self · (inner) ego · inner being · true being · essential nature · animating principle · life force · vital force · inner man/woman · persona · identity · personality · individuality · make-up · subconscious · anima ·.

2. Emotional or intellectual energy or intensity especially as revealed in a work of art or an artistic performance.

synonyms: inspiration · feeling · emotion · passion · animation · intensity · fervour · ardour · enthusiasm · eagerness · warmth · energy · vitality · vivacity · spirit · spiritedness · commitment · fervency · ardency · passionateness

3. the essence or embodiment of a specified quality.

The third definition equates soul with essence. While this usage may be widespread, this is most unfortunate as, in this secular age, it appears to have caused an aversion to an essential definition because of the ethereal association it has acquired. This has led to Wittgenstein's family resemblance concept, and its consequent vagueness, gaining currency. Essence will therefore form no part of the essential definition of soul. Definition 2 does not do this and is acceptable, abbreviated to be just emotional or intellectual energy or intensity. However, one of the synonyms listed, namely life-force expresses this more succinctly and so soul will instead be defined as *life-force*. This is more generic and reflects something that can be sensed in the four dimensions (three spatial, one time) that we have ready access to. It does not preclude it coming from a further dimension but does not require it. This neither requires nor precludes any religious belief and would seem to have the capacity to be agreed by people ranging from atheist to devoutly religious, without requiring either to adopt the convictions of the other. This leaves out of its definition anything that could cause debate or confusion on such matters.

This produces a definition of soul as *life-force*.

References

Mill, J. S. (1874). *A system of logic, ratiocinative and inductive*. Harper & Brothers.

Oxford. (*Dictionaries online* [Online], Oxford. Available: http://oxforddictionaries.com [Accessed].

Chapter 5
Defining Meaning and Truth

This chapter defines meaning using the steps outlined in the definitional refining method in Chap. 10.

5.1 Define 'Meaning'

Step 1 Define derivative or component terms

This is a derivative term with the root verb 'mean' and the noun-forming suffix 'ing'.

Step 2 Survey lexical usage

Lexical usage will be sourced from the following dictionary sources:

A range of dictionaries that have been well known for many years that were available (in 2013/14) online (Cambridge, Collins, Longman, Macmillan, Macquarie, Merriam-Webster, Oxford)

1. A range of various online dictionaries (BusinessDictionary.com, Dictionary.com, TheFreeDictionary, Wiktionary) and
2. The Concise Oxford Dictionary (Fowler & Fowler, 1964) – as a comparator for how these definitions may have changed over the last 50 years.

Lexical usage of both 'mean' and 'meaning' is surveyed in Tables 5.1 and 5.2.

Step 3 Analyse lexical usage

The main sense of the word 'mean' from Table 5.1 is the intension to convey, refer to or signify something. The word is also used in the phrase "that means", for which the term 'implies' could be substituted, however that is defining a phrase rather than a word and so will not be pursued. It is also used in the phrase "mean to

S. K. McGrath, *Speaking Management*,
https://doi.org/10.1007/978-981-16-2213-7_5

Table 5.1 Definitions of 'mean'

Dictionary	Definition of mean (All sourced on 15/7/2018)
Business	Arithmetic average
Cambridge	(v) To express, intend or to have a result (adj.) Not generous, not kind, violent, good, bad quality, mathematical average (n) mathematical average, middle of two completely different ways
Collins	(v) what it refers to or what its message is, exact explanation Means to = importance to (adj.) unwilling to spend much money, unkind, cruel, shabby, excellent (n) average of a set of numbers, halfway between extremes (v) to intend to convey or express, to denote, connote; signify; represent, to produce or cause, have the importance of
Concise Oxford	(v) purpose, have in mind (adj.) equally far from two extremes, half-way; inferior, poor, shabby, stingy (n) condition, quality, virtue, course, equally removed from two opposites, the term between the first and last terms of arithmetical, geometrical etc. progression, (pl) that by which a result is brought about, pecuniary resources, in every possible way or at any cost.
Dictionary.com	(v) to intend to express or indicate, (adj.) offensive, selfish, or unaccommodating; nasty; malicious: small-minded or ignoble: penurious, stingy, or miserly: inferior in grade, quality, or character: low in status, rank, or dignity: of little importance or consequence: unimposing or shabby: small, humiliated, or ashamed: in poor physical condition. troublesome or vicious; bad-tempered: *Slang*. skilful or impressive: (n) midway between two extremes, intermediate, arithmetic mean
Longman	(v) to have or represent a particular meaning, to intend to say or do something, result in something, be familiar, say something seriously, how important somebody/something is (adj.) cruel, not generous, average, poor (n) the mean (implying mathematical), the/a mean between something and something
Macmillan	(v) to have a particular meaning; to communicate a particular meaning, feeling or piece of information; to be evidence that something exists; to intend something bad or harmful; to make something necessary or to make it happen

(continued)

Table 5.1 (continued)

Dictionary	Definition of mean (All sourced on 15/7/2018)
Macquarie	(v) **1.** to have in the mind as in intention or purpose (often with an infinitive as object): **2.** to intend for a particular purpose, destination, etc.: **3.** (*usually passive*) to intend or require (that something should happen): **4.** to intend to express or indicate : **5.** (of words, things, etc.) to have as the signification; signify. (adj.) **1.** inferior in grade, quality or character: **2.** low in station, rank, or dignity. **3.** of little importance or consequence. **4.** unimposing or shabby: **5.** without moral dignity; small-minded or ignoble: **6.** penurious, stingy, or miserly: **7.** pettily offensive or unaccommodating; nasty. **8.** small, humiliated, or ashamed: **9.** troublesome or vicious, as a horse. **10.** (of one involved in a competitive activity, as sport, business, warfare, etc.) sufficiently accomplished and determined to make success very difficult for an opponent: **11.** *Colloquial* powerful, effective, having a vicious energy: (n) **1.** something intermediate; that which is midway between two extremes: **2.** *Mathematics***a.** a quantity having a value intermediate between the values of other quantities; an average, especially the arithmetic mean.**b.** either the second or third term in a proportion of four terms. **3.** *Logic Obsolete* the middle term in a syllogism. *–adjective* **4.** occupying a middle position or an intermediate place. **5.** intermediate in kind, quality, degree, time, etc.
Merriam-Webster	(v) **1 a** : to have in the mind as a purpose : INTEND **b** : to design for or destine to a specified purpose or future **2** : to serve or intend to convey, show, or in-dicate : SIGNIFY

(continued)

Table 5.1 (continued)

Dictionary	Definition of mean (All sourced on 15/7/2018)
Oxford	**(v) 1** Intend to convey or refer to (a particular thing); signify. *1.1* (of a word) have (something) as its signification in the same language or its equivalent in another language. *1.2* Genuinely intend to express (something) *1.3* mean something to Be of a specified degree of importance to (someone) **2** Intend (something) to occur or be the case. *'they mean no harm'* **2.1 be meant to do something** Be supposed to do something. **2.2** often **be meant for** Design or destine for a particular purpose. **2.3 mean something by** Have something as a motive or explanation in saying or doing. **2.4 be meant to be** Be generally considered to be. **3** Have as a consequence or result. **3.1** Necessarily or usually entail or involve. *Origin* Old English mænan, of West Germanic origin; related to Dutch meenen and German meinen, from an Indo-European root shared by mind. (adj.) • **1** *British* Unwilling to give or share things, especially money; not generous. • **2** Unkind, spiteful, or unfair. **2.1** *North American* Vicious or aggressive in behaviour. *'the dogs were considered mean, vicious, and a threat'* • **3** (especially of a place) poor in quality and appearance; shabby. **3.1** (of a person's mental capacity or understanding) inferior. *'it was obvious to even the meanest intelligence'* **3.2** *dated* Of low birth or social class. **4** *informal* Very skilful or effective; excellent. (n) **1** The value obtained by dividing the sum of several quantities by their number; an average. **2**A condition, quality, or course of action equally removed from two opposite extremes.

(continued)

Table 5.1 (continued)

Dictionary	Definition of mean (All sourced on 15/7/2018)
The free dictionary	**(v)** **1. a.** To be used to convey; denote : **b.** To act as a symbol of; signify or represent : **2.** To intend to convey or indicate : **3.** To have as a purpose or an intention; intend: **4.** To design, intend, or destine for a certain purpose or end: **5.** To have as a consequence; bring about: **6.** To have the importance or value of: (adj.) **1.** **a.** Lacking in kindness; unkind: **b.** Cruel, spiteful, or malicious: **c.** Expressing spite or malice: **d.** Tending toward or characterized by cruelty or violence: **e.** Extremely unpleasant or disagreeable: **2.** Ignoble; base: **3.** Miserly; stingy: **4.** **a.** Low in value, rank, or social status: **b.** Common or poor in appearance; shabby: **5.** Slang **a.** Hard to cope with; difficult or troublesome: **b.** Excellent; skillful: (n) **1.** Something having a position, quality, or condition midway between extremes; a medium. **2.** *Mathematics* **a.** A number that typifies a set of numbers, such as a geometric mean or an arithmetic mean. **b.** The average value of a set of numbers. **3.** *Logic* The middle term in a syllogism. **4. means** *(used with a sing. or pl. verb)* A method, a course of action, or an instrument by which an act can be accomplished or an end achieved. **5. means** *(used with a pl. verb)* **a.** Money, property, or other wealth: **b.** Great wealth:

do" for which 'intend' could be substituted. There is another sense it is used in, as stingy or nasty, which will also not be here defined as it is not contested. However, even with this seemingly divergent usage, it is still possible to find a common

Table 5.2 Definitions of 'meaning'

Dictionary	Definition of meaning (n) (All sourced on 15/7/2018)
Business	Not given
Cambridge	What it expresses or represents, also importance or value
Collins	The thing or idea that it refers to or represents, the thoughts or ideas that are intended to be expressed, having a purpose that is worthwhile
Concise Oxford	What is meant, expressive, significant
Dictionary.com	1. what is intended to be, or actually is expressed or indicated; signification; import: 2. the end, purpose, or significance of something:
Longman	The thing or idea that a word, expression or sign represents; the thoughts or ideas that someone wants to understand from what they say, do, write etc.; the quality that makes life, work etc. seem to have a purpose or value; the nature or importance of something
Macmillan	the thing, action feeling, idea etc that a word or words represent
Macquarie	Not available
Merriam-Webster	**1 a** : the thing one intends to convey especially by language : PURPORT **b** : the thing that is conveyed especially by language : IMPORT **2** : something meant or intended : AIM **3** : significant quality; especially : implication of a hidden or special significance **4 a** : the logical connotation of a word or phrase **b** : the logical denotation or extension of a word or phrase
Oxford	**1** What is meant by a word, text, concept, or action . **1.1** *mass noun* Implied or explicit significance. **1.2** *mass noun* Important or worthwhile quality; purpose.
The free dictionary	**1.** **a.** The denotation, referent, or idea associated with a word or phrase: **b.** Something that is conveyed or intended, especially by language; sense or significance: **2.** An interpreted goal, intent, or end: **3.** A sense of importance or purpose :
Wiktionary	1. The symbolic value of something. 2. The significance of a thing. 3. (*semantics*) The objects or concept that a word or phrase denotes, or that which a sentence says. 4. (*obsolete*) Intention .

(continued)

Table 5.2 (continued)

Dictionary	Definition of mean (All sourced on 15/7/2018)
Wiktionary	(v) 1. To intend . 1. (*transitive*) To intend, to plan (to do); to have as one's intention. [from 8th c.] 2. (*intransitive*) To have intentions of a given kind. [from 14th c.] 3. (*transitive, usually in passive*) To intend (something) for a given purpose or fate; to predestine. [from 16th c.] 2. To convey meaning. 1. (*transitive*) To convey (a given sense); to signify, or indicate (an object or idea). [from 8th c.] 2. (*transitive*) Of a word, symbol etc: to have reference to, to signify. [from 8th c.] 3. (*transitive*) To have conviction in (something said or expressed); to be sincere in (what one says). [from 18th c.] 4. (*transitive*) To result in; to bring about. [from 19th c.] 5. (*transitive*) To be important (to). (adj) 1. (obsolete) Common; general. 2. Of a common or low origin, grade, or quality; common; humble. 3. Low in quality or degree; inferior; poor; shabby. 4. Without dignity of mind; destitute of honour; low-minded; spiritless; base. 5. Of little value or account; worthy of little or no regard; contemptible; despicable. 6. (*chiefly Britain)* Ungenerous; stingy, tightfisted; North American English: cheap; formal: niggardly, penurious, miserly. 7. Disobliging; pettily offensive or unaccommodating; small. 8. Selfish; acting without consideration of others; unkind. 9. Causing or intending to cause intentional harm; bearing ill will towards another; cruel; malicious. 10. Powerful; fierce; harsh; damaging. 11. Accomplished with great skill; deft; hard to compete with. 12. (*informal, often childish*) Difficult, tricky. (n) 1. (*now chiefly in the plural*) A method or course of action used to achieve some result. [from 14th c.] 2. (*obsolete*, *in the singular*) An intermediate step or intermediate steps. 3. Something which is intermediate or in the middle; an intermediate value or range of values; a medium. [from 14th c.] 4. (*music*, *now historical*) The middle part of three-part polyphonic music; now specifically, the alto part in polyphonic music; an alto instrument. [from 15th c.] 5. (*statistics*) The average of a set of values, calculated by summing them together and dividing by the number of terms; the arithmetic mean. [from 15th c.] 6. (*mathematics*) Any function of multiple variables that satisfies certain properties and yields a number representative of its arguments; or, the number so yielded; a measure of central tendency. 7. (*mathematics*) Either of the two numbers in the middle of a conventionally presented proportion, as *2* and *3* in *1:2=3:6*.

essence. From the etymological analysis below, that essence can be expressed as an extension of 'half-way' and 'in-mind' to common, or well below the best or second rate, which in monetary terms is stingy. It is of more use to seek an essential definition of the sense of the word we are concerned with here. This less-than-desirable situation of having two quite different meanings for the same word just has to be accepted as an accident of history. This is a case where the context of the use of the word in a particular sentence has to provide the indicator as to which sense of the term is being used.

This leaves the potential definition of "intend to convey, refer to or signify" to be considered. To 'refer to' is something that can be done without any connotation of explanation, such as pointing and so will also not be selected. 'Signify' is potentially suitable but has been used in defining 'definition' and a separate distinct meaning is being sought so that the two terms do not overlap causing confusion. That leaves the tentative definition of the verb 'mean' as "intend to convey".

The main sense of the word 'meaning' from Table 5.2 is what is meant (by a word, text, concept, or action). This points to communication occurring across more than words i.e. across all the senses, and so its definition will not be limited to words only. This is in contrast to definition which can only apply to words. The root word 'mean' will be selected rather than 'expressed' or 'represented', as required by the definitional refining method, and this also avoids double definition. It is a secular sense that is referred to here, but there is another meaning that appears often in Table 5.2 and that is purpose, which indicates it is commonly used in an ethereal sense. That means that the error identified as Issue 5 (see Sect. 6.5) has been made in previous usage and so will be excluded from the definition here. Its ethereal usage will be addressed in considering the phrase 'the meaning of life' in existentialism below.

This enables tentative definitions to be proposed.

Step 4 Develop a connotative (intensional) conventional definition

In line with Group Rule 2(d), the verb will be defined first, and the noun then defined in terms of the verb as follows:

<u>mean (verb):</u> = *intend to convey*

<u>meaning (noun):</u> = *what is intended to be conveyed*

Note: These definitions allow for the circumstance where it is not possible to express all meaning in words. They can also be applied generically to words, concepts, actions, pictures, diagrams and works of art.

Step 5 Report academic review of definitions

Various views of meaning have been proposed in various 'isms' and those relevant to definition are considered in 8(d) below after first considering etymology.

Step 6 Remove unwarranted inclusions

There are no such inclusions remaining.

Step 7 Remove mixed content/process meanings

None present.

Step 8 Reduce divergence/consider additional inclusions

Checks (a) and (d) are appropriate for this term.

Step 8(a) Consider historical usage

The etymology of these words extracted from Harper (2017 in 'M') on 11 July 2018 is as follows:

mean (n.)
"that which is halfway between extremes," early 14c., from Old French *meien* "middle, means, intermediary," noun use of adjective from Latin *medianus* "of or that is in the middle" (see **mean** (adj.2)). Oldest sense is musical; mathematical sense is from c. 1500. Some senses reflect confusion with *mean* (adj.1). This is the *mean* in *by no means* (late 15c.).

mean (v.2)
"calculate an arithmetical mean," 1882, from **mean** (n.).

mean (v.1)
"intend, have in mind," Old English *mænan* "to mean, intend, signify; tell, say; complain, lament," from West Germanic **mainijan* (source also of Old Frisian *mena* "to signify," Old Saxon *menian* "to intend, signify, make known," Dutch *menen*, German *meinen* "think, suppose, be of the opinion"), from PIE **meino-* "opinion, intent" (source also of Old Church Slavonic *meniti* "to think, have an opinion," Old Irish *mian* "wish, desire," Welsh *mwyn* "enjoyment"), perhaps from root ***men-** (1) "to think." Conversational question *you know what I mean?* attested by 1834.

mean (adj.1)
"low-quality," c. 1200, "shared by all," from *imene*, from Old English *gemæne* "common, public, general, universal, shared by all," from Proto-Germanic **ga-mainiz* "possessed jointly" (source also of Old Frisian *mene*, Old Saxon *gimeni*, Middle Low German *gemeine*, Middle Dutch *gemene*, Dutch *gemeen*, German *gemein*, Gothic *gamains* "common"), from PIE **ko-moin-i-* "held in common," a compound adjective formed from collective prefix **ko-* "together" (Proto-Germanic **ga-*) + **moi-n-*, suffixed form of PIE root ***mei-** (1) "to change; exchange." Compare second element in **common** (adj.), a word with a sense evolution parallel to that of this word.

Of things, "inferior, second-rate," from late 14c. (a secondary sense in Old English was "false, wicked"). Notion of "so-so, mediocre" led to confusion with **mean** (n.). Meaning "inferior in rank or status" (of persons) emerged early 14c.; that of "ordinary" from late 14c.; that of "stingy, nasty" first recorded 1660s; weaker sense of "disobliging, pettily offensive" is from 1839, originally American English slang. Inverted sense of "remarkably good" (i.e. *plays a mean saxophone*) first recorded c. 1900, perhaps from phrase *no mean* _______ "not inferior" (1590s, also, "not average," reflecting further confusion with *mean* (n.)).

mean (adj.2)
"occupying a middle or intermediate place," mid-14c., from Anglo-French *meines* (plural), Old French *meien*, variant of *moiien* "mid-, medium, common, middle-class" (12c., Modern French *moyen*), from Late Latin *medianus* "of the middle," from Latin *medius* "in the middle" (from PIE root ***medhyo-** "middle"). Meaning "intermediate in time" is from mid-15c. Mathematical sense is from late 14c.

meaning (n.)
"sense, import, intent," c. 1300, from **mean** (v.).

Summarising and interpreting this, the original usage of the word as being half-way between extremes (average or what most values lie closest to) was extended in two different and independent ways. One was being average or second class, which was further stretched to nastiness. The other was to where a group collectively reaches an average position that is taken to representing understanding 'in-mind'.

The essence of 'half-way-ness' that spawned these variations has disappeared from the two derivatives 'meanness' and 'meaning', but not without trace.

Step 8(b) Consider field/ specialty usage
See 8(d)
Step 8(c) Practitioner usage
See 8(d)
Step 8(d) Competing concepts & frameworks

Various views of meaning have been proposed in various 'isms' and significant ones relevant to definition are considered here. Each will be examined to see if the tentative definition accommodates their explicit or implied definition of meaning or requires modification for it to do so, and whether any of the definitional issues identified in this book can be found.

5.2 Essentialism

The idea of essence originated from Plato. The Oxford dictionary defines essentialism as "a belief that things have a set of characteristics which make them what they are, and that the task of science and philosophy is their discovery and expression; the doctrine that essence is prior to existence". The approach taken here in defining 'meaning' aligns with the method of definition contained in the first part of this statement, which refers to secular essence and is independent of the doctrine in the second part of the statement that presumes an ethereal view of essence. That issue is discussed extensively in addressing Issue 5 in 6.5, has no impact on the definitional method applied here, and so will not be further considered here. Essence has been defined above as *a property or group of properties of something without which it would not be what it is*. Essentialism is not primarily concerned with meaning other than incidentally as a result of its confusion with essence. Consideration of essentialism therefore requires no alteration to the definition of meaning.

5.3 Existentialism

The key statement of existentialism was made by Sartre (1973) (1905–1980) in saying "existence precedes essence", reversing Plato's order. This is dissected in Issue 5 in 6.5, identifying the definitional error of 'dual simultaneous meanings' (ethereal and secular) of the term 'essence' and enumerating the silent qualifiers in both Plato's and Sartre's statements, demonstrating how both can be true.

However there are other terms used in discussing existentialism which are also similarly definitionally confused and require attention here. The term 'meaning', like 'essence', has dual simultaneous ethereal and secular usage, and to compound that problem, the two terms have effectively come to be regarded as synonymous.

Søren Kierkegaard (1813–1855), the 'father of existentialism', said:

> What I really need is to get clear about what I must do, not what I must know, except insofar as knowledge must precede every act. What matters is to find a purpose, to see what it really is that God wills that I shall do; the crucial thing is to find a truth which is truth *for me*, to find *the idea for which I am willing to live and die*. (...) I certainly do not deny that I still accept an imperative of knowledge and that through it men may be influenced, but then it must come alive in me, and this is what I now recognize as the most important of all (Kierkegaard et al., 1978).

He uses the term 'purpose' here and does not mention 'meaning', but the introduction of ethereal essence can be seen in the reference to God's will. While the quotation would lose none of its secular meaning if "what it really is that God wills" was omitted, its inclusion effectively states that purpose isn't possible without reference to God and that ethereal purpose is pre-eminent over secular purpose.

A similar ambiguity of meaning arises for the word 'fate' in the following excerpt:

> In existentialism you choose your own fate, and you determine what you (in essence) are: even if you avoid decisive choices, or acts, you are responsible for that avoidance. You also create your own values. There is no authoritative tablet of stone bearing God's unambiguous commandments for the good life. Even if there was once such a thing, it no longer has authority for modern man, because— in Nietzsche's dramatic declaration—'God is dead'. There are in fact Christian Existentialists— including the first Existentialist, Søren Kierkegaard— but for them, too, God's will is objectively unknowable (Gravil, 2007).

The dual simultaneous meanings of the word 'fate' are eternal ethereal fate, and the secular consequences of our actions (or inactions).

It would be useful to invoke the 'spirit' (dare I say 'essence'?) of Descartes' mind-body distinction for definition only. Then we may know exactly what it is we are all talking about without needing to find a linkage between them in the definitional domain that condemns us to 'eternal' confusion by regarding their dual meanings to be inseparable and simultaneous with a hierarchy hinting at the need for Derridean deconstruction.

Before returning to the definition of meaning, there is another aspect of existentialism that bears upon it namely subjectivity, which is evident in both quotations above. If we choose your own fate and our own values, then we can choose actions (or inaction) accordingly. These will have consequences but may or may not lead to the fate imagined, as we cannot absolutely know what outcomes (fate) our actions will produce. If God is actually dead, as Nietzsche said, and we are all alone and responsible for ourselves and our choices, what else will guide us if our fate is so subjective and unique to us? Without either someone to tell us, some authority figure or organisation) or adequate introspection, we may, either without any thought whatsoever or even with a little knowledge of and belief in existentialism, just do what we feel like and imagine that whatever outcome results, that is our fate.

This is something much less than Kierkegaard's idea "for which I am willing to live and die" and tends towards justifying an arbitrary and whim dependent 'I can do what I like' approach. The former represents a serious internal conviction in something outside of self that could be labelled 'mature'. The latter could be labelled as 'justified' if it referred to resisting moves to restrict one's reasonable personal liberty, but 'immature' if used to justify acting upon whims with no consideration for others. The immature view implies that no matter what misunderstandings I may have, I will pursue them regardless. That view simply ignores the boundaries of reality or even that any boundaries exist. Meaning for me may be subjective, but once it starts to impact other people, it isn't any longer; I will run up against boundaries that will be imposed simply by the mere existence of other people. Popper's world view would hold that we relate to people in his conceptual World 3 (where things can be put objectively so others can see), not in his World 2 (inside our heads). However this interpretation of subjectivity has more to do with relativism than existentialism and requires clarity around a definition of truth, which must be compatible with the definition of meaning. This is dealt with below in considering relativism.

The term 'meaning' is used in both ethereal and secular senses; secular meaning is descriptive whereas 'the meaning of life' is prescriptive and ethereal. The ethereal meaning makes no sense if the tentative definition of 'meaning' derived above is accepted; it begs the illogical question of who is conveying what to whom. There is no 'what is intended to be conveyed' of life. The clear ethereal invocation of the phrase 'meaning of life' invites confusion with the secular sense of the term. And it does so when there is another word that could be used that better expresses the intent of the phrase, namely 'purpose', as was used by Kierkegaard. There is no need to appropriate ethereal meaning to a secular term when there is already another secular term 'purpose' that adequately expresses what is intended, and no need to suffer the resulting confusion. The phrase 'purpose of life' adequately expresses the intent without inducing confusion. The phrase 'meaning of life' is internally contradictory, contains a belief (see Issue 5 in Sect. 6.5) and has the effect of forcing association of meaning/ purpose with essence, bringing with it the ethereal interpretations of these terms which are implicitly assumed to be valid and to predominate over the secular. That phrase will therefore be rejected here. It is an understanding arising from a definitional error that would be best expunged from the English language, something that would occur should proper attention be paid to definition.

Consideration of these aspects of existentialism therefore provides no reason to alter the tentative definitions, which enable clear distinction between meaning, essence and purpose.

5.4 Defining True and Truth

The Oxford dictionary defines relativism as "the doctrine that knowledge, truth, and morality exist in relation to culture, society, or historical context, and are not absolute". The concept of truth bears on definition and so it will be defined, and its logical implications considered before specifically addressing relativism itself.

A survey of dictionaries was done and there was surprising commonality of definition. The Tables are therefore not included. This confirmed that even though there is scholarly debate about truth, there is little confusion or disagreement in the lexical sources surveyed, justifying the default position of commencing with the Oxford dictionary which defines:

- 'true' as being in accordance with fact or reality,
- 'reality' as the state of things as they actually exist, as opposed to an idealistic or notional idea of them and
- 'truth' as the quality or state of being true.

These are close to essential definitions. Uncertainty associated with interpretations of reality will be avoided by omitting it and using 'fact', and quality will be selected rather than state because a definition of truth, not 'in truth' is being sought. This produces an essential definition of truth as *the quality of being in accordance with the facts*. This aligns with the definition which Popper adopted from Tarski in 1935 which used the term "correspondence to" rather than "accordance with" the facts (Popper, 1992; Popper, 1995).

This definition implies that truth may be stated definitely or absolutely when correspondence is found. It follows from this, and from good scientific practice, that the limits of that truth need to be stated, in case it may not be a truth outside those boundaries and context. It also follows that any extrapolation requires further testing/ observation/ facts to determine truth in these wider circumstances.

This corresponds with the findings of the papers in Part II, detailing the false presumptions of the genericity of various IT definitions and processes having confused project management outside that field. We may be unaware of whether there is a wider group outside our own 'world' or whether that wider group might agree or not, and we may or may not choose to investigate that. And depending upon whatever our personal standard of proof might be, we may well accept something as being true for a wider environment when it isn't. That will have unknown consequences that are unlikely to be helpful in the long run.

This leads to the seemingly trivial but quite important conclusion that truth can only be stated absolutely when all boundaries i.e. all elements of context, are made fully explicit. This implies the need to make statements of "true for" rather than just presuming the single term 'universally'.

It also follows that truth is absolute within its circumstances and there is no such thing as relative truth. Truth is absolute, notwithstanding that it may at times be difficult to establish, or that many truths may be established that do not provide a clear overall picture, and that there may be many true facts established along the way to reaching an erroneous verdict; but it is simply the definitional aspect only that these comments are concerned with here. If truth is absolute, then the terms 'absolute truth' and 'relative truth' are illogical and should not be used. Rather, the circumstances (boundaries and context) should be specified. **Truth is relative to context but absolute within it.** It can therefore be both relative and absolute; the silent qualifiers of context just need to be stated. The argument between the two apparently competing, dichotomous positions then simply vanishes.

Use of the word 'universal' in association with truth is potentially quite confusing. It begs the question as to which universe is being referred to. Something might apply within one universe that doesn't apply in another. This gets recursive, leading nowhere and devolving into word games. Consequently, there can never be universal truth, which means truth always needs to have a suffix describing where it has been found. However, it can be definite or absolute within its circumstances. The problem is just with the words used where the signification of them has not been fully agreed or the context of competing usages not specified. The term 'universal' has been used above as an adjective, but Plato used it as a noun and ascribed ethereal essence to it. This analysis has found that the concepts of essence and meaning have been thoroughly confused between their dual simultaneous usages, ethereal and secular, with the former taking precedence over the latter, causing confusion. The term 'universal' is closely aligned with both of those terms and appears to have suffered the same fate. For these reasons, use of the term 'universal' when describing truth is avoided here.

Not all facts come from physical laboratory observations; conceptual facts can be established or agreed by various means. These range from mathematical proof, through observing people's presence or absence or actions or adherence to rules, to sensing 'what people might think' i.e. collectively agree. Once values are, for example, written into a code of conduct, or a particular attitude becomes widely accepted in a group or organisation, it represents an agreement that behaviour can be assessed against it, to determine whether conformity is present or absent, true or false. It will be absolute, as decisions made against such agreements may involve imposing penalties. Penalties are either imposed or not; they cannot be half-imposed i.e. relative, even though the severity of the sanction may be relative to the seriousness of the offence. It will also not matter for people within that group if a broader group does not agree the same things; they are within that group and so will be governed by its rules, written and unwritten. Another example is, of course, agreement on the signification of words.

It is also worthwhile to note that the above consideration of truth is one case where treating objects and concepts in the same way is beneficial, unlike definition itself where this has been problematic, as identified in Issue 7 (See Sect. 6.7). Note also that the term 'true' is more commonly applied to physical observations and events that occur, whereas the term 'correct' is more likely to be used for concepts where assessment is relative to some agreed benchmark.

Having considered the definition of truth and its logical implications, and as a result having identified various flaws in relativism, the concept itself can now be explicitly considered in relation to the tentative definition, and a position stated.

It is worthwhile discussing the difficulty of determining truth. If truth is being in accordance with the facts, this begs the question as to which facts. There is a difference between an individual's Popperian World 2 facts that exist only in their own heads, which can stem from beliefs, and all relevant facts observed by others that can be agreed between people. This begs the further question of whether all the necessary facts were collected, and who the others are (which group), and perhaps what the size of that group might be, which matters in determining what a population may accept.

The question of standard of proof is super-ordinate to all of these considerations. There is a question of what standard an individual/ group/ whole society might require, what methods they use before accepting something as fact, and correspondence with that as being true (or correct), and whether they bother to state the contextual qualifiers.

This highlights the difficulty of establishing fact and truth, but this has no impact on the definition of truth itself.

5.5 Relativism

Relativism, according to Baghramian and Carter (2015), is

> the view that truth and falsity, right and wrong, standards of reasoning, and procedures of justification are products of differing conventions and frameworks of assessment and that their authority is confined to the context giving rise to them… the truth of claims attributing these properties (of some classes of things) holds only once the relevant framework of assessment is specified or supplied. Relativists characteristically insist, furthermore, that if something is only relatively so, then there can be no framework-independent vantage point from which the matter of whether the thing in question is so can be established.

The approach taken to definition in this book concurs with this aspect of relativism that is concerned with boundaries and context, but it does not concur with the extension of that which is evident in the Oxford definition of it that considers "truth, and morality exist in relation to culture, society, or historical context, and are not absolute".

According to Baghramian and Carter (2015), Comte developed what has become the battle cry of relativism "all is relative" in 1976. This assertion implies that the concept of relative truth makes sense, which it does not, as shown above, and the following steps were taken to preclude this:

1. the term "true for" rather than 'relative to' was used
2. suffixes qualifying the circumstances were proposed rather than a prefix qualifying the meaning of the base term and
3. use of the term 'universal' was avoided.

The (il)logical extension of this relativist battle cry is problematic. If truth were actually relative, as the battle-cry would hold, and as the Oxford definition states, then there can be no basis for assessing the value or morality or truth of any position anyone may hold. This then becomes the ideal philosophy for anyone who just wants to believe or justify anything they like. The illogicality of this position becomes evident when contexts or boundaries clash i.e. differ from the perspective of the entities involved. For example, it may well be that some things regarded as 'moral principles' are true in the context of humanity, insofar as individuals abiding by them may advantage the interests of the whole human race. But they may require restraint of particular individual desires and a particular individual may consider that view untrue for or irrelevant to them. They may simply be ignorant of why it may be true or relevant. Ignorance is not a determinant of truth. The twisting of the meaning of the battle-cry contains the hidden presumption of infinite knowledge in every individual. Any actions that impact on others can have at least three contexts – mine, theirs and what might be good for the overall group. Things that are 'moral' are generally good for a group and require self-restraint by individuals. Once my actions affect other people, then the world is no longer the context in which I wish to see it and my boundaries are impacted. Definition is concerned with describing things and their boundaries or context, not with resolving what beliefs may or may not be best for any group of people. However, being rigorous about definition can avert false beliefs and unnecessary debate.

It is not difficult to state our (perception of) truth absolutely (dogmatically) within our boundaries or context and imagine or wish those to be unlimited. But to believe they are unlimited is a fantasy.

This consideration of relativism provides a definition of truth which is clearly distinguishable from meaning and so provides no reason to alter the tentative definitions.

5.6 Nominalism

The Oxford dictionary defines nominalism as: "The doctrine that universals or general ideas are mere names without any corresponding reality". Rodriguez-Pereyra (2016) notes that "Nominalism comes in at least two varieties. In one of them it is the rejection of abstract objects; in the other it is the rejection of universals". Nominalism deals with what is meant by universals and abstract objects rather than with the definition of meaning itself. Such issues are dealt with above in considering the problem of universals and provide no reason to change the tentative definition.

5.7 Nihilism

The Oxford dictionary defines nihilism as "the rejection of all religious and moral principles, in the belief that life is meaningless". According to Pratt (2018):

> Nihilism is the belief that all values are baseless and that nothing can be known or communicated. It is often associated with extreme pessimism and a radical skepticism that condemns existence. A true nihilist would believe in nothing, have no loyalties, and no purpose other than, perhaps, an impulse to destroy.

This fuels relativism and existentialism but is primarily concerned with argument about an ethereal belief. This is not the province of definition and we are here dealing with arriving at a secular understanding of meaning. It also considers the meaning of life which, as pointed out earlier, is a definitional error which should be stated as the purpose of life to avoid introducing an unnecessary ethereal dimension to the term 'meaning'. Nihilism is not relevant to the definition of meaning and so provides no reason to change the tentative definition.

This concludes Step 8 of the definitional method that was commenced in 5.1.

Step 9 Check against the five rules

The definitions are operational rather than by genus and difference and so a check against the 5 rules is not appropriate. Nevertheless, they do actually satisfy them.

Step 10 Report the derived definition

The derived definitions are as follows:

- mean (v) = *intend to convey*
- meaning (n) = *what is intended to be conveyed*
- meaning of life = *nil*. The purpose of life is a separate question that does make sense.
- Truth = *the quality of being in accordance with the facts*

5.8 Observation

These supposedly deep philosophical questions concerning meaning turn out to be grounded in nothing more than definitional mistakes, creating much ado over something we've just rushed past – noises we haven't agreed the meaning of.

References

Baghramian, M. & Carter, J. A. (2015). *Relativism* [Online], The Stanford Encyclopedia of Philosophy. Available: https://plato.stanford.edu/entries/relativism/. Accessed 15 July 2018.

BusinessDictionary.com. (*Online dictionary* [Online]. Available: http://www.businessdictionary.com [Accessed].

Cambridge. (*Online dictionary* [Online]. Available: http://dictionary.cambridge.org/dictionary/british [Accessed].

Collins. (*English dictionary* [Online]. Available: http://www.collinsdictionary.com/dictionary/english [Accessed].

Dictionary.com. (*Online dictionary* [Online]. Available: http://dictionary.reference.com [Accessed].

Fowler, H. W. & Fowler, F. G. (1964), *The concise Oxford dictionary of current English*, Clarendon Press, .

Gravil, R. (2007). *Existentialism*. Humanities-Ebooks.

Harper, D. (2017). *Online etymology dictionary*. Douglas Harper.

Kierkegaard, S., Hong, E. H., Hong, H. V., & Malantschuk, G. (1978). *Søren Kierkegaard's journals and papers Volume 5 Part 1 - 1829-1848*. Indiana University Press.

Longman. (*Dictionary of contemporary English online* [Online]. Available: http://www.ldoceonline.com [Accessed].

Macmillan. (*Dictionary* [Online]. Available: http://www.macmillandictionary.com [Accessed].

Macquarie. (*Dictionary online* [Online], Sydney. Available: http://www.macquarieonline.com.au [Accessed].

Merriam-Webster. (*Online dictionary* [Online], Britain. Available: http://www.merriam-webster.com [Accessed].

Oxford. (*Dictionaries online* [Online], Oxford. Available: http://oxforddictionaries.com [Accessed].

Popper, K. R. (1992). *Unended quest: An intellectual autobiography*. Routledge.

Popper, K. R. (1995), The open society and its enemies: Volume 2 Hegel and Marx, Routledge, .

Pratt, A. (2018). *Nihilism* [Online], Internet Encyclopedia of Philosophy. Available: http://www.iep.utm.edu/nihilism/. Accessed 20 July 2018.

Rodriguez-Pereyra, G. (2016). *Nominalism in Metaphysics* [Online], The Stanford Encyclopedia of Philosophy (Winter 2016 Edition), Edward N. Zalta (Ed.). Available: https://plato.stanford.edu/cgi-bin/encyclopedia/archinfo.cgi?entry=nominalism-metaphysics [Accessed].

Sartre, J. P. (1973). *Existentialism is a humanism*. Eyre Methuen.

TheFreeDictionary. (*Online dictionary* [Online]. Available: http://www.thefreedictionary.com [Accessed].

Wiktionary. (*Online dictionary* [Online]. Available: http://en.wiktionary.org [Accessed].

Chapter 6
Philosophical Examination of the Ten Linguistic Traps/Issues

Each of the ten linguistic traps is examined individually. The approach taken is to first explain the issue, then identify how it arose from the papers in Part II, give examples of its occurrence within management where possible, and consider its philosophical background before developing definitional axioms and/or rules to counteract it.

6.1 Issue 1 Fact v Opinion (Attitudes)

***This deals with whether the inclusion of attitudes should be accepted in definitions* or not.**

There is little opportunity for attitudes to intrude into the definition of physical objects such as a table or a cup, but the same cannot be said for terms like ethics, essence, governance and program. For example, interviews with project management practitioners (reported in McGrath and Whitty (2019)) conducted as part of the research covered in this book found that some held the opinion that a program must be transformational while others contradicted that. This was causing problems and wasting time within one organisation. Attitudes also affect colloquial use of the term 'ethics', which presumes that ethics equates to 'good' ethics. There can also be 'bad' ethics and the presumption of 'good' can confuse the definition of the basic term and its subsequent usage, as mentioned in the ethics paper in Chap. 13. Similar confusion can result from including an opinion about ethereal or religious matters in the definition of essence, and the difficulty this creates is sufficiently serious to warrant it being identified as a separate definitional issue. The view that 'good' ethics should form part of the definition of governance was also noted in McGrath and Whitty (2020c) which reported interviews of practitioners on their understanding of governance, finding that it was a confusing factor in resolving a satisfactory

S. K. McGrath, *Speaking Management*,
https://doi.org/10.1007/978-981-16-2213-7_6

definition of governance and project governance. Such a view of 'good' governance overlooks the fact that even a brutal dictatorship will have governance, some aspects of which would be considered 'good'. It is therefore erroneous to include good ethics in a definition of governance.

This issue has not received much overt consideration in the writings of major philosophers on the subject of definitions other than **John Stewart Mill** (JSM) who was very clear, saying "But to impose upon the facts in the first instance the yoke of a theory, while the grounds of the theory are reserved for discussion in a subsequent stage, is not a course which a logician can reasonably adopt" (Mill, 1874). **Aristotle** left open the possibility of introducing value judgements to definition by allowing the value judgement of ethereal belief to infiltrate definition as elaborated in the section below dealing with essence. **Popper** identified "a logical mistake which is connected with the close analogy between the *meaning* of our words, or terms, or concepts, and the *truth* of our statements or propositions" (Popper, 2002). He noted that definitions link meaning and truth (Popper, 2002). This is based on accepting the view that meaning comes from its original meaning "because we learned it correctly from a true authority" (Popper, 2002). This is debateable as we often have differing understandings of the same concepts, and/or of the same word labelling the concept, as **Wittgenstein** recognised, and as also evidenced by the analyses of contested terms in Part II. We also might have learned it from someone who was also confused. However, Popper later concluded somewhat similarly to Wittgenstein that "truth is above human authority" (Popper, 2002) and that we should:

> give up the idea of ultimate sources of knowledge and admit that all knowledge is human; that it is mixed with our prejudices, our dreams, and our hopes; that all we can do is grope for truth even though it is beyond our reach (Popper, 2002).

While hopes and dreams are important in living our lives, this statement goes much further than Aristotle and presumes that value judgements must enter into definition. **Derrida** similarly considered "that our perception of unconscious traces occurs long 'after the event' " (Derrida & Spivak, 1976). These statements refer to perception, not to definition and so it appears that Derrida also did not make that distinction. While perceptions are vitally important for communication and in deciding what action to take living our daily lives, they are riddled with value judgements and their suitability for inclusion in definition is another matter entirely.

Based upon the outcomes of the definitional papers in Part II as well as the above sources, opinion/value judgement/normative matters are best excluded from definition. Allowing their inclusion has contributed to confusion and conflict about the concepts discussed in those papers in Part II. Chapter 10 gives a method for excluding these which was successfully applied in all the chapters in Part II, as well as in the other definitional papers referred to in this book. The difficulty with Popper's association of meaning with truth becomes evident if we separate out the assumption of the need for an authority or original use to determine or 'fix' the definition, and accept that there is no authority, so the best we can do is reach agreement on what the words we use actually signify.

Magee and Searle (1987) mention that many of the words that trouble us in philosophy and ethics are words like good and beautiful and that Wittgenstein was suspicious of these words, thinking part of our failure was in looking for some essence of goodness or beauty. While there may be difficulty in looking for the essence of goodness or beauty, there is a more significant problem in looking for absolute right and wrong or good and bad which does not exist and can only be a matter of opinion. It is absolutist, pre-evolutionary thinking which overlooks consideration of who or what the matter under consideration is 'good' for, as mentioned in Part II Chaps. 12 and 13; what is good for the larvae of the ichneumonidae wasp feeding within the live bodies of caterpillars is not good for those caterpillars. There is no absolute 'good' here, unless one makes a value judgement on which entity has the greater value, or on the overall value (to humans) of a food chain that we sit on top of. As Darwin and Beer (2008) point out, "natural selection works solely by and for the good of each being". As such, natural selection works on self-interest, not on morality or value judgement.

To be blinded by this mistaken search of conflicting opinions for an absolute truth is simply to accept a false premise, which can only lead to a poor theory with little explanatory power – such as Wittgenstein's family resemblance theory, as will be discussed separately below. The approach of determining secular essence is much more realistic (Issue 5), but it does require a definitional refining method setting out a process that can resolve competing views. This is what has been done in the chapters of Part II in redefining governance and further testing the method in defining stakeholders, accountability and responsibility, power, ethics, leadership, strategy, management and strategic management.

Definitional laziness can produce the excitement and drama of emotional conflict. However, it is more productive to persist in considering and reaching agreement on what we think the contested terms we use actually mean. Failing to reach such agreement simply perpetuates confusion in discussion, producing the farcical situation where none of us really has a clue what we are all talking about. In this respect, we can empathise with both Popper and Wittgenstein; it makes no sense. It correlates with Wittgenstein's non-sense about which, to paraphrase the last line of his Tractatus, we might all be justifiably implored to shut up.

This question of reaching agreement is a crucial one. It is one that is so obvious but is so easily overlooked. As **Wittgenstein** himself said:

> The aspects of things that are most important for us are hidden because of their simplicity and familiarity. (One is unable to notice something—because it is always before one's eyes.) The real foundations of his enquiry do not strike a man at all. Unless *that* fact has at some time struck him. —And this means: we fail to be struck by what, once seen, is most striking and most powerful (Wittgenstein & Anscombe, 1958).

In summary, the issue of inclusion of opinion in definition was clearly identified by Mill and was not adequately identified or addressed by the other philosophers considered here. Furthermore, clarity did result from excluding opinion from definition (as distinct from debate) of both ethics and governance, as well as of all the other subjects dealt with in the definitional papers in Part II. For the purposes of gaining understanding and enlightenment about any entity or phenomenon, a definition is best served by taking great note of any person's experience with it and little note of their opinion of it, unless the phenomenon we are seeking to understand is their emotional reaction to it.This leads to proposing the following:

Axiom 1: ***A definition states what a group of people have agreed a particular sound will represent or signify***. This means that there is no absolute correct sound or absolute correct definition of what that agreed sound means; correctness of definition can only be judged relative to that agreement. If agreement has not been reached, or different groups have agreed different things, there will be contention about correctness. Words are meaningful only insofar as we have agreed their meaning or signification.

Definitional rule 1 ***Exclude attitudes from definition***. Accommodate them after definitions have been agreed, not before.

However, Axiom 1 raises a further question about senses other than sound. Nuances in looks, gestures, tones and actions can completely change the meaning of spoken words. We have five senses available to us, all of which can potentially be used in determining the meaning of any communication. So, while speech may at times convey the full meaning, there will be many cases in which it cannot, and in which speech or words will therefore convey only part of the meaning. This leads to a further axiom:

Axiom 2 ***Meaning does not come from words alone***. We have five senses, each with its own capacity to give us information about the external world. We use all senses to derive internal meaning, which we call understanding. The senses that the spoken and written word do not use therefore also contribute to meaning and in some cases, words may have difficulty in, or be incapable of, expressing or communicating the full meaning.

6.2 Issue 2 Meaning v Representation

This issue deals with whether the meaning we communicate is in the terms we use, or in what those terms represent or signify.

The issue became evident in considering the term governance, which is generally considered to be of great importance, but is a concept that has no physical existence. It exists only in its instantiations, which may or may not be in written form. This issue (together with Issue 4) emerged from attempting to reconcile various project management frameworks (such as PMBOK and PRINCE2). The essence of project management had become confused by overlooking the relationship of words to meaning. It was then realized this had created some of the difficulty for project management practitioners in offering definitions of governance, as noted in Chap. 10). Adopting a 'words equals meaning' approach to project management leads to conflicting positions on the very basic question of what a project actually is, as detailed in McGrath and Whitty (2019), McGrath and Whitty (2020b); it differs between PMBOK and PRINCE2, with one defining it as an endeavour and the other defining it as an organisation. This makes it obvious that words can only represent meaning and cannot actually be meaning. Adopting a 'words represent meaning' approach allows truth to be sought through realising that each framework represents meaning but does not have a mortgage upon it.

Philosophically, this gets to the question of whether we think we are defining the thing itself or the word labelling the thing. This may seem abstract, until one realises the differences between major philosophers on the subject. This issue may not have been recognized by **Aristotle** but it has been part of philosophical thinking since the seventeenth century. Cohen (2016) said "It is important to remember that for Aristotle, one defines things, not words". When taken at face value, this seems reasonable; it indicates that we are not just playing word games and that words actually stand for something. But it invites the view that the words we use to describe something are actually that thing, which, of course, they cannot be; they can only represent or signify it in speech.

In the seventeenth century, **Thomas Hobbs** very clearly expressed the dangers of inappropriate signification and definition and the consequent compounding with the passage of time. He mentioned use of speech as signs as well as abuses of speech which included "inconstancy of the signification of their words; by which they register for their conceptions that which they never conceived, and so deceive themselves" (Hobbes, 1996). He also said:

> a man that seeketh precise truth had need to remember what every name he uses stands for, and to place it accordingly; or else he will find himself entangled in words, as a bird in lime twigs; the more he struggles, the more belimed. ... men begin at settling the significations of their words; which settling of significations, they call *definitions*, and place them in the beginning of their reckoning... For the errors of definitions multiply themselves, according as the reckoning proceeds, and lead men into absurdities, which at last they see, but cannot avoid, without reckoning anew from the beginning; in which lies the foundation of their errors. ... So that in the right definition of names lies the first use of speech; which is the acquisition of science: (Hobbes, 1996).

John Locke was also aware of the distinction between words and what they signify in saying that terms should be "reduced in their signification... to determined collections of the simple ideas they do or should stand for" Locke (1690). **John Stuart Mill** said "Definitions are properly of names only, and not of things" (Mill, 1874). He also said:

> To fix the connotation of a concrete name, or the denotation of the corresponding abstract, is to define the name. When this can be done without rendering any received assertions inadmissible, the name can be defined in accordance with its received use, which is vulgarly called defining not the name but the thing. What is meant by the improper expression of defining a thing ... is to define the name, subject to the condition that it shall denote those things (Mill, 1874).

Thus Mill clearly distinguishes between defining the name and defining the thing. The word 'abstract' in the paragraph above is taken here to mean an instance of i.e. abstraction of the attributes contained in the connotation determined for a concrete name, albeit that that concrete name may label an abstract concept. The word 'vulgar' is also taken to mean 'common'.

Neither **Wittgenstein** nor **Popper** followed Mill in this respect, pursuing instead absolute meaning in words themselves, taking the lead from Aristotle, even though Wittgenstein seems to have been aware of the distinction in saying "descriptions ought to take the form: 'The word .... Signifies'" (Wittgenstein & Anscombe, 1958).

Wittgenstein seems to have rushed past the difficulty of gaining agreement. "26… One thinks that learning language consists in giving names to objects… 27. We name things and then we can talk about them" (Wittgenstein & Anscombe, 1958).

Ferdinand de **Saussure** introduced the concept of a word being a sign of a two-sided psychological identity comprised of a signifier and a signified (Saussure, 1966). **Derrida** adopted Saussure's concept of the sign (Derrida, 1970) and developed his deconstruction of structuralism from it (Derrida & Spivak, 1976).

In more recent times, with the prevalence of modernism and the pervasion of the influence of Wittgenstein and his family resemblance concept, as further discussed below, the importance of this distinction has been largely overlooked or forgotten. The analyses in the chapters of Part II indicates the importance of the two-faced aspects of words as signs – the signifier (the word) and signified (what it represents), which is equivalent to the realisation that words *represent* meaning, they do not equal it. But Aristotle's requirement to state the essence of what the thing is, tends to overcome the representational aspect of words that he overlooked in saying that we define things rather than words. It effectively says the closer that definition of the word can be to the essence of the thing itself, the less the confusion.

This leads to proposing the following:

Axiom 3 ***A word simply provides the label or*** ***signifier*** ***for what is*** ***signified*** ***by its agreed definition***. A word can only represent something; it cannot actually be it.

6.3 Issue 3 Word v Phrase Meanings

This issue deals with whether recognising silent or assumed qualifying words that provide context should be regarded as a necessary part of definition or not.

It would seem to be almost self-evident that it should be, but the definitional chapters in Part II of this book, as well as other definitional papers referred to in Part I, found it is so often not done that it was identified as a separate definitional issue. These papers found definitional competition within and between various fields, with one field desiring its definition of a particular term to be regarded as generic and supreme above all others. This resulted from either not considering whether it adequately expressed the essence of the term across other fields or from assuming a qualifier (context) that the proponent did not recognise and which needed to be made explicit. For example, overlooking this issue led to the fathers of the term using both governance and corporate governance synonymously (See Chap. 10), simply because their context was private corporations and the need for government departments to have governance was overlooked, unforeseen or not considered to present any terminological problem. The error here was in adding the unwarranted qualifier "corporate". A similar thing was found in stakeholder theory, which implicitly assumed a company rather than an activity base, as documented in Chap. 17, causing confusion in application to government departments. The error here was in not recognizing and adding the qualifier 'corporate' before 'stakeholder theory'.

This issue has also historically not received overt consideration in the writings of major philosophers on the subject of definitions. However, overlooking this has caused difficulties. **Bertrand Russell** developed his theory of descriptions (RTD) (Russell, 1905) to deal with the problems of co-referring and non-referring expressions. These only start to become problematic if it is assumed that words are meaning rather than just labels representing meaning and the context or qualifiers are overlooked. The problem of referring to the same object (Venus) in two different ways (morning and evening star), or the issue of good versus bad feelings about governance depending upon which side of it you are on, as stated by one of interview participants in McGrath and Whitty (2020c), is easily resolved if the context of the label assignment is made clear by stating the silent or assumed qualifiers. Similarly, the problem of non-referring expressions (referring to non-existent things) also vanishes when it is recognized that words are not meaning but just simply label or represent or signify it and that the full context needs to be made explicit. Searching for absolute truth in and applying Boolean logic to statements containing words which represent only what a group of people think they have agreed those words will signify, is an exercise that cannot help but throw up insoluble conundrums when people have differing understandings of what is signified. Logic, and what can be agreed upon, can sometimes be two very different things. Identification of the existence of a conundrum may simply indicate that there is a problem with the representational framework, which might represent meaning well enough for practical use but isn't really fully correct as it is still a human representation of something, not the thing itself.

For example, a unicorn doesn't exist, but a governance doesn't either. Neither can be captured and put on display. The latter term is a useful construct in our heads that enables regulation for the common good, keeping everyone happy to some degree. Ideas or concepts have existence in the human "mind" or "consciousness" that is neither physical (apart from electrical impulses) nor mystical. But they do have an impact upon human disposition and behaviour, simply because they are independent concepts that can be held in our thinking. They signify or represent a meaning that it would be helpful if we all agreed on. A unicorn is easily drawn and converted into an object of fantasy. A governance can't be drawn; it can only be represented abstractly.

The deconstruction technique of (Derrida & Spivak, 1976) is another case where difficulty has occurred. This seeks the point of inversion in a text where the inbuilt hierarchy can invert itself because of the undecidability of meaning. This inversion point, according to Kleinberg (2013), is found by deconstructing or taking apart the text to identify subconscious bias (normativity) and looking at the pieces to recognise if and where some have been given prominence over others for historical/ cultural/ other reasons. Kleinberg (2013) also notes that deconstruction is a method of enquiry that asserts that all writings are full of confusions and contradictions, and even a writer cannot overcome these by deliberate effort to convey meaning. Deconstruction can therefore never end and so meaning is undecidable.

This, in effect, condones, builds upon, and even reifies the family resemblance concept of Wittgenstein. Both have the common effect of perpetuating loose definition of conceptual terms. That concept of Wittgenstein's is dealt with in more detail in Sect. 7.1.

The need to apply deconstruction to find such an inversion, if there is any such need at all, can be either reduced or avoided if we apply the Mangle, identifying silent or hidden qualifiers, providing the basis for reaching agreement as demonstrated in the chapters of Part II. This has provided a means of clarifying meaning, contradicting, or one could say, deconstructing this aspect of deconstructionism. As noted in Issues 1 and 2 above, words do not have absolute meaning of themselves, but we can simply agree what they mean, then judge understanding of meaning against that and move on, without becoming stuck in an unending infinite deconstructive loop.

This leads to proposing the following:

Definitional Rule 2 ***Identify any silent or assumed qualifiers.***

6.4 Issue 4 Dogma v Human Framework

Note that the Oxford English Dictionary (OED) (accessed on 28 December 2018) defines a framework as an essential supporting structure of a building, vehicle, or object. It also defines dogma as a principle or set of principles laid down by an authority as incontrovertibly true. A human framework is therefore a framework developed by man rather than by God and so its authority can be questioned, and it may not necessarily be incontrovertibly true.

This issue deals with the nature of our beliefs about things and whether those should be regarded as absolute truth or as a framework constructed by some human being(s) to represent aspects of the world.

With the question framed in that way, the answer again may seem obvious, until one asks the question "what if those beliefs are religious dogma?" In project management, the issue arises in relation to approaches, practices and beliefs common to IT having spread inappropriately to other parts of the project management world, causing confusion. One example is the focus of MSP on the internal organisational transformation resulting from an IT change project. This leads to difficulty in applying MSP to engineering infrastructure organisations where no such transformation occurs (McGrath & Whitty, 2020a). Dogmatic applications require such a transformation to be found, which it can be in the transformational affect that infrastructure projects have upon communities; but this is artificial because it doesn't apply to the delivery organisation when it's supposed to. This causes further confusion when it overlaps with a stakeholder management framework. These and many other such instances are described in McGrath and Whitty (2019), McGrath and Whitty (2020b), McGrath and Whitty (2020a). This issue was realized (together with Issue 2) in reflecting on all Part II chapters and the other definitional papers referred to in this book collectively and recognising the difference between underlying meaning or truth and the human framework we use to explain it. This issue also reflects into Issues 3 and 10.

Within project management, various frameworks are promoted with some degree of fervour that may help in increasing sales, but that is not helpful in reaching a common understanding across frameworks. The power of dogma became apparent in McGrath and Whitty (2019), where a particular project management system (PRINCE2) had been reified to the point of practitioners accepting it as dogma, leading to superseded interpretations of the terms program and portfolio from an out-of-date manual being adopted, causing ongoing confusion. It became evident that frameworks provide belief systems which lead their followers to take action in accordance with those beliefs which they believe are 'right'.

As noted in Issue 2, **John Stuart Mill** regarded words in a language as a means of signifying something. This can be viewed as recognizing language as providing a framework for representing things; a verbal means of expressing our feelings, notions or ideas. Furthermore, as noted earlier, words (language) are only one means by which we communicate. We also communicate with gestures, body language and touch, each within their own framework of representation. So it is evident that the speech framework cannot be a complete framework for the expression of meaning, as per Axiom 2, above.

Derrida considered that deconstruction meant the dismantling of excessive loyalty to any idea and learning to see the aspects of the truth that might lie buried within its opposite. Derrida and Caputo (1997) expressed this as "explore what it omits, forgets, excludes, expels, marginalizes, dismisses, ignores, scorns, slights, takes too lightly, waves off, is just not serious about!" Guarding against excessive loyalty to any idea or framework is a most useful aspect of deconstructionism and this is consistent with the approach taken in the Mangle, which guards against this problem by requiring exclusion of all normative matters.

This leads to proposing the following:

Definitional Rule 3 ***Exclude beliefs from definition***. Accommodate them after definitions have been agreed, not before (This is the same as Rule 1 with beliefs substituted for attitudes. Both attitudes and beliefs can be regarded as opinions).

6.5 Issue 5 Secular Essence v Ethereal Essence (Beliefs)

This issue addresses whether use of an ethereal interpretation of essence should be excluded from definitions or not.

It emerged indirectly from preparation and submission of the power papers in Chapters 11 and 12, because of their implied challenge to Wittgenstein's family resemblance theory (see Sect. 7.1). That theory implies that what the Mangle achieves is not possible. The reasoning for that theory is that if essence includes ethereal essence, that cannot be verified, therefore any form of essence cannot be universally determined. While this argument is quite obviously illogical, saying that because a word has two different senses that disproving one sense of it disproves the other, it is nevertheless pervasive. The many definitional chapters in Part II and the other definitional papers referenced in this book contradict this position by successfully using essence in defining a wide range of terms including governance, program, stakeholders, accountability, responsibility, power, ethics, leadership, strategy, management and strategic management. These essential secular definitions were made possible by excluding ethereal essence. However, there is still a residual in governance, for example, as found in the practitioner interviews, where the concept was reified or considered reverently, as would befit a relationship to an ethereal entity, without anyone being really confident they knew what it was or how to define it (McGrath & Whitty, 2020c).

A secular understanding of essence considers what a thing is within the limitations of the four dimensions we have sensual access to. Going beyond this into other dimensions involves an ethereal understanding of the term. Essence is defined above as *A property or group of properties of something without which it would not be what it is.* The definition is equally applicable to both secular and ethereal essence. This means that another qualifying word is necessary (Issue 3) to identify which sense of essence is being referred to.

The following discussion indicates how these two understandings have arisen philosophically, how they have become inseparable causing confusion, enabling the secular interpretation to be discounted or over-ridden by the ethereal one. In this, we have a situation where two different and almost mutually exclusive understandings from different dimensions have been assumed and applied to the same term. This is a pernicious form of polysemy that can be expressed as two terms having 'dual simultaneous meanings' with the 'higher order' ethereal meaning gazumping the secular meaning without any subconscious awareness that this has even happened. This has ensured that the rules resulting from Issues 1 (fact versus opinion), 3 (word versus phrase meanings) and 4 (dogma versus human representation) have all been contravened.

Aristotle used the term essence in both secular and ethereal senses and his secular use is examined here before considering his ethereal use of the term. He considered that everything contains an essence or an essential feature that enables it to be identified. We can therefore know what a thing is and what its natural role is. This essence of a thing must remain the same as its attributes change over time. Aristotle asks what features something must lose to not be what it previously was (Whitty, 2013). Aristotle also says:

> what belongs to a thing in respect of itself belongs to it in its essence (*en tôi ti esti*)" for we refer to it "in the account that states the essence" (*Posterior Analytics*, 73a34–5). He reiterates these ideas in Z.4: "there is an essence of just those things whose logos is a definition" (1030a6), "the essence of a thing is what it is said to be in respect of itself" (1029b14). (Cohen, 2016).

(Cohen, 2016) also notes:

Some maintain that Aristotle's theory is ultimately inconsistent on the grounds that it is committed to all three of the following propositions:

(i) Substance is form.
(ii) Form is universal.
(iii) No universal is a substance

All of these cannot be so and Cohen (2016) takes the following position:

the indefinability of particulars makes it impossible for substantial forms to be particulars. … Aristotle's claim that a substantial form is an individual (tode ti) does not exclude its being a universal (katholou). Universals are contrasted with particulars (kath' hekasta), not individuals (although Aristotle does sometimes ignore the distinction between tode ti and kath' hekaston). What makes something a tode ti is its being a fully determinate thing, not further differentiable; what makes something a kath' hekaston is its being a particular thing, unrepeatable, and not predicated of anything else. There is thus the possibility of a universal tode ti—a fully determinate universal not further divisible into lower-level universals, but predicated of numerous particulars. … Aristotle's point may be that since form is predicated of matter, a substantial form is predicated of various clumps of matter. But it is not the substance of those clumps of matter, for it is predicated accidentally of them. The thing with which it is uniquely correlated, and of which it is the substance, is not one of its instances, but is the substantial form itself. This conclusion should not be surprising in light of Aristotle's claim in Z.6 that 'each substance is one and the same as its essence'. A universal substantial form just is that essence (Cohen, 2016).

This accords with Whitty (2013), whose analysis of Aristotle concluded that the essence of something is derived from its form which means more than its shape; it refers to its functional structure, and the way it is organised to function. This is similar to Governance which is the Gestalt, the emergent quality formed from the relationship the parts have with each other i.e. the parts create a form.

And in De Anima he is perfectly explicit that the soul, which is the form or essence of a living thing, "is a cause in three of the ways we have distinguished" (415b10)—efficient, formal, and final (Cohen, 2016).

In H.6, Aristotle returns to the problem of the unity of definition and offers a new solution based on the concepts of potentiality and actuality. He begins by pointing out (recalling the language of Z.17) that the things whose unity he is trying to explain are those "which have several parts and in which the totality is not, as it were, a mere heap, but the whole is something besides the parts" (1045a8–10). His task is to explain the unity of such complexes. The problem is insoluble, he says, unless one realizes that "one element is matter and another is form, and one is potentially and the other is actually." Once one realizes this, "the question will no longer be thought a difficulty" (1045a20–25) (Cohen, 2016, S13).

And since proper definables are universals, it remains to be seen how the proposed solution applies to them. After all, universals are not material objects, and so it is not clear how they can be viewed as hylomorphic compounds. But Aristotle has at his disposal a concept that can do this perfectly, viz., the concept of intelligible matter (hulê noêtê)… Aristotle goes on (1045a33) to introduce matter into the current context. If this is so, we may conclude that the material component in the definition of a species is intelligible matter (Cohen, 2016).

Elsewhere, he explicitly describes genus as matter: “the genus is the matter of that of which it is called the genus” (I.8, 1058a23). So a species too, although it is not itself a material object, can be considered a hylomorphic compound. Its matter is its genus, which is only potentially the species defined; its differentia is the form that actualizes the matter.

Summarising all of this, substance is essence is form; the form of a hylomorphic compound may be accidentally predicated of matter; that form is potentiality (e.g. governance, to direct and control if properly related/ coupled) and matter is actuality; material may refer to its material or its structure or its ‘intelligible matter’, making it the kind of thing that it is. Aristotle’s essence can therefore be understood to be the form of the thing qualified by its material or structure or its ‘intelligible matter’ and the precedence of causes in any definition is formal followed by material, with the efficient and final causes generally not being relevant to definition.

However, in saying the soul is the essence of a living thing, Aristotle sowed the seed for soul to be regarded as a proxy for essence. But this is only an association; if substance and essence are the same, ascribing the term soul to be the essence of one class of entity looks beyond the four dimensions and five senses we have ready access to and ignores other characteristics within those dimensions and senses that could have been used. For example, he does not actually say that intellectual concepts, which will have an essence, must have a soul. Nevertheless, later philosophers have been induced into equating essence with soul, as will be demonstrated in further discussion of this issue below, producing uncertainty in treating it as physical or secular, to the point where the ethereal dimension is seen to predominate and almost over-rule purely secular consideration. This leads to the circumstance of one term having two very different applications of the same definitions within different contexts. This requires resolution if we desire definitional clarity.

This confusion in the definition of essence and the predominance of the ethereal over the secular view of essence lead **Popper** away from the concept and into an irreconcilable tangle between definition and diarrhesis (as further discussed in Sect. 7.3). It has also allowed acceptance of Wittgenstein’s family resemblance concept. This indicates the need for the secular definition of soul developed above. That definition does not preclude soul from being the essence of living things, but just leaves out any required extra-dimensional or extra-sensory belief. It is therefore independent of any particular belief, in a similar way to **JSM** defining an animal as being something which possess attributes of sensation and voluntary motion. It also takes no position on the completely separate argument concerning ethereal existence or otherwise of the soul. It just defines the term ‘soul’ in a way that says what the concept is, without specifying where it comes from or what belief system may surround it. It is then compatible with having either secular or ethereal qualifier attached to it so that we know what we are talking about.

Whitty (2013) noted that **Locke** held the view that classification takes the pragmatic form of conventional names which we use to cover or represent the experience. We cannot claim to know the real essence of a thing, only the nominal essence through the mediated terms of our senses, which has more to do with our experience of it than with the thing itself. There are primary qualities in the object and in the experience itself e.g. hardness, and secondary qualities produced by something in the object without actually being in the object itself e.g. colour. This reinforces the additional difficulty of our particular perceptions of things being different from others because of our different experiences of it Whitty (2013). However as far as essence is concerned, this difficulty can be accommodated by distinguishing between physical and ethereal perception and excluding the latter and its associated value judgements from definition, thereby removing one source of disagreement and confusion. Locke can be regarded as having advocated definition in terms of secular essence by saying that terms should be "reduced in their signification… to determined collections of the simple ideas they do or should stand for" (Locke, 1690).

The 'essence' of what Popper was getting at with his concept of *diarrhesis* was generating understanding by dividing the subject space into intelligible portions. This aligns with Aristotle's intent with the secular aspect of his concept of essence, as observed by (Naraniecki, 2009).

However, the ethereal connotation of the term 'essence' introduced beliefs/ value judgements/ explanations beyond the four dimensions we have ready access to. This association has been in place since the Stoics, whose philosophy influenced Aristotle. As shown above, Aristotle accepted an ethereal dimension to essence but did not universally require it.

There is also a possible connection between ethereal essence and intuition because of the uncertain source of the latter. Intuition can be attributed to the combination of sense inputs or to some ethereal reality or to both. Popper's reservation about Aristotle's infallibility of intuition is understandable when it is considered that peoples' ethereal 'realities' may be quite different, and intuition can be very difficult to distinguish from strong desire at times, whereas processing of sensory input is generally reliable and may have been what Aristotle was referring to.

Derrida and Spivak (1976) also had difficulty with essence. Deconstruction seeks the point in a text where the inbuilt hierarchy inverts itself because of the undecidability of meaning, as mentioned in discussing Issue 3. If we were to focus on actually agreeing the essential signification of our conceptual terms, we would have done no more than getting to the point where we could all know what it is we and others are actually talking about, facilitating communication by reducing unnecessary confusion. Deconstructionism capitulates on agreeing essential meanings of conceptual terms.

The concept of **existentialism** provides a very clear demonstration of this definitional error. Sartre concluded that "existence precedes essence" (Sartre, 1973), based on the reasoning that human beings have no essence before their existence because there is no Creator. This means that he justified this conclusion on the basis that essence was ethereal but then expressed his reversal of Plato's statement using a secular understanding of the term. It is possible to restate both positions by inserting the missing qualifiers:

Plato: Ethereal essence precedes existence.
Sartre: Existence precedes secular essence.

This removes the metaphysical confusion from Sartre's statement, taking it out of the realm of meta-physics and leaving Plato's statement as metaphysical and making sense, whether one believes in God or not. The modified statement of Sartre's requires no belief in God but also does not contradict such a belief. A person's essence or key character traits can still be described whether an ethereal soul exists or not. This leads to the conclusion that the conversion and reification of Sartre's unqualified statement into an 'ism' (existentialism) is grounded in nothing more than a definitional error. The same applies to Plato's unqualified statement.

However, there is also a secular sense to Plato's metaphysical statement that is not contentious. When a person consciously creates or makes or does something or causes something to happen, they will first have had an idea or conception of it. Of course, a person can also unconsciously create, where there is no intent and the bringing into existence is accidental, such as unintended consequences. That conscious idea or conception that precedes the bringing into existence will deal with the function it will perform and the characteristics it must have to fulfil that desired function. The secular part of Plato's words could therefore be expressed by adding the missing qualifiers as follows:

Plato further re-written: The idea of secular essence precedes existence, where there is an intention to create.

This describes planning and leaves ethereal/ metaphysical aspects to be debated separately. Note that Sartre's modified statement still applies to both intentional and unintentional creation as it takes the position of all observers, including the creator, be they secular or ethereal, once the creation is done.

It is therefore evident that confusion is reduced if the definition of any term is approached through seeking its secular essence.

Possible criticisms of this position would be to question whether this is even possible, or to claim that it is an idealistic over-simplification to think that quite divergent usages of some terms could possibly have the same essence. An example that may prompt such criticisms and appear, at first sight, to make this position seem untenable is the use of the word 'ball'. When referring to a ball, would it mean a ball to play some sort of sport with, or a dance which is held in a ballroom? How could any plausible argument possibly be based on finding a common essence across these two meanings of the same word?

However, there are three possible answers to this:

1. There is actually a common element, and that is fun, as borne out by considering another common usage "we had an absolute ball!". Playing ball-games is fun, as is dancing. So there is actually a common feature or essence in all of them - as being a short-hand way of referring to activities that are fun to take part in, one being a game and one a dance. It is just symbolized by the word ball which was named after something you can have fun with that just happens to be round(ish allowing for Rugby) and happens to provide a physical object that can be used to symbolize or represent things.

2. The concern here is only to remove ambiguity from the management environment (where clarity/ removal of ambiguity is actually an advantage), not from all environments. The example is not from a management environment and so this criticism is invalid.
3. Considering the hidden or silent qualifiers as well as context, the problem is actually between ball-game and ball-room and both have simply become abbreviated in common usage.

Consider the management example of regulations existing in two government departments, one in a democracy and one in a dictatorship; what is the common essence there? It is the fact that both sets of regulations form part of the governance system of their organisation. Ethics can be written into governance arrangements, but it is those arrangements that then form part of governance, not the ethics themselves; they can be either 'good' or 'bad'.

Two further examples demonstrate the same thing. The term 'card' can be, say a nine of diamonds in a card game, a red or yellow card in a football game or a punched computer card. All of these are a piece of (possibly laminated) cardboard, with a pattern appropriate for the circumstances. Specifying the context removes uncertainty regarding what sort of card it is. Furthermore, the cards all symbolize something and the particular card provides the physical means of signifying the intended concept. Similarly, a 'tap' can be a knock, a water outlet, the thread on the inside of a metal sleeve or a piece of metal on the bottom of a shoe. All of these have the connotation of letting something out, whether it be sound, water or a bolt.

These examples demonstrate just how easy it can be to fail to find secular essence. Just because it may be difficult to identify does not excuse failing to adequately look for it or failing to adopt a perspective that allows it to be found. It may be that there are some terms or usages that are particularly resistant to this approach of finding common secular essence by examining uses across different contexts. But it is difficult to avoid the utilitarian position of maximising the greater good, concluding that if we can greatly reduce confusion by adopting this position, that we should do so. Any remaining difficulties can be viewed from the perspective of Issue 8 which deals with precision versus clarity; here clarity rather than full theoretical precision would be selected.

This approach could be further criticised for just being convenient. However, the alternative is to ignore the importance of context/ boundaries/ environment/ limits in any problem, which is not a scientific approach. In this light, it is worth remembering that Newton's theory had small errors which went unexplained for some centuries until Einstein's theory of relativity. But Newton's theory actually enabled the industrial revolution to occur, producing the standard of living we have today. Had such an objection been sustained then, it may have prevented the industrial revolution occurring. Ideas do not have to be fully correct to be useful.

The Mangle seeks essential definitions that exclude normative considerations, thereby selecting secular essence and excluding ethereal essence. Its success in resolving definitional difficulties across a range of subjects, as documented in the chapters of Part II and the other published definitional papers referred to in this book, indicates that the approach works.

This leads to proposing the following:

Axiom 4 ***The closer the signification of a word comes to the important attributes that a thing must have (i.e. essence) for that label (signifier) to be correctly assigned to it, the closer it gets to accurately representing the auditory part of meaning contained in the written word***, and the less the confusion that can result. The closer it comes to representing the meaning received from all five senses, the closer it comes to representing the full meaning.

Axiom 5 ***Some words such as essence have dual simultaneous meanings that are secular (four dimensional) and ethereal (extra-dimensional) and the 'higher order' ethereal meaning will gazump the secular by subconscious default unless the issue is called out.*** Defining in terms of secular essence removes the dependence of definition on matters of ethereal belief. Ethereality emerges from seeking definition/ meaning in dimensions other than those that are physically accessible to us.

Definitional Rule 4 ***Exclude ethereal significations from the definition of unqualified terms with dual simultaneous meanings such as 'essence' by adding the qualifiers 'ethereal' or 'secular' to them.*** Accommodate the ethereal after definitions have been agreed, not before (Note: This is effectiveley the same as rule 3 with ethereal essence substituted for beliefs).

6.6 Issue 6 Intension v Extension

This issue deals with the method of definition and addresses the question of whether intension or extension should be the first choice of definitional method when definitions are contested.

Definition by extension lists all the items or instances the thing may include or be found in. Definition by intension lists the minimum attributes the thing must have. The former runs the risk of omission and the latter runs the risk of selecting the wrong attributes. However, as Copi and Cohen (1990) state, "the extension of a term is determined by its intension, but the reverse is not true... intension must determine extension". This means that the risk of omission in definition by extension is avoided if the correct intension is identified, indicating that definition by intension is generally preferable. This conclusion was reached in developing and using the Mangle to resolve conflicting definitions of governance terms in Chap. 10. The problem of definition by extension also became apparent in the range of definitions of governance given by practitioners, as reported in McGrath and Whitty (2020c). These definitions included oversight, decision-making, structure, approvals, way finding, management of risk, gates, Quality Assurance (QA). These are all extensions or instantiations of the term, but they do not tell us what the essence of governance actually is, whereas definition by intension does tell us that. The intensional definition derived using the Mangle defines governance as "the system by which an entity is directed and controlled".

Definition by intension is equivalent to definition of secular essence, the philosophical background to which has been detailed above in discussing Issue 5, requiring no further enumeration here.

This leads to proposing the following:

Definitional Rule 5 ***Define by intension rather than by extension where-ever possible.***

6.7 Issue 7 Objects v Concepts

This issue addresses whether a common understanding of objects and concepts can be reached using the same linguistic approach or not.

The realization that this may be an important distinction arose from reflection upon how it may have been possible for so many different conceptions to be in circulation about what various management terms are thought to mean. A wide range of understandings of governance was found in both the academic literature and the practitioner interviews reported in McGrath and Whitty (2015), McGrath and Whitty (2020c). The same was found for other management terms, such as ethics, stakeholders, strategic management and power which are considered in Part II. In searching for an explanation, it was noticed that there is one key word in the label 'essentially contested concept' given by Gallie (1956) and that is the term concept. That implies that the only terms that are contested are concepts i.e. we don't have difficulty reaching agreement on what we understand by the terms we use to label objects we can see. This suggests that there is a process we use for reaching agreement on labels we assign to objects and that that process works. It also suggests that whatever process we use for agreeing what we understand by a label given to a conceptual term doesn't always work. That led to the following analysis.

Concepts are thoughts which have no physical existence detectible by our five senses i.e. they cannot be seen, touched, heard, smelt or tasted; there is nothing that can be pointed at to verify that we have reached a common understanding. So the verification process we use for objects cannot work for concepts and a separate means of verification is needed for them.

One means of doing this is to rely on authority, i.e. believe a person we think seems to know a lot about the subject. That may produce a result that is not contested, but it also may not. We have no way of knowing whether that person may have learned their understanding from someone who was also confused or whose experience covered only some of the possible circumstances the term can be applied to.

Another way is to rely upon what everybody else thinks. But we have no idea where the view originated, or the motivation of the initiator, or the standard of proof they may have thought necessary, or even whether there was any proof at all – it may have just suited the initiator's convenience, or they may have simply overlooked communicating their context.

There are so many things that can go wrong with reaching agreement on a common understanding of conceptual terms that it became evident that the readily available means, the commonly accepted process, is inadequate, and a different and more reliable process of reaching agreement is required. The Mangle fills this process gap by providing a verification process for concepts that is unnecessary for physical objects, which we can verify agreement on by pointing at.

This need for an additional process for verifying that we do have a common understanding of conceptual terms, does not appear to have been previously recognised as a philosophical issue of any importance.

The word 'concept' has been defined above as an abstract idea. It is necessary to distinguish between a grammatical object and a physical object as a grammatical object is itself a concept that can include physical objects as well as concepts. In addressing this issue of the distinction between objects and concepts, only physical objects are dealt with here.

The notion of what a concept is in relation to its philosophical background was considered by Whitty (2013), who said:

> **Kant** shunned the relativist view that everyone experiences everything completely differently and felt that there must be some commonality or common grounding of experiences… **Locke** introduced the idea that our knowledge of the world comes to us through our senses... In computing terms, **Hume** has discovered that we have an operating system that provides a platform for all the other mental software to run on. But **Kant** is asking: what is it that enables us to proceed with running this mental operating system? There must be a mental BIOS that needs to be run in order for the mind to proceed to come to know something (Whitty, 2013).

He further considered this BIOS (Basic Input Output System) comprises:

> Kant's four 'pure categories of the understanding' which are; quality (unity, plurality, and totality), quantity (reality, negation, and limitation), modality (possibility, existence, and necessity), and relation (inherence, causality, community, and correlation) … (and) The application of these categories *is* thinking. … using these cognitive powers is literally what understanding is (Whitty, 2013).

He then summarizes Kant's view of concepts as follows:

> Kant puts forward the case that we build our most basic mental concepts on fundamental axioms which we hold as unquestionably true. They intuitively feel right… We build our ideas and concepts on them. The first axiom is that we distinguish 'between' things, between one object and another in the mind… the mind cannot come to know any other concepts without the spatial axiom. The second basic axiom is the mental capacity to make distinctions 'within' things. So within the ideas we hold in our mind there are certain dynamics which we call changes or motions or actions, and the experience of observing this is what we call temporality or time (Whitty, 2013).

Temporality is necessary for concepts to exist and for physical objects to be observed. However, concepts exist only in our thoughts and this makes verifying our collective understanding of them more difficult than it is for physical objects we can point to.

Difficulty with the issue of linguistic treatment of objects and concepts occurs most noticeably in **Derrida**'s concept of deconstruction. Kleinberg (2013), in commenting on deconstruction with respect to text, notes that the first step is to examine the text for moments that betray when the inbuilt hierarchy inverts itself, creating aporia or undecidability of meaning and the second step is to locate the moment where the seemingly dependent term turns out to be foundational for the dominant term. This presumes that there must always be some binary hierarchy present, some struggle between two opposites, in all terms. This may be possible for some concepts but is a step too far for terms representing physical objects.

This need to find an inversion in deconstruction only exists because we are chasing a phantom that emerges only when we haven't agreed on what is signified by the signifier when we are considering conceptual terms. The Mangle provides a means of doing this without needing to rely on deconstruction. If we were to focus on actually agreeing the essential meanings (signifiers) of our conceptual terms, we would have done no more than get to the point where we could all know what it is we and others are actually talking about, facilitating communication by reducing unnecessary confusion. If there is still anything left of deconstructionism's point of inversion beyond that, the amount of potential confusion will have at least been much reduced. As mentioned in Issue 5, deconstructionism capitulates on agreeing essential meanings of conceptual terms.

Derrida also saw the subjectivity of language as its principal problem. He thought that absolute truth could not be found through language because of the undecidability and subjectivity of language, and that words could not be pinned down to a single definite meaning because of their invisible trace, according to Kleinberg (2013). But, of course there will be subjectivity if the meanings of conceptual terms haven't been agreed. If it were true that meaning differs from reader to reader, from time to time, on every word, then there would indeed be no possibly of having a shared truth that we can all access. But then there would be no point at all to any language we may have, as none of them could serve any useful purpose. But language does serve the useful purpose of enabling communication; we don't actually have too much difficulty agreeing on the signifiers of physical objects we can point to and say "that's what a 'such n such' is" in whatever language we happen to speak. This means that the fundamental premise of deconstructionism, of subjectivity of language generally, is false. Expression of subjectivity using language is a general occurrence that language accommodates, but introduction of subjectivity into definition is not universally so, as evidenced by the relative ease of reaching agreement on what labels denoting physical objects signify. Introducing subjectivity into definition simply causes confusion. This effectively deconstructs deconstructionism.

There is shared knowledge we can all access in the physical sciences such as engineering, otherwise things (physical structures) fall down, leaving the reality of failure, injury, loss of life, destruction and litigation. That is a reality check not necessarily present in the social sciences until long after the social construction is installed, and the causes of any failure are then very difficult to trace. However, the consequences for injury and loss of life of any failed social system, such as Nazism, can be much greater than the failure of any physical structure. The physical sciences are constantly grounded in an immediacy of reality that the social sciences are not, or at least not until the consequences become evident and attempts to identify and attribute cause and effect become possible. By that time the 'thought architects' who conceived it, and the 'thought engineers' who figured out how to implement it (if anyone actually did so) may well be long gone and the trace of the idea very difficult to determine.

If the meaning of both signifier and the signified in language is really "the relationship between two palimpsests (such that) reading then resembles those X-ray pictures which discover, under the epidermis of the last painting, another hidden picture of the same painter or another painter, no matter" (Derrida & Spivak, 1976), then how could we have ever learned to speak and agree on any terms at all, let alone to the level we currently do. The proposition may be esoterically appealing for concepts, but it is inapplicable at a physical level. The only heat likely to be applied will be emotional and that certainly won't reveal the palimpsest; it is far more likely to hide it and/ or result in (possibly murderous) conflict.

An aspect of deconstruction that Kleinberg (2013) focuses on is seeking the point of inversion, or the point at which the writer's assumed social hierarchy is exposed. He does this by examining only the text for moments that betray when the inbuilt hierarchy inverts itself, as mentioned in discussing Issue 3, to expose the arbitrary or constructed nature of that hierarchy. This presumes there is an inbuilt hierarchy in everything. This may be so for some concepts but falls down for physical objects which simply exist and are allocated a sound to signify them. Any hierarchy determined according to any criteria for objects can only be between objects and will refer to a relationship between them rather than a definition of them. This is quite different to finding the inversion point for a concept.

Wittgenstein overlooked this issue through adopting as his basis for analysis a primitive language dealing with a builder and assistant communicating about physical objects. In this, he took the lead from Augustine, and was only secondarily concerned with the names of certain actions and properties. He saw "the remaining kinds of word as something that will take care of itself" (Wittgenstein and Anscombe, 1958). However, it is within these types that concepts fall and there is an additional difficulty in reaching agreement on concepts that physical objects do not have because the simple means of verification, namely pointing, is not possible. The processes of teaching and learning that preoccupied him as an educator have little to do with what is agreed before there is something to teach.

These considerations lead to proposing the following:

Axiom 6 ***Concepts require an additional definitional process to physical objects for agreement to be reached, as they cannot be pointed at, to collectively verify meaning***. The Mangle provides this. (Note that this does not refer to grammatical objects which can include both physical objects and concepts.)

Definitional Rule 6 ***Use the Mangle to resolve contention for conceptual terms***. It provides a triangulation process to verify that a common understanding of concepts has been reached. It also provides a means of incorporating any new realizations or applications. It is not necessary to apply it to objects which can be seen/touched; their physical existence automatically generates agreement upon the signification of any term used to represent them.

6.8 Issue 8 Detail v Overview

This issue considers the relationship between depth and breadth; between detail and overview.

It addresses the level of precision required to provide clarity sufficient to generate agreement on definition (what is signified) by considering two opposing philosophical views, one that increasing precision universally obscures meaning, and the other that it clarifies it.

An example of this occurring in project management is in the definitions of a project found in practitioner reference documents. PMI publications define it broadly as an activity whereas PRINCE2 and MSP define it as an organisation, focusing on just one aspect or detail of what is involved in many, but not all projects. Similarly, PRINCE2 claims to be about and for projects yet does not adopt a project lifecycle, choosing instead to use a product development cycle. It also uses the iterating part of one 'stage' of that cycle to base its whole process upon, having the effect of requiring an extraordinarily detailed, bottom-up approach without any strategic perspective or overview.

However, the first inkling of the importance of this distinction came from Chap. 16 dealing with distinguishing accountability from responsibility, in which McGrath and Whitty (2018) observed "Universal definition of terms can produce clarity whereas universal application of different understandings of a term cannot". This raised the issue of how to accommodate Karl **Popper**'s philosophy which promotes clarity but decries definition, claiming it goes to increasingly impractical detail, towards the point of infinite regress (Popper, 2002). He was concerned with induction, which he said "Hume had shown was invalid because it led to an infinite regress" (Popper, 1979). He deals with the issue of precision versus clarity somewhat inconclusively in saying:

> although clarity is valuable in itself, exactness or precision is not: there can be no point in trying to be more precise than our problem demands. Linguistic precision is a phantom, and problems connected with the meaning or definition of words are unimportant (Popper, 2002).

He considered that "a definition can only reduce the meaning of the defined term to that of undefined terms" and concluded "this Wittgensteinian belief is nonsense" (Popper, 2002).

This raises the question as to how we can reach this point of clarity that he valued without defining what we understand to be the meaning of the labels we give our concepts. Where is the threshold between clarity and detail? He uses a process he calls diarrhesis which subdivides the conceptual space, but he doggedly refused to acknowledge a place for definition. He also said that no diarrhesis is final (Popper et al., 2008).

Popper (2002) proposed his Table of Ideas showing how he considered truth and meaning were related. That table is reproduced below as Fig. 6.1.

I will enumerate the left-hand side in full, using his capitalisation:

> IDEAS that is DESIGNATIONS or TERMS or CONCEPTS may be formulated in WORDS which may be MEANINGFUL and their MEANING may be reduced, by way of DEFINITIONS to that of UNDEFINED CONCEPTS and the attempt to establish (rather than reduce) by these means their MEANING leads to infinite regress (Popper, 2002).

This enumeration indicates Popper overlooked the possibility that there are some contested concepts, so we do not get the opportunity to progress through increasing precision to the point of infinite regress as we can't even get to the point of agreeing in very general terms what the labels we give them signify. So, we are stuck with no original use or authority to fall back on. We have words to describe contested concepts, all of them meaningful to someone but not necessarily to everyone.

Another example, although unrelated to management, demonstrates very well a further problem with the table. It is the definition of an animal mentioned earlier as

	IDEAS	
	that is	
DESIGNATIONS or TERMS or CONCEPTS		STATEMENTS or PROPOSITIONS or THEORIES
	may be formulated in	
WORDS		ASSERTIONS
	which may be	
MEANINGFUL		TRUE
	and their	
MEANING		TRUTH
	may be reduced, by way of	
DEFINITIONS		DERIVATIONS
	to that of	
UNDEFINED CONCEPTS		PRIMITIVE PROPOSITIONS
	the attempt to establish (rather than reduce) by these means their	
MEANING		TRUTH
	leads to an infinite regress	

Fig. 6.1 Popper's table of ideas. (Sourced from Popper (2002))

"all things which possess attributes of sensation and voluntary motion" (Mill, 1874) (Book IV Chap. IV §2). This definition was sufficiently clear to include an ape, a bear, a mouse, a bird or a human. There was no infinite regress there, unless the pedantic step of defining sensation and voluntary motion was pursued. We could therefore say that it defined an animal in terms of other undefined concepts, but the definitions were sufficiently clear to not need further definitional effort in the direction of infinite regress.

Nevertheless, sense can be made of this inconsistency if we distinguish (i.e. make a diarrhesis) between defining for the purpose of usage and defining for the purpose of understanding the internal workings of the entity or phenomenon labelled by the term. If we accept the former purpose, we need go only as far as facilitates communication and we then do not reach infinite regress. If we accept the latter purpose, then it is possible we may get to infinite regress. Popper was apparently focusing on the latter purpose in his table.

The following revision of the left-hand side of the table (with changes underlined/ struck-through) would accommodate the definitional difficulties and render the table more generic:

> IDEAS that is DESIGNATIONS or TERMS <u>are used to label</u> CONCEPTS and may be formulated in WORDS which may <u>or may not be generally AGREED</u> and <u>the lack of agreement on</u> their MEANING may be <u>leading to prevention of adequate</u> DEFINITIONS. The attempt to ~~establish (rather than~~ reduce~~) by these means~~ their MEANING leads to an infinite regress.

Here the underlying meaning is separated from the representation or formulation of it in words. By not distinguishing between the label of the concept, the words representing it, and the thing itself, Popper's view of definition would be considered 'vulgar' by John Stuart Mill. Perhaps he was over-reacting to Wittgenstein's obsession with the mechanics of language, which erupted in the famous poker incident, as documented in Edmonds and Eidinow (2001). Popper stated "if philosophy was all about word puzzles, I would not have gone into it". However, he does not appear to have recognised language as just a framework for representing things (Issue 4), even though he wrote a whole book about the myth of the framework. As Popper points out in that book, it may well be difficult for people to communicate when they have different frameworks (Popper & Notturno, 1994), but an aversion to definition will generate unnecessary difficulty. He may well have been referring to what would now colloquially be termed a paradigm rather than a framework, where a framework is an unemotive term referring to some structure of thought, whereas a paradigm has the connotation of being a framework that is strongly believed in or is so deeply ingrained that it is assumed to be true and/ or we may not even be aware of having it.

(Popper, 1995) claimed that "the attempt to define terms would only increase the vagueness and confusion". This statement suffers greatly from being a universal statement. It also overlooks the process versus content distinction dealt with below in Issue 9. It simply demonstrates that Popper must have had a completely different view (or definition) of definition. This statement may have been true in the political example he chose to demonstrate his point, of political speeches becoming much longer, to the point of defining every single word they use. But this is an extreme example that pursues understanding of components rather than understanding of usage. It is only words that lack agreement on what is signified by the term where clarification is necessary; otherwise, what is the purpose of language if, no matter what we say, nobody knows anything of what we mean. That would simply render communication impossible. Of course, it may be difficult to know when we have a different understanding of a concept to somebody else, but on the majority of words, that difficulty does not exist and there is no need to clutter the verbal space with definitions of those terms, or proceed towards pedantic infinite regress any further than the point where agreement can be reached. The falsity of this universal claim of Popper's is also evident from the number of successful applications of the Mangle in Part II and in the definitional papers referred to in this book, and in resolving significations for 'essentially contested terms', in the terminology of Gallie (1956).

Popper was most critical of definitions, saying:

> The following passage from Crossman's *Plato Today* is characteristic of a view held by many contemporary philosophers of repute, for example, by Wittgenstein [46]. 'if we do not **know precisely the meaning of the words** we use, we cannot discuss anything profitably. Most of the futile arguments on which we all waste our time are largely due to the fact that we each have our own vague meanings for the words we use and assume that our opponents are using them in the same senses. If we defined our terms to start with, we could have far more profitable discussions…'. This passage is very characteristic of one of the prejudices which we owe to Aristotle, of the prejudice that language can be made more precise by the use of definitions (Popper, 1995).

I contend that Aristotle was correct, and that Popper was mistaken in inferring that increasing precision was the problem, as was Wittgenstein, as the quotation from him bolded above indicates, exposing the workings of his mind in thinking that words = meaning. The chapters of Part II and the other definitional papers referred to in Part I indicate that the problem is rather in lack of agreement on what conceptual terms signify (Issue 1/ Axiom 1). Describing what is meant in sufficient detail to arrive at an understanding sufficient for the purpose of communication (or system use) will rarely involve the infinite regress that can be encountered in seeking to understand ever increasing levels of detail/ precision about the structure or workings of an entity – a problem Popper was most concerned with as a philosopher of science.

Focusing on agreement rather than on precision implies a relative rather than an absolute concept of truth. Truth or accordance with the facts can be established deductively for (i.e. relative to) a particular entity or system being considered, but it cannot be established inductively for a class of such entities or systems in ignorance of all their relevant, particular circumstances.

Popper's Table of Ideas may have been useful in relation to induction, but it is not fully generic, and his definition of definition is problematic. It also represents a somewhat deterministic over-simplification if we are looking to influence opinion by making emotional sense as well, rather than just being intellectually, rationally, pedantically correct.

It is also worth noting that Popper's diarrhesis is not to be confused with (scientific) reductionism. The former goes down only as far as is necessary (often only one level) to divide the space into parts where (macro) sense can be made. The latter divides the subject space (often down many levels) to make (micro) sense of its elemental components. The former produces functionality, as Popper's World 3 concept exemplifies, and the latter produces understanding of detailed workings, but not necessarily of usage or system performance.

Clarity of meaning or at least of labelling and of what we understand the label to signify is necessary to allow the meaningful discussion and criticism which Popper advocates. It is interesting to note that this can often be achieved by applying just one further level of diarrhesis, in this case, recognizing a distinction between the purposes of communication and achieving understanding of an entity.

Derrida, according to Pathak (2014), questioned the finality of signifiers, asserting that we keep moving from one signifier to another and the ultimate meaning or supposed signified remains elusive; there is always some lack, some incompleteness and so no entity is a unified whole. This makes micro-sense but not macro-sense and effectively prioritizes understanding ahead of use and does not produce clarity. If what is signified is not final i.e. constant and depends on our developing associations with and feeling for it, then the understanding of labels we give things can change over time, defeating the purpose of communication that allocation of a label serves. The detail that this aspect of deconstruction provides is therefore counter-productive to definition and does not result in clarity.

Furthermore, prioritizing understanding ahead of use can paralyse action. One does not have to understand everything about the micro-structure of something (for example a medicine) for it to be useful. The same applies for organisms. Lack of finality may be universally true for an organism in the progression of Kantian time, but at any given time, it does physically exist in Kantian space in whatever fullness it happens to be in. Any other organism has to deal with it as a complete entity, without focusing too much on seeking to understand any one particular detail of it. This dealing may range from ignoring it to mating with it, or from killing it to being killed by it. Its internal physiological state and biological processes inevitably change and will always be incomplete, simply because it is alive, but that is of little relevance to any other organism dealing with it; it must therefore be regarded by others as a unified whole. If we want to understand its internal workings, then we may need to know the details of its biological processes. But if we just want to deal with it immediately in the here and now, we only need to accept its existence and do so fairly quickly.

Separating understanding for the purpose of using or dealing with a system from understanding for the purpose of understanding internal workings or sub-systems enables the level of detail appropriate to the task at hand to be determined. This diarrhesis exposes the falsity of both the absolute Popperian argument that increasing precision always leads to infinite regress and the notion that deconstruction can produce clarity.

The Mangle effectively offers an alternative paradigm to deconstruction for conceptual terms through the same process that falsifies text deconstruction; namely reaching agreement on what conceptual terms mean, through stripping them to their essence. This, in conceptual terms, is analogous to pointing. It removes the need to perpetuate dichotomies and confusion through chasing undecidability through the detail of finding hierarchical inversion. It avoids unending esoteric discussions of text deconstructionism that cannot tell us what we should do. The precision inherent in deconstruction does not provide clarity of use or decidability on what we should do.

This leads to proposing the following:

Axiom 7 ***Clarity is more important than precision in reaching agreement on definition, but precision may be useful to reach a point of clarity, albeit that it may obscure matters if taken beyond that point***. Infinite regress does not occur if we seek only the detail necessary to agree usage and do not pursue deeper understanding of the internal workings of an entity or concept.

Axiom 8 ***Connections between divisions or component parts also require labelling and definition***. Properties or characteristics of systems that emerge from having made those connections comprise the 'whatever it is' that is more than the sum of the parts.

Definitional Rule 7 ***Use precision only to the point where clarity is reached***. If clarity is not reached, go back up a level. Precision regarding sub-systems or components does not produce clarity at the system level. Further precision is required only if an understanding of the internal workings of parts or sub-systems of an entity is being sought.

Definitional Rule 8 ***In defining a system, recognize the connections between its parts***.

6.9 Issue 9 Process v Content

This issue is concerned with whether it is beneficial to separately consider process and content or not.

The need to distinguish between these two things was identified in Chap. 10 in considering whether decision-making should be included in the definition of governance or not. It was excluded because it is a process that is broader than and not unique to governance, and a definition of governance should say what it is rather than one aspect of how it is done, which would then have required definition by extension rather than by intension. The author had also had experience of this distinction being used successfully in practice for gaining user acceptance during the introduction of a new project management methodology: it enabled existing content knowledge to be respected and a process for dealing with it to be introduced. The philosophical distinction this aligns with is between epistemology and ontology. Resolving process, including boundaries and definitions, deals with how we come to know things, i.e. epistemology. This then establishes the basis for gaining knowledge of content, for knowing what we know, i.e. ontology.

Popper (1995) said that definitions "do not contain any knowledge whatever, not even an opinion; they do nothing but introduce new arbitrary shorthand labels; they cut a long story short. In practice, these labels are of the greatest usefulness". Popper recognised the problem but did not escape from it himself. Identifying boundaries and clearly labelling them does contain knowledge of where the boundaries of consistency or coherence lie. It therefore provides a process for determining knowledge or truth, or rather, it provides knowledge of the process of labelling or categorising our thinking (diarrhesis) as distinct from gaining knowledge of the content of the particular subject or concept being considered (which Popper would not admit to calling definition). Knowledge is knowledge, whether it is of process or of content. Furthermore, the difficulty is not in finding a shorthand label; we have plenty of them and the real difficulty is in agreeing what those labels (of conceptual terms) actually signify. Consciously separating process from content is itself a subclassification that can achieve clarity, as Popper himself did with identifying and labelling his Worlds 2 and 3.

Whitty (2013) noted that **Hume** classified propositions into two types; analytic propositions, which refer to the structure of the relation of things and can be known *a priori* (i.e. without depending on our experience) (e.g. mathematics); and synthetic propositions that are concerned with things we observe that cannot be known *a priori* so an experience (of the senses) is required to determine their truth. Hume concluded that we habitually see cause or infer cause everywhere. This is similar to **Aristotle** distinguishing between things that are "better known to us" and things that are "better known in themselves," and maintaining that we should begin our study of a given topic with things better known to us and arrive ultimately at an understanding of things better known in themselves (Cohen, 2016). Whitty (2013) likened Hume's view to having a mental subroutine that we habitually run and are insensible of running it. We cannot actually know anything because our observations are so personal and subjective. The cause and effect habit of mind creates a feeling that we know, but we as individuals cannot have enough information in the moment to truly know. In other words, we need a process that provides some surety that we are not just accepting some particular content knowledge as universally applicable just because it seems to us that it is. The Mangle developed in Chap. 10 provides such a process for verifying the genericity of content. It accommodates **Mill**'s view as noted above that the truth of the representation is to be sought and cannot be determined by any authoritarian decree.

The need to separate content from process is not one that is readily apparent, and it can be much more engaging to just jump into the emotionality surrounding competing content than it is to be bothered with following some unemotional, potentially boring process of first determining definitions. It can also be argued that following such a process will straight-jacket people and stifle their creativity. The obvious response is that we can, as anyone who seriously poses such a question seems to wish, all waste our time arguing about process; but that simply prevents us from getting to the real work of understanding content. The process stuff should be just that - simply procedural. But because it is unattractive to sort that out first, we keep bumbling around in a confused haze, seeking to justify the lack of discipline with woolly arguments like freedom of creativity or Wittgenstein's family resemblance theory or with the popularised theory of pragmatism, which has been corrupted into the opposite of its original purpose, as identified by Rescher (2016). If so much of our creativity has to go into sorting out turmoil over process, we may have little time left for applying our creativity productively.

This leads to proposing the following:

Axiom 9 ***Diarrhesis can facilitate definition by enabling sense to be made within divisions that cannot be made without them***. Knowledge therefore does come from establishing boundaries and divisions (diarrhesis) (such as Popper did with his three worlds).

Axiom 10 ***One such diarrhesis that can reduce confusion in definition is the separation of epistemology from ontology, through distinguishing between content (what we know) and process (how we know it).*** This can avoid enshrining non-generic content within a process that may potentially be generic.

Definitional Rule 9 ***Consider process and content separately***; this supports exclusion of non-generic content from definition. The Mangle sorts out process, leaving the focus on content and true genericity.

6.10 Issue 10 Set v Sub-Set

This issue is concerned with definitive statements being made for a whole set based upon extrapolation from a sub-set.

This issue became evident from McGrath and Whitty (2020c) dealing with confusion of governance terminology. It was found to occur most notably in practice in the mistaken assumption that some aspects of the IT sub-set of project management are generic to all forms of project management, as demonstrated in McGrath and Whitty (2019) dealing with practitioner views of program, as well as analysis of PRINCE2 and MSP in McGrath and Whitty (2020b), McGrath and Whitty (2020a). For example, early versions of MSP stated that programs were transformational. This generalised from the IT sub-set of programs to all programs in general. While IT programs often bring about transformational change to the organisations they are delivered in, they do not do so for most conventional maintenance programs or for infrastructure organisations that routinely deliver programs of projects without internal transformation. What applied to most of the sub-set did not apply to the full set. Later versions of MSP corrected the definition but left the internal process upon which MSP is based untouched. Further examples include the definition of project as an organisation rather than as a more generic activity, and the use of an IT product rather than a generic project basis for the whole PRINCE2 management process, and are explained in the papers referred to above.

This is reflected philosophically in **Mill** noting "the great danger in all things philosophical is not so much of embracing falsehood for the truth, as of mistaking part of the truth for the whole" (Mill et al., 1987). Examples of this occurring in the philosophy of Popper and Derrida were mentioned above in discussing the detail versus overview dichotomy (Issue 8).

To establish whether a definition or an observation made for a sub-set applies universally at the next level up, it needs to be tested in that wider environment/ context. Truth cannot be established universally through induction inferring from what happened previously in terms of cause and effect, but it can be established with reference to a particular system relative to its usage and boundary conditions (context).

This leads to proposing the following:

Definitional Rule 10 ***Identify the context within which the term is being defined and refrain from making any generalisations that have not been tested outside that context***. This is similar to definitional rule 2 which deals with making assumed or silent qualifiers explicit. Both rules deal with making context explicit. The Mangle provides a recognized way of doing this.

6.11 Consequent Philosophical Problems

Before a coherent philosophical position on definition and a theory of meaning concerning management terms can be articulated, there are philosophical problems arising from conflict within and between the positions taken by previous major twentieth century philosophers, identified in analysing the issues above, that require resolution. These are Wittgenstein's family resemblance concept, the philosophical difference between Popper and Wittgenstein that famously erupted in the poker incident, internal difficulties in Popper's philosophy including the diarrhesis versus definition question, the philosophy of Derrida and the general philosophical trend away from definitions.

The next chapter will attempt to reconcile these based on the position that all of them dealt with real problems that their system of thinking addressed and so there must have been a truth (reasoned line of argument) in all of them within the boundaries of their consideration, in-so-far as they were aware of them. These boundaries will be examined for occurrences of the above 10 issues. This will rely not only upon the empirical and analytical work reported on here, but also on advances in technology, geology, archaeology, and evolutionary theory that have occurred since these philosophies were developed.

References

Cohen, S. M. (2016). Aristotle's metaphysics., In Zalta, E. N. (Ed.), *The Stanford encyclopedia of philosophy* (Winter 2016 Edition).

Copi, I. M., & Cohen, C. (1990). *Introduction to logic*. Macmillan.

Darwin, C., & Beer, G. (2008). *On the origin of species*. Oxford University Press.

Derrida, J. (1970). *Structure, sign, and play in the discourse of the human sciences* [Online]. Available: http://www5.csudh.edu/ccauthen/576f13/DrrdaSSP.pdf. [Accessed 26 April 2018].

Derrida, J., & Caputo, J. D. (1997). *Deconstruction in a nutshell: A conversation with Jacques Derrida*. Fordham University Press.

Derrida, J., & Spivak, G. C. (1976). *Of grammatology*. Johns Hopkins University Press.

Edmonds, D., & Eidinow, J. (2001). *Wittgenstein's poker: The story of a ten-minute argument between two great philosophers*. Faber.

Gallie, W. B. (1956). Essentially contested concepts. *Proceedings of the Aristotelian Society, 56*, 167–198.

Hobbes, T. (1996). *Leviathan*. Oxford University Press.

Kleinberg, E. (2013). *Derrida and deconstruction – basic introduction and demonstration* [Online]. Available: https://www.youtube.com/watch?v=N8BsnfjtNCg. [Accessed 3 May 2018].

Locke, J. (1690), "An essay concerning human understanding", *In:* Manis, J. (Ed.), Electronics Classics Series, Hazleton, pp.

Magee, B. & Searle, J. (1987). *Bryan Magee talks to John Searle about Wittgenstein* [Online]. Available: https://www.bing.com/videos/search?q=wittgenstein&&view=detail&mid=E4F4484E5D59D9E78DDBE4F4484E5D59D9E78DDB&rvsmid=C58CB8F0496A11CA44AFC58CB8F0496A11CA44AF&fsscr=0&FORM=VDQVAP. [Accessed 7 March 2017].

McGrath, S. K., & Whitty, S. J. (2015). Redefining governance: From confusion to certainty and clarity. *International Journal of Managing Projects in Business, 8*(4), 755–787.

McGrath, S. K., & Whitty, S. J. (2018). Accountability and responsibility defined. *International Journal of Managing Projects in Business, 11*(3), 687–707.

McGrath, S. K., & Whitty, S. J. (2019). A typology of meanings: Practitioners views of 'program'. *Journal of Modern Project Management, 7*(20), 228–245.

McGrath, S. K., & Whitty, S. J. (2020a). The suitability of MSP for engineering infrastructure. *The Journal of Modern Project Management, 7*(4), 348–368.

McGrath, S. K., & Whitty, S. J. (2020b). The suitability of PRINCE2 for engineering infrastructure. *The Journal of Modern Project management, 7*(4), 312–347.

McGrath, S. K., & Whitty, S. J. (2020c). What do project management practitioners think governance is? A study on perceptions in Queensland, Australia. *International Journal of Managing Projects in Business, 13*(5), 961–980.

Mill, J. S. (1874). *A system of logic, ratiocinative and inductive*. Harper & Brothers.

Mill, J. S., Bentham, J., & Ryan, A. (1987). *Utilitarianism and other essays*. Penguin.

Naraniecki, A. J. (2009). *"Popper re-appraised: New perspectives on karl popper's method and its applications"*, PhD PhD, Griffith University.

Pathak, A. K. (2014). *Jacques derrida & deconstruction* [Online]. Available: https://www.youtube.com/watch?v=STydy9wbAo0. [Accessed 3 May 2018].

Popper, K. R. (1979). *Objective knowledge: An evolutionary approach*. Clarendon Press.

Popper, K. R. (1995). *The open society and its enemies: Volume 2 Hegel and Marx*. Routledge.

Popper, K. R. (2002). *Conjectures and refutations: The growth of scientific knowledge*. Routledge.

Popper, K. R., & Notturno, M. A. (1994). *The myth of the framework: In defence of science and rationality*. Routledge.

Popper, K. R., Shearmur, J., & Turner, P. N. (2008). *After the open society: Selected social and political writings*. Routledge.

Rescher, N. (2016). *Pragmatism in philosophical inquiry: Theoretical considerations and case studies*. Springer.

Russell, B. (1905). On denoting. *Mind, 14*(56), 479–493.

Sartre, J. P. (1973). *Existentialism is a humanism*. Eyre Methuen.
Saussure, F. d. (1966). *Course in general linguistics*. McGraw-Hill Book Co..
Whitty, S. J. (2013). Thinking in slow motion about project management. In N. Drouin, R. Muller, & S. Sankaran (Eds.), *Novel approaches to organizational project management research: translational and transformational*. Copenhagen Business School Press.
Wittgenstein, L., & Anscombe, G. E. M. (1958). *Philosophical investigations*. Basil Blackwell.

Chapter 7
Resolution of Consequent Philosophical Problems

7.1 Wittgenstein's Family Resemblance Concept

This concept holds that some terms have quite varied usages such that it is not possible to determine essence or "What is common to them all" (Wittgenstein &Anscombe, 1958), and that there are instead, similarities or resemblances which may or may not be present, in the same way that family characteristics may be present or not in the physical appearance of individual family members. This concept arose as a challenge to publication of the power papers in Chaps. 11 and 12. The definition of essence via the Mangle has formed part of the basis for resolving contest in all of the analytical definitional papers referred to in this book as well as in the other chapters of Part II dealing with governance and related groups of terms. The following discussion outlines the flaws in the family resemblance concept.

John Stuart Mill (1806–1873) was critical of the concept of resemblance in definition that Wittgenstein would later develop. He said:

> But when a name is in common use, the difficulty is … of ascertaining and fixing the connotation with which it is already used… But the vulgar (including in that term all who have not accurate habits of thought) seldom know exactly what assertion they intend to make, what common property they mean to express, when they apply the same name to a number of different things. All which the name expresses with them, when they predicate it of an object, is a confused feeling of resemblance between that object and some of the other things which they have been accustomed to denote by that name… This rough general impression of resemblance is, however, made up of particular circumstances of resemblance; and into these it is the business of the logician to analyse it; to ascertain what points of resemblance among the different things commonly called by the name, have produced in the common mind this vague feeling of likeness; and have given to the things the similarity of aspect, which has made them a class, and has caused the same name to be bestowed upon them. (Mill, 1874)

This points out the need to qualify the term to the particular circumstances it is used in, then look at the meaning in context with the qualifications used to

S. K. McGrath, *Speaking Management*,
https://doi.org/10.1007/978-981-16-2213-7_7

understand what the essence of the term really is. This is the task the Mangle performs. Mill further says:

> In attempting to rectify the use of a vague term by giving it a fixed connotation, we must take care not to discard (unless advisedly, and on the grounds of a deeper knowledge of the subject) any portion of the connotation which the word, in however indistinct a manner, previously carried with it. For otherwise language loses one of its inherent and most valuable properties, that of being the conservator of ancient experience; the keeper-alive of those thoughts and observations of former ages, which may be alien to the tendencies of the passing time. (Mill, 1874)

Wittgenstein (2007) himself also warns against mixing terminology, noting that "philosophical puzzlement occurs by using the terms from one language-game as if they belonged to another e.g. judging moral or religious talk as if it were scientific"

Use of Wittgenstein's 'family resemblance' concept has been advocated by Haugaard (2010) who argued that "there is no single best definition of power". He considered:

> pragmatic criteria of usefulness, rather than essence, define better or worse usage. When moving language games, the relationship between signifier and referent changes, which leads to confusion, unless the family resemblance nature of power is understood (Haugaard, 2010).

Wittgenstein himself used the examples of games to justify his family resemblance concept. He looked for something common in them, some essence and found none. He considered board-games, card-games, ball-games, Olympic games, and so on. He considered and rejected amusement, competition (in the process confusing play with games), skill, luck and found no common essence, only a resemblance in some changing features (Wittgenstein &Anscombe, 1958) (Sections 66 & 67).

Looking closely, as Wittgenstein exhorted, but without falling into the trap of ostensive definition which consumes much of his lead up to this point, enables a different conclusion. Copi and Cohen (1990) point out that "The primary way of learning to use language is by observation and imitation, not by definition" and "the process of frequently hearing the word when the object it denotes is present." They go on to say "But such a process would not be a definition at all … it would be the primitive, pre-definitional way of learning to use language"(Copi & Cohen, 1990). In the governance paper summarised in Chap. 10, McGrath and Whitty (2015) note in discussing this quotation that this statement refers to an object and governance is an intangible concept, not a tangible object. Demonstrative learning and definition may suffice for objects which are present for all to see, but such methods present difficulties when used in defining abstract concepts. Wittgenstein in his Philosophical Investigations falls into this trap and does not get out of it. As Copi and Cohen (1990) further note:

> the set of all attributes the speaker believes possessed by the objects denoted by that word. But this set plainly varies from individual to individual and even from time to time for the same individual – and thus cannot serve the purposes of definition.

Wittgenstein then compounds this error by extrapolating into children's "language games" (Wittgenstein & Anscombe, 1958), thereby falling into a further trap of classifying language as a competitive activity. While language may be used competitively in debate, that is not its sole or universal purpose – refer to Hobbes's four uses of language. Language is, at its heart, a means of communication and cooperation. Children play with things, but can clearly distinguish, as Wittgenstein did not, the difference between playing with things and playing a competitive game. Children's play with objects can progress to the level of mastery where competition becomes possible. But this is opposite to the view that in play with objects, competition is missing. Such a misconception does become possible if one views language as a competitive activity. Undoubtedly there is an association between games and playing, but it is a loose one that is not exclusive.

These two mistakes undermine the legitimacy of using Wittgenstein's argument on essence in relation to definitions. His argument can be completely invalidated if a definition that does capture the essence of the term 'game' can be developed, and the next paragraph proceeds to do just that.

In Magee and Searle (1987), various potential essences of the term 'game' were rejected including pastimes and diversions because some can be grim and some people derive their livelihood from them, such as at gaming tables in Las Vegas. Wittgenstein himself rejected amusement in the quotation above. These are unsuitable candidates for essence as they do not cover all circumstances. However just because an essence may not be readily apparent or an unsuitable one may have been chosen does not prove one does not exist. Listening to the remainder of the Magee and Searle (1987) interview, the essential elements that constitute all of these types of activities called games were actually given. They are assembled here into an essential definition of the word 'game' as a competitive activity with rules players are obliged to follow, or, more succinctly, *a competitive rule governed activity*. The two essential features are that it is competitive, and it is rule governed. This definition passes no judgement on whether the players follow the rules or not or whether they get caught or not or whether the consequences are frivolous or dire or whether there are associated with grim or happy emotions or whether the activity is physical or mental or whether it is played on a board or on a marked field or even somewhere not demarcated at all or even whether the rules are written down or not. It is non-normative and contains the essence of what a game is. It does not overlook the distinction between games and play or confuse learning a language with defining words. It appears Wittgenstein was misled by his assumptions into not adequately looking for essence.

Wittgenstein may also have been misled by his tendency towards mysticism, which he stated as "There are indeed, things that cannot be put into words. They make themselves manifest. They are what is mystical" (Wittgenstein et al., 1974). Understanding sourced from other senses apart from hearing may be unseen but is not mystical. Furthermore, it is worthwhile contrasting this statement of Wittgenstein's with Mill's clarity regarding definition, in expressing an equivalent sentiment as "The meaning of a term actually in use is not an arbitrary quantity to be fixed, but an unknown quantity to be sought. … To fix the connotation of a concrete name, or the denotation of the corresponding abstract, is to define the name" (Mill, 1874).

It was possible to derive the definition of 'game' above just by excluding all the silent or assumed qualifiers that describe whatever sort of game it is. The result is entirely compatible with Wittgenstein's observations but reaches a very different conclusion. Yes, as Wittgenstein notes, all sorts of things drop out and others get added in when considering the word with a different silent or assumed qualifier. But that is just due to the simple fact that the definition of a word and a phrase are different. The additional word is actually necessary to make the distinction. All superfluous characteristics do drop out when one searches for just the essence of the word rather than for the essence of a series of phrases. The essences of all the phrases using a common term will be different by at least some nuance, otherwise the qualifying terms used would not have been needed.

To make a further point, Wittgenstein's 'language game' view would actually be excluded by the definition of 'game' above, as language is a cooperative not a competitive activity unless we are contesting something. This simple example indicates again the dangers of proof by induction contained in Wittgenstein and Anscombe (1958) P31, referred to above. Picking the wrong essence provides no justification for a false view. This leads into the very circumstance that Wittgenstein describes:

> If I am inclined to suppose that a mouse has come into being by spontaneous generation out of grey rags and dust, I shall do well to examine those rags very closely to see how a mouse may have hidden in them, how it may have got there and so on. But if I am convinced that a mouse cannot come into being from these things, then this investigation will perhaps be superfluous. (Wittgenstein & Anscombe, 1958)

There are two other presumptions stated in Wittgenstein's works that are problematic/ erroneous. The first is the statement in his Tractatus: "5.6 The limits of my language mean the limits of my world" (Wittgenstein et al., 1974). This suffers from the logical positivism he was pursuing along with Bertrand Russell in attempting to establish a logical correspondence between language and mathematics. Although he later renounced his Tractatus, his later work did not escape this thinking. He evidently considered language was reality, rather than just one means of representing it and communicating about it. He appears to have had no concept of language as being just one of a number of frameworks we use to represent the world. This led to lengthy futile analysis of grammatical forms seeking understanding of something that just isn't there to be found, examining the 'grey rags and dust'. The realisation that speech is just one of a number of sensory frameworks we use to determine meaning did not become widely known until the work of Bandler and Grinder (1975) in family therapy and the deductive proof in the thought experiment of Sypniewski (2008), where the same characters used or responded to the same words "Look! there's snake in the grass" in different contexts, demonstrating that the meaning of the same words could vary with context.

The second is that Wittgenstein in his later work, as observed by Magee and Searle (1987), says that because the sum total of the possible uses of a word constitutes its meaning, in the end what language and words mean depend on 'forms of life', on the social contexts within which they are used, so all the criteria of meaning are not personal or private at all. They are social. There are at least three problems with this. Firstly, this presumes definition by extension is the only valid definitional method and ignores definition by intension (Issue 6), which implies essence (Issue 5). Secondly it promotes mysticism around circumstances where just following simple grammatical rules can produce understanding, as outlined in the chapters of Part II. Thirdly it ignores the confusion resulting from silent or assumed qualifiers (Issue 3). Furthermore, this issue was resolved by Popper's distinction between second and third worlds, which addressed Issue 1.

It could be argued that a different interpretation of the above two presumptions might make sense of them. This argument would be that Wittgenstein was simply stating that we are all limited by the bounds of our private language, but language is social and so private language is a non-sense. He says "And sounds which no one else understands but which I appear to understand might be called a 'private language' " (Wittgenstein & Anscombe, 1958). While language is social, this does not mean it needs to remain confused in contested areas. That is exactly why a process is needed for agreeing conceptual terms. Wittgenstein therefore inadvertently promotes 'private language' rather than rendering it invalid for the reasons given in the above two paragraphs.

Magee observes on Wittgenstein:

> His first book, *Tractatus Logico-Philosophicus*, which was published in 1921, was the text most influential on the Vienna Circle. He came subsequently to regard it as mistaken, and mistaken primarily because it incorporated a false theory of meaning. He thereupon set out to investigate the different sorts of ways in which we can be mislead by our own use of language, having been so mislead himself, and this nourished a new school of philosophy, usually called 'linguistic analysis'. (Magee, 1973)

Using a mini-Mangle approach produced an essential definition of the word 'game' above, which bars Wittgenstein's 'language game' from actually being considered a game. One could equally well have defined 'beautiful' as a form that pleases human eyes, without getting into all the various ways it may be found in nature, art and architecture.

The family resemblance theory has simply reified the confusion that can result when the trap of defining by extension is fallen into.

Having established the fundamental flaws in Wittgenstein's language game argument and disproven it by developing an essential definition of the term used to justify it, it will be considered no further and will play no part in the definitional philosophy developed here.

7.2 Popper v Wittgenstein

The conflict between Wittgenstein and Popper can be reduced to conflict over words and meaning and so needs to be understood in considering definition. Here again, this is relevant to the philosophical basis of the Mangle which has been successfully used to reconcile definitional conflict in many groups of terms.

Naraniecki (2009) has achieved significant insight into Popper through analysis of his unpublished as well as his published work. He also identified difficulties with Popper's view of definition and provided an exposition of it as follows:

> Popper turned from definition to the notion he called *diarrhesis*, and he claimed to have appropriated it from Plato's Laws (932e). *Diarrhesis* mean a 'division'. Explaining the advantage of *diarrhesis* over the definition of a word in that knowledge derived from definitions are impossible as 'definitions are an attempt to lay down some "absolute" meaning of a term in advance'. *Diarrhesis*, however, holds the meaning of a concept is always *ad hoc* and pertains to the current problem under discussion. Thus the distinctions developed and the term used can only be understood in regard to the argument into which they are situated (Naraniecki, 2009).

This is very similar to Wittgenstein's 'family resemblance' concept. Naraniecki further comments:

> Popper states that 'distinctions' (*diarrhesis*) may always be refined, that is, carried one step further; but one should do so only if the needs of the discussion require it. ... What Popper was aiming at with his understanding of *diarrhesis* appears in practice what Aristotle originally meant when he introduced the term 'definition' which was intended as a statement regulating the extension and designate of a given name. However, for Popper the Aristotelian origins of the problem of definitions occurs in Aristotle's understanding of induction not as being 'a method of inferring natural laws from particular individual instances' which he associated with the inductivism of the Vienna Circle, 'but a method by which we are guided to the point whence we can intuit or perceive the essence or the true nature of a thing' (Naraniecki, 2009).

This provides an account as to how Popper ended up in a self-contradictory position. It corresponds with Issue 5, dealing with the attribution of ethereal dimension to essence.

Naraneicki also noted:

> The problem is of applying a meta-linguistic theory designed for formal mathematical languages to ordinary human languages... Popper applied a theory from one field of inquiry to that of another... A definition of truth for ordinary languages of every day usage is not possible according to Popper, yet he rightly saw that with caution, Tarski's semantic theory can confer theoretical benefits on the understanding of human communication beyond the narrow field of semantics. In 1944 Tarski even stated that: *I happen to believe that the semantic conception does conform to a very considerable extent with the common-sense usage*" (Naraniecki, 2009).

Accepting this, the relationship of language to mathematics is dealt with in Sect. 8.3 in developing an emergent theory of meaning.

Naraniecki also considered Popper also had an "evolutionary" view that meaning comes from our childhood "by listening to adults" (Naraniecki, 2009). Popper therefore had a similar view of language acquisition to Wittgenstein. This view fails to recognise imitation and definition as two methods of how we come to understanding what a word signifies or is a sign to. To propose that meaning comes from one alone is to fall into the error of induction. Imitation comes first and definition comes later as we mature:

> The primary way of learning to use language is by observation and imitation, not by definition' and 'the process of frequently hearing the word when the object it denotes is present... But such a process would not be a definition at all … it would be the primitive, pre-definitional way of learning to use language' (Copi & Cohen, 2009).

Erroneous generalisations provided a starting assumption for both men and while their chain of reasoning diverged, as evidenced by the poker incident, it also led to their views coalescing as noted by Naraniecki (2009). Furthermore,

> Wittgenstein's opposition to a private language very closely reflects some of Popper's arguments concerning "knowledge in the objective sense" … For Wittgenstein, unless we can appeal to some larger social gathering there is no difference between my thinking that I am actually using the word correctly and my actually using the word correctly (Naraniecki, 2009).

This supports surveying existing usages in pursuit of meaning, as included in the Mangle, and then reaching shared agreement.

Popper, according to Naraniecki considered:

> It is only in direct relation to the process of a problem situation in which we attempt to reduce error and by extension harm that we form meaning and accept the meaning on the basis of a correct or successful outcome' (Naraniecki, 2009).

For contested terms, we have not achieved the successful outcome of reaching agreement. This does not require arbitrary determinism in advance; rather it just requires closer consideration, as John Stuart Mill put it:

> The meaning of a term actually in use is not an arbitrary quantity to be fixed, but an unknown quantity to be sought. … To fix the connotation of a concrete name, or the denotation of the corresponding abstract, is to define the name (Mill, 1874).

This implies that language is a product of meaning, not the other way around, as both Popper and Wittgenstein held. It is a response to us directing another's attention to something.

It would not have been possible for Russell, Wittgenstein and to a lesser degree Popper to have pursued their view of definitions without presuming JSM's 'vulgar' view of definition. The research for this book failed to find any evidence that they viewed definition as representing rather than being meaning. Wittgenstein and Russell were concerned with the mathematics of words which led them in a deterministic direction that overlooked the physical object/ concept distinction and the confusion present in understanding conceptual as distinct from physical terms. To take this 'words = meaning' approach, they would have had to have been either unaware of the significance of or ignored what JSM had to say about definition quoted above. Russell's problems of co-referring and non-referring expressions in his theory of descriptions do not arise if the full meaning of what the words represent within their context is taken into account; in other words, if the assumed or silent qualifiers are stated and it is recognized that the signification of words depends upon human agreement.

It appears that neither philosopher regarded language as just one of a number of frameworks for expressing meaning (Issues 2 and 4); others include gestures and sound. Recognising language as a framework allows understanding of the positions of both philosophers and helps avoid the problem of determinism, differing interpretations of which led to their disagreement. It also highlights the Aristotelean need for definitions.

The position taken here draws on Popper's principle of diarrhesis and attempts to implement his view of expressing things understandably but without accepting his aversion to calling that definition. He must have been talking about the signifier rather than the signified and that, in so doing, he also had to have accepted the view that words = meaning rather than just representing it. When that distinction is drawn, infinite regress can occur if we are attempting to find meaning in a word. And we could chase its traces (to use Derrida's term) ad-infinitum. However, if we just take it to the level where it is possible to agree what we are all talking about, what it is that is just the essence of what we understand the label we give it to signify in an auditory sense, then we do not get into infinite regress and that supports the principle of clarity that Popper advocated. It stops at the point of utility rather than at a point enabling understanding of the workings of the entity (Issue 8).

Popper's progression to an infinite loop is similar to Derrida's concept of the ongoing possibility of inversion of the dominant hierarchy. That infinite regress can be avoided by simply going only as far as necessary to agree or establish recognition.

7.3 Popper's Philosophy

Popper took an anti-definitional stance and so any argument that definition is essential has to reckon with that aspect of his philosophy. Here again, this is relevant to the philosophical basis of the Mangle which has been successfully used to reconcile definitional conflict in many groups of terms.

7.3.1 Diarrhesis Versus Definition

Popper said:

> The myth of the framework can be stated in one sentence, as follows:
>
> A rational and fruitful discussion is impossible unless the participants share a common framework of basic assumptions or, at least, unless they have agreed on such a framework for the purpose of the discussion. … I mean by 'framework' here a set of basic assumptions,

> or fundamental principles – that is to say, an intellectual framework. (Popper & Notturno, 1994).

This could be construed to align with the views of Hobbes and Mill on definition but is quite at odds with Popper's stated view of definition:

> I am, as you know, a conscious and determined enemy of definitions: definitions are attempts to lay down some ('absolute') meaning of a term in advance, as it were, of a discussion, without explicit reference to the problem under discussion. I replace definition (except right-to-left abbreviations) by what I call diarrhesis (see Plato, Laws, 932e: 'division' or 'distinction') which is always ad hoc, with respect to the needs of a discussion of a certain problem… No diarrhesis is final, or formal: it is always possible that the problem in hand may require further distinctions (Popper et al., 2008).

The analyses in the chapters of Part II and in the definitional papers referred to in Part I found problems arising precisely because of this sort of thinking. It was absolutely necessary to exclude reference to the particular problem under discussion, namely normative references and the interpretation of terms used by particular fields with reference only to their field, which generally involved silent or assumed qualifiers. Furthermore, if we don't come to discussions with some absolute meaning or common understanding of our terms, then it would be impossible to communicate verbally at all.

The passage Popper refers to from Plato's Laws that prompted his idea of diarrhesis deals with distinguishing poisoning causing injury from poisoning causing death, and further divides the former into two types, physical injury and mental injury – "sorceries and incantations and spells". Plato then divided the appropriate punishment for such crimes into two further categories; doctors and lay-persons (Plato & Bury, 1967, S933a & d). These passages do not relate to definition at all, but Popper evidently used the division principle contained within them as the model and philosophical justification for his position.

Popper applied the principle of diarrhesis in conceptualising his three worlds – 1 objects, 2 subjective thought or consciousness and 3 objective contents of thought (Popper, 1979). His subdivision of thinking into two categories – Worlds 2 and 3 – neatly bypasses the normative problem of universality of right and wrong (the view that there is absolute right and wrong), differentiates between concepts and our personal views of them, and also happily accords with the idea of separating issues from personalities. This simple device of establishing a new classification provides clear subdivisions or boundaries that enables consistency of pattern to be recognised and apparent contradiction or inconsistency to be explained. So establishing the boundaries of what we are talking about is an important issue for removing incoherence. However, he did not seem to regard this as definition but did say "coherence cannot establish truth, but incoherence and inconsistency do establish false-hood" (Popper, 2002).

Popper's diarrhesis accords with Kant's distinguishing between things using the spatial axiom and within things using the axiom of time. Our judgements on those are based on quality, quantity, modality and relation. Kant's axioms and categories of understanding correspond to classifying the thinking space into divisions where sense can be made.

In conceptualising, labelling and describing his three worlds, Popper has, according to the Oxford definition given earlier, defined, as he has "marked out the boundary or limits of", even though he refers to it as diarrhesis. Furthermore, he has done so without progressing to infinite regress. Popper's distinction between definition and diarrhesis can be seen as some sort of (partial) recognition of the distinction between the concept of words = meaning and the concept of words representing meaning.

He seems to have considered that definition must necessarily chase undefined terms back to their source hence creating an infinite regress. He attempted to avoid definition by creating as many divisions or distinctions as is necessary to make sense of what was being spoken about. Many subdivisions may be necessary if we are seeking a full **understanding** of the internal workings of a phenomenon or entity, and he was principally concerned with the philosophy of science, but this is unnecessary for verbal communication. Furthermore, as noted above, it also does not accommodate contested terms which have competing definitions.

In attempting to understand and resolve the diarrhesis versus definition question, his view of deduction rather than induction will be accepted and employed; induction "has been called 'Hume's problem'… Popper's seminal achievement has been to offer an acceptable solution to the problem of induction. In doing this he has rejected the whole orthodox view of the scientific method" (Magee, 1973). Various aspects of Popper's philosophy are analysed below.

7.3.2 *Empiricism v Rationalism*

The approach taken here addresses the empiricism (all knowledge is based on experience derived from the senses) / rationalism (opinions and actions should be based upon reason and knowledge rather than on religious belief or emotional response) conundrum, allowing both to apply but in different portions of our linguistic space. Rationalism has been faulty because of poor definitional practices rather than because of any abstract fifth dimensional mystical notions. We have simply treated physical existence and the existence of mental concepts in the same way; and that has not worked very well for many concepts.

Verbal communication can only successfully occur when the communicants all agree upon what the words being used actually signify. This becomes very quickly evident when two people with no knowledge of each other's language attempt to communicate.

It is relatively easy for a group to agree sounds signifying physical objects that can be seen or touched or pointed at or generally experienced through our senses, and this provides the basis for empiricism. This is evidenced by the fact that over 7000 surviving languages have independently evolved (Lewis et al., 2017) and it is possible to translate between them. Language evolves in a particular geographic area among inhabitants who have to interact. So different groups of people have agreed upon different sounds to signify the same object.

However, the same easy process of coordination or error correction does not exist for mental concepts and an additional means of doing so is required to achieve clarity about them. Such a process has been developed here; that is to recognize and make explicit any silent/ assumed qualifiers to provide a basis for reaching agreement. This process, the Mangle, is described in Chap. 10.

The Mangle approach relies on an economy of words; an Ockham's Razor approach; an assumption that if a word does not signify a nuance of its base term, then it would not have been necessary to develop that word to express it in the first place.

Use of the approach developed here, as encapsulated in the Mangle, can avert or correct some linguistic mistakes that occur in the normal uncontrolled machinations of language development. Those machinations can be regarded as occurring in two ways; one legitimately extending the language by developing new or nuanced terms not expressible by a single root term alone, and the other making mistakes causing confusion by failing to recognize silent/ assumed qualifiers.

One could conclude that this calls for language regulation such as occurs in France via the Academie francaise. However, an alternative approach would be to focus on 'essentially contested concepts' and other circumstances where definitional contention and confusion is known to exist and apply the Mangle method of Chap. 10 to produce clarity in a transparent way that facilitates moving towards agreement.

As mentioned in Chap. 4, it is important for both objects and concepts to be defined by essence where possible. This limits the difficulty and confusion that may be caused in reaching agreement on what is signified by a conceptual term.

The Mangle focuses on intensional definition = essence and the processes built into it identify and strip away silent/ assumed qualifiers.

This approach simply applies a Popperian diarrhesis to the linguistic communication space. The common factor for both physical and conceptual terms is reaching agreement on what they signify, but the additional feature necessary for conceptual terms is to make the silent/ assumed qualifiers explicit.

It is only when we are sufficiently rational that we can be as definite and confident and factual in mental concepts as we can be with objects we can see, touch and point to. The position adopted here is therefore both empiricist and rationalist. Both are part of the same linguistic space and because a conundrum has existed around them, neither fully understands or adequately represents reality. Empiricism has overlooked things that are physical but indetectible to human senses, and rationalism has been confused by both mystical notions and poor definitional practice. They are both frameworks of thinking that are insufficient.

7.3.3 Nominalism Versus Essentialism

Popper argues for nominalism (universals are mere names with no corresponding reality) and against essentialism (everything has attributes necessary to its identity and function). He says "Aristotle's essentialist definitions … serve to substitute a long formula for a short one" (Popper, 1995). In this respect both nominalist and essentialist approaches agree. Popper (1995) says "For Aristotle's essentialist definitions are the principles from which all our knowledge is derived; they thus contain all our knowledge". This latter phrase appears to be an unsubstantiated assertion that suffers from being a universal statement, which only requires a simple example of knowledge not contained in a definition, such as that presented above regarding knowledge of boundaries or process, to negate. Popper's statement could be rendered correct by inserting 'means of agreement on' (i.e. distinguishing between content and process) before 'all our knowledge'.

Popper notes "I have called it 'essentialism' – which tries to link meaning and truth so closely that the temptation to treat both in the same way becomes almost irresistible" (Popper, 2002), and he presents the following to demonstrate that they should not be treated this way:

> According to essentialism (especially Aristotle's version of it) a definition is a statement of the inherent essence or nature of a thing. At the same time, it states the meaning of a word – of the name that designates the essence (Popper, 2002).

This then requires a further distinction between the words used to label a concept and the concept itself, as Popper noted here but did not explore further, and as John Stuart Mill had previously done, as noted above. Failing to make this distinction produces confusion between signifier and signified (Issue 1) as well as between process and content (Issue 9); the process of coming to know what we know about a concept through all of its instantiations or applications, and our understanding or what we know of the content matter of the concept itself.

Naraniecki (2009) said "It is very difficult to arrive at a clear understanding of what Popper meant by 'essentialism' as his arguments concerning the problem of essences constantly evolved". Naraniecki (2009) said "Popper's opposition to essentialism is based on the understanding that we cannot know if objects have *de re* (*about the thing*) essences". That is only true if it is presumed that essence has an ethereal dimension. Essence is defined above in non-ethereal terms and, as mentioned earlier, Popper's interpretation of Aristotle as requiring a ethereal dimension is a mistake that has led to confusion. Naraniecki (2009) continues "Even though Popper did not like to speak of essences, he did not consider himself to be a nominalist. In relation to the problem of essences, however, his fallibilism would force a nominalist stance". But not fully embracing a nominalist stance seems to have also led Popper away from adopting the signifier/ signified view of definition.

Naraniecki (2009) also noted that "Popper's ethical theories are presented as if they were epistemological theories, thereby revealing a tendency in Popper's thought to disguise ethical and subjective convictions as epistemological principles… Popper's arguments in the social sciences are often justified by empirical support from biology or analytic support from logic or geometry. Such arguments analogously applied to the social sciences however, are not demonstrable and are used to develop Popper's ethical position". This indicates several issues; he introduced value judgement into his concept of definition, accepted proof by analogy and his mind-set was appropriate to the physical sciences.

Popper also, as mentioned above, did not adopt the signifier/ signified view of definition. As Naraniecki (2009) says, "For Popper, language was the means by which humans receive knowledge of the external world". Naraniecki (2009) also notes:

> Popper's anti-essentialism cannot be a doctrine against ontological existence of essences in the world, or against our capacity to have knowledge of such entities. It is rather an impossibility of our ability to have scientific or rational knowledge of essences. As we cannot have scientific knowledge of essences it is thus not possible to refute their existence. Popper's anti-essentialism may have appeared, following Aristotle, to have seen the need to define *things* and not *words*, which gave rise to his disputes with the linguistic philosophies of the neo-positivists in Cambridge and Vienna. However, Popper did not follow Aristotle in linking the notion of essence (*to tie n einani*) with the notion of definition (*horismos*) as is evident from Aristotle's *Topics* 'a definition is an account (*logos*) that signifies an essence… In Popper's view philosophy cannot, as Wittgenstein claims, purge our language of linguistic puzzles through the clarification of meaning, so that science can get on with the business of investigating facts. For Popper, *horismos* would be reduced to *diarrhesis* in relation to the scientific task of searching for invariants.

So Popper did not link essence with definition as Aristotle did because of the impossibility of refuting the existence of an ethereal essence. Aristotle used essence in both secular and ethereal senses and Popper focused on its ethereal dimension which he felt should be excluded from consideration. This means that Popper effectively accepted a definition of essence from a dimension outside time and three-dimensional space which left him in the position of having to attack the very thing that going to the next level of diarrhesis (distinguishing between secular and ethereal essence) would have solved.

Russell (2005) noted similarly in saying that "Metaphysicians, ever since Aristotle, have interpreted syntactical differences metaphysically".

In the definitional work outlined in the chapters of Part II, definitional confusion was found in every field investigated. It is therefore perhaps not surprising to find it was present in ancient times as well.

Popper's three world conception provides more precision around the thought process, more precise definition, providing two categories of thought which assists us in reaching agreement on what it is we are actually talking about. It provides two regions where some consistency of pattern can be observed, versus considering it as one whole region where there is no consistency of pattern. That categorisation does itself provide some conceptual knowledge, contradicting the absolute nominalist view that universals or general ideas are mere names without any corresponding reality. The nominalist statement may be true, as asserted, but for content only, not for process.

Definition for Popper appears to have had a connotation of precision. He refers to labelling as if it is completely arbitrary. This may be so in some cases for the original use of the term, but to assume it continues to be so for every subsequent use of the term, especially after its use has become established, is akin to believing in the tabular razor, which he decries. Once a term is in circulation, we are constrained by previous usage and any usage contrary to that can be regarded as unreasonable and excluded; the confusion that its gaining currency may induce is worth avoiding. As Popper points out:

> Thus the Aristotelean claim that intellectual intuition is a source of knowledge as opposed to opinion, unerringly and indubitably true, and that it furnishes us with definitions which are the safe and necessary basic premises of all scientific deduction is baseless in every single one of its points. And a definition turns out to be nothing but a sentence that tells us that the defined term means the same as the defining formula, and that each can be replaced by the other (Popper, 1995).

However, we nonetheless have to deal with all those opinions. The way to do so without making any value judgements that would be subject to conjecture, is simply to make sure we describe what any contested or misunderstood term means without any silent or assumed qualifiers; that is to say, simply apply the Mangle to them. Applying a diarrhesis distinguishing between internal knowing (feeling) resulting from intuition and the feeling resulting from strong desire would remove Aristotle's claim from being fully baseless. This approach would regard Aristotle's truth of intuition as referring to things that we sense through the human condition to be true.

7.3.4 Overall Evaluation

Popper's focus on clarity is therefore accepted here, but without his hang-up about definition. His distinction between diarrhesis and definition is rejected as artificial and invalid.

Popper's definitional philosophy relied on six mistakes/ invalid assumptions, as follows, all of which were identified in the ten definitional issues (traps) above:

1. Accepting the inclusion of value judgement in definition, i.e. not distinguishing between opinion and fact in definition and excluding the former (Issue 1).
2. Inadequate distinction between signifier and signified (Issue 2).
3. Equating essence with soul or ethereal dimensions (Issue 5).
4. Overlooking some aspects of context, leading to omitting necessary qualifications e.g. drawing conclusions on language based on analysing conceptual terms without checking their applicability to physical objects, or claiming universality for infinite regress when that is not the case for physical objects (Issue 7).
5. Precision versus clarity – Not distinguishing between understanding and usage (Issue 8).
6. Not distinguishing between process and content (Issue 9).

Popper was not alone in making such mistakes, as indicated above and below. It is also interesting and ironic to note that all these mistakes involve not proceeding with just one further level of diarrhesis.

In contradiction with Popper, three methods of definition are here accepted:

1. General definition where various extensions are listed.
2. Essential definition which defines essence by stating the intension of the term.
3. Diarrhesis which clarifies the definitional space by dividing or segmenting it into chunks that enable sense to be made

Note that:

Methods 1 and 2 are distinguished by Copi and Cohen (1990).
Method 1 is commonly used in dictionaries.
Method 2 is also used in dictionaries and is heavily used in the Mangle in Chap. 10 to achieve consistency by removing duplication and value judgements and by considering all possible usages.
Method 3 is used when identifying silent or assumed qualifiers, dividing the communication space up into homogeneous chunks. (Note that a similar concept is mentioned in different terms in Copi and Cohen (1990) effectively using the same technique to clarify extensions changing with time, pointing out that fixing the extension of a term in time also fixes its extension. They also note that the reverse is not true).

Carrying Popper's insistence that definition produces infinite regress to its logical conclusion would mean that we can never know what it is we are talking about. While this may often be true for concepts, it is actually contradicted by the fact that we have in our language development managed to agree commonly accepted meanings of words denoting physical objects which we are not attempting to explain (Issue 7). We simply need to address the question 'how far do we need to go to avert avoidable confusion and conflict'?

Popper's development of the concept of diarrhesis may have been sparked by Plato, but making the process conscious and transparent (and one could mischievously say defining it) by giving it label, was a major realisation whose significance is both profound and easy to overlook as well as under-estimate.

The research that prompted this book arose from attempting to solve a problem of disagreement on terminology. This aligns with Popper's view that:

> we do not start from observations but always from problems: from practical problems, or from a theory which has run into difficulties – that is to say, a theory which has raised, and disappointed, certain *expectations*. Once we are faced with a problem, we proceed by two kinds of attempt. We attempt to guess, or to conjecture, a solution to our problem. And we attempt to criticize our usually somewhat feeble solutions. Sometimes a guess or a conjecture may withstand our criticism and our experimental tests for quite some time. But as a rule, we find that our conjectures can be refuted, or that they do not solve our problem, or that they solve it only in part. And we find that even the best solutions – those able to resist the most severe criticism of the most brilliant and ingenious minds – soon give rise to new difficulties, to new problems. Thus we may say that our knowledge grows as we proceed from old problems to new problems by means of *conjectures and refutations* – by the refutation of our theories or, more generally, of our *expectations* (Popper and Notturno, 1994).

Support for not rejecting any reasonable usage of a word can also be found in Popper (1979) where he mentions Churchill's epistemology in glowing terms – taking cross bearings to get independent testimony to reality, rather than considering that actual existence is metaphysically dependent on the observer's senses. In a physical sense, we can determine where something is by taking bearings from independent positions. In a linguistic sense, we can determine what something is by corroborating the observations of more than one person. This can be directly translated into something meaningful for concepts, which inhabit Popper's Worlds 2 and 3. We can only verify the meaning of any concept by considering it from different perspectives; different fields; different areas of study. Only by this process can we reduce or refine or remove the non-essential elements from our description of the concept to whatever its essential features are, so we can then obtain agreement on it. So, triangulating meanings to reach agreement on 'what is it?' is actually taking an essentialist approach. Once a conceptual term has a label that is commonly accepted, thought to be commonly understood and used regardless, then the concept itself becomes objective rather than subjective and therefore becomes part of Popper's World 3. If we can't determine what it is, so that our World 2 can account for it, then we are in trouble. Popper's praise of Churchill's cross-bearing approach in effect calls for a definitional cross-check for this purpose, and the method developed in Chap. 10 includes such a check.

7.4 Derrida's Philosophy

Derrida developed the concepts of deconstruction, logocentrism and aporia. Deconstruction has been described under Issue 3 as seeking the point of inversion were meaning become indeterminable. Logocentrism is "the metaphysics of phonetic writing" (Derrida & Spivak, 1976). Aporia is "an irresolvable internal contradiction or logical disjunction in a text, argument, or theory" (Oxford). The conflict between deconstruction and definition evident in Issue 3 has also been discussed in Issue 7. Pathak (2014) also notes this in saying that Derrida questioned the finality of signifiers, considering there is always some lack or incompleteness. The definitional papers referred to in this book, as well as the chapters of Part II use the Mangle described in Chap. 10 to successfully reconcile definitional conflict in governance and other groups of related terms. Deconstructionism was deconstructed in Issue 7 through applying the diarrhesis of dividing linguistic space into terms denoting physical objects and those denoting conceptual terms.

There are both useful aspects and deficiencies in Derrida's philosophy. The deficiencies in his theory of deconstruction are:

1. It makes generalisations about the undecidability of concepts that do not apply to physical objects/ entities (Issue 7).
2. It allows and encourages the introduction of normative matters of human relationships into definitions via their trace, producing complication and confusion (Issue 1).

3. This masks the need to agree definitions of conceptual terms, condones deficient definition and supports reifying confusions such as the family resemblance concept.
4. The intellectual exercise of everywhere seeking the point of inversion, presumes there is an implied hierarchy in every text/ sentence/ word, which cannot be so for those dealing only with physical objects. It also seems to default (or have a trace) back to, and therefore super-imposes, a simplistic, binary choice view of the world, which is almost Marxist in presuming an all-pervading and eternal struggle between oppressor and oppressed, the worker and the bourgeoise.
5. It invites "complexification" (Derrida & Caputo, 1997) beyond the point of usefulness.

These aspects of his theory of deconstruction dealing with the written word will therefore not form any part of the definitional philosophy adopted here. However the following aspects of his philosophy dealing with speech are most useful:

1. The 'two-faced' aspects of words as signs – the signifier and signified, as originally developed by Saussure. This corresponds with the finding from the definitional and empirical work here that words do not equal meaning but rather represent it (Issue 2).
2. Taking deconstruction to be a discourse to discover what the other person's unconscious assumptions are (their trace) and to then 'deconstuct' both their views and my views. This corresponds with one of the key ideas incorporated within the Mangle. This facilitates separating fact from opinion (Issue 1) as well as encouraging investigation of all previous uses of particular terms.
3. A less rigorous interpretation of deconstruction than the seeking of an inversion point taken by Kleinberg (2013) which is the identification of subconscious bias (normativity), by taking things apart and looking at the pieces to recognise if and where some have been given prominence over others for historical/ cultural/ other reasons. As Derrida and Caputo (1997) say, it is about "cracking nutshells wherever they appear". There is a parallel with governance – what makes it all work is the system part, which accommodates the directing and controlling part of the definition that draws people's attention.

7.4.1 *Impact of the Mangle on Derrida's Philosophy*

The Mangle takes the mis-mash of usage from multiple sources to determine essence which then produces definition with all the traces, all the impurities, contaminants or infecting agents, distilled/ flung/ shaken/ crushed/ separated out. This resolves definition first, leaving increased clarity when discussing or writing about concepts. It separates definition from discussion, removing the normativity of value judgements and placing them squarely in the field of discussion, where they can be explicitly dealt with, rather than being implicitly included and unknowingly concealed in presumed definition. It offers an alternative paradigm for conceptual terms through the same process that falsifies text deconstruction; namely reaching agreement on what the conceptual terms mean, through stripping them to their essence, which, in conceptual terms, is analogous to pointing. Using the Mangle removes the need to perpetuate dichotomies, conundrums and confusion through chasing undecideability through hierarchical inversion within text. It also avoids the endless esoteric discussions of text deconstructionism that cannot tell us what we should do.

7.5 Summary Evaluation of All Considered Philosophers' Positions

In summary, the position presented here on the philosophers considered above in relation to their views on definition is as follows:

Aristotle used the concept of essence in both secular and ethereal senses and not making this clear led to subsequent misinterpretation. His view that truth can arise from intuition is neither false nor universal, as intuition or 'gut feeling' can so easily be mistaken for strong desire. Aristotle's and Hobbes's views on the importance of definition are accepted. Whitty's interpretations of Hume, that we have a mental subroutine that we habitually run and are insensible of running it, and of Kant, in that we have a mental BIOS for running it which represents things and feelings to our minds, are accepted. John Stuart Mill's view, that language is a means of expression of what we feel our concepts mean, is accepted. Language is therefore regarded as just another framework we use to communicate and represent meaning. Seeking absolute meaning in words, as Wittgenstein attempted, is an error. His view on family resemblance as applied to definition is rejected. His doubts on the ability of philosophy to address absolute moral questions are considered to be fully justified. His later view that language is something that is under our collective control is accepted. Popper's acceptance of Tarski's definition of truth as correspondence with the facts is accepted. Popper's views on the desirability of simplicity and clarity of expression as well as on the need to not divide or define further than is necessary to achieve clarity are also accepted. Popper's concept of diarrhes is most useful and basically constitutes definition.

7.6 Observations on Philosopher Positions

Identification of the same initial error in both Wittgenstein's and Popper's work (presuming words were meaning rather than just representing it) enabled a conclusion alternative to both of theirs to be reached by simply distinguishing between process and content, in a similar way to separating epistemology from ontology. This allowed the validity of the concept of Aristotelean essence to be retrieved from the current Wittgensteinian view of family resemblance and from the corrupted view of pragmatism documented by Rescher (2016).

From the analysis conducted here, it became apparent that influential twentieth century philosophers regarded language as meaning rather than as just signifying something requiring agreement, and that this approach still persists and permeates contemporary philosophical thinking. This does not affect objects we can verify our understanding of by seeing and touching, but it becomes quite important when we move beyond objects to abstract concepts.

Reification of concepts to the point of considering them dogmatically universally true can result in overlooking the simple grammatical device of making sure we define a word rather than a phrase (a word with a silent or assumed qualifier). This became evident in developing resolutions of meaning for the many contested concepts addressed in the definitional papers referred to in Part I, as well as in the chapters of Part II. Overlooking this simple factor led to both Wittgenstein and Popper realising in their different ways that we simply haven't known what it is we are talking about; with Wittgenstein constantly asking people he met "What do you mean by that?" (Edmonds, 2002) and Popper saying "if philosophy was all about word puzzles, I would not have gone into it" (Edmonds & Eidinow, 2001).

We can avoid trouble if we just agree what our conceptual words signify, and Chap. 10 gives a process to enable this to occur (the Mangle).

In the words of Magee:

> Many different twofold distinctions have been applied in the history of philosophy … and none of them should be driven too hard: what can make them particularly misleading is that, whichever of them is applied, large-scale figures usually straddle the divide. But one of the dualisms which runs through most of the subject's history is that between a view of philosophy which sees it as an attempt to understand our use of concepts, and a view of philosophy which sees it as an attempt to understand the world. Obviously it is impossible to understand the world without the use of concepts, and therefore people on both sides of the distinction will usually believe with some justification that they are doing both jobs (Magee, 1973).

This work does not really attempt to do either deliberately, but perhaps does both some extent accidentally, by simply attempting to get agreement on what we all mean by any particular conceptual term and the context we are considering it within, before we start to debate it.

7.7 The Trend Away from Definitions

There has been a trend in recent years away from definitions, as evidenced by Pothos and Hahn (2000) noting that "Despite the wealth of evidence to the contrary, much research overtly or covertly continues to promote the case for definitions."

As indicated above, this work has found definitional confusion has been wasting academic and practitioner resources in project management and related fields and this has resulted at least in part from Wittgenstein's family resemblance concept.

The inversion of the Peirce's original conception of pragmatism as being rigorous analysis to select the principles that are most successful, into political expediency independent of principles, as noted by Rescher (2016), may also have contributed.

The trend away from definitions results from looseness of thinking, as well as from convoluted, complicated reasoning, ignoring the advice of earlier sages (Aristotle and Mill) who it is now evident knew better after all. Regarding that part of their advice as being out of date and no longer modern and needing a post-modernism label to address, appears to be an act of hubris, that, as this book demonstrates, has resulted in the almost inevitable confusion identified here in so many areas. The trend away from definition has achieved hamartia on a grand scale.

References

Bandler, R., & Grinder, J. (1975). *The structure of magic: A book about language and therapy*. Science and Behavior Books.

Copi, I. M., & Cohen, C. (1990). *Introduction to logic*. Macmillan.

Copi, I. M., & Cohen, C. (2009). *Introduction to logic*. Pearson education.

Derrida, J., & Caputo, J. D. (1997). *Deconstruction in a nutshell : A conversation with Jacques Derrida*. Fordham University Press.

Derrida, J., & Spivak, G. C. (1976). *Of grammatology*. Johns Hopkins University Press.

Edmonds, D. (2002). *Address on Wittgenstein's poker* [Online], C-SPAN. Available:. https://www.c-span.org/video/?168613-1/wittgensteins-poker. Accessed 8 Mar 2017.

Edmonds, D., & Eidinow, J. (2001). *Wittgenstein's poker : The story of a ten-minute argument between two great philosophers*. Faber.

Haugaard, M. (2010). Power: A 'family resemblance' concept. *European Journal of Cultural Studies, 13*(4), 419–438.

Kleinberg, E. (2013). *Derrida and deconstruction – basic introduction and demonstration* [Online].. Available: https://www.youtube.com/watch?v=N8BsnfjtNCg.. Accessed 3 May 2018.

Lewis, M. P., Simons, F. G., Fennig, D. C., & Summer Institute of Linguistics. (2017). *Ethnologue® : Languages of africa and europe*. SIL International.

Magee, B. (1973). *Popper*. Fontana.

Magee, B. & Searle, J. (1987). *Bryan Magee talks to John Searle about Wittgenstein* [Online].. Available: https://www.bing.com/videos/search?q=wittgenstein&&view=detail&mid=E4F4484E5D59D9E78DDBE4F4484E5D59D9E78DDB&rvsmid=C58CB8F0496A11CA44AFC58CB8F0496A11CA44AF&fsscr=0&FORM=VDQVAP.. Accessed 7 Mar 2017.

McGrath, S. K., & Whitty, S. J. (2015). Redefining governance: From confusion to certainty and clarity. *International Journal of Managing Projects in Business, 8*(4), 755–787.

Mill, J. S. (1874). *A system of logic, ratiocinative and inductive*. Harper & Brothers.

Naraniecki, A. J. (2009). *Popper re-appraised: New perspectives on karl popper's method and its applications*. PhD Griffith University.

Oxford (*Dictionaries online* [Online], Oxford. Available: http://oxforddictionaries.com. Accessed.

Pathak, A. K. (2014). *Jacques derrida & deconstruction* [Online].. Available: https://www.youtube.com/watch?v=STydy9wbAo0. Accessed 3 May 2018.

Plato, & Bury, R. G. (1967). *Plato*. Harvard University Press.

Popper, K. R. (1979). *Objective knowledge: An evolutionary approach*. Clarendon Press.

Popper, K. R. (1995). *The open society and its enemies: Volume 2 Hegel and Marx*. Routledge.

Popper, K. R. (2002). *Conjectures and refutations : The growth of scientific knowledge*. Routledge.

Popper, K. R., & Notturno, M. A. (1994). *The myth of the framework : In defence of science and rationality*. Routledge.

Popper, K. R., Shearmur, J., & Turner, P. N. (2008). *After the open society : Selected social and political writings*. Routledge.

Pothos, E. M., & Hahn, U. (2000). So concepts aren't definitions, but do they have necessary or sufficient features? *British Journal of Psychology, 91*(3), 439–450.

Rescher, N. (2016). *Pragmatism in philosophical inquiry : Theoretical considerations and case studies*. Springer Berlin Heidelberg.

Russell, B. (2005). *History of Western Philosophy*. Routledge.

Sypniewski, B. (2008). Snake in the grass. *Language, Communication and Social Environment (Russian), 6*, 33–54.

Wittgenstein, L. (2007). *A lecture on ethics*. Quodlibet.

Wittgenstein, L., & Anscombe, G. E. M. (1958). *Philosophical investigations*. Basil Blackwell.

Wittgenstein, L., Macguiness, B. F., Pears, D. F., & Russell, B. (1974). *Tractatus logico-philosophicus*. Routledge & Kegan Paul.

Chapter 8
Development of a Theory of Meaning for Conceptual Terms

Having considered the philosophical influences behind all ten definitional issues identified, developed axioms and definitional rules from them, and then proposed resolutions to the philosophical problems they highlighted, a theory of meaning (MTOM) which encapsulates all of this and reflects contemporary society and the current state of scientific knowledge can now be developed. To put this in context of broader social views, consideration will first be given to the relative merits of clarity and ambiguity, the concept of qualia and the relationship of mathematics to the definitional problem before finally stating a definitional position.

8.1 Clarity over Ambiguity

Both clarity and ambiguity can be a hindrance in some circumstances and advantageous in others. Furthermore, clarity and ambiguity produce different behaviours. Clarity works well for building things both physical and intellectual, where we are constrained by 'laws of nature' that cannot be broken and so can be considered within our environment as absolute and in which emotion plays no part. Ambiguity works well for relative matters such as marketing, advertising, politics, the arts, and psychology, and in these matters, emotion can play a legitimate and pivotal role.

This means that we need to use both in appropriate circumstances. Ambiguity in matters which are absolute produces an ontological problem of not knowing where to look next. Ambiguity can also result from the epistemological problem of not having clear, generally accepted essential definitions. The work reported in this book arose from the field of management and while emotion can play an important role in the application of management theory to particular environments, the empirical and analytical work covered in this book indicates that ambiguity causes confusion in circumstances where clarity works best. Ambiguity therefore needs to be kept out of theory development, at least in defining the basic terms we wish to discuss.

S. K. McGrath, *Speaking Management*,
https://doi.org/10.1007/978-981-16-2213-7_8

This is particularly so when we are dealing with the human-machine interface, where we need to be more structured; the machine won't accommodate our feelings, it will just respond to our actions.

However, ambiguity can also sustain markets for competing frameworks and products. Consequently desire for its resolution via application of the Mangle may vary considerably between professional practitioners and product, framework and training suppliers. Nevertheless, ambiguity in management terminology can inhibit productivity. Circumstances where application of the Mangle can reduce confusion are documented in Chaps. 10, 11, 12, 13, 14, 15, 16 and 17 of Part II.

8.2 Qualia

If full comprehension of something only emerges after we have processed all our sensory input, we need a word that describes that comprehension, that perception, the totality of the sensory experience of it. That word would be qualia.

Qualia (singular 'quale') in common modern usage are "properties of experiences", according to Byrne (2016) who credits American pragmatist C. I. Lewis for introducing the term in 1929 in *Mind and the World Order* as "recognizable qualitative characters of the given". The later definition is more succinct and is also an essential definition and so will be accepted.

Whitty (2013) gives ideas and concepts as examples of qualia or mentally perceptual features. Pain is another. These are formed in our brains in response to our sensory experiences and so are properties of those experiences.

Here, qualia are taken to be the evaluation of the subjective sense experiences we are conscious of; our overall impression or awareness that is developed from all the senses but does not actually have a visible physical existence anywhere; the totality of our comprehension or experience of a particular thing. Intuition and 'sixth sense' are taken to be qualia.

When we consider any concept, we are likely to have difficulty describing it as there is no physical entity to be seen. Furthermore, we can become stuck or loop recursively when we attempt to describe all of the meaning coming from all of the senses when using only one of them (sound = words).

This adopts an Aristotelean view as opposed to a Platonic view. A Platonic approach leads to mysticism as it holds that we can never know the ultimate ideal of perfection and it will always be beyond our comprehension and experience. An Aristotelean approach however offers the recognition of the whole as being something besides the parts, which implies essence, so that the key characteristic(s) can be identified in various instantiations of a particular concept, enabling it to be recognised (as distinct from being fully internally understood). Whitty (2013) points out the difficulties of the Platonic approach, noting that groups define the essence of 'chairness' as "a seat with a back, all of which is elevated approximately knee height off the floor" and it is impossible to sit in this ideal chair because it is suspended in mid-air and any attempt to connect it to the ground renders it a particular chair rather than a universal form.

So qualia are in effect, our comprehension of things, the sum total of all the impulses being processed across synapses in our brains plus our responses (including emotional reactions) to them, as a result of our instinctive application of Kant's four pure categories of understanding – quality, quantity, modality and relation. It is our sense-making mechanism, combining and processing information from all five senses, the thing that we as humans do almost instinctively about things we have previously experienced; provided our minds have not been previously hijacked or desensitized, through familiarity or other means, to that particular thing. It is not a thing that exists separately elsewhere. Aristotle would contradict Plato in saying that 'chairness' isn't there; it is distributed across all chairs and is a human experience of things. As Diogenes of Sinope said, "I've seen Plato's cups and table, but not his cupness and tableness" (Davernport, 1979).

To relate this to governance, which triggered this investigation, there are numerous and various governance arrangements (moving parts of the governance machine) that organisations have in place. However governance itself is an emergent behaviour, which can be experienced by the human brain as a universal or qualia, but which does not actually exist as a separate entity anywhere. The concept of it exists and is spread across all implementations of it. The word governance refers to the system formation of the various governance arrangements that result in the emergent behaviour of being able to direct and control an entity. But these ideas of direction and control are human constructs that exist only as concepts and describe the key activities that we understand to comprise the essence of governance, together with the system for bringing them about. However, any change in direction and control can be explicitly measured, and also 'felt', as evidenced by this observation drawn from an empirical investigation of governance "The overall feeling (of participants) can be broadly summarised as indicating that you get good feelings if the governance is good and you don't if it isn't" (McGrath & Whitty, 2020). The participants did not distinguish between bad governance and an absence of governance, regarding them as equivalent.

Using the governance analogy above, while qualia cannot have a separate physical existence that we can see, we can if we feel so inclined, just all agree on what the word qualia represents and leave it at that. So once we have an initial feeling or sense of something, we can label that as a quale. That's as far as we should go, otherwise we are deterministically proceeding in the belief that further reduction (compartmentalisation) will universally bring increased understanding. There is a point beyond which further reduction takes things out of focus, rendering them opaque, falling into the trap of Issue 8. To go further also tempts the mistake of ascribing an ethereal essence beyond a descriptive essence (Issue 5). This is akin to the view of Artificial Intelligence researcher Marvin Minsky who regards it as a mistake to:

> attempt to reify "feeling" as an independent entity, with an essence that's indescribable… feelings are not strange alien things. It is precisely those cognitive changes themselves that constitute what "hurting" is… The big mistake comes from looking for some single, simple, 'essence' of hurting, rather than recognizing that this is the word we use for complex rearrangement of our disposition of resources. (Minsky, 1998)

In other words, we use a particular conceptual word to describe or represent the state of having a particular sense of the nature of an experience and we should avoid seeking ethereal essence. Qualia is a label of a group that any single feeling or perception can be categorised as belonging to, but the diversity of feelings or perceptions that the term can be applied to make it meaningless to reify it into some form of ethereal existence. It's just a useful label for our sense of experience. Qualia, like essence and governance, is a useful concept with no actual physical existence.

Minsky does not accept that there is any deep or essential difference between thinking and feeling. He considers emotions are not alternatives to thinking; they are simply different types of thinking. It is worth noting that the Mangle in Chap. 10 doesn't exclude emotion either; it just defines without making any value judgement.

This concept of qualia is of relevance to Issue 8 and Axiom 8 and so reference to it will be included in the final statement of definitional position below.

8.3 Mathematics and the Definition of Conceptual Terms – Omitted Variables (OVB), Autoregression and Endogeneity

Consideration of this subject enables the linkage/trace of the origins of the 'words equal meaning' approach embodied in the work of Russell and Wittgenstein (Issue 2) to come full circle and be brought to a close.

An **omitted variable bias (OVB)** is an error that occurs when a mathematical equation leaves out one or more relevant variables, producing a biased or incorrect answer. If meaning is a function of the words we use, then to fully express that meaning, all variables contributing to that meaning must be included, and irrelevant ones excluded.

An omitted definitional variable was identified in Issue 3 –silent or hidden qualifiers. This can result from abbreviation or imprecision for the sake of convenience resulting in accidental omission. It can occur within professional fields, geographical areas, sub-cultures and even in individuals omitting (sometimes unconsciously) the qualification of some particular key aspect of their environment. A prime example of this is the interchangeable use of governance and corporate governance by the fathers of governance terminology, which is also an example of Issue 10 (drawing a conclusion about a set from a sub-set when the conclusion is not applicable to wider application.). When a term is picked up outside the particular community it was developed in and applied more broadly, confusion is likely to result where environmental conditions (context) are different. A further example is Popper's exclusion of the process of identifying boundaries (diarrhesis) from definition, which is also an example of Issue 9 (not separating process from content).

Extraneous or irrelevant variables can also be included in definition/meaning, which could be regarded as the inverse of an OVB issue. This can occur where an opinion/attitude/belief has been included in definition, such as identified in Issues 1, 4 and 5. These are normative matters and can include moral, cultural or religious value beliefs and value judgements (Issue 5 – attribution of ethereal meaning to secular words) or belief in the genericity of certain aspects of IT project management to the whole of the project management field (exemplifying Issues 4, 9 and 10). As noted in defining the term 'normative' above, it is the business of definition to adequately describe things, not to impose norms. Note that "addition of extraneous variables does not lead to biased coefficients. However, adding extraneous (or "junk") variables to the model will result in inflated standard errors and all the problems they create" (Williams, 2015).

These OVB problems in definition can create a further OVB problem in communication as well; that is not realising that others have a different definition of the same conceptual word, as expressed in Axiom 1. Communicable words simply constitute an agreement on what particular noises will signify. Contention between subgroups over the meaning of a word, such as occurs for contested terms, can confound communication and indicate that agreement is missing.

There is also a further omission that can modify the meaning of words and govern or over-ride their place in communication, and that is other sensory input. Where this exists, it will determine the full meaning of both what is conveyed and what is received (understood). The senses apart from hearing, namely sight, touch, taste and smell, have their own ways (frameworks) for communicating meaning (e.g. gestures and body language for sight). In other words, there are aspects of meaning that words may not completely capture i.e. elements of communication or meaning that are missing from words.

These omissions and inclusions can be expressed succinctly in a semi-mathematical way as follows:

$$\text{Meaning in words} = \text{Fn}(\text{essence, context})[\text{Note: This is the province of definition}]$$

$$\text{Meaning communicated} = \text{Fn}(\text{words, agreement on their signification, over} - \text{riding sensory input})$$
$$[\text{Note: This is the province of communication}]$$

Where Fn = a function of.

Given these missing and/or unwarranted variables that can confuse meaning in our use of words, and the number of ways in which these confusions can occur, it makes little sense to regard words as having absolute meaning of themselves or to regard them as always comprising the totality of meaning. Such an approach was attempted by Russell and Wittgenstein who considered that all we had to do was develop sufficient true statements, express them mathematically, solve all the simultaneous equations and their totality would produce the ultimate theory of meaning (Wittgenstein et al., 1974, Section 6.343). This approach has an inherent OVB problem. Wittgenstein did eventually recant from this position and developed his family resemblance concept, but that did not step outside the realm of the words = meaning approach. It was therefore similarly subject to OVB. One could possibly set out to prove that the approach of Russell and Wittgenstein was correct when all the other missing variables are included, but this would be an enormous and almost incomprehensible investigation of little value, given the above reasoning.

To restate the problem in another way, the evolution of language has generated omitted and extraneous variable mutations that has produced confusion which has not helped human communication, cooperation and consequently survival. Once this mistake was made, it then generated a further problem which can also be expressed in mathematical terms as **autoregression**, where future understandings and conclusions are based upon past events. Subsequent understandings are generated having cause and effect (causal) relationship with the prior-period data values and on a stochastic (random) term (normative matters – value judgements and beliefs). This can vary randomly, producing random answers. This is another way of saying that understanding of meaning strays further away from essence, the more such definitional mistakes are made.

A further way of expressing or labelling this is in econometric terms, as an endogeneity problem. **Endogeneity** occurs where an external (exogenous) variable outside the model (such as different sensory frameworks, context or normative matters – value judgements and beliefs) is correlated with both the independent variable (meaning) and the dependent variable (auditory representation via words).

These considerations demonstrate that there is some mathematical link that can be made between language and mathematics; but it is not the absolute one that Russell and Wittgenstein imagined. This section has demonstrated that following a mathematical approach to words (that just represent agreements) will be stymied by disagreements and will be unproductive, as Witgenstein eventually sensed. The product of that thinking, his family resemblance concept, proceeds in that same unproductive direction and definitional clarity would be greatly served by its abandonment.

8.4 Generic Applicability

The position taken here is that resolving agreement on conceptual terms using a transparent process can provide a basis for agreement and resolve unnecessary contention. This has been determined deductively in the Chapters of Part II, which have provided a basis for agreeing cross-field definitions of governance, accountability, stakeholders, strategic management, power and ethics. These investigations were conducted within the management environment for circumstances where achieving clarity is desirable and productive.

8.5 Definitional Position

Having reconciled with the views of the major philosophers on the subject of definition, the position that emerges from this work can now be stated. This philosophical position on definition and meaning is in direct opposition to Wittgenstein's family resemblance concept. It comprises the ten axioms and ten definitional rules developed from the ten issues identified above. These axioms and rules are listed together below, with embellishments added to Axioms 1, 2 and 8 following the philosophical considerations above.

Definitional Axioms

1. ***A definition states what a group of people have agreed a particular sound/ word will represent or signify***. This means that there is no absolute correct sound or absolute correct definition; correctness of definition and of assignment of the label to instances where the signification is found can only be judged relative to that agreement. If agreement has not been reached, or different groups have agreed different things, there will be contention over correctness. Words are meaningful only insofar as we have agreed their meaning/signification. Contention over definition indicates agreement hasn't been reached yet. Overlooking or rushing past this critical point has delivered confusion and philosophical linguistic tangles, from Aristotle to Wittgenstein. All we can do is identify contention and just sort it out, recognising that full knowledge of any concept is spread across many individuals. That requires a new process for doing so, which the Mangle provides. We just have to regain control of the human tool we call language, rather than letting it control us.
2. ***Meaning does not come from words alone***. We have five senses, each with its own capacity to give us information about the external world which we use to derive internal meaning regarding impact on us, which we call understanding. The senses that the spoken and written word do not use can also contribute to meaning and, in some cases, words may have difficulty expressing or communicating that meaning.
3. ***A word simply provides the label or signifier for what is signified by its agreed definition.*** A word can only represent something; it cannot actually be it.
4. ***The closer the signification of a word comes to the important attributes that a thing must have (i.e. essence) for that label (signifier) to be correctly assigned to it, the closer it gets to accurately representing the auditory part of meaning contained in the written word***, and the less the confusion that can result. The closer it comes to representing the meaning received from all five senses, the closer it comes to representing the full meaning.
5. ***Some words such as essence have dual simultaneous meanings that are secular (four dimensional) and ethereal (extra-dimensional) and the 'higher order' ethereal meaning will gazump the secular by subconscious default unless the issue is called out***. Defining in terms of secular essence removes the dependence of definition on matters of ethereal belief. Ethereality emerges

from seeking definition or meaning in dimensions other than those that are physically accessible to us.

6. ***Concepts require an additional definitional process to physical objects for agreement to be reached as they cannot be pointed at, to collectively verify meaning***. The Mangle provides this. (Note that this does not include grammatical objects, which can refer to both physical objects and concepts.)
7. ***Clarity is more important than precision in reaching agreement on definition, but precision may be useful to reach a point of clarity***, albeit that it may obscure matters if taken beyond that point. Infinite regress does not occur if we seek only the detail necessary to agree usage and do not pursue deeper understanding of the internal workings of an entity or concept.
8. ***Connections between divisions or component parts also require labelling and definition***. Properties or characteristics of systems that emerge from having made those connections comprise the 'whatever it is' that is more than the sum of the parts. This can be expressed as qualia. Qualia have no physical existence but the word provides a useful conceptual term to describe the extra bit that we feel or sense that is otherwise difficult to give a general name to or to find an essence of.
9. ***Diarrhesis can facilitate definition by enabling sense to be made within divisions that cannot otherwise be made***. Knowledge therefore does come from establishing boundaries and divisions (diarrhesis) (such as Popper did with his three worlds).
10. ***One such diarrhesis that can reduce confusion in definition is the separation of epistemology from ontology, through distinguishing between content (what we know) and process (how we know it)***. This can avoid enshrining non-generic content within a process that may potentially be generic.

Definitional Rules

1: ***Exclude attitudes from definition***. Accommodate them after definitions have been agreed, not before.

2: ***Identify any silent or assumed qualifiers***.

3: ***Exclude beliefs from definition***. Accommodate them after definitions have been agreed, not before (This is the same as rule 1 with beliefs substituted for attitudes. Both attitudes and beliefs can be regarded as opinions).

4: ***Exclude ethereal significations from the definition of unqualified terms with dual simultaneous meanings such as 'essence' by adding the qualifiers 'ethereal' or 'secular' to them***. Accommodate the ethereal after definitions have been agreed, not before (This is the same as rule 3 with ethereal essence substituted for beliefs).

5: ***Define by intension rather than by extension where-ever possible***.

6: ***Use the Mangle to resolve contention for conceptual terms***. It provides a triangulation process to verify that a common understanding of concepts has been reached. It also provides a means of incorporating any new realizations or applications. It is not necessary to apply it to objects which can be seen/touched; their physical existence automatically generates agreement upon the signification of any term used to represent them.

7: ***Use precision only to the point where clarity is reached.*** If clarity is not reached, go back up a level. Precision regarding sub-systems or components does not produce clarity at the system level. Further precision is required only if an understanding of the internal workings of parts or sub-systems of an entity is being sought.

8: ***In defining a system, recognize the connections between its parts.***

9: ***Consider process and content separately.*** This supports exclusion of non-generic content from definition. The Mangle sorts out process, leaving the focus on content and true genericity.

10: ***Identify the context within which the term is being defined and refrain from making any generalisations that have not been tested outside that context.*** This is similar to rule 2 which deals with making assumed or silent qualifiers explicit. Both rules deal with making context explicit. The Mangle provides a recognized way of doing this.

8.6 Application

The validity of previous definitions or usages of a term can be determined by looking for evidence of any of the above ten issues/axioms/rules having been violated or transgressed. They can all cause ambiguity/linguistic confusion. If any of these are found, then the particular usage requires adjustment. The means of doing this proposed here is application of the Mangle as outlined in Chap. 10.

8.7 Features of the Mangle

The features of the Mangle that enable it to remove ambiguity and confusion are that it:

1. uses a rigorous transparent process to arrive at definitions, providing both a basis for supporting the derived definitions as well as a means of challenge
2. produces internal consistency between terms in the group of terms defined
3. defines by intension where possible, avoiding the problems of defining by extension
4. ensures a wide range of perspectives are canvassed including historical use and so it effectively triangulates
5. exposes silent and assumed qualifiers
6. removes opinion/normative matters from consideration in definition, leaving those matters for subsequent discussion once we know what we are talking about

7. places definition firmly in Popper's World 3, removing it from his World 2 by accepting only non-normative arguments i.e. by removing value judgements
8. 'deconstructs' the term rather than the text, looking for points of disagreement rather than hierarchical inversion
9. ensures epistemology is addressed before ontology, avoiding ontological error that the existence of definitional contention indicates exists
10. accommodates Popper's diarrhesis (categorization through the process of division or distinction), without accepting Popper's aversion to labelling this process as definition.

It is also worth noting that the Mangle process is self-correcting because every element deals with removing epistemological error; so, no matter how rudimentary a mini-Mangle application of it may be conducted, it will tend towards facilitating ontological agreement.

References

Byrne, A. (2016). Inverted qualia. In E. N. Zalta (Ed.), *The Stanford encyclopedia of philosophy* (Winter 2016 Edition).

Davernport, G. (1979). *Herakleitos and diogenes*. Grey Fox Press.

McGrath, S. K., & Whitty, S. J. (2020). What do project management practitioners think governance is? A study on perceptions in Queensland, Australia. *International Journal of Managing Projects in Business, 13*(5), 961–980.

Minsky, M. (1998). *Edge interview with Marvin Minsky: Consciousness is a big suitcase* [Online]. Available: https://www.edge.org/3rd_culture/minsky/minsky_p4.html. Accessed 27 Mar 2018.

Whitty, S. J. (2013). Thinking in slow motion about project management. In N. Drouin, R. Muller, & S. Sankaran (Eds.), *Novel approaches to organizational project management research: Translational and transformational*. Copenhagen Business School Press.

Williams, R. (2015). *Specification error: Omitted and extraneous variables* [Online]. University of Notre Dame. Available: https://www3.nd.edu/~rwilliam/stats2/l41.pdf. Accessed 19 July 2018.

Wittgenstein, L., Macguiness, B. F., Pears, D. F., & Russell, B. (1974). *Tractatus logico-philosophicus*. Routledge & Kegan Paul.

Chapter 9
Implications of This Theory

There are a number of implications of this definitional position which are dealt with below.

9.1 The Converse of Diarrhesis

It is worthwhile exploring the converse of Popper's diarrhesis insight in sub-classifying the thinking world. That is the tendency for particular specialities to think their world is actually the wider universe and attempt to apply their thinking biases, opinions and beliefs to it. This approach can result in attempts to have something accepted as universal that is actually not. This is actually an inductive approach. It can lead to errors ranging from small misunderstandings between two people, to, for example, Wittgenstein's error in classifying language as a competitive activity. We may find a particular person difficult to understand or to deal with, and then generalise that to all men/women/children/adults/old people/people of a certain race or creed, to resolve our difficulty. We may then propose an explanatory theory which we then proceed to apply, omitting all the silent qualifiers surrounding the particular person and the circumstances we encountered them in. Or we may talk about generic project methodology and PRINCE2 together, omitting the silent 'IT' qualifier and not considering the fact that the IT parentage of PRINCE2 has made it very difficult to apply in infrastructure projects, where it has had very little successful adoption. There is a simple grammatical rule which helps avoid this error and that is to make assumed qualifiers explicit. While the rule is simple, its application can be quite difficult, as we are often unaware we are assuming a qualifier. But applying that rule can avoid a sub-set of meaning being confused with or taken for universal truth.

S. K. McGrath, *Speaking Management*,
https://doi.org/10.1007/978-981-16-2213-7_9

9.2 The Problem of Universals

This problem dissolves upon accepting that:

1. words simply represent what a group of people agree they will signify within the four dimensions we have ready access to and
2. universals or qualia or the sum total of the processing of all our senses in relation to some object or concept, do not have to be ethereal; they are concepts that exist in our thinking but have physical existence in our brains that cannot be 'seen' without sophisticated equipment.

Again, applying a diarrhesis solves the problem by simply specifying whether the existence is physical or conceptual. Concepts exist in our thoughts, once we understand what the word denoting the concept signifies, via whatever physical means of biological and electromagnetic impulses that exist in our brain to produce the phenomenon called understanding. These are actually physical processes, but they are hidden in our heads such that we cannot see them. So the diarrhesis is effectively between what we can physically see and what we can't, for the purposes of communication.

This means that both opposing positions on universals are wrong without the necessary silent qualifiers and both are right when these are added; universals do have conceptual existence that cannot be seen, and universals have no physical existence that can be seen. They may be conceptually found in things (objects or concepts) simply as a property of those things.

The existence of concepts neither requires nor precludes ethereality, yet we have comprehensively confused ourselves with it for millennia. The omission of silent qualifiers was understandable in former times without the access to the technology and modern knowledge of the human body, but it is not today.

Ethereality, or any normative matter (opinion or claim derived from our cultural values and beliefs rather than from evidence), is a legitimate topic for discussion, but any such discussion is best deferred until we have defined our words such that we can all know what each other is talking about. Universals are concepts that emerge from observing the functioning of combinations of things (objects and/or other concepts). We just need to agree what the words we use to label them will be and what they will signify, then move on. The notion that we can invent and agree on a word like chair-ness and that there can then be some ultimate perfect chair-ness that only godliness can aspire to is untenable. This in itself demonstrates the dysfunctionality of allowing ethereality into definition.

9.3 Essentially Contested Concepts

Gallie's 'essentially contested concepts' is a symptom of acting as though 'words = meaning' that does not require any further enumeration or subclassification, but rather application of the Mangle to individual instances to remove them.

9.4 The Relationship Between Language and Mathematics

Russell and Wittgenstein identified the parallel between language and mathematics but pursued it in a way that did not provide explanatory power and so did not produce a satisfactory outcome. They effectively assumed correlation between meaning and the signifier, overlooking the signified. They did not recognize that words signifying conceptual terms represent only a past agreement (that may be absent) and consequently fell into the OVB problem of Sect. 8.3.

9.5 Support for the Mangle

Wanderer (2007) notes:

> General semantics points out how we 'create reality' by selecting things to notice from Out There, selecting things to relate them to from In Here, and creating a Picture in Our Head from all that. One major problem is that we tend to think the picture we have created is a representation of what's happening Out There, when so much of that picture comes from stuff already In Here.

The Mangle provides a way of aligning individually created realities.

Support for the approach taken in the Mangle can also be drawn from the work of Sypniewski (2008) in rejecting the idea that 'words equal meaning' and in exposing the importance of context. He noted "that Saussure (as do most traditional linguists) does not think that the surroundings are at all important" and holds "another pervasive abstraction in traditional linguistics. All communications are assumed to be flawless". He further observes that "Abstractions such as this, by eliminating "distracting details", are supposed to make observations easier and thought processes clearer. By eliminating important details, our observations are made harder and our thought processes cloudier" (Sypniewski, 2008). He considers "HSL (Hard Science Linguistics) admonishes us to study people communicating in the real world. We cannot afford to neglect the surroundings in our models because the surroundings, together with the other elements of a linkage, model the real world" (Sypniewski, 2008). He further notes "The listener is not the tabula rasa of traditional linguistics but has senses and experience" (Sypniewski, 2008).

This constitutes rejection of the 'words equal meaning' concept, where the same words are presumed to convey the same meaning regardless of the surroundings. Meaning and signification are not the same thing and so it is dangerous to associate meaning with definition alone. Meaning is something besides its contributing sensory parts. But we must all understand the same signification of a term regardless of the other meanings/nuances we extract from the environment and from our other sensory frameworks, otherwise it is pointless having language. Language exists to enable us to consistently convey something. The alternative idea that it exists so that we don't know what we are talking about is untenable.

> A clear conception means a determinate conception; one which does not fluctuate, which is not one thing today and another tomorrow, but remains fixed and invariable, except when, from the progress of our knowledge, or the correction of some error, we consciously add to it or alter it. Mill (1874)

Sypniewski (2008) is not exhorting us to adopt a position of definitional laxity. To do so would simply drop back into the confusion of Wittgenstein's family resemblance idea, which was developed in times preceding recognition that speech is just one of a number of sensory frameworks we use to communicate meaning. The Mangle gives a method of sorting out the signification of our words without pretending that the words give the full meaning. We only need to understand exactly what the words signify so that we don't unnecessarily confound the determination of meaning. The Mangle is a means of dealing with polysemy. It provides a means of reaching agreement.

The Mangle resulted from an analysis of one word – governance. It is quite different to, but has significant parallels with the work relating transformational grammar and family therapy by Bandler and Grinder (1975), both in form and in application.

The parallel in form, using their terminology, is that the Mangle exposes the transformation of the surface structure of the contested term that is required to move to the deep structure which contains the full picture and is where sense can be made. It does this by identifying the structural difficulties of the language use surrounding them – its generalisations, deletions and distortions, which are herein expressed as omissions, value judgements and unwarranted inclusions.

The parallel in application is that the Mangle has provided a basis for resolving conflict across many areas of management, as documented in Part II. Any such area can be regarded as a portion of the human family that is having an 'essentially contested concept' issue with the rest of the family group. The Mangle provides a means for the family member to resolve their issue with the rest of society/the world in a way that doesn't generate further difficulty.

9.6 Observations on the Axioms and Rules

The problems highlighted by this research and the solution developed suggest that there may be potential beneficial implications well beyond the field of management and project management. So it is perhaps worthwhile to extend the theory of meaning in Chap. 8 by extracting some meta-axioms and meta-rules and stating them in a way that is potentially suitable for wider application.

Meta-axioms

The following meta-axioms have been derived from considering all of the conclusions drawn collectively as follows:

1. **Truth is relative to context but absolute within it.**
2. **Communication isn't what you think you meant. It's what the other person thinks you meant**. What you think you meant is just talking (flapping your gums while making some noise) or writing.
3. **Consequently, many disagreements are simply misunderstandings or miscommunication over the signification (meaning) of terms.**
4. **Any application of the Mangle will tend towards facilitating understanding and agreement** – whether it's application is 'full', 'midi' (full formal structure with just a single dictionary selected) or 'mini' (neither full formal structure nor tabulation of multiple lexical sources i.e. a single widely recognized dictionary (e.g. Oxford) is selected and eclectic observations made, with a mental post-check that all Mangle steps have been covered and axioms and definitional rules followed). The triangulation process this requires is self-correcting. Even if mistakes in reasoning are made – the process provides transparency, enabling identification and correction (see meta-rule 1 below).
5. **Referring in definition to context outside the four dimensions we have ready access to (the three spatial dimensions plus time) introduces difficulty and confusion that can take millennia to resolve** (see meta-rules 3–5 below).

Meta-rules

Two meta-rules arise from the first four meta-axioms as follows:

1. **Apply the Mangle to any disagreement first to make sure you actually have one before drawing any conclusions or taking any verbal or physical action (from meta-axiom 3. Note that this extends and is superordinate to definitional rule 6).**
2. **Detach from any desire to have a personal or group view accepted as generic without first applying some form of the Mangle to it.**

Several further meta-rules emerge from definitional rule 6 and are developed below.

Wherever we have agreed for whatever reason in the past that a particular noise/word will have multiple different significations, we have to take the extra step of using context to determine which one is being used. This is the case for the word 'mean' which can signify arithmetic average, nasty, excellent, dreadful or what I intended to say. Although there is a common essence of stretching all these meanings from ‘half-way’ and ‘in-mind’, each of the derivative uses has its own essence that can also be determined. It follows that in determining definitions, an insufficient search for essence should not be the default position.

However, it is where context cannot be seen that much greater confusion can arise. Such is the case for the words ‘essence’, ‘meaning’ and ‘universal’; three words that are of great importance to philosophical discourse. All of these terms are commonly understood in both secular and ethereal senses at the same time, without the grammatical context necessarily indicating which is being used.

So it is not so much a matter of removal of ethereality that is the problem; it is rather of making it explicit when a ethereal interpretation (context) is being used and of not allowing the meaning to flip-flop randomly with an inherent presumption that the ethereal interpretation must always over-ride the secular. If, as Nietzsche said “God is dead” (Nietzsche et al., 2010), then we haven’t buried him properly in our minds and he has resurrected. Proffering God is generally done for things that are otherwise difficult to explain; and surely definition can be explained. Furthermore, removing the ethereal dimension and any presumption of it from definition only can have no impact at all on whether God exists or not or on what the purpose of life may be. It is simply saying that presuming an ethereal dimension on some key words has caused so much confusion that it would be advisable to stop doing it; and to then do something else that doesn’t cause confusion. This can be done by implementing the following meta- rules:

3. **Add the qualifying term ‘secular’ or ‘ethereal’ to any use of the word essence.**
4. **Substitute the word ‘purpose’ for any ethereal connotation of the word ‘meaning’**, thereby abandoning and allowing to become obsolete any reference to the illogical ‘meaning of life’.
5. **Add the qualifier ‘in the secular sense’ or ‘in the ethereal sense’ after any use of the word ‘universal’.**

Note that this discussion is irrelevant to the ‘does God exist’ question, upon which no statement is made here. It is simply clarifying the dimensional context that is generally omitted/unspoken/silent.

9.7 Robustness of the Language Tool

The success of the many applications of the Mangle documented in this book seems to indicate there is a robustness of the (English) human language system, even with the presence of all the ten usage mistakes identified above. There was not a single case where a satisfactory essential definition could not be determined by continuing the analysis until an acceptable intersection of all sets of meanings could be found, even with the presence of these possible usage mistakes. This seems to indicate that common usage somehow imposes an underlying rigor that induces some sort of innate collective intelligence akin to Adam Smith’s invisible hand. This hints at the possibility of the concept of unfoldment in (Bohm, 1980) being present in the language system. This has not been pursued here, other than using physical unfoldment to remove ethereal confusion. It was possible to do this using quite basic techniques without needing to resort to quantum mechanics. However this observation on that outcome does raise the possibility that if one wished to develop an understanding of the apparently self-correcting nature of language usage, the concept of enfoldment (or the related term implicate order) may be worth exploring.

It is also worth noting that the human language usage system is effectively a classification system and so is subject to the advantages and disadvantages of such systems, as outlined in Sect. 3.4.

References

Bandler, R., & Grinder, J. (1975). *The structure of magic: A book about language and therapy*. Science and Behavior Books.

Bohm, D. (1980). *Wholeness and the implicate order*. Routledge and Kegan Paul.

Mill, J. S. (1874). *A system of logic, ratiocinative and inductive*. Harper & Brothers.

Nietzsche, F. W., Common, T., & Chapco, B. (2010). *Thus spoke Zarathustra*. Feedbooks.

Sypniewski, B. (2008). Snake in the grass. *Language, Communication and Social Environment (Russian), 6*, 33–54.

Wanderer, R. (2007). General semantics: A compendium of definitions. *ETC: A Review of General Semantics, 64*(3), 193–204.

Part II
Resolving Terminology Confusion in Management and Project Management

The purpose of this Part II is to comprehensively test the theory developed in Part I. The first Chap. 10 describes development of a method of doing this. The following chapters effectively test this method by applying it to a wide range of terms whose meanings have not been universally agreed within the field of management, including governance, power, ethics, leadership and management. Each chapter either contains a case study on one such group of terms or considers the group's definitional space. Existing terminology confusion is documented before either carrying out or summarising the analytical work of determining the essence of meaning of the contested terms. This is done by applying the method, canvassing the range of usages, and developing definitions of the various concepts to provide a transparent means for avoiding linguistic confusion. Where appropriate, the resulting definitional space is then mapped, resulting in depiction of various mechanisms and models that are also subsequently tested. All Part II chapters, other than those summarising previously published peer-reviewed papers, have been written to academic journal standard and format, fully justified and referenced. The outcome of all this work was that all applications of the method were successful. This indicates the veracity of the method and provides a comprehensive body of knowledge for resolving definitional confusion across the field of management. Disagreements over opinions can quickly descend into attempts to influence in favour of one competing opinion over another, and the outcome then ceases to depend upon truth or logic. To avoid this, the chapters have all been written to exclude normative considerations. Consequently, as stated in the book's introduction, its findings cannot be logically challenged on the basis of predisposition, preference, bias or opinion; its findings can only be logically challenged by identifying any issue missed, or by finding some flaw in its reasoning. Then for any such challenge to be useful, it would also have to propose an adjusted meaning that accommodates all the previously documented considerations as well as the new issue or flaw identified. The definitions proposed here therefore provide a rigorous and transparent starting point for subsequent agreement to be reached. The subjects dealt with in this Part are contested concepts selected from across the management lexicon. The chapters are as follows: 10. Governance. 11. Power and its exercise. 12. Enablers, mechanisms, tools and channels of power. 13. Ethics, morality, values, principles and beliefs. 14. Who are 'good' ethics good for. 15. Leadership and strategic management. 16. Accountability and responsibility. 17. Stakeholders. The lexicon in Part III contains all the terms defined in Parts I and II. There are other published definitional papers that have produced definitions by using this approach, as well as by surveying existing documents or experienced practitioners. These are more specialist project management papers and so summaries of them have not been included in this book. However, the definitions they produced have been included in the Part III lexicon.

Chapter 10
Governance

This chapter summarises McGrath and Whitty (2015) and reproduces portions of it. That paper developed what was dubbed ‘the Mangle’ and applied it to governance and its associated terms to remove definitional confusion from the field of governance.

The lack of an agreed definition of governance was first established as documented in Biesenthal and Wilden (2014), Ahola et al. (2014), Pitsis et al. (2014), Cepiku (2013). A pre-existing methodology for resolving the definitions of a group of conceptual terms was then sought, but none was found. This left no option but to develop one.

The difficulties of definition were then analysed and it was realised that a purely linguistic approach would be insufficient as the methodology required would need to be capable of developing internally consistent definitions for groups of terms. Furthermore, it needed to accommodate the group of governance terms not being simply a collection of unique, tangible objects that can be observed and classified; it is a collection of terms dealing with abstract concepts which have the potential to overlap. A systems approach was therefore overlayed upon the linguistic approach, thereby enabling terms to be uniquely identified, in the same way as physical objects. The methodology was therefore designed to combine three elements; a systems approach, linguistics and logic. Linguistics determined some initial group criteria and the initial process of defining the individual terms. An over-arching systems approach determined group criteria to ensure consistency. Logical criteria were then developed for reducing any discovered divergence of meaning. Furthermore, references were restricted, as far as possible, to academic, peer-reviewed papers, to remove the influence of opinion and marketing.

Twelve different dictionaries were then selected to give a comprehensive starting group of potential definitions for all terms to be included in any analysis. On the recommendation of Copi and Cohen (1990), intensional definition was preferred, by genus and difference where possible but with operational and synonymous definition also being accepted. Definition by extension was avoided where possible

S. K. McGrath, *Speaking Management*,
https://doi.org/10.1007/978-981-16-2213-7_10

because of the ease of omitting key attributes. The Copi and Cohen (1990) five supplementary rules were also adopted, namely that the definition:

1. States the essential attributes of the species
2. Avoids circularity
3. Is neither too broad nor too narrow
4. Avoids ambiguous, obscure or figurative language
5. Is affirmative rather than negative.

10.1 The Definitional Method

The method has now been applied to multiple groups of terms, resulting in the following slight modifications being identified:

1. Step 2 should have an additional qualification at the end stating "that has produced a definition by intension, not specific to any extension." (Identified in Chap. 15 Stakeholders and Chap. 17 Leadership and strategic management)
2. Step 10 the word "adopted" should be "derived", (Identified in Chap. 15 Stakeholders and Chap. 17 Leadership and strategic management)

   The full method including these slight modifications is as follows:

10.1.1 Group Rules Pre-definition

1. Select the group of terms to be defined.
2. Determine the order of definition as follows:
   (a) Identify any inconsistencies within the group that may require one term to be defined before another.
   (b) Where a compound term is to be defined, define the component terms first.
   (c) Where a derivative term is to be defined, define the root term first.
   (d) Where a term has a noun and a verb form, define the verb first.
3. Consider any terms that are likely to be used in definition that may themselves require prior definition.

10.1.2 Steps to Determine a Connotative (Intensional) Conventional Definition of Each Term

1. Define derivative or component terms using the root or component definitions that have previously been defined by this process or are clear and accepted in their meaning. (This obviates the need to proceed through the remaining definitional steps unless there is other reason to do so, such as confusion in the meaning of the compound or derivative term itself).
2. Survey lexical usage (This and the following two steps may be omitted if there is a known comprehensive academic review of definitions of the term that has produced a definition by intension, not specific to any extension). Note this updates this step in McGrath and Whitty (2015) in accordance with the observations of Chap. 15.
3. Analyse this to determine the main contenders for inclusion in the definition.
4. Develop a connotative (intensional) conventional definition. (This may be synonymous, operational or by genus and difference).
5. Report and analyse any known academic review of definitions of the term
6. Remove unwarranted inclusions.
7. Remove divergence of meaning resulting from mixing content and process by removing any reference to content (for generic conceptual terms).
8. Remove any remaining divergence of meaning and for operational definitions, consider the need for additional inclusions, by checking against the following, as appropriate to the particular term:
   (a) Historical usage
   (b) Field/specialty usage – the definition most generic to as many fields as possible will be selected
   (c) Practitioner usage (via practitioner literature, considering the influence of opinion and marketing)
   (d) Competing concepts & frameworks (considering the influence of opinion and marketing)
9. Check any resulting definitions by genus & difference against the Copi and Cohen (1990) five rules and discard any which do not satisfy them. These rules are:
   1. States the essential attributes of the species
   2. Avoids circularity
   3. Neither too broad nor too narrow
   4. Avoids ambiguous, obscure or figurative language
   5. Affirmative rather than negative.
10. Report the derived definition.

10.1.3 Group Rules Post-definition

1. Cross-check terms defined in this group for any inconsistency and resolve.
2. Cross-check any terms defined in this group known to be used interchangeably with other terms outside the group and resolve any inconsistency.

10.2 Application of the Method

The terms selected for definition, in order, were govern, governance, government, organisational governance, organisational governance arrangements, corporate governance and project governance.

10.2.1 Key Definitional Issues

Key issues addressed in working through the method for these terms were:

- Government can either control directly or it can regulate, just setting the bounds within which people can exercise freedom and discretion. Regulation is an alternative or indirect method of control. It is a subset not a characteristic of control and was therefore not included in any of the definitions.
- Usage of the terms power and authority overlap. They were identified as also requiring definition and this is done in Chap. 11. To avoid confusion, neither term was included in any of the definitions.
- Decision making also overlaps with and is required by both direction and control. Consequently, it was not included in any of the definitions. However allocating authority to make decisions on all matters the entity deals with is part of its governance and was included under organisational governance arrangements.
- Lord Cadbury (1992), the father of corporate governance, did not distinguish between governance and corporate governance. His remit from government was to look at (misbehaviour of) private companies. This oversight was identified and corrected in the resulting definitions.
- The following items were found to have been previously erroneously arranged under the governance banner: leadership, strategy, ethics, decision making, rationalising, relationships, coordinating. Ethical arrangements may or may not be included in organisational governance arrangements, albeit that the purpose of having governance arrangements is to ensure good ethics/behaviour. Governance is the mechanics of constraints on doing things, not the determination of what to do. Governance is the means, not the purpose.
- Accountability was taken to be part of the definition of organisational governance rather than of governance itself as a dictator may have no accountability but will still have governance. Similarly, a machine can be governed but not held to account.

10.2.2 Summary of Definitions

The following definitions resulted from application of the derived method:

- Govern = direct and control.
- Governance = the system by which an entity is directed and controlled.
- Government = an entity that controls a geographic area.
- Organisational governance = the system by which an organisation is directed, controlled and held to account.
- Organisational governance arrangements = an entity's structure (component parts, inter-relationships), positions (roles, responsibilities, pay levels and numbers), rules (written and unwritten, including policies, procedures, codes, methodologies and conventions), decision making processes (including financial and other delegations, as well as approval processes), records and reporting arrangements (annual, financial, progress, assurance, audit, regulatory, stakeholder). (Note the need for records and audit to be added was identified in McGrath and Whitty (2020)).
- Corporate governance = the organisational governance of a corporation = the system by which a corporation is directed and controlled and held to account.
- Project governance = the organisational governance of a project = the system by which a project is directed and controlled and held to account.

Note that McGrath and Whitty (2015) said

> It should also be noted that the term public governance has deliberately not been included in the terms defined above as it is an unnecessary product of the confusion resulting from failing to distinguish between the terms governance and corporate governance.

However, in the intervening time, this term has gained more usage and so a definition consistent with the method is included here as well as in the Appendix I lexicon, to avoid usage of the internally contradictory term 'public corporate governance'.

- Public governance = the organisational governance of a publicly owned (i.e. government) entity = the system by which a publicly owned (i.e. government) entity is directed, controlled and held to account.

10.2.3 Framework for Governing an Organisational Entity

Figure 10.1 gives a diagrammatic framework for governing an organisational entity. It provides a conceptual representation of the above definitions. Note that it updates Figure 2 of McGrath and Whitty (2015) with the addition of records and audit, as determined in McGrath and Whitty (2020).

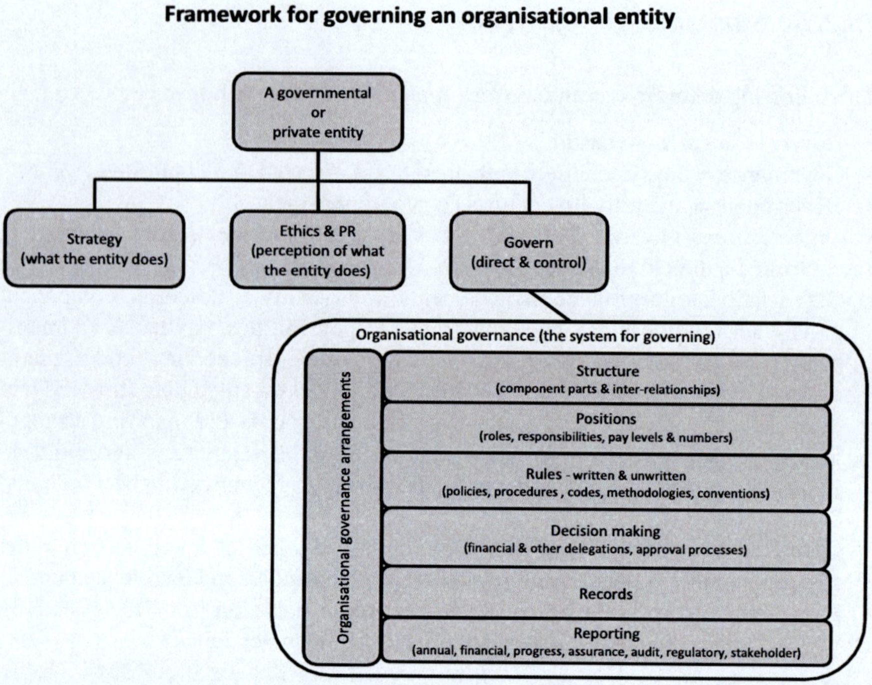

Fig. 10.1 Framework for governing an organisational entity

10.3 Observations and Conclusions

It was possible to develop a group of governance terms applicable across the whole governance ambit – national and international, covering private and governmental organisations as well as higher level political power structures of whatever nature; democratic, autocratic, monarchical, dictatorial, communist or other form.

The paper eschewed the conventional approach to governance of considering agency theory, stewardship theory, stakeholder theory, transaction cost theory and/or resource dependence theory. That did not in any way inhibit its derivation of robust definitions.

Applying the definitional method resulted in the exclusion, or rather, relegation to organisational governance arrangements, of some terms that had previously been purloined into definitions of governance. This separated process from content and disentangled corporate governance from the more generic governance term.

The preoccupation of the originators of the modern usage of the term 'governance' (Cadbury, 1992; Tricker, 1984) with the joint-stock company model had the effect of arrogating the term governance to accounting and legal purposes. It is perhaps not surprising that confusion has followed for those not working in the joint-stock company environment from an accounting and or legal perspective.

This paper identified other terms that are the subject of similar definitional confusion. These were power, ethics and strategy, stakeholders, responsibility and accountability. These are considered in other chapters in this Part.

References

Ahola, T., Ruuska, I., Artto, K., & Kujala, J. (2014). What is project governance and what are its origins? *International Journal of Project Management, 32*(8), 1321–1332.

Biesenthal, C., & Wilden, R. (2014). Multi-level project governance: Trends and opportunities. *International Journal of Project Management, 32*(8), 1291–1308.

Cadbury, A. (1992). *Report of the committee on the financial aspects of corporate governance* (p. 90). Burgess Science Press.

Cepiku, D. (2013). Unraveling the concept of public governance: A literature review of different traditions. In L. Gnan, A. Hinna, & F. Monteduro (Eds.), *Conceptualizing and researching governance in public and non-profit organizations*.

Copi, I. M., & Cohen, C. (1990). *Introduction to logic*. Macmillan.

McGrath, S. K., & Whitty, S. J. (2015). Redefining governance: From confusion to certainty and clarity. *International Journal of Managing Projects in Business, 8*(4), 755–787.

McGrath, S. K., & Whitty, S. J. (2020). What do project management practitioners think governance is? A study on perceptions in Queensland, Australia. *International Journal of Managing Projects in Business, 13*(5), 961–980.

Pitsis, T. S., Sankaran, S., Gudergan, S., & Clegg, S. R. (2014). Governing projects under complexity: Theory and practice in project management. *International Journal of Project Management, 32*(8), 1285–1290.

Tricker, R. I. (1984). *Corporate governance: Practices, procedures and powers in british companies and their boards of directors*. Gower.

Chapter 11
Power Defined (Part 1): Power and Its Exercise

11.1 Introduction

This research originated from the area of governance at the interface between organisations and their projects, where it became clear that an understanding of the exercise of power was necessary. A definition of power was sought, and it soon became evident that there was no commonly accepted definition. A similar problem had previously been encountered regarding governance itself and a method had recently been successfully applied there to achieve definitional consistency (McGrath & Whitty, 2015). That method adopted a purely definitional approach and is applied here to see if it might resolve the contestability of definitions of power. A detailed definitional analysis was completed, and it became evident that this could be expanded to include many other non-contested terms. This developed into a comprehensive mapping of power terms into a model, and it was then found that previous and contemporary power theories could easily be located within it.

This work is reported over two Chapters. Chapters 11 reviews the contested nature of power, points out the inadequacy of single term definitions, considers desirable attributes of any analysis method, outlines the philosophical approach taken, adopts an appropriate method then applies it to determine the group of power terms to be defined, before proceeding to define legitimacy, authority, power and influence. Chapter 12 defines the remaining terms, namely direct, control, regulate and regulation, before arranging all the defined terms together with other non-contested terms into a diagram or model representing the machinery of power. Several thought experiments are conducted on this model before considering means of driving it.

The definitional approach taken is strictly non-normative, non-behavioural and non-institutional, thereby avoiding the issues of the morality, strategies and outcomes of exercising power. Consequently, these chapters offer no evaluation of social or political theory; They simply define and then attempt from these definitions to understand the consequent mechanics of power within an internally

S. K. McGrath, *Speaking Management*,
https://doi.org/10.1007/978-981-16-2213-7_11

consistent definitional framework. The work of others, is surveyed, not to evaluate their theory or conclusions, but to cover the field sufficiently to ensure no view that could potentially invalidate the derived definitions is excluded.

11.2 Definitional Confusion Regarding Power Terminology

Power is a term that is often used synonymously with authority and has also been defined differently within different fields of study. It has been considered by some to be an "essentially contested concept" (Sadan & Flantz, 1997; Lukes, 1974; Nye, 2011; Dowding, 2012; Lukes 2005). Turner (2005), while not explicitly mentioning these exact words, comes very close, noting "we use the term in ordinary parlance confident that we know what it means until we are asked to define it", and reiterating the view of Fiske and Dépret (1996) "of endless difficulties in trying to define it." Turner (2005) also notes that "power and influence are not properly distinguished in standard theory" and that "It has proved difficult to differentiate consistently (power) from related constructs of influence, compliance, control, dominance, authority, status and rank". Fiske and Dépret (1996) also paraphrased Lukes (1986) as follows: "every attempt at reaching a single definition of power has failed, and is likely to fail". This may be so until one steps outside social theory, accepts that machines also have power and realises that the method of learning language does not serve as definition (Copi & Cohen, 1990).

11.3 Is Power Really an Essentially Contested Concept?

The description of some concepts as essentially contested was developed by Gallie in his 1956 publication and he gave four tests for a concept to qualify as such. The first test requires that "it must be appraisive in the sense that it signifies or accredits some kind of valued achievement" (Gallie, 1956). There is no achievement implied by the word power that makes any linguistic or grammatical sense. The word is not appraisive and so it fails to warrant proceeding to the other three tests, which all relate to this achievement (Gallie, 1956). Furthermore, even if it did not fail this test, a claim to essential contestability can only be sustained if "it is quite impossible to find a general principle for deciding which of two contestant uses of an essentially contested concept really 'uses it best' " (Gallie, 1956). This Chapter develops such a general principle while reviewing academic definitions of power below. Therefore, on these two grounds, power cannot be considered an 'essentially contested concept'. It has, of course, been contested and this is addressed below.

11.4 Why Is Definition of the Word Power Important?

A concept is an idea held in the mind of an individual. Terms are written or spoken representations of concepts. A term can be either a word or a phrase, and the meaning of a phrase is determined by first defining the component words. In this work, definitions are sought that would not be disputed by anyone using the particular word. The definitions derived here do not have to be sufficient for everyone's purposes, just not in conflict with the basic intent of their usage. This approach seeks to maximise alignment between the general understanding of a concept and the meaning of the term (word or phrase) used to describe it.

Much can be denoted or signified by the word power; political power, biological power, personal power, mechanical power, the power of beautiful forms, and so on. There is no common meaning across these different types of power. But these terms are contingent upon having a common understanding of the word power. It appears that much of the contest around the meaning of this word stems from desire to define the different types of power, such as political power or power-to or power-over, rather than just defining the word power itself. The approach taken here is to remove the confusion of defining a word as a phrase with an assumed or silent qualifier. We describe a physically strong man as powerful and do not say we are talking about biological power. We describe a prime minister as powerful and do not say we are talking about political or social power. We say a car is powerful and do not say we are talking about mechanical power.

Any attempt to develop a conceptual definition that covers all the different types of power must be nebulous and not at all amenable to representation in any model. If the terms (words and phrases) used in describing the concepts involved in the various types of power were defined uniquely and unambiguously, it would then be possible to develop a representation or model by working through the implications of the definitions. This, in turn, would make it possible to map approaches to exercising power in particular circumstances, identifying gaps and alternative options. The way power is exercised can become an issue in itself, complicating resolution of conflict in circumstances ranging from personal to international. So the existence of such a model or mapping technique would facilitate dispassionate evaluation of conflict situations, providing a basis for separating out emotive issues.

While a definitional exercise alone can produce clarity, exploring the implications by developing a representation of the derived definitions adds to the effectiveness of the approach. Together they have the potential to reduce waste resulting from confusion and unnecessary and avoidable disagreement, and consequently increase productivity.

This work defines the word power and terms related to it, analyses the implications of these definitions and develops a model that can be used to indicate other ways of exercising power that may not have been immediately apparent.

11.5 The Ontology of Definition

There are words commonly used in definition whose meaning is not disputed. Such words are:

- Concept = an abstract idea (Oxford).
- Term = a word or phrase used to describe a thing or to express a concept (Oxford).
- Meaning = What is meant by a word, text, concept or action (Oxford). (Defined in Chap. 5 as what is intended to be conveyed).
- Definition = A statement of the exact meaning of a word (Oxford). (Defined in Chap. 4 as a statement of what is signified by a term).
- Process = A series of actions or steps taken in order to achieve a particular end (Oxford).

A further necessary term has been defined by McGrath (2019) (See Chap. 4 above) as:

- Essence = A property or group of properties of something without which it would not be what it is.

There is a further important term that, while not contested, can benefit from increased specificity and it will be defined more closely:

- Content = [mass noun] The material dealt with in a speech, literary work etc. as distinct from its form or style (Oxford). This is a definition by genus and difference. The difference refers to particular, specific extensions, although inclusion of etc indicates possible wider applicability. This will be made clear by genericising both genus and difference. Content will therefore be defined as the material or subject matter dealt with in or by a process, form or style.

A term (word or phrase) used to denote a concept is a written or linguistic representation of the meaning of that concept that applies to all its content areas. It is a model in words of the meaning of a concept. A concept exists in peoples' minds. The term representing it exists in sound waves or on a printed page. While using the same term to denote a concept, people can have different understandings or experiences of it.

The content that a term is applied to can have nuances, types, classifications and sub-classifications, all of which may have different value in different circumstances. For a concept to be universally understood, the definition of the term denoting it needs to accommodate all of these content areas without being dependent upon or hostage to any one of them. The definition of a concept must therefore be done in terms of the essence that all of its instantiations possess.

Here, definition will be done in words that represent the essence of a concept as closely as possible so that essence and definition become indistinguishable. If a definition does not express the essence of a concept or particularises it, then there is a discrepancy between the two, requiring resolution.

11.6 Approach

McGrath and Whitty (2015) (see Chap. 10) proposed a set of terms to remove confusion from governance terminology and in so doing demonstrated the pitfalls of defining contested conceptual terms within the bounds of one single field and in isolation from other terms. This also effectively demonstrated the difficulty in progressing from defining objects to defining concepts. As Heidegger (1962) noted "It has long been known that ancient ontology works with 'Thing-concepts' and that there is a danger of 'reifying consciousness' …. Why does this reifying always keep coming back to exercise its dominion?" Interestingly, as Stolorow et al. (n.d.) note, Heidegger himself later fell into this very same difficulty in hypostasizing his own concept of being.

Copi and Cohen (1990) also noted that "The primary way of learning to use language is by observation and imitation, not by definition" and "the process of frequently hearing the word when the object it denotes is present." They go on to say "But such a process would not be a definition at all … it would be the primitive, pre-definitional way of learning to use language". Copi and Cohen (1990) also commented on the difficulty presented by opinion in defining "subjective connotative" definition which they state is

> The set of all attributes the speaker believes possessed by the objects denoted by that word. But this set plainly varies from individual to individual and even from time to time for the same individual – and thus cannot serve the purposes of definition.

Clegg (1989) also noted "In constructing, representing and making sense of a concept like power, we can never be free from the matter of words". Clegg (1989) also noted that

> Habermas … argues … that the search for consensus is inherent to community expressed through language, because such a speech-community can be built only on trust, not power… Power would act as a barrier to the free and unconstrained realisation of the human interest in achieving rational thought or enlightenment.

Dowding (2012) also identifies the difficulty of normative argument as follows:

> We need to make our concepts as non-normative as possible so as not to conceal that normative disagreement within a conceptual one. To try to hide one's normative commitments by the conceptual mixing of the extensionality of a term and its normative connotations is an ideological sleight of hand. Such tricks might work for a while, but I am convinced that careful analysis will always reveal the trickster's games in the end. And we can all be exposed as tricksters if we are not careful.

Once a unique identifier is accepted for a physical object, confusion regarding its identification is removed. While the same can also apply for intellectual concepts, these require something more intellectually as there is no physical object to point at. Recognising and reaching agreement on the identification or existence of a concept is not the same thing as reaching agreement on what the concept itself actually is or what it means, especially within the context of other similar and possibly competing terms. Different people will have different opinions. Aside from random variation, opinions are also subject to the tendency of, or at least the possibility for, people to construe such concepts to advantage themselves, either deliberately or inadvertently. So the method of arriving at a commonly accepted definition for a conceptual term, and particularly for a contested one, must necessarily contain some additional processes to guard against this.

Taking into account usage of a term across multiple fields provides some form of triangulation regarding commonality of meaning and usage. Defining terms as a group at least avoids doubling up or overlapping and thereby confusing meaning. Doing both can potentially remove past and prevent future confusion and conflict. Keeping definitions non-normative can reduce confusion by quarantining value-judgements and opinion to discussion of the various extensions of those concepts, rather than being inherent in their definitional intension. The adopted method includes these features.

The epistemology of the method chosen below is objectivist and uses a positivist theoretical perspective that seeks to define objective content, essence or intrinsic nature of the particular concept. However, no claim is made here that the derived definitions describe anything existential as far as the concepts themselves are concerned. The definitional method used makes no provision for judgement of the content of the concept. The content is distinguished from the process of determining an acceptable meaning within the bounds of the 'language game' of English, in this case. This process does exist; it has sounds with energy that can be measured, heard and felt, forming words that have meaning to us. It simply seeks the essence of a concept that exists in peoples' minds, behind the range of definitions used and defines non-normatively using accepted English grammatical process to determine meaning. It proposes definitions which, if agreed and adopted, have the potential to remove unnecessary debate and confusion.

This approach accepts the post-modernist view that truth is dynamic and that many forces (the meta-apparatus of society) will continually shape it, causing it to change over time. "Where modernism played with the elements of reality … it did not challenge the concept of reality itself." (Appleby, 1996). However, while there may be no absolute truth, if we are a society that wants to build transportation systems, education systems, health systems and so on, we need to construct a set of terms within our English language game that will direct the actions of people in a particular way that serves society best in these endeavours.

One of the ways to construct a particular truth is to agree upon certain terms and promulgate them through the various societal apparatuses to construct a discourse that leads to productivity. This means developing a discourse that all can participate in, with shared understanding of meaning, removing accidental and undetected differences. This position is therefore midway between (or partly both) realist and post-modernist, as this apparatus (ensuring consistency and universality of terminology) can satisfy people's need for order rather than disorder or chaos. It does this by removing unnecessary conflict, which, although it may be one (and only one) source of innovation, is also a significant inhibitor of productivity.

This work therefore seeks to remove definitional overlap and confusion from a group of terms concerning power.

11.7 Method

The features outlined above are included in the method of developing consistent definitions for a group of terms that was developed by McGrath and Whitty (2015), who surveyed the literature and were unable to locate any previous such method. Their method will therefore be adopted. It is set out below.

Group rules pre-definition:

1. Select the group of terms to be defined.
2. Determine the order of definition as follows:
    a. Identify any inconsistencies within the group that may require one term to be defined before another.
    b. Where a compound term is to be defined, define the component terms first.
    c. Where a derivative term is to be defined, define the root term first.
    d. Where a term has a noun and a verb form, define the verb first.
3. Consider any terms that are likely to be used in definition that may themselves require prior definition.

Steps to determine a connotative (intensional) conventional definition of each term:

1. Define derivative or component terms using the root or component definitions that have previously been defined by this process or are clear and accepted in their meaning. (This obviates the need to proceed through the remaining definitional steps unless there is other reason to do so, such as confusion in the meaning of the compound or derivative term itself).
2. Survey lexical usage (This and the following two steps may be omitted if there is a known comprehensive academic review of definitions of the term that has produced a definition by intension, not specific to any extension).
3. Analyse this to determine the main contenders for inclusion in the definition.
4. Develop a connotative (intensional) conventional definition. (This may be synonymous, operational or by genus and difference).
5. Report and analyse any known academic review of definitions of the term
6. Remove unwarranted inclusions.
7. Remove divergence of meaning resulting from mixing content and process by removing any reference to content (for generic conceptual terms).
8. Remove any remaining divergence of meaning and for operational definitions, consider the need for additional inclusions, by checking against the following, as appropriate to the particular term:
    a. Historical usage
    b. Field/specialty usage – the definition most generic to as many fields as possible will be selected
    c. Practitioner usage (via practitioner literature, considering the influence of opinion and marketing)
    d. Competing concepts & frameworks (considering the influence of opinion and marketing)

9. Check any resulting definitions by genus & difference against the Copi and Cohen (1990) five rules and discard any which do not satisfy them.
10. Report the ~~adopted~~ derived definition. (Note: this change corrects what appears to have been a typographical error in the source paper, in which all applications of the method used the word 'derived')

11.8 Group Rules Post Definition

1. Cross-check terms defined in this group for any inconsistency and resolve.
2. Cross-check any terms defined in this group known to be used interchangeably with other terms outside the group and resolve any inconsistency.

The five rules for checking a definition by genus and difference, sourced from Copi and Cohen (1990) are as follows:

1. States the essential attributes of the species
2. Avoids circularity
3. Neither too broad nor too narrow
4. Avoids ambiguous, obscure or figurative language
5. Affirmative rather than negative.

Lexical usage will be sourced from the following dictionary sources:

1. A range of dictionaries that have been well known for many years that were available (in 2013/14) online (Cambridge, Collins, Longman, Macmillan, Macquarie, Merriam-Webster, Oxford)
2. A range of various online dictionaries (BusinessDictionary.com, Dictionary.com, TheFreeDictionary, Wiktionary) and
3. The Concise Oxford Dictionary (1964) – as a comparator for how these definitions may have changed over the last 50 years.

This method will now be applied to the power arena.

Note that for ease of reading, derived definitions and subsequent refined and other contributing definitions are shown in pale grey highlight in the text. Similarly, the main contenders for inclusion in the derived definition are also shown in pale grey highlight in the Tables in the Appendix which survey lexical usage.

11.9 Group Rules Pre Definition

Group pre-definition rule 1 – Select the group of terms to be defined

Terms with contested or overlapping meaning commonly used in this area are: power, authority, influence, direct, control, regulate and regulation. The term legitimacy is also used in association with authority and although not contested in common parlance, it has been contested academically and so will be included in the group to be selected for definition. The terms compliance, dominance, status and rank do not have contested or overlapping meaning and so will not be included.

Group pre-definition rule 2 – Determine the order of definition

Rule 2 (a) – Identify group term inconsistencies
Authority and power are often used interchangeably. While it could be argued that this work is all about power and so it should be defined first, lack of authority can prevent some forms of power from being exercised. For example, a political party in a democracy may be capable of exercising power but will not get the opportunity to do so if not elected. Authority will therefore be defined before power. Influence is also used in a way that may affect the exercise of power, however it is less compelling and so will be defined after power.

Rule 2(b) – Compound terms
The group contains no compound terms.

Rule 2(c) – Derivative terms
Legitimacy and legitimate have the same stem 'legitim' with the suffixes '-ate' forming the adjective and '-acy' forming the noun. Legitimacy is usually used in the sense of denoting that something is legitimate and so the adjective legitimate will be defined before the noun legitimacy. The verb form is also dependent upon the adjective form and so will be ignored.

Regulate will be defined ahead of its derivative regulation.

Rule 2(d) – Define verb form of term before the noun form
Again, regulate will be defined before regulation.

Some authority must exist for legitimacy to be measured against and so authority will be defined first. Influence can affect the use of power and the exercise of authority and so will be defined next and before the more procedural terms (direct and control) and the regulatory terms, which will be last as they are outputs of the other terms. Direct will be defined ahead of control as one needs to have a direction to control against. Thus the order of definition will be as follows: legitimate, legitimacy, authority, power, influence, direct, control, regulate, regulation.

Group pre-definition rule 3 – Definitional terms requiring prior definition

There are no other terms outside this group that have multiple meanings and are commonly used in defining power.

11.10 Define 'Authority'

Step 1 Define derivative or component terms

This is not a derivative or compound term.

Step 2 Survey lexical usage

Lexical usage is surveyed in Table 11.1 in the Appendix.

Step 3 Analyse lexical usage

The definitions included in Table 11.1 are for the uncountable form only. Countable forms such as 'an authority' or 'the authorities' will be taken to have consequential definitions; one who has or those who have authority. Some definitions indicate authority has been taken to be a particular type of or differentiation of power, while some say it is a type of right and others are ambivalent regarding which it is. Many of the definitions are judicial.

The Business Dictionary definition is appealing but verbose. The later Oxford definition is concise and encompasses many of the other definitions and so will be adopted with the omission of power, which unnecessarily introduces the confusion between power and authority mentioned in the definition of power below. The Merriam-Webster definition includes the additional terms orders and decisions which are not covered by enforcing obedience and are legitimate inclusions. This leaves a definition that does not mention command and control, as numbers of the other definitions in Table 11.1 do, however these are implied by the terms used and so do not need to be explicitly mentioned. The ability to commit resources also does not need to be mentioned as this is a consequence of being in a position to give an order.

Step 4 Develop a connotative (intensional) conventional definition

Authority will therefore be tentatively defined as '*The right to make decisions, give orders and enforce obedience*'. This is a definition by genus and difference, with the differences being operational.

Step 5 Report academic review of definitions

There are reviews of the definition of this term within the field of organisational studies. These are considered below. The term has also been used interchangeably with power and those academic sources are canvassed there.

Casey (2008) says "Authority is a type of power that can be distinguished in particular by the presence and effect of legitimacy. Authority is exercised over others at the same time as its operation is accepted by those over whom it is exercised". This does not actually define the word itself without a corresponding definition of power. It needs to be defined independently. The tentative definition does include legitimacy through its use of the phrase 'the right to' and does not conflict with this encyclopaedic reference.

It is also necessary to ensure the definition of the English language word is as generic to as many fields as possible and so circumstances other than organisational need to be considered. It is possible to attribute authority to someone who is not actually an authority, and to follow (obey) their advice, judgements, decisions or opinions. This may be considered to be actually illegitimate, but the person following may be unaware of this, that is they may legitimately follow an illegitimate authority. However, that is a matter of value judgement, which is here being abstained from. The point is that authority can be ascribed informally in people's heads as well as by formal organisational role statement. The definition needs to allow for but not be drawn in by that issue, otherwise we end up in the normative area, evaluating questions such as rationality and irrationality, which are irrelevant to the actual meaning of the English language words. These questions are also addressed in depth by others and have no bearing upon the point being made here. The tentative definition covers both circumstances without presuming an organisational context.

Another area of consideration is the legal area and the concept of content independent reasons for action. This is overviewed by Gur (2007) who refers to (H.L.A.) Hart's basic characterisation of this notion, as follows:

> Content-independence of commands lies in the fact that a commander may issue many different commands to the same or to different people and the actions commanded may have nothing in common, yet in the case of all of them the commander intends his expressions of intention to be taken as a reason for doing them. It is therefore intended to function as a reason independently of the nature or character of the actions to be done.

Joseph Raz … provides a similar explanation…:

> A reason is content independent if there is no direct connection between the reason and the action for which it is a reason. The reason is the apparently "extraneous" fact that someone in authority has said so…

This sense of possible disconnection between reason and action is not precluded by the proposed definition and so provides no reason to alter it.

Step 6 Remove unwarranted inclusions

There are no unwarranted inclusions remaining.

Step 7 Remove mixed content/process meanings

None present.

Step 8 Reduce divergence/consider additional inclusions

Historical check (a) and field/speciality usage (b) are the appropriate checks for this term.

Step 8(a) Consider historical usage

As described in Step 5 of the definition of power, authority and influence have historically been used somewhat interchangeably. This interchangeability has persisted to the current day, as evidenced by the definitions in Table 11.1. Given the historical and current confusion or ambivalence, there is no compelling historical reason to not clear this up. Macfarlane (2014) points out that

> The constitutional position was reinforced by the Magna Carta in 1215 … England was a limited monarchy, based on the voluntary acquiescence of the people, and where the King himself was bound by the same laws as his countrymen. England was an association of free men held together by mutual contracts.

In other words, the King actually had some of his authority removed. While still acknowledged as the head of the country, authority was removed to the legal system and a parliament, which actually administered the country while the aristocracy and middle classes, in Britain at least, controlled the various means of production. So while the monarch was still at the top of the social pile, he or she no longer actually directly controlled anything much as the authority had been delegated. Ruling, for the monarch, therefore came to not include governing, with its associated direct control. This separation of powers was formally expounded by Locke (Locke and

Macpherson, 1980) in the eighteenth century. This is also reinforced by Russell (1938) who points out that ownership is not the same thing as control.

Step 8(b) Consider field/specialty usage

Note that this term applies only to living things and not to machines.

(i) Governance perspective – the question of legitimacy

French and Raven (1959) include legitimate power as one of their five bases of power. However Galinsky et al. (2015) regard legitimacy as a moderator or qualifier of power, noting that "legitimacy can refer to how power is acquired or how it is exercised". Legitimacy has the connotation of being acknowledged or accepted. Power exercised with authority (as per the tentative definition), such as in governing of a country, can be considered legitimate. Power exercised without authority, such as invasion or coup cannot be considered legitimate, but does take over authority and so acquires legitimacy, as some form of civil administration has to continue. So legitimacy is associated with authority but not necessarily with power.

The word 'right' in the derived definition implies legitimacy as well as a licence or permission to act. The word 'enforce' implies the use of force or some form of compulsion which could result in a person or persons doing something they do not want to do, or not doing something they do want to do. The use of 'right' and 'enforce' together mean legitimate (as distinct from illegitimate) exercise of power through force or compulsion. The degree and nature of that force is a normative matter outside the purview of this work. Continued tenure of an incumbent in any position with authority derives from conformity with both the law and any organisational governance requirements that may exist. Contravention of these may affect the tenure of the occupant rather than the existence of the position itself, with outcomes ranging from dismissal to dictatorship, dependent upon the opinions of other organisational participants.

Options open to any social action group seeking to achieve change include attempting to obtain or influence formal authority, attempting to have formerly unauthorised activity officially condoned, and attempting to make formerly illegitimate activity made legitimate. This again makes obvious the existence of a relationship between authority and legitimacy.

These considerations provide no reason to alter the derived definition.

(ii) Strategy

The policies, approaches, strategies and actions that people in positions of authority may choose to pursue, which are not subject to the regulation of law or organisational governance, may be ethical or not and may produce the desired outcome or not. However, this deals with content rather than process and provides no reason to alter the derived definition.

(iii) Individual perspective

One can lack the formal authority to do something but do it anyway, as in exercising initiative. Authority can be self-given or offered by others, either tacitly or formally through some form of organisation. Offered authority is then either self-accepted or not. The derived definition accommodates all these circumstances.

(iv) Living things

Any authority beyond that which is self-given comes from another person or living thing. In the case of some animals, a pecking order is established based upon perceived and sometimes actual might. The lack of authority that a pecking order imposes on those lower in the order may not diminish their physical power, but does limit their social ability to exercise it, as documented by Mazur (1973). However a large, unconstrained, carnivorous, hungry wild animal will not give any man authority over it and will use its superior physical power to dominate (eat). A strong physical body with a weak mind may therefore gain authority within its environment by physical means. A weak body with a strong mind (such as man) may get authority to exercise substantial organisational power by intellectual means. Again, this consideration provides no reason to alter the derived definition.

(v) Law

Consider the legal field which is concerned with the law as well as the control, judgement and prohibition terms mentioned in Table 11.1. The derived definition does not conflict with any of these.

Step 9 Check against the five rules

This is a definition by genus and difference and satisfies Rules 1 to 5.

Step 10 Report the derived definition

The derived definition is as follows:

- Authority = The right to make decisions, give orders and enforce obedience.

11.11 Define 'Legitimate' and 'Legitimacy'

Step 1 Define derivative or component terms

Legitimate is the root term of legitimacy and so will be defined first.

Step 2 Survey lexical usage

Lexical usage is surveyed in Tables 11.2a and 11.2b.

Step 3 Analyse lexical usage

We will consider the adverb form only as the verb form in most of the lexical sources is defined in terms of the adverb.

Many of the references are to law. However, legitimacy is also conferred by things other than law, such as professional body rules, standards or examinations. Therefore, no reference to law will be accepted, nor will reference to any other field such as theatre or religion, except for some generic reference to the source making the activity legitimate. Any reference to heredity, monarchy or wedlock will also be excluded as they are not generic. Similarly, any sources making the activity legitimate will be excluded (law, rule, standard, custom, code, behaviour, principles etc). Having excluded all of these, to make the definition complete, it will be necessary to include some generic reference to the deciding source that makes the activity legitimate as well as the target group it applies to, apart from saying what it actually is.

Words used to define the word legitimate in Table 11.2a are acceptable, recognised, genuine, valid, conforming, allowed, reasonable, sensible, proper, regular, in accordance with, normal, justified, sanctioned, authorised, fair, official and in compliance with.

The phrases in accordance or compliance with are unnecessarily formal and other words in the group express this more succinctly anyway. Authorised will not be selected as it does not cover the norms of acceptable group behaviour which may vary depending on the circumstance for which there may be no formal authority. Sanctioned will not be used because of similar connotations. Justified will not be selected as it has an association with accountability that is not present in all circumstances. Circumstances of unexpressed and emergent group norms are not official and so this will not be selected. Reasonable, sensible, proper, regular and fair will not be selected as some group norms may not be any of these things, yet still be condoned by the group. Genuine has a wider sense and meaning than is applicable to being legitimate and one could be genuinely illegitimate as well, so it will not be used. Allowed has the connotation of something being prevented, which is not the case when something that is not legitimate occurs, and so it will be excluded. Valid is a term more relating to reason and one can have a valid reason for taking action that is not considered legitimate. Something can be normal and not be considered legitimate in some circumstances. This leaves three candidates; acceptable, recognised and conforming. Recognised is too formal and not everybody might recognise a particular action as having the same acceptability. Acceptable is more generic than conforming with something but describes an approach to an action rather than the action itself. This leaves acceptable as the only word remaining that is both specific and general enough for generic use.

Step 4 Develop a connotative (intensional) conventional definition

There is one other word that does not appear in Table 11.2a and that is condoned. This is similar to authorised and sanctioned which were both ruled out, however condoned does not have the connotation of formal authority which caused these two words to be ruled out. However condoned has the association of being approved of by somebody. The word accepted does not say whether the action is approved of. It may be just not objected to without being approved of and we need to consider the case of an action that is neither approved of nor disapproved. Such an action could not be considered illegitimate but does not really carry the force or imprimatur that would actually justify it being labelled as legitimate and so the positive sense of being condoned will be selected.

Legitimacy will therefore be defined in terms of being condoned. This requires the addition of by whom, for which a generic specification is those with those with authority in the particular circumstance, taking into account the distinction between power and authority as set out in the definitions derived below. This covers organisational and parental use as well as influence. It is a definition suitable for further testing.

Most of the lexical sources define legitimacy consequentially to the definition of legitimate, as the quality or state or fact of being legitimate. The choice is between three words; quality state and fact. The word fact will be avoided as it has a connotation of determinism. Quality is more general than state and so will be selected.

Legitimate will therefore be tentatively defined as condoned by those with authority in the particular circumstance Legitimacy will be consequentially defined as the quality of being legitimate, or the quality of being condoned by those with authority in the particular circumstance.

Step 5 Report academic review of definitions

There has been significant academic debate over what legitimate and legitimacy actually mean. Suchman (1995) "synthesises the large but diverse literature on organisational legitimacy" and proposes "Legitimacy is a generalized perception or assumption that the actions of an entity are desirable, proper, or appropriate within some socially constructed system of norms, values, beliefs, and definitions" Suchman (1995). This definition is verbose and has the unfortunate iteration of having another 'definition' within it. It also includes much about the means of measurement which were specifically excluded from the proposed definition to make it generic. However it does not conflict with the proposed definition and so provides no reason to alter it.

Step 6 Remove unwarranted inclusions

There are no such inclusions remaining.

Step 7 Remove mixed content/process meanings

None present.

Step 8 Reduce divergence/consider additional inclusions

Addition of acquiescence by the group subject to whatever authority was considered but rejected on the grounds that while acquiescence of the group is necessary for authority to be exercised, the group does have some opportunity for input into establishing that authority, and a criminal offender will not willingly acquiesce in the wishes of authority.

Step 9 Check against the five rules

The definitions are both synonymous and by genus and difference and satisfy Rules 1 to 5.

Step 10 Report the derived definition

The derived definitions are as follows:

- Legitimate = condoned by those with authority in the particular circumstance.
- Legitimacy = the quality of being legitimate = the quality of being condoned by those with authority in the particular circumstances.

11.12 Define 'Power'

Step 1 Define derivative or component terms

This is not a derivative or compound term.

Step 2 Survey lexical usage

Lexical usage is surveyed in Table 11.3 in the appendix.

Step 3 Analyse lexical usage

Many of the definitions in Table 11.3 are specific to legal, political, governmental, religious or supernatural, familial, astrological, mathematical or specific technical areas, including optics and electricity. To arrive at a generic definition, all these will be excluded. The definitions in Table 11.3 also do not distinguish between power, authority, control or influence, which are all used liberally throughout. To keep the definition generic, any reference to these competing terms will also be excluded. These exclusions rule out practically all the Table 11.3 definitions, with one common exception that was mentioned in most dictionaries, namely the ability or capacity to do something or to act.

To act is to do something, whether the activity be physical or mental (exerting influence). Furthermore, to act, one must be both capable of acting (having the energy and/or skill and/or knowledge required at the particular time) and have sufficient authority to do so, whether this be legitimate, assumed, usurped or imposed. Authority has been defined above. Capacity covers all of energy, skill and knowledge, whereas the latter terms do not include each other. Ability and capability are similar to capacity and while any one of these could be selected, capacity will be chosen as it is more generic, covering machines as well as living things.

To propose a general meaning, it is also necessary to separate content from process. It is a generic process that is being defined here which will then be applicable to many different content areas and so any reference to content will be excluded. Many such areas have been excluded above, however this also means excluding intentionality, so that the definition will be non-normative, covering both its proper (moral) and improper use (abuse).

Step 4 Develop a connotative (intensional) conventional definition

Power will therefore be tentatively defined as 'the capacity to act'; this is independent of whether that capacity is exercised through force, authority or influence.

Step 5 Report academic review of definitions

Database searches on "power" returned thousands of items and it was impractical to analyse this number. To exclude irrelevant items, all EBSCO databases were searched on 25/10/2015 for the terms "power" and "define" in the title. 223 were found, returning 124 unique items and none contained any such review. A similar search was done for "definition of power" from 2010 onwards. 99 were found, returning 59 unique items and these were examined. Most either had no direct relationship between these two terms or were about defining power in particular circumstances, rather than in defining the term generally. Four relevant items were found. Two were academic peer reviewed papers; (Dowding, 2012) surveying power definitions generally and (Salthe, 2010) considered power from a thermodynamic perspective. Salthe (2010) used the (Merriam-Webster) definition from Table 11.3, which is referred to and dealt with in Section 8(b) below.

The third was Galinsky et al. (2015) which defined social power as "asymmetric control over valued resources in a social relationship". Removing the specificity of this definition to social science leaves a definition of power itself as the asymmetric control of valued resources. This cannot be accepted as a generic definition as it confuses power with authority, does not apply in any complete sense to mechanical power and power exerted through influence does not actually control the resources influenced. Galinsky et al. (2015) note that "Power is often conceptualised as the capacity to influence others." While this may not be incorrect, it does not accommodate machine power.

The fourth item was a book by Nye (2011) who stated:

> Power is a contested concept. No one definition is accepted by all who use the word, and people's choice of definition reflects their interests and values. Some define power as the ability to make or resist change. Others say it is the ability to get what we want.

He then referred to

> The dictionary which tells us that power is the capacity to do things and in social situations to affect others to get the outcomes we want. Some people call this influence, and distinguish power from influence, but this is confusing because the dictionary defines the two terms as interchangeable.

This is not useful; it does not mention which dictionary 'the' dictionary is and does not admit the possibility that common usage, as reflected in some dictionaries, may be inconsistent or confused and include mixed concepts. Nye (2011) notes that "behavioural definitions judge power by outcomes that are determined after the action". He considers defining power in terms of the resources that can produce outcomes but does not pursue this as he identifies the paradox that this does not always produce the desired outcomes. This includes intentionality, which is being excluded here. He also considers hard and soft power, along with other normative issues which are being avoided here. He distinguishes between behavioural (relational) and resource-based definitions and the three aspects of relational power: commanding change, controlling agendas and establishing preferences. These views of power need to be accommodated, but they are not suitable for use in the definition. Once an adjective is used before any term, it becomes an extension of meaning rather than an intensional definition of the primary term.

This leaves the general paper by Dowding (2012) to be examined. Dowding (2012) says "Power is a contested concept; of that there is no doubt." He argues that definitions should be non-normative, noting that "power is a somewhat morally neutral concept" and that "I am opposing those who want to moralize concepts so that actions they consider justified are only described in a language with positive normative connotations". He notes that "explanation always entails prediction ... Explanation is about patterning the universe through descriptive or causal inferences. It follows, however, that prediction and therefore explanation are in themselves normative". He does describe normative approaches to power, including conflictual versus consensual theory, zero-sum and positive-sum concepts as well as soft power versus hard power. However Dowding (2012) does not himself present a definition, adopting the view, in effect, that it is many things dependent upon the circumstances. He rather suggests "elements that might be used in its definition, such as 'resources', 'intensions', 'persuasion', 'force', and so on."

The selected method has a non-normative approach and so intentionality will be excluded from definitions here. It has become apparent that this is much more difficult for concepts than it is for anything within the physical field of view. There is therefore nothing in this academic review that would present a conflict with the tentative definition of power derived above. However Dowding (2012) goes on to say "Any term that is used in our ordinary language is likely to carry normative implications that cannot simply be rendered irrelevant by some formal definition." While acknowledging this view, it is a non-normative definition of power that is being proposed here and which, if agreed and commonly used, could remove unnecessary debate around the concept.

His suggestions for inclusion in a definition of power will now be addressed. Intention and persuasion apply only to living subjects of the application of power and so cannot be included in its generic definition. Resources may be controlled by having the authority (legitimate or usurped) to do so, but control of resources is not a universal aspect of the application of all power and so cannot not form part of its definition. Physical force does form part of the mechanical definition of power but is not part of intellectual power and so also cannot form part of its generic definition. So none of these suggestions can be included.

This concludes the review of EBSCO sources and consideration can now turn to other items located in the references of the above four items and from other general reading and searches.

Russell (1938) wrote of the impulse to power, noting "When a moderate degree of comfort is assured, both individuals and communities will pursue power rather than wealth" and referred to the presumption of economic motivation as "This error in orthodox and Marxist economics". His impulse to power has some similarities with Nietzsche's "will to power", but his treatise is concerned with understanding the various forms of power, to propose means of "taming" it. He was writing before the outbreak of the Second World War and defined power as "the production of intended effects". This definition is applicable to social science but is not fully appropriate for mechanical power and so cannot be adopted here. It also does not accommodate the eventuality that unintended effects may be produced.

Nietzsche and Kaufmann (1968) declare "This world is the will to power and nothing besides" presupposing, as Denneson (n.d.) notes, "that humans are always attempting to inflict their wills upon others". Again, this view is limited to the human dimension, does not accommodate mechanical power and is too narrow for generic definitional use here. Nevertheless, the derived definition does not conflict with this view.

No contemporary discussion of power would be complete without consideration of the views of Michael Foucault. These are expressed in Foucault and Gordon (1980). "Power is that concrete power which every individual holds, and whose partial or total cession enables political power or sovereignty to be established..."

This unfortunately defines power in terms of itself. He also says (Foucault & Gordon, 1980)

> What means are available to us if we seek to conduct a non-economic analysis of power? ... We have the assertion that power is neither given, nor exchanged, nor recovered, but rather exercised, and that it only exists in action.

In other words, individuals and institutions have power and this exists only through its exercise. That presents no difficulty to there being a conceptual difference between power and authority.

He also says (Foucault & Gordon, 1980) "We have another assertion that power is ... above all a relation of force. If power is to be exercised, what sort of exercise does it involve? In what does it consist? What is its mechanism?" He concludes "power is essentially that which it represses. Power represses nature, the instincts, a class, individuals" and (Foucault & Gordon, 1980) "[If it's force] should we not analyse it in terms of struggle, conflict and war?" He also offers a third contention that it is a contest of strength (Foucault & Gordon, 1980) and a fourth view that it is "production, accumulation, circulation and functioning of a discourse" (Foucault & Gordon, 1980). A fifth view offered is that "The essential role of the theory of right, from mediaeval times onwards, was to fix the legitimacy of power" and that this "translates and puts in motion relations that are not relations of sovereignty but of domination" (Foucault & Gordon, 1980). He also says it is "the multiplicity of force relations immanent in the sphere in which they operate and which constitute their own organization" (Foucault, 1978). This is similar to his "relation of force" above, but with his later conclusion that power was not necessarily repressive and could also be productive.

While Foucault's considerations have been taken into account in building a generic model of power in Fig. 12.1 (Chap. 12), there are several difficulties with attempting to use any of the above statements in a formal definition.

Firstly, while expression of the intent of human power over other humans may be repression or prevention, mechanical power is not that which it represses. The power of machines is real physical power – the ability to act when provided with the right inputs or conditions (fuel, oil, water). While this can be used to develop implements of torture or destruction, their primary function is to provide a service to mankind by assisting in doing things – whether for construction or destruction. The intent of creating machines with power is not repression – unless they are incorporated into weapons. Furthermore, there is atomic power that releases rather than suppresses nature. Of course, as Merquior (1985) notes, Foucault did change his focus from power in the negative terms of repression to considering that it also produces (Foucault & Gordon, 1980). However, a generic definition is being sought to avoid any potential "essential contestability" Gallie (1956) and so extensions that limit a definition of power to the human interaction realm will need to be excluded.

Secondly the view of power as a circulating discourse does not accommodate well the biological reality that as one is fed and consequently grows up, one's personal biological power increases, without it flowing from other people – that is unless the food parents give their children is regarded as part of the circulating discourse. This becomes somewhat abstract and also does not apply to machines, unless one also takes the view that the components needed to make a machine all flow from people. However, as one grows, one's capacity to accept and exercise authority and influence (generally) increases. Authority and influence can circulate, however one has to be alive with a certain capacity (power) to be even in the game. Similarly a machine has to be assembled and fuelled to be ready to act.

Thirdly Foucault describes the concept of power exercised by individuals in a network influencing each other as being one of the "relations of power" (Foucault & Gordon, 1980). He appears to have not always distinguished power from its circulation, at times seeming to regard power and authority synonymously, as is commonly done in everyday use today, as evidenced by the examination of lexical use in Table 11.3.

For any power to be useful, it needs to be harnessed or controlled or governed (e.g. as the governor on an engine does) and so this is a different concept to power itself. Authority needs to be generated to allow or govern the exercise of power. Both authority and power are needed, and machines do not exist unless created and controlled (authorised) by man. So while Foucault's definitions cannot be used in definition here, they are extensions into the social realm which do not actually conflict with the tentative definition, which is by intension.

In 'standard' power theory as enumerated in French and Raven (1959), there are five types of power: reward, coercive, legitimate, expert and referent. Raven later added informational. All of these are relative to human agents only. Nevertheless, the derived definition does not conflict with these five types denote pre-existence of different circumstances that provide some particular capacity for action to occur. The French and Raven approach can be regarded as symptomatic, observing manifestations or mechanisms, in other words, extensions which are not in conflict with the tentative definition by intension.

Sayer (2012) says "In English we use it both to refer to a capacity or potential that some thing, person or institution possesses, and sometimes to refer to the exercise of that capacity, perhaps 'over' something else". He also argues causality is inherent in power:

> 'Power', in its broadest everyday sense, serves as a summarising term for situations where some change is made to happen, or perhaps prevented. It is also sometimes attributed to specific objects as a property or potential they possess that may or may not be exercised. It is not a thing. There is no such thing as power-as-such, just powers of concrete particulars (Harré and Madden 1975) ... A cause is simply whatever produces change. It does not have to be material; it can be ideational, whether spoken or unspoken. (Sayer, 2012)

Sayer (2012) argues persuasively "that students of power should embrace causality and normativity". He considers:

> full acknowledgement of our sentience and consequent capacity for suffering and flourishing is inhibited by scientistic tendencies in accounts of social life which revel in a certain coldness and the academic cultural capital associated with a refusal of everyday language, whether through a positivistic suspicion of values, emotion and feeling, or a preference for reducing persons to bodies and as wholly reducible to products of subjectivation. The situ-

ation is made worse by the hegemony of positivist framings of the issue in terms of is-ought problem. (Sayer, 2012)

The approach taken here is deterministic only insofar as following grammatical 'oughts' facilitates understanding and productivity and so this view can be accepted. Sayer alludes to the nature of power rather than directly defining it, but this does not result in any contradiction of the tentative definition. He also notes that Foucault did not acknowledge causality and was concerned with the how and not the why (Sayer, 2012). These chapters are focused on the 'what'.

Turner (2005) says "The standard theory is that power is the capacity for influence". While this again is appropriate for human actors only, it also does not distinguish authority, but nevertheless does not conflict with the derived definition. He also says

> The most general meaning of power found in the literature and everyday thinking is that it is the capacity to cause effects, to have an impact on or change things, to do 'work' either in the physical or social world. At this level of abstraction, power belongs to things as well as people and affects things as well as people.

He later says "I shall term power as impact". He also talks of "Power to affect the world and power through people" which only "emerges from human social relationships, from the capacity of people to organise themselves into groups, institutions and societies." While the derived definition makes no mention of these things, it certainly does not preclude them, as organisation into a group is usually done for the purpose of enhancing the capacity to act.

Turner (2005) then reverses the standard theory which proposes that the control of resources produces power which produces influence which produces psychological group formation. His three-process theory places group formation at the start, which produces influence, producing power which then controls resources. He claims the power is generated from influence. However this is not true of machines and is also not true of conquest, where attempts to influence have not been made or have failed. Nevertheless, this reverse of the standard theory does not conflict with the derived definition which is free of both precondition and causality.

Sadan and Flantz (1997) also give a brief history of power theories while making "no pretension to survey all the existing literature in the field". They cover power as a factor of domination (Weber, 1947), the extension of this to ruling elites by Dahl (1961), the Bachrach and Baratz (1963) overt and covert dimensions and the addition of the latent dimension by Lukes (1974). Sadan and Flantz (1997) state "Power is exercised by human agents" and so provide only instantiations to be accommodated within a definition of power, none of which conflict with the derived definition.

Lukes (2005) notes "unending disagreements about how to define it", then states "Power is a capacity, not the exercise of that capacity (it may never be, and never need to be, exercised)". This contains a key element of and is very close to the definition derived above. Lukes (1974) presents three views, which he labels dimensions of analysing power from a decision making perspective (Lukes, 2005). It is worth noting that McGrath and Whitty (2015) rejected decision making as a component of their definition of governance, relegating it to being only a component of what they defined as "organisational governance arrangements". So analysing decisions made (first dimension), considering background values and agendas (second dimension) and any latent conflicts that may impact (third dimension) provides a framework for managing or exercising power, which is not a definition of it.

Clegg (1989) proposes another three-dimensional model of power circulating as in an electric circuit board with three interacting circuits. He labels these episodic, dispositional and facilitative, with the first being considered micro and the latter two macro. This also does not conflict with the derived definition as a capacity. See the notes under Fig. 12.1 (Chap. 12) for details of how these relate to the model proposed after deriving definitions for the group of power terms. Clegg and Haugaard (2009) note "After World War II, the consensual view of power, as a capacity for action, as 'power to', came to the fore…" They note in contemporary perceptions of power there is "the tendency for normative issues to intrude". The definitional method used here is designed to exclude normative issues and the derived definition is virtually the same as the post-war consensus. Clegg et al. (2014) note "However in its most general sense power constitutes simply a capacity for action, which is *power to*."

Morriss (2002) regards power as ability, which does not conflict with the tentative definition, although the more generic term capacity rather than ability has been selected to cover machines. Morriss (2002) also distinguishes between the concepts of ability and ableness, referring to ability as meaning one "can" do something, and ableness as the "all-in can", which "combines the "can" of ability with the presence of an opportunity. Capacity covers both words, whether the opportunity is present or not.

Allen (1998) and Allen (1999) set out to "develop a satisfactory feminist account of power" and achieves this in a non-normative way by defining three types of power as follows:

- 'power to' as "the ability of an individual to attain an end or series of ends" (Allen, 1998, 1999).
- 'power over' as "the ability of an actor or a set of actors to constrain the choices available to another actor or set of actors in a nontrivial way" (Allen, 1998, 1999) and
- 'power with' as "the ability of a collectivity to act together for the attainment of a common or shared end or series of ends" (Allen, 1998, 1999).

All of these definitions have a qualifier on the noun and so cannot serve as a definition of the word itself. They are types of power rather than the essence of power itself. However she does go on to give a broad definition of power encompassing all three types as follows: "the ability or capacity of an actor or set of actors to act" (Allen, 1998, 1999). Removing the aspects of this definition that restrict it to the human social dimension leaves a definition almost identical to the definition proposed above. She also notes "the entomology of the term: 'power' is derived from the Latin *potere* and the French *pouvoir*, both of which mean *to be able*." (Allen, 1998, 1999)

Pansardi (2012) ignores 'power with' and argues that 'power to' and 'power over' are "two analytically distinguishable aspects of a single and unified concept of social power". However to reach this conclusion, she resorts to "reserving the specific use of the term *power* for what individuals are able to do in a social context" Pansardi (2012). This cannot be accepted in a generic definition for public usage.

'Power with' also corresponds with the observations of Dowding (2003) on revealed preference analysis when he says "One cannot conclude that because a group of individuals do not promote some end x they have no interest in promoting x. They may simply face a collective action problem". Again, this provides nothing that can be used in a generic definition. Dowding (2003) concurs with the tentative definition in rejecting the proposal of Barry (2002) to equate power with resources, but for a completely different reason; it is not sufficiently generic to cover inanimate objects and animals.

Pansardi (2012) also refers to "the classical definition proposed by Dahl, according to which A has power over B to the extent that he can get B to do something that B would not otherwise do". This definition works only for human social situations and so cannot be used as a generic definition. Dahl (1957) himself says:

> First let us agree that power is a relation, and that it is a relation among people. Although in common speech the term encompasses relations among people and other animate and inanimate objects, we shall have our hands full if we confine the relationship to human beings.

This may be so in terms of covering all the different power relationships there may be between people and in the world generally, but insofar as actually defining the meaning that captures the essence of a single English word, it is not generic and so this definition of power as a relation must be rejected.

In Step 3 above, the choice between ability, capability and capacity was discussed and capacity chosen as it is more generic, covering machines as well as living things.

Haugaard (2010) argues a Wittgensteinian 'family resemblance' concept, considering "there is no single essence that unites all these usages" Haugaard (2010). These usages refer to all the various types (extensions) of power and no attempt is made here to find a common essence among these types. The attempt here is simply to define the minimum common (essence of the) English language meaning of a single word, power. The essences or 'substances' of the various types of power (such as gravitational power, electrical power, political power and mechanical power) are so completely different that attempting to 'distil' a common essence across them is most certainly futile. However, to do so would also be seeking the essence of a group of phrases rather than of a single word. It must be possible to determine a minimum common meaning that captures the essence represented by the noun 'power', as this is what enables its use across these various types. The evidence does point to this being insufficient for many fields without a qualifying adjective or suffix, but this does not invalidate the meaning of the noun. If it were to do so, it would end up as a dialect or private language game, which the definitional effort here seeks to avoid and which Haugaard (2010) himself describes as "inherently meaningless".

For the above reasons, "The idea that power is a family resemblance concept entails that there can be no single best definition of power" (Haugaard, 2010) is here contradicted. The family resemblance exists because of the common use of the noun power. There must be a definition representing the essence of the concept denoted by the English language word power for it to be so used.

Haugaard (2010) further argues " 'essential contestedness' of power does not stem from observations of empirical reality … but … from their 'moral and political perspectives' ". Thus, what is at issue is a normative debate concerning moral right and wrong. This accords with the endeavour here to define non-normatively. However he also maintains there are "language games" around various power theories and states:

> One of the greatest sources of confusion in the power debates arises from the all-too-prevalent tendency for social scientists to be unaware when they move concepts from one language game to the next. In the power debate, the most frequent confusion in this regard is between normative and analytical usages. Haugaard (2010)

While much confusion arises from this source, the analytical and normative uses can hardly be described as two separate language games. They may be separate games, but not separate language games; the within-fields or subfields jargon may be different, but there is a meta-language game also being played, and that is the common tongue that is being used, which in our case is English. It is useful to distinguish by the type of content rather than its language, and to not invite confusion by conceptually mixing these two together under a single umbrella term 'language game'.

While concepts are not deterministic, the grammatical rules of the English language game are, and we either all either agree on the meaning of a word or we don't. The word game does exist; it has sound energy that can be measured. The rules already exist (English grammar) and the label assigned to the word game being played here is simply English.

So to use its existing grammatical rules, as noted above, arriving at a single denotative definition of power by extension, or by including any qualifiers, is impossible, but a connotative, intensional definition as per the adopted method is quite possible and in fact essential. This is based upon Copi and Cohen (1990) and summarised in McGrath and Whitty (2015) (See Chap. 10). This is not playing separate language games across the various power fields; rather, there are different instantiations of content. But within any content area, although some terminology used may be unique, we all need to play the same English language game, abide by its grammatical rules and agree on the meaning of the words we use. If we don't do this, we are inventing private language and our confusion over terminology will never be resolved.

This review of academic literature therefore finds no reason to alter the definition derived above.

A common feature evident across the types or categories or characterisations or dimensions or means of exercise or effects of power is that they all rely upon using a sometimes-unspoken qualifier with the term power, in other words, a phrase. Terms such as 'power-over', a phrase whose essence could be said to be domination, 'expert power', a phrase whose essence could be said to be knowledge, or 'political power' a phrase whose essence could be said to be social interaction, have no common meaning or essence. These phrases describe types or aspects of power rather than actually defining the meaning of the simple English language word power, albeit that Galinsky, Nye, Turner, Lukes and Sayer all came very close to this. Such categorising may be necessary for developing social theory, but this work is not here seeking to evaluate such theory. It is simply concerned with determining a simple, working, generic definition of a single English language word, for which such categorisation is irrelevant. For that word to be used across all these phrases, it must have its own unique essence. It is this essence, of this single English language word 'power', that is being defined here, not the meaning within social science of the multitude of categorisations or characterisations of the word that are possible.

The practice of omitting the qualifier can legitimately occur when repeated use is necessary within any field or community of interest. But this can cause a problem if this abbreviated or encrypted usage of a word is taken outside, where it is not understood in the same way. If it is clarity of communication that is being sought here, this sort of abbreviation or shorthand is a laxity that is unhelpful. It can also invite normative considerations to creep into our understanding of words, as well as generate avoidable contest between fields for their particular usage to prevail. If, by simply avoiding this practice, some amount of confusion and conflict in the world could be reduced, why would we not do so? It is a very simple rule that would seem almost elementary to apply in any practice purporting to have any scientific aspect to it, and it cannot possibly be productive to do otherwise. There may appear to be little point in stepping back to re-evaluate when one doesn't realise one needs to, when there is a desire to "just get on with it"; but there is no sensible reason to add unnecessary contest over the meaning of the words to legitimate contest over normative issues. The practice of omitting the qualifier of a concept is destructive to the productivity of the wider social machine.

In summary, there is support within the academic sources for the proposed definition and the discussion of all the types or categories or characterisations or dimensions or means of exercise or effects of power has found no reason to alter it.

Step 6 Remove unwarranted inclusions

There are no such inclusions of this term remaining.

Step 7 Remove mixed content/process meanings

None present. As mentioned in Step 3 above, the definition has excluded intentionality (content), so that it (the process only) covers both its proper and improper use (abuse).

Step 8 Reduce divergence/consider additional inclusions

Historical check (a) and field/speciality use (b) are the appropriate checks for this term.

Step 8(a) Consider historical usage

In the fifth century BC (Sun & Cleary, 1988) claimed "Knowledge is power". This is a synonymous definition. However as is evident from Hobbes (1996) below, there are many other synonyms for power and so this cannot suffice as a generic definition. Knowledge can be regarded as one of a number of capacities that enable action.

In the early sixteenth century Machiavelli wrote *The Prince* (Machiavelli & Constantine, 2009). This was the first modern treatise on political philosophy and was about the exercise of power. It was concerned with the rule of Princes or sovereigns, and with how a Prince might acquire and maintain his position. It contains no definition of power.

In the seventeenth century Hobbes (1996) defined "The power of a man" as "his present means to obtain some future apparent good". This is much too narrow a definition to suffice here. However insofar as "to obtain" implies action and some capacity is required to achieve it, this is not in conflict with the derived definition. He also mentions natural power of body and mind, servants, friends, riches, reputation, popularity, success, affability, prudence, nobility, eloquence and form. These can be regarded as capacities and not in conflict with the derived definition.

Also in the seventeenth century, John Locke refuted Sir Robert Filmer's justification of the divine right of kings over the life and death of his subjects. Locke (1821) refers to this as "absolute power" and "royal authority" and attacks its basis of "fatherly authority" supposedly handed down from Adam. At that time, Kings were considered to have both the power and the authority to execute subjects. This accords with Foucault's view of juridical power (James 2011) and presents no difficulty for the derived definition.

In the eighteenth century, Adam Smith was concerned with power, but principally with respect to the division of labour. He says (Smith & Butler-Bowden, 2010)

> Wealth, as Mr Hobbes says, is power. … the power of purchasing a certain command over all the labour, or over all the produce of labour which is then in the market … it enables him to purchase or command. The exchangeable value of everything must always be precisely equal to the extent of this power which it conveys to the owner.

Smith is concerned with a particular aspect of power and refers to it rather than defining it. This is too limiting to be useful here and the intensional definition covers Smith's extension anyway.

So there is no historical reason to alter the definition derived above.

Step 8(b) Consider field/specialty usage

Table 11.3 contains definitions relevant to law, mechanics, politics, government, the military, mathematics, engineering, science, finance, energy, electricity, physics, religion, sociology, psychology, astrology and family. The derived definition does not conflict with any of the Table 11.3 definitions relative to these fields. Strength is another descriptor that was not selected as it is also compatible with the capacity to act. Power, as the time rate of doing work, or energy emitted or transmitted Merriam-Webster is still a measure of capacity to act.

This is compatible with the approach taken in sport and the fitness industry, as indicated by Ohtake (2012),

> Power and work capacity are one … and are often used interchangeably. Work capacity is the amount of work that can be performed in a given period of time. The more work that can be done, the greater the work capacity (i.e. more power). Power provides the foundation for any type of fitness or sport.

So examination of usage in this wide range of fields does not indicate any need to change the derived definition.

Step 9 Check against the five rules

This is a definition by genus and difference and satisfies Rules 1 to 5.

Step 10 Report the derived definition

The derived definition is as follows:

- Power = the capacity to act.

11.13 Define 'Influence'

Step 1 Define derivative or component terms

This is not a derivative or compound term.

Step 2 Survey lexical usage

Lexical usage is surveyed in Table 11.4 in the appendix.

Step 3 Analyse lexical usage

Many of the definitions in Table 11.4 use the word 'power' which has already been defined and so will be excluded to avoid circular definitions and mixing concepts.

Step 4 Develop a connotative (intensional) conventional definition

In line with Group Rule 2(d), the verb will be defined first and the noun then defined in terms of the verb.

Influence (verb):

There is a group of synonyms in Table 11.4 that generally apply to people only. These include persuade, induce, motivate, drive (to action), impel, bias and sway. A person may be influenced by events that have no element of persuasion or inducement. Impel is appealing as it describes inciting a person to action as well as affecting internal motivation and it also includes the possibility of constraint or coercion, but a person can be influenced without necessarily feeling impelled. This group collectively covers various means and degrees of force, from gentle to substantial and from ethical to corrupt, avoiding intentionality, but individually, none are really fully inclusive of the others and none are fully applicable to inanimate objects such as planets and magnets.

There are two other synonyms from Table 11.4 that do apply to people, things and animals namely, to affect or have an effect upon. However, a definition in these terms would be a little too short to be fully meaningful, calling for a qualification, such as opinions, thoughts, behaviour, conduct, decisions (all applying to people and animals, and none being inclusive of all the others), movement, actions (applying also to things, and action is inclusive of movement).

The Wiktionary definition "to affect by gentle action" is appealing, however some action that influences is not gentle. Bullying influences people's behaviour and whether physical, emotional or mental, can hardly be said to be gentle, and the gravitational pull of the earth on a human body falling from a height towards it is quite powerful, with an outcome that cannot be described as gentle. So, gentleness will not be included.

The Longman's definition "to affect the way someone or something develops, behaves, thinks, etc. without directly forcing or ordering them" is also appealing, but a little too verbose. A shorter form that encapsulates this meaning will be proposed as follows: To affect the thoughts or actions of an entity.

This is a process definition, free of intentionality, covering all forms of action, whether operating with obvious force or without direct or apparent effect. It acknowledges that one can be emotionally affected by something without being compelled to act physically and whether affected emotionally or impelled to act, one has been influenced. It covers covert influence as well as that which is overtly and publicly exercised.

Influence that has no effect is not successful influence, but it is still influence. It may also have a completely opposite effect to that desired, turning the target away from the influencer's desired action. The proposed definition is independent of the outcome and accommodates this, as well as the circumstance of two magnet ends of the same polarity being placed together, influencing each other by repelling. It also covers the historical ethereal, occult, spiritual and moral aspects mentioned in Table 11.4 as well, as all these things may affect the way a person thinks and acts.

Note that affecting the outcome of a process involves affecting the thoughts or actions of the person carrying it out, or introducing some chemical, mechanical or animal intervention at a particular time, all of which require a person to initiate, design or act in some way. The proposed definition accommodates this.

Influence (noun):

Defining the noun in terms of the verb results in the following definition: The effect of one entity upon another. This covers range of intentionality – whether good, bad or neither, as well as living and inanimate entities, including magnetic and gravitational. It covers action both sensibly and insensibly exercised, operating without any direct or apparent cause.

The tentative definition of influence will therefore be "to affect the thoughts or actions of an entity" (v) and "the effect of one entity upon another" (n).

Step 5 Report academic review of definitions

Not relevant here where there is no significant or generally recognised contention regarding meaning.

Step 6 Remove unwarranted inclusions

There are no such inclusions remaining.

Step 7 Remove mixed content/process meanings

None present.

Step 8 Reduce divergence/consider additional inclusions

Checks (a) and (b) are appropriate for this term.

Step 8(a) Consider historical usage

Historical usages appear in Table 11.4 and as noted in Step 4, the proposed definitions accommodate these.

Step 8(b) Consider field/specialty usage

Step 4 has dealt with astronomical, magnetic, spiritual, occult and moral perspectives of these terms, noting that the definition accommodates all of these.

Step 9 Check against the five rules

The definitions are operational rather than by genus and difference and so a check against the 5 rules is not appropriate. Nevertheless, they do actually satisfy them.

These definitions are generic, satisfy Rules 1 to 5 and do not conflict with the above lexical usage.

Step 10 Report the derived definition

The derived definition is as follows:

- Influence = (v) to affect the thoughts or actions of an entity and (n) the effect of one entity upon another.

11.14 Summary of Definitions

The initially accepted definitions were:

- Concept = an abstract idea (Oxford).
- Term = a word or phrase used to describe a thing or to express a concept (Oxford).
- Meaning = What is intended to be conveyed.
- Definition = A statement of what is signified by a term.
- Process = A series of actions or steps taken in order to achieve a particular end (Oxford).

The derived definitions are as follows:

- Content = [mass noun] The material or subject matter dealt with in or by a process, form or style.
- Legitimate (a): condoned by those with authority in the particular circumstance.
- Legitimacy (n): the quality of being legitimate, or the quality of being condoned by those with authority in the particular circumstance.
- Authority: the right to make decisions, give orders and enforce obedience
- Power: the capacity to act (whether exercised through authority, force or influence)
- Influence: (v) to affect the thoughts or actions of an entity and (n) the effect of one entity upon another.

11.15 Analysis and Conclusion

Application of the selected method to the remaining terms is found in Chap. 12 and so analysis and conclusions of all definitions including the three definitions in this Chapter appear there. Chapter 12 also develops a diagrammatic view of the definitions, expanded to show the parts of the machinery of power, indicating its means of exercise, enablers, mechanisms and tools. These tools are then enumerated in a table showing for each tool the channels through which it may be applied.

Appendix

Table 11.1 Definitions of 'authority'

Dictionary	Definition of authority (All sourced on 11/1/14 ex Macquarie 24/4/2018)
Business	1. Institutionalized and legal power inherent in a particular job, function, or position that is meant to enable its holder to successfully carry out his or her responsibilities.
	2. Power that is delegated formally. It includes a right to command a situation, commit resources, give orders and expect them to be obeyed, it is always accompanied by an equal responsibility for one's actions or a failure to act.
Cambridge	The moral or legal right or ability to control
Collins	The power or right to control, judge, or prohibit the actions of others
Concise Oxford	The power or right to enforce obedience
Dictionary.com	The power to determine, adjudicate, or otherwise settle issues or disputes; jurisdiction; the right to control, command, or determine.
Longman	The power you have because of your official position, official position to do something
Macmillan	The power to make decisions or tell people what to do
Macquarie	The right to determine, adjudicate, or otherwise settle issues or disputes; the right to control, command, or determine.
Merriam-Webster	The power to give orders or make decisions: the power or right to direct or control someone or something. The power to influence or command thought, opinion, or behaviour
Oxford	The power or right to give orders, make decisions, and enforce obedience
The free dictionary	1 The power to enforce laws, exact obedience, command, determine, or judge.
	2 Power assigned to another; authorization
Wiktionary	The power to enforce rules or give orders.

Table 11.2a Definitions of 'legitimate'

Dictionary	Definition of legitimate (All sourced on 6/9/2016 ex Macquarie on 24/4/2018)
Business	Acceptable or recognized as genuine, valid, or conforming to established codes, customs, rules, or standards of conduct.
Cambridge	**Adjective**
	Allowed by law
	Reasonable and acceptable
	Verb
	To make something legal or acceptable
Collins	*adj*
	1. born in lawful wedlock; enjoying full filial rights
	2. conforming to established standards of usage, behaviour, etc
	3. based on correct or acceptable principles of reasoning
	4. reasonable, sensible, or valid:
	5. (Law) authorized, sanctioned by, or in accordance with law
	6. (Government, Politics & Diplomacy) of, relating to, or ruling by hereditary right:
	7. (Theatre) of or relating to a body of famous long-established plays as distinct from films, television, vaudeville, etc:
	vb
	8. (*tr*) to make, pronounce, or show to be legitimate
Concise Oxford	**Adjective**
	Born in lawful wedlock;
	Lawful, proper, regular, conforming to standard type;
	(of sovereign's title) based on strict hereditary right;
	Logically admissible.
	Verb
	Make legitimate by decree, enactment or proof;
	Justify, serve as justification for.

(continued)

Table 11.2a (continued)

Dictionary	Definition of legitimate (All sourced on 6/9/2016 ex Macquarie on 24/4/2018)
Dictionary.com	**adjective**
	1. according to law; lawful:
	2. in accordance with established rules, principles, or standards.
	3. born in wedlock or of legally married parents:
	4. in accordance with the laws of reasoning; logically inferable; logical:
	5. resting on or ruling by the principle of hereditary right:
	6. not spurious or unjustified; genuine:
	7. of the normal or regular type or kind.
	8 Theatre. of or relating to professionally produced stage plays, as distinguished from burlesque, vaudeville, television, motion pictures, etc.:
	verb (used with object), legitimated, legitimating.
	9. to make lawful or legal; pronounce or state as lawful:
	10. to establish as lawfully born:
	11. to show or declare to be legitimate or proper:
	12. to justify; sanction or authorize:
	His behavior was legitimated by custom.
	noun
	13. the legitimate, the legitimate theater or drama.
	14. a person who is established as being legitimate.
Longman	**Adjective**
	1 fair or reasonable:
	2 acceptable or allowed by law:
	3 a legitimate child is born to parents who are legally married to each other
	Verb
	the usual American form of LEGITIMIZE
Macmillan	1. fair and reasonable
	2. allowed by the law, or correct according to the law
	3. a legitimate child is born to parents who are legally married
Macquarie	**1.** according to law; lawful.
	2. in accordance with established rules, principles, or standards.
	3. of the normal or regular type or kind.
	4. in accordance with the laws of reasoning; logically inferable; logical:
	5. born in wedlock, or of parents legally married.
	6. resting on or ruling by the principle of hereditary right:
	7. genuine; not spurious.
	8. *Theatre* relating to or denoting plays or acting with a serious and literary purpose.
Merriam-Webster	: allowed according to rules or laws
	: real, accepted, or official
	: fair or reasonable

(continued)

Table 11.2a (continued)

Dictionary	Definition of legitimate (All sourced on 6/9/2016 ex Macquarie on 24/4/2018)
Oxford	1. ***ADJECTIVE***
	1. conforming to the law or to rules:
	2. able to be defended with logic or justification; valid:
	3. constituting or relating to serious drama as distinct from musical comedy, revue, etc.:
	2. ***VERB***
	1. make lawful or justify:
The free dictionary	*adj.*
	1.
	a. Being in compliance with the law; lawful:
	b. Being in accordance with established or accepted rules and standards:
	c. Valid or justifiable:
	d. Based on logical reasoning:
	2. Born of legally married parents:
	3. Of, relating to, or ruling by hereditary right:
	4. Of or relating to drama of high professional quality that excludes burlesque, vaudeville, and some forms of musical comedy:
	tr.v. (-māt′) **le·git·i·mat·ed, le·git·i·mat·ing, le·git·i·mates**
	To make legitimate, as:
	a. To give legal force or status to; make lawful.
	b. To sanction formally or officially; authorize.
	c. To demonstrate or declare to be justified.
Wiktionary	Adjective
	1. In accordance with the law or established legal forms and requirements; lawful.
	2. Conforming to known principles, or established or accepted rules or standards; valid.
	3. Authentic, real, genuine.
	4. Lawfully begotten, i.e., born to a legally married couple.
	5. Relating to hereditary rights.

Table 11.2b Definitions of 'legitimacy'

Dictionary	Definition of legitimacy (All sourced on 6/9/2016 ex Macquarie on 24/4/2018)
Business	No definition given.
Cambridge	The quality of being legal
	The quality of being reasonable and acceptable
Collins	The quality or state of being legitimate
Concise Oxford	Not defined
Dictionary.com	The state or quality of being legitimate.
Longman	Not defined
Macmillan	1. the fact that something is legal
	2. the fact that something is fair and reasonable
Macquarie	The state or fact of being legitimate
Merriam-Webster	The quality or state of being legitimate
Oxford	1. Conformity to the law or to rules:
	1.1 (With reference to a child) the quality of being legitimate:
	2. Ability to be defended with logic or justification; validity:
The free dictionary	The quality or fact of being legitimate.
Wiktionary	The quality of being legitimate or valid; validity.

Table 11.3 Definitions of 'power'

Dictionary	Definition of power (All sourced on 7/1/2014 ex Macquarie 24/4/2018)
Business	1. Ability to cause or prevent an action, make things happen; the discretion to act or not act. Opposite of disability, it differs from a right in that it has no accompanying duties.
	2. Law: (1) An instrument transferring or vesting legal authorization. (2) The ability conferred on a person by law to determine and alter (by his or her own will) the rights, duties, liabilities, and other legal relations, of himself or others.
Cambridge	1. ability to control people and events:
	2. the amount of political control a person or group has in a country:
Collins	1. ability or capacity to do something
	2. *(often plural)* a specific ability, capacity, or faculty
	3. political, financial, social, etc, force or influence
	4. control or dominion or a position of control, dominion, or authority
	5. a state or other political entity with political, industrial, or military strength
	6. a person who exercises control, influence, or authority
	7. a prerogative, privilege, or liberty
	8. 1 legal authority to act, esp in a specified capacity, for another
	2 the document conferring such authority
	9. 1 a military force
	2 military potential
	10. (*mathematics*)
	1. the value of a number or quantity raised to some exponent
	2. *another name for* exponent (sense 4)
	11. (*statistics*) the probability of rejecting the null hypothesis in a test when it is false. The power of a test of a given null depends on the particular alternative hypothesis against which it is tested
	12. (*physics*, *engineering*) a measure of the rate of doing work expressed as the work done per unit time. It is measured in watts, horsepower
	13. 1 the rate at which electrical energy is fed into or taken from a device or system. It is expressed, in a direct-current circuit, as the product of current and voltage and, in an alternating-current circuit, as the product of the effective values of the current and voltage and the cosine of the phase angle between them. It is measured in watts
	2 (*as modifier*) ⇒ a power amplifier
	14. the ability to perform work

(continued)

Table 11.3 (continued)

Dictionary	Definition of power (All sourced on 7/1/2014 ex Macquarie 24/4/2018)
Concise Oxford	Ability to do or act, vigour, energy, active property, government influence, authority (over), authorisation, delegated authority, influential person, body or thing, deity, large number or amount, mechanical energy, capacity for exerting mechanical force.
Dictionary.com	1. ability to do or act; capability of doing or accomplishing something.
	2. political or national strength.
	3. Great or marked ability to do or act; strength; might; force.
	4. The possession of control or command over others; authority; ascendancy.
	5. political ascendancy or control in the government of a country, state.
Longman	1 the ability or right to control people or events
	2 the position of having political control of a country or government
	3 the ability to influence people or give them strong feelings
	4 the right or authority to do something:
	5 a natural or special ability to do something
	6 energy that can be used to make a machine work or to make electricity – nuclear/wind/solar etc power
	7 the ability to earn money, buy things etc
	8 the physical strength or effect of something
Macmillan	1. the ability to influence or control what people do or think
	a. the ability to achieve something or to make something happen
	b. a natural or unusual ability for doing something
	2. political control of a country or government
	a. official or legal authority to do something
	b. a country that is able to influence other countries because of its economic or military strength
	3 energy obtained from oil, coal, the sun etc, used for operating equipment and machines
	a. the supply of electricity to your home, office, community etc
	4. physical force or strength
	5. the ability of a machine or vehicle to operate quickly and effectively

(continued)

Table 11.3 (continued)

Dictionary	Definition of power (All sourced on 7/1/2014 ex Macquarie 24/4/2018)
Macquarie	**1.** ability to do or act; capability of doing or effecting something.
	2. (*usually plural*) a particular faculty of body or mind.
	3. political or national strength: *the balance of power in Europe.*
	4. great or marked ability to do or act; strength; might; force.
	5. the possession of control or command over others; dominion; authority; ascendancy or influence.
	6. political ascendancy or control in the government of a country, etc.
	7. legal ability, capacity, or authority.
	8. delegated authority; authority vested in a person or persons in a particular capacity.
	9. a written statement, or document, conferring legal authority.
	10. someone or something that possesses or exercises authority or influence.
	11. a state or nation having international authority or influence.
	12. a military or naval force.
	13. (*often plural*) a deity or divinity.
	14. *Theology* a member of the sixth order of angels.
	15. *Colloquial* a large number or amount.
	16. *Physics* the time rate of transferring or transforming energy; work done, or energy transferred, per unit of time.
	17. mechanical energy, as distinguished from hand labour.
	18. *Electricity* the rate, per unit of time, at which electrical energy is transferred by an electric circuit; the SI unit of power is the watt.
	19. electric current, especially as supplied to domestic and commercial customers by an energy provider: *the power's off.*
	20. a particular form of energy: *nuclear power*; *electrical power.*
	21. *Mathematics* the product obtained by multiplying a quantity by itself one or more times.
	22. *Optics* the magnifying capacity of a microscope, telescope, etc., expressed as ratio of diameter of image to object.
	–verb (*t*) **23.** to supply with electricity or other means of power.
	24. (of an engine, etc.) to provide the force or motive power to operate (a machine).
	–verb (*i*) **25.** to move with a surge of power.
	–adjective **26.** providing electricity.
	27. operated using a power source and mechanism, in addition to the usual manual labour, the source being electricity, compressed air, internal combustion engines or the like.
	28. associated with a managerial or executive style.
	–phrase **29. power down,** *Colloquial* to switch off a computer or peripheral device.
	30. power one's way, *Colloquial* to draw on reserves of strength and energy to gain a victory.
	31. the power behind the throne, the person who is really in control, although appearing to defer to someone else.
	32. the powers that be, those in authority. [*Phrase Origin:* from the New Testament (Romans 13:1): 'Let every soul be subject unto the higher powers. For there is no power but of God: the powers that be are ordained of God.']
	33. power up, *Colloquial* to switch on a computer or peripheral device.

(continued)

Table 11.3 (continued)

Dictionary	Definition of power (All sourced on 7/1/2014 ex Macquarie 24/4/2018)
Merriam-Webster	: the ability or right to control people or things
	: political control of a country or area
	: a person or organization that has a lot of control and influence over other people or organizations
	Full Definition of *POWER*
	1 *a (1)* : ability to act or produce an effect *(2)* : ability to get extra-base hits *(3)* : capacity for being acted upon or undergoing an effect
	b : legal or official authority, capacity, or right
	2 *a* : possession of control, authority, or influence over others
	b : one having such power; *specifically* : a sovereign state
	c : a controlling group.
	d archaic : a force of armed men
	e chiefly dialect : a large number or quantity
	3 *a* : physical might
	b : mental or moral efficacy
	c : political control or influence
	4 *plural* : an order of angels — see CELESTIAL HIERARCHY
	5 *a* : the number of times as indicated by an exponent that a number occurs as a factor in a product.
	b : CARDINAL NUMBER
	6 *a* : a source or means of supplying energy; *especially* : ELECTRICITY
	b : MOTIVE POWER
	c : the time rate at which work is done or energy emitted or transferred
	7 : MAGNIFICATION 2b
Oxford	1 the ability or capacity to do something or act in a particular way:
	2 the capacity or ability to direct or influence the behaviour of others or the course of events:
	political or social authority or control, especially that exercised by a government.
	authority that is given or delegated to a person or body.
	the military strength of a state.
	a state or country, especially one viewed in terms of its international influence and military strength.
	a person or organization that is strong or influential within a particular context.
	a supernatural being, deity, or force.
	3 physical strength and force exerted by something or someone.
	capacity or performance of an engine or other device.
	denoting a sports player, team, or style of play that makes use of power rather than finesse
	the magnifying capacity of a lens.
	4 energy that is produced by mechanical, electrical, or other means and used to operate a device.
	electrical energy supplied to an area, building, etc.
	[as modifier] driven by electrical energy.
	5 *Physics* the rate of doing work, measured in watts or less frequently horse power.

(continued)

Table 11.3 (continued)

Dictionary	Definition of power (All sourced on 7/1/2014 ex Macquarie 24/4/2018)
The free dictionary	1. The ability or capacity to perform or act effectively.
	2. A specific capacity, faculty, or aptitude. Often used in the plural.
	3. Strength or force exerted or capable of being exerted; might.
	4. The ability or official capacity to exercise control; authority.
	5. A person, group, or nation having great influence or control over others.
	6. The might of a nation, political organization, or similar group.
	7. Forcefulness; effectiveness.
	8. *Chiefly Upper Southern U.S.* A large number or amount.
	9. a. The energy or motive force by which a physical system or machine is operated.
	b. The capacity of a system or machine to operate.
	c. Electrical or mechanical energy, especially as used to assist or replace human energy.
	d. Electricity supplied to a home, building, or community.
	10. *Physics* The rate at which work is done, expressed as the amount of work per unit time and commonly measured in units such as the watt and horsepower.
Wiktionary	1. (*social*) Effectiveness.
	1. (*countable*) Capability or influence.
	Control, particularly legal or political (jurisdiction).
	3. (*chiefly in the plural*) The people in charge of legal or political power, the government.
	4. Influential nations, companies, or other such bodies.
	2. (*physical, uncountable*) Effectiveness.

Table 11.4 Definitions of 'influence'

Dictionary	Definition of influence (All sourced on 7/1/2014 ex Macquarie 24/4/2018)
Business	Effect of the fluctuation in the value of an independent (such as income) variable on the value of a dependent variable (such as consumption).
Cambridge	the power to have an effect on people or things, or a person or thing that is able to do this:
Collins	noun
	1. an effect of one person or thing on another
	2. the power of a person or thing to have such an effect
	5. power or sway resulting from ability, wealth, position, etc
	4. a person or thing having influence
	5. an ethereal fluid or occult power regarded as emanating from the stars and affecting a person's actions, future, etc
	verb *(transitive)*
	7. to persuade or induce
	8. to have an effect upon (actions, events, etc); affect
Concise Oxford	Noun: Flowing from stars of etherial fluid affecting character and destiny of man,
	Action insensibly exercised [insensible = too small or gradual to be perceived
	Verb: Exert or have an effect upon
Dictionary.com	*noun* 1. the capacity or power of persons or things to be a compelling force on or produce effects on the ac-tions, behavior, opinions, etc., of others.
	2. the action or process of producing effects on the actions, behavior, opinions, etc., of another or others.
	3. a person or thing that exerts influence.
	verb (used with object), in·flu·enced, in·flu·enc·ing.
	7. to exercise influence on; affect; sway
	8. to move or impel (a person) to some action

Longman	**Noun**
	1 the power to affect the way someone or something develops, behaves, or thinks without using direct force or orders:
	2 someone or something that has an influence on other people or things
	Verb [transitive]
	To affect the way someone or something devel-ops, behaves, thinks etc without directly forcing or ordering them.
Macmillan	1. the effect that a person or thing has on someone's decisions, opinions, or behaviour or on the way something happens
	2. a person or thing that has an effect on someone or something
Macquarie	1. invisible or insensible action exerted by one thing or person on another, especially by people in power.
	2. power of producing effects by invisible or insensible means.
	3. a thing or person that exerts action by invisible or insensible means.
	4. *Astrology*
	a. the supposed radiation of an ethereal fluid from the stars, regarded in astrology as affecting human actions and destinies, etc.
	b. the exercise of occult power by the stars, or such power as exercised.
Merriam-Webster	: the power to change or affect someone or something: the power to cause changes without directly forcing them to happen
	: a person or thing that affects someone or something in an important way
	Full Definition of *INFLUENCE*
	1 *a* : an ethereal fluid held to flow from the stars and to affect the actions of humans
	b : an emanation of occult power held to derive from stars
	2 : an emanation of spiritual or moral force
	3 *a* : the act or power of producing an effect without apparent exertion of force or direct exercise of command
	b : corrupt interference with authority for personal gain
	4: the power or capacity of causing an effect in indirect or intangible ways
	5: one that exerts influence

(continued)

Table 11.4 (continued)

Dictionary	Definition of influence (All sourced on 7/1/2014 ex Macquarie 24/4/2018)
Oxford	*noun*
	1 *[mass noun]* the capacity to have an effect on the character, development, or behaviour of someone or something or the effect itself
	– the power to shape policy or ensure favourable treatment from someone, especially through status, contacts, or wealth
	– a person or thing with the capacity to have an influence on someone or something
	2 *Physics*, *archaic* electrical or magnetic induction.
	verb have an influence on
The free dictionary	**1.** A power affecting a person, thing, or course of events, especially one that operates without any direct or apparent effort
	2. Power to sway or affect based on prestige, wealth, ability, or position
	3.
	a. A person who exerts influence
	b. An effect or change produced by influence.
	4.
	a. A determining factor believed by some to affect individual tendencies and characteristics understood to be caused by the positions of the stars and planets at the time of one's birth.
	b. Factors believed to be caused by the changing positions of the stars and planets in relation to their positions at the time of one's birth.
	tr.v. in·flu·enced, in·flu·enc·ing, in·flu·enc·es
	1. To produce an effect on by imperceptible or intangible means; sway.
	2. To affect the nature, development, or condition of; modify.

Wiktionary	Noun
	1. The power to affect, control or manipulate something or someone; the ability to change the development of fluctuating things such as conduct, thoughts or decisions.
	2. An action exerted by a person or thing with such power on another to cause change.
	3. A person or thing exerting such power or action.
	Verb
	1. (*transitive*) To affect by gentle action; to exert an influence upon; to modify, bias, or sway; to persuade or induce.
	2. (*intransitive*) To exert, make use of one's influence.
	3. (*transitive, obsolete*) To cause to flow in or into; infuse; instill

References

Allen, A. (1998). Rethinking power. *Hypatia, 13*(1), 21–40.

Allen, A. (1999). *The power of feminist theory: Domination, resistance, solidarity*. Westview Press.

Appleby, J. O. (1996). *Knowledge and postmodernism in historical perspective*. Routledge.

Bachrach, P., & Baratz, M. S. (1963). Decisions and nondecisions: An analytical framework. *American Political Science Review, 57*, 641–651.

Barry, B. (2002). Capitalists rule OK? Some puzzles about power. *Politics, Philosophy & Economics, 1*(2), 155–184.

BusinessDictionary.com. *Online dictionary* [Online]. Available: http://www.businessdictionary.com

Cambridge. *Online dictionary* [Online]. Available: http://dictionary.cambridge.org/dictionary/british

Casey, C. J. (2008). Authority. In S. Clegg & J. R. Bailey (Eds.), *International encyclopedia of organization studies*. SAGE.

Clegg, S. (1989). *Frameworks of power*. Sage.

Clegg, S., & Haugaard, M. (2009). *The Sage handbook of power*. SAGE.

Clegg, S., Flyvbjerg, B., & Haugaard, M. (2014). Reflections on phronetic social science: A dialogue between Stewart Clegg, Bent Flyvbjerg and Mark Haugaard. *Journal of Political Power, 7*(2), 275–306.

Collins. *English dictionary* [Online]. Available: http://www.collinsdictionary.com/dictionary/english

Concise Oxford Dictionary. (1964). *Concise oxford dictionary*. Oxford University Press.

Copi, I. M., & Cohen, C. (1990). *Introduction to logic*. Macmillan.

Dahl, R. A. (1957). The concept of power. *Behavioral Science, 2*(3), 201–215.

Dahl, R. A. (1961). *Who governs? Democracy and power in an american city*. Yale University Press.

Denneson, T. J. (n.d.). *Society and the individual in Nietzsche's the will to power*. Available: http://infidels.org/library/modern/travis_denneson/power.html. Accessed 13 July 2016.

Dictionary.com. *Online dictionary* [Online]. Available: http://dictionary.reference.com

Dowding, K. (2003). Resources, power and systematic luck: A response to barry. *Politics, Philosophy & Economics, 2*(3), 305–322.

Dowding, K. (2012). Why should we care about the definition of power? *Journal of Political Power, 5*(1), 119–135.

Fiske, S. T., & Dépret, E. (1996). Control, interdependence and power: Understanding social cognition in its social context. *European Review of Social Psychology, 7*(1), 31–61.

Foucault, M. (1978). *The history of sexuality*. Pantheon Books.

Foucault, M., & Gordon, C. (1980). *Power/knowledge: Selected interviews and other writings, 1972–1977*. Vintage Books.

French, J. R. P., & Raven, B. (1959). The bases of social power. In D. Cartwright (Ed.), *Studies in social power*. Research Center for Group Dynamics, Institute for Social Research, University of Michigan.

Galinsky, A. D., Rucker, D. D., & Magee, J. C. (2015). Power: Past findings, present considerations, and future directions. In M. Mikulincer, P. R. Shaver, J. A. Simpson, J. F. Dovidio, M. Mikulincer, P. R. Shaver, J. A. Simpson, & J. F. Dovidio (Eds.), *APA handbook of personality and social psychology, Volume 3: Interpersonal relations*. American Psychological Association.

Gallie, W. B. (1956). Essentially contested concepts. *Proceedings of the Aristotelian Society, 56*, 167–198.

Gur, N. (2007). Are legal rules content-independent reasons? *Problema, 11*(5), 175–210.

Haugaard, M. (2010). Power: A 'family resemblance' concept. *European Journal of Cultural Studies, 13*(4), 419–438.

Heidegger, M. (1962). *Being and time*. Harper & Row.

Hobbes, T. (1996). *Leviathan*. Oxford University Press.

James, R. (2011). *Juridical, disciplinary and biopolitical power: Basic background on foucault* [Online], UNC, Charlotte. Available: https://www.youtube.com/watch?v=X31ayDsG67U. Accessed 20/01/2016.

Locke, J. (1821). *Two Treatises of Government, etc*. Whitmore and Fenn.

Locke, J., & Macpherson, C. B. (1980). *Second treatise of government*. Hackett Pub. Co.

Longman. *Dictionary of contemporary English online* [Online]. Available: http://www.ldoceonline.com

Lukes, S. (1974). *Power : A radical view*. Macmillan, [S.l.].

Lukes, S. (1986). *Power*. New York University Press.

Lukes, S. (2005). *Power: A radical view*. Palgrave Macmillan.

Macfarlane, A. (2014). *The invention of the modern world*. The Fortnightly Review.

Machiavelli, N., & Constantine, P. (2009). *The Prince*. Vintage Books.

Macmillan Dictionary [Online]. Available: http://www.macmillandictionary.com

Macquarie Dictionary online [Online], Sydney. Available: http://www.macquarieonline.com.au

Mazur, A. (1973). A cross-species comparison of status in small established groups. *American Sociological Review, 38*(5), 513–530.

McGrath, S. K. (2019). *What is project governance? Disclosing the source of confusion and revealing the essence of governance*. PhD Thesis, University of Southern Queensland.

McGrath, S. K., & Whitty, S. J. (2015). Redefining governance: From confusion to certainty and clarity. *International Journal of Managing Projects in Business, 8*(4), 755–787.

Merquior, J. G. (1985). *Foucault*. Fontana Press/Collins.

Merriam-Webster *Online dictionary* [Online], Britain. Available: http://www.merriam-webster.com

Morriss, P. (2002). *Power: A philosophical approach*. Manchester University Press.

Nietzsche, F. W., & Kaufmann, W. (1968). *The will to power*. Random Press, [S.l.].

Nye, J. S., Jr. (2011). *The future of power*. Perseus Books, Public Affairs.

Ohtake, S. (2012), Maxworkouts

Oxford Dictionaries online [Online], Oxford. Available: http://oxforddictionaries.com

Pansardi, P. (2012). Power to and power over: Two distinct concepts of power? *Journal of Political Power, 5*(1), 73–89.

Russell, B. (1938). *Power: A new social analysis*. Allen and Unwin.

Sadan, E., & Flantz, R. (1997). *Empowerment and community planning: Theory and practice of people-focused social solutions*. Hakibbutz Hameuchad.

Salthe, S. N. (2010). Maximum power and maximum entropy production: Finalities in nature. *Cosmos & History, 6*(1), 114–121.

Sayer, A. (2012). Power, causality and normativity: A critical realist critique of foucault. *Journal of Political Power, 5*(2), 179–194.

Smith, A., & Butler-Bowden, T. (2010). *The wealth of nations*. Capstone Publishing.

Stolorow, R. D., Atwood, G. E., & Orange, D. M. (n.d.). *Heidegger's nazism and the hypostatization of being*. Available: http://www.georgeatwood.com/heideggers-nazism-and-the-hypostatization-of-being.html. Accessed 20 Feb 2016.

Suchman, M. C. (1995). Managing legitimacy: Strategic and institutional approaches. *Academy of Management Review, 20*(3), 571–610.

Sun, T., & Cleary, T. F. (1988). *The art of war*. Shambhala.

TheFreeDictionary Online dictionary [Online]. Available: http://www.thefreedictionary.com

Turner, J. C. (2005). Explaining the nature of power: A three-process theory. *European Journal of Social Psychology, 35*(1), 1–22.

Weber, M. (1947). *The theory of social and economic organization*. The Free Press.

Wiktionary *Online dictionary* [Online]. Available: http://en.wiktionary.org

Chapter 12
Power Defined (Part 2): Enablers, Mechanisms, Tools and Channels of Power

12.1 Introduction

This Chapter follows *Power defined – Part 1: Power and its exercise* (Chap. 11) as its second part dealing with the enablers, mechanisms, tools and channels of power. Part 1 provided the philosophical basis for the definitional process followed in both Parts and it defined the terms authority, power and influence. The definitions derived were as follows:

- Legitimate (a): condoned by those with authority in the particular circumstances.
- Legitimacy (n): the quality of being legitimate, or the quality of being condoned by those with authority in the particular circumstances.
- Authority (n): the right to make decisions, give orders and enforce obedience.
- Power (n): the capacity to act (whether exercised through authority or influence).
- Influence (v): to affect the thoughts or actions of an entity and (n) the effect of one entity upon another.

This Part 2 defines the remaining terms: direct, control, regulate and regulation before developing a diagrammatic view of the definitions, expanded to show the parts of the machinery of power, indicating its means of exercise, enablers, mechanisms and tools. These tools are then enumerated in a table showing for each tool the channels through which it may be applied. Several thought experiments are then conducted on this and means of driving the machinery of power are considered before determining the location of previous and contemporary power theories within this framework.

S. K. McGrath, *Speaking Management*,
https://doi.org/10.1007/978-981-16-2213-7_12

Note that the same dictionary sources are again employed as follows:

(1) A range of dictionaries that have been well known for many years that were available (in 2013/14) online (Cambridge, Collins, Longman, Macmillan, Macquarie, Merriam-Webster, Oxford)
(2) A range of various online dictionaries (BusinessDictionary.com, Dictionary.com, and TheFreeDictionary, Wiktionary)
(3) The Concise Oxford Dictionary (1964) – as a comparator for how these definitions may have changed over the last 50 years.

12.2 Define 'Direct'

Step 1 Define derivative or component terms

This is not a derivative or compound term.

Step 2 Survey lexical usage

Lexical usage is surveyed in Table 12.1 in the Appendix.

Step 3 Analyse lexical usage

Only the verb form will be considered as the noun form, meaning being to the point, is uncontroversial. The derivative noun using the noun-forming suffix 'ion' will adopt the noun form of the derived verb.

Words used in Table 12.1 to define 'direct' include control, command, order, instructions, point and show. Of these, command, order and instructions have some promise. Control will not be used as is one of the group of terms still to be uniquely defined. Direction will also not be used as it includes the term being defined. Being a director or giving a direction has the connotation of having formal authority. However leadership can be exercised without this, such as through having expert knowledge. A manager may make procedural decisions, but these will often be subject to the approval of a director. To avoid potential confusion, neither management nor operations will be included. Leadership will also not be included as, while a leader may direct, he or she may also lead by other means, such as inspiring their followers. Both will be separately defined elsewhere (Chap. 15).

Accountability will also be defined elsewhere (Chap. 16) and is linked to the director role and implies the requirement to make decisions. However, accountability spans many roles and its inclusion would unnecessarily co-mingle concepts that require separate and unique definition. There are also aspects of the unknown and of consequent risk in giving a direction, as well as in governing and so risk and uncertainty will not be included. Any reference to governing will also not be included as governance has already been defined in McGrath and Whitty (2015) in terms of directing (Chap. 10). To keep the definition generic, any familial references will be rejected and any reference to geographic course, straight lines and pointing will be avoided in favour of more broad terms.

In practice, everyone at whatever level will have things they can direct themselves, and things they manage according to set rules. For example, a tradesman directs how he does his work, but usually does not direct the other building activity that goes on around him. Similarly, a director of a large infrastructure project who decides the order in which construction will proceed will have procurement rules he must follow. A company chairman leads a company in a particular direction but must still ensure ASIC rules are complied with. The definition therefore has to be applicable to any level. Strategic direction and goal setting will similarly not be included.

Common themes across Table 12.1 which do not have any of the above difficulties identified thus far are giving orders, commands or instructions. Orders will be selected as it encompasses the other two terms, covering nuances ranging from a military command to giving someone instructions or directions. The term has the connotation of autonomy, of not needing to seek anyone's permission, however this is implied by being able to give the order. It also has the connotation of authority, however one cannot successfully give an order without the subject accepting one's authority, and so it does not need to be included.

Step 4 Develop a connotative (intensional) conventional definition

This leaves the definition of the verb 'direct' as "to give orders". This is an acceptable operational definition.

Step 5 Report academic review of definitions

Not relevant where there is no significant or generally recognised contention regarding meaning.

Step 6 Remove unwarranted inclusions

There are no such inclusions of this term remaining.

Step 7 Remove mixed content/ process meanings

None present.

Step 8 Reduce divergence/ consider additional inclusions

None of the four checks are necessary for this term.

Step 9 Check against the five rules

The definition is operational rather than by genus and difference and so a check against the 5 rules is not appropriate. Nevertheless, it does actually satisfy them.

Step 10 Report the derived definition

The derived definition is as follows:

- Direct (v) = to give orders.
- Direction (n) = an order.

12.3 Define 'Control'

Step 1 Define derivative or component terms

This is not a derivative or compound term.

Step 2 Survey lexical usage

Lexical usage is surveyed in Table 12.2 in the Appendix.

Step 3 Analyse lexical usage

Words used in Table 12.2 to define control include order, limit, rule, command, direct, check, curb, restrain, restrict, dominate, command, regulate and dictate or determine the behaviour of. In a sense, all of these words provide a definition of the term by extension, as none could be said to not be included by the term. However all of these have the connotation, as expressed in some of the above definitions, of making somebody or something do what you want or ensuring that action or function occurs in a particular way, so a definition by intension would have to be expressed in these terms.

Several mention power to make decisions, which will be referred to as authority, as defined above. This aligns with 'dictate', as does the usage of the word 'direct' which has also been defined above as to give orders. Again, these would be relevant to a definition of the term by extension but not by intension.

Note that regulate is mentioned in several of the definitions in Table 12.2 as one means of control.

Step 4 Develop a connotative (intensional) conventional definition

To control can therefore be defined as "to ensure that actions occur in a particular way". This covers requiring people to act and/ or activities to be conducted in a particular way.

Step 5 Report academic review of definitions

Not relevant where there is no significant or generally recognised contention regarding meaning.

Step 6 Remove unwarranted inclusions

No such inclusions remain.

Step 7 Remove mixed content/ process meanings

None present.

Step 8 Reduce divergence/ consider additional inclusions

Field/ specialty check (b) is the only check appropriate for this term.

Step 8(b) Consider field/ specialty usage

The definition is appropriate for people, animals and machines.

Step 9 Check against the five rules

The definition is operational rather than by genus and difference and so a check against the 5 rules is not appropriate. Nevertheless, it does actually satisfy them.

Step 10 Report the derived definition

The derived definition is as follows:

- Control (v) = to ensure that actions occur in a particular way.

12.4 Define 'Regulate'

Step 1 Define derivative or component terms

This is not a derivative or compound term.

Step 2 Survey lexical usage

Lexical usage is surveyed in Table 12.3 in the Appendix.

Step 3 Analyse lexical usage

Most of the definitions in Table 12.3 are in the general form of a sub-set of control, namely control by some particular method. Words used in this Table to define regulate include control, maintain, set, adjust, direct or govern (the control words) by a rule, principle, law, restriction, method or as required or in a particular way (policy or method).

Control is the most common word used and the other terms, maintain (in the sense it is used above), set and adjust are covered by the definition of control above. Also, direct and govern have been separately defined and so the term control will be used in the first part of the definition.

Step 4 Develop a connotative (intensional) conventional definition

Table 12.2 also includes definitions that could be taken to be the purpose or intension of regulating something, that is, to bring order, method, or uniformity. However, as uniformity can be obtained by means other than regulating, such as armed force, or government undertaking activities directly (rather than by regulation), a definition by intension would result in too broad a definition here, and so the means of regulating need to be defined by extension.

To regulate will therefore be defined as "control by rule, principle, law, restriction, policy or method". This is a definition by genus and difference.

Step 5 Report academic review of definitions

Not relevant where there is no significant or generally recognised contention regarding meaning.

Step 6 Remove unwarranted inclusions

There are no such inclusions of this term remaining.

Step 7 Remove mixed content/ process meanings

None present.

Step 8 Reduce divergence/ consider additional inclusions

None of the four checks are necessary for this term.

Step 9 Check against the five rules

This is a definition by genus and difference and satisfies Rules 1 to 5.

Step 10 Report the derived definition

The derived definition is as follows:

- Regulate = control by rule, principle, law, restriction, policy or method.

12.5 Define 'Regulation'

Step 1 Define derivative or component terms

Regulation is derived from the root word 'regulate' with the suffix '-ion' added. '-ion' is a noun forming abstract suffix. Abstract suffixes may denote "act, state, quality, etc." (Nesfield).

In this case, state or quality are inapplicable, without the qualification of a preceding adjective, such as good or bad. Regulation could be defined as "the act of regulating", but this does not seem complete; it is satisfactory for the uncountable sense of the word, but not for the countable sense. Passing an act of parliament (using a different sense of the word act) containing a regulation is only one way that a government may regulate activity or behaviour; it can also offer inducements rather than legislating prevention. So the countable form of the noun is more limited in scope than either the uncountable form or the verb and it would therefore be appropriate to select a sub-set of the attributes of the verb by a process of elimination.

While establishing a guiding principle can regulate an activity, regulations are generally more detailed, specifying exactly what will or will not happen and so (countable) regulations are not really principles. Regulations may also say what will happen and so restriction will not be selected. It could be argued that regulations express or set policy, but policy is much broader than regulation and so will also not be selected. This leaves rule, law, and method, all of which do describe a particular government regulation. So the countable form could be defined as "a rule, law or method". However, given the above difficulty, an analysis of lexical usage will still be conducted.

Step 2 Survey lexical usage

Lexical usage is surveyed in Table 12.4 in the Appendix.

Step 3 Analyse lexical usage

The lexical usage confirms the suitability of the above derivative definitions. Analysis of Table 12.4 shows use of the term 'process' could also be used for the uncountable sense. However, this is covered by the word 'method' anyway.

Step 4 Develop a connotative (intensional) conventional definition

The definition for the uncountable form then becomes "the act or process of regulating". This is an acceptable synonymous definition.

The definition of the countable form remains as as "a rule, law or method". This is an acceptable operational definition.

Step 5 Report academic review of definitions

Not relevant here where there is no significant or generally recognised contention regarding meaning.

Step 6 Remove unwarranted inclusions

There are no such inclusions of this term remaining.

Step 7 Remove mixed content/ process meanings

None present.

Step 8 Reduce divergence/ consider additional inclusions

As per the root term 'regulate', none of the four checks are necessary for this term.

Step 9 Check against the five rules

The definition is synonymous rather than by genus and difference and so a check against the 5 rules is not appropriate. Nevertheless, it does actually satisfy them.

Step 10 Report the derived definition

The derived definition is as follows:

Regulation = a rule, law or method (countable) and the act or process of regulating (uncountable).

12.6 Group Rules Post Definition

Cross check 1 Consistency within group

1. The definitional method has not resulted in any inconsistency between terms in this group.
2. Cross check 2 Consistency with terms outside the group

There is no known overlap of meaning of any of the above group of terms with any other term outside the group that would prevent the definitions being accepted.

12.7 Summary of Definitions

The derived definitions are as follows:

- Legitimate (a): condoned by those with authority and accepted by their affected group.
- Legitimacy (n): the quality of being legitimate, or the quality of being condoned by those with authority and accepted by their affected group.
- Authority: (n) the right to make decisions, give orders and enforce obedience
- Power: (n) the capacity to act (whether exercised through authority, force or influence)
- Influence: (v) to affect the thoughts or actions of an entity and (n) the effect of one entity upon another.
- Direct: (v) to give orders, commands or instructions
- Direction: (n) an order, command or instruction
- Control: (v) to ensure that actions occur in a particular way.
- Regulate: (v) control by rule, principle, law, restriction, policy or method.
- Regulation: (n) a rule, law or method (countable) and the act or process of regulating (uncountable).

12.8 Building the Machinery of Power

If these power terms can be drawn in a map that adequately represents the full power space, this would support the veracity of the definitions and highlight any inconsistencies. This was done and the result appears in Fig. 12.1.

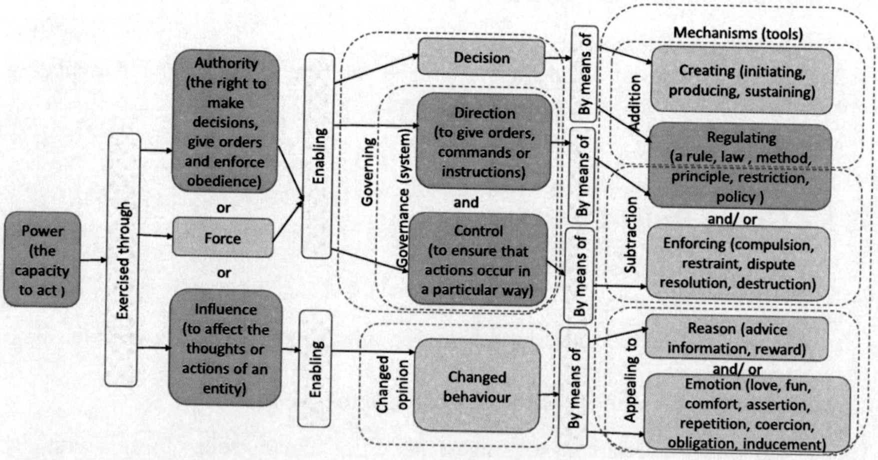

Fig. 12.1 The machinery of power

This figure was developed by starting with the terms just defined. However, including only these terms would have given only a partial picture of the power arena. There are many terms associated with power whose meanings are not contested, confused or commonly understood in contradictory ways, and these do not require the analysis engaged in above. Consequently, all these terms were listed and the relationships between them considered to determine logical groupings. These were then iterated to remove inconsistencies until no identifiable contradiction remained.

The first group selected was the means of exercise. This then enabled follow-on groupings of like terms describing different mechanisms or tools. These were then categorised into broader groups that were labelled enablers.

The mechanisms were subdivided into tools which were then further subdivided into what was labelled as channels. This served to classify the multiplicity of terms relating to power that are currently in use as there were far too many to be presented in a diagrammatic extension of Fig. 12.1. These appear in Table 12.5.

Notes on the Fig. 12.1 Model are as follows:

(1) Terms formally defined in these chapters are shown in darker grey boxes and other uncontested terms are shown in lighter grey.
(2) The dotted boxes indicating governing and governance came from the McGrath and Whitty (2015) definitions (See Chap. 10).
(3) The view of Foucault (1978) as analysed in James (2011) is accommodated in the dotted boxes in the right-hand column. His "right of death" flows through to enforcement. His "power over life" is accommodated by the top and bottom dotted boxes on the right-hand side, resolving the difficulty of considering this as not acting through formal institutions. Resistance flows across the top of the diagram, in the same way as governmental power. Subversion flows across the bottom of the diagram. The model applies to both individuals and community and so no distinction is drawn between his two types of normative power; (self) discipline, which flows through to the subtraction dotted box, and bio-political power or administration, which flows through to the addition dotted box. Individuals everywhere can flow through the top (authority) part of this diagram e.g. in parenthood. The opinion box accommodates his (and Locke's) view regarding matters that need to be governed and those which can be left to opinion.
(4) French and Raven (1959) theory is accommodated with expert and referent power being considered as capacities that increase power on the left. Their other categories, considered as tools, appear in the bottom right, except for legitimate, which falls into the boxes above it. Obligation was added to the bottom right-hand box as it is not necessarily reward or coercive or corrupt and may result from circumstances such as family ties or normal business favours returned. Assertion and repetition were also added as these are not necessarily coercive, such as existing belief or un-true myth, repeated and believed. Fun or enjoyment has also been added as it can also change opinion, and advice is not necessarily just information.

(5) The three power circuits of Clegg (1989) are accommodated as follows: micro or episodic power corresponds with flow across the bottom of diagram through opinion; dispositional power aligns with the subtraction elements of governance and facilitative power with the producing element of governance. As Clegg (1989) notes, power may exist in any or all of these.
(6) Nietzsche's "will to power" (Nietzsche & Kaufmann, 1968) is not shown as this provides motivation or intentionality to drive the machine of power, but does not describe its mechanisms.
(7) Lukes' three dimensions do not appear in the model. Normative considerations have been excluded and, as Clegg (1989) notes, "Lukes … endorses moral relativism". However, his three dimensions have been used below as an investigative process in considering how to drive the machinery of power.
(8) Authority is considered legitimate and no moral position is taken on the means of its acquisition or exercise, such as invasion or rigged elections. Similarly, no view is taken of groups that consider themselves to be oppressed by whatever factor – war, gender, age, ethnicity, sexual preference, social group or class. The model simply looks at what power is, how it is exercised, what its enablers are, and what its tools or mechanisms are.
(9) The power to, over and with, as proposed in Allen (1998) and Allen (1999) is partially accommodated within the model. 'Creating' corresponds to 'power to' and regulating and enforcing corresponds to 'power over'. However the flow across the bottom from influence to reason and emotion does not exactly correspond with the collective action and solidarity aspects that motivated development of the 'power with' category. Nevertheless, it does not exclude it, but points to its incompleteness compared to the whole gamut of influence, and perhaps to its normative feminist intention. However, once organisation of a movement comes into play, this is actually 'power to' being exercised across the top of the diagram to the mechanism of creating. Also Pansardi (2012) states that "acts of resistance are undoubtedly cases of *power over*", however, this cannot be so as those resisting have no formal power. The 'power over' is being exercised by others. Resistance occurs in response to 'power over'. The subjects of oppression have two choices, to submit or to resist in some way by taking (creating) some form of action (resistance). Resistance is not explicitly mentioned either in Fig. 12.1 or Table 12.5 as it is 'power to', exercised as an action of creating something, taken in response to enforcement or 'power over' exercised by another.

It is evident from the above notes that the model accommodates all theories of power surveyed. This confirms the observation on the disparate positions of many previous authors "that all these perspectives all contain acute observations concerning significant aspects of power" by Haugaard (2010).

Table 12.5 in the Appendix expands Fig. 12.1 by itemising channels through which each of the tools of power can be applied.

Notes on Table 12.5 are as follows:

(1) All tools can be used with 'good' or 'bad' intent and can have 'good' or 'bad' outcomes.

(2) No distinction is made between individuals and groups. Groups comprise individuals and this is a fractal application.
(3) Channels may apply to individuals, groups, organisations, roles, functions, items, actions or base motivations.
(4) Governments must deal with all tools of power, whether taking direct action, regulating, or choosing not to intervene. Individuals in their own lives must similarly deal with all tools of power.
(5) Individual government departments as well as private and public companies must deal with all 'power tools' they have access to.
(6) Individuals must, in their personal lives, deal with all 'power tools', whether taking direct action, regulating, or choosing not to intervene.
(7) Project, Program, Portfolio, Asset, Operations and General management are all categories of management, not tools of power.
(8) While project management aligns with creating, and general management aligns with regulating and enforcing, any management (or strategy) is not a mechanism, tool or channel: Strategy and management are techniques for selecting mechanisms, tools and channels.

12.9 Testing the Machinery of Power

Applying the chosen method has covered the first three of the four Popper (1992) 'tightness' criteria for scientific theory (Popper, 1992) as follows:

(1) Internal consistency, through group rules pre and post definition
(2) Ensuring logical form without tautology, through Step 6 Removing unwarranted inclusions, Step 7 Removing divergent meanings and Step 9 Checking against the Copi and Cohen (1990) five rules
(3) Comparison with other theories, through checking term usage across multiple fields in Step 8.

Given that this work has extended beyond definition into proposing what is, in effect, a new framework for dealing with power terminology, it is necessary to satisfy Popper's fourth requirement, namely to test this theory by way of empirical applications of the conclusions that can be derived from it. The device of the thought experiment will be used to do this. A number of thought experiments are conducted below. These are drawn from a range of circumstances across general and project management, covering private and public companies as well as government departments.

12.9.1 Government

12.9.1.1 Political Parties

Within a democracy, in the absence of a coup, force is not an option for changing government, and so power is exercised only through the other two remaining ways – authority and influence. Politicians and their parties have their own organisational and personal power (capacity to act) which they use to influence voters to give them authority via election. Success substantially increases their power as it vests control of the machinery of government for a term of office.

A political party seeking a democratic term of office does not have access to all mechanisms of power. Any new regulation or enforcement measures have no way of being approved in a neutralised caretaker period and no new proposal can be initiated (actually created). So the party must use the portion of the creation mechanism that is available to it, namely creating a campaign, and attempting to sway the electorate with the other two available mechanisms – emotion and reason, and may use whatever tools and channels they wish within those mechanisms.

12.9.1.2 Advocacy

Similarly, an advocate seeking to promote a particular social cause, whether in an election period or not, does not have regulation and enforcement available and must use the same three mechanisms as a political party, create a campaign and appeal to emotion and reason.

12.9.1.3 Political Party Leadership

The circumstances surrounding the downfalls of Prime Ministers Kevin Rudd, Julia Gillard and Tony Abbott in Australia will be briefly considered. All had the authority of office but reached the point where they did not succeed in influencing a sufficient number of their colleagues and/ or voters to their view of the world, resulting in their authority being removed and them suffering a consequent reduction in (removal of) their capacity to act (power).

12.9.1.4 Government Ministers and Department Heads

Government ministers have the enablers of power at their disposal – the machinery of their government department, the authority to govern it, make decisions, and drive the governance system, directing and controlling as they see fit. They also have the attention of the media which can be utilised in any attempt to change community perceptions, behaviour or attitudes. They also have all five mechanisms of power legitimately available and cannot avoid pressure to make decisions on any one of them. Similarly, a government department head, at the direction of the minister, has access to all five mechanisms.

This short analysis of government examples has found no difficulty in mapping the instances considered to the means of exercise of power outlined in Fig. 12.1, providing no reason to reject it.

12.9.2 General Management

12.9.2.1 Private and Public Companies

Private and public companies operate within a regulatory and enforcement framework they do not control, and so these mechanisms are not available to them externally. This is the case even if the company provides security or enforcement services. Companies may navigate creatively though the legislative environments they operate within, exploiting loopholes, creating competitive advantage and seeking market domination where they can, however they can still be gazumped by government action. Internally, the only form of regulation and enforcement they can control is their own governance. Within their external environment, these companies have only three mechanisms available: they create by producing products or services to customers, and they may seek to influence these customers, as well as regulators, using reason and emotion.

12.9.2.2 Company Chair and CEO

A company chair has all five mechanisms legitimately available internally and three externally, as mentioned above. All available mechanisms will need to be used or addressed in some way.

This short analysis of general management provides no reason to reject the model.

12.9.3 Project Management

Project managers also operate within a regulatory and enforcement framework they do not control and so, as outlined for general management above, have all five mechanisms legitimately available internally and only three externally, as mentioned above. All available mechanisms will need to be used or addressed in some way. The others need to be addressed via risk management.

This short analysis of project management provides no reason to reject the model.

Having found no negation of the model from any of the above thought experiments, consideration can now be given to how the machine of power might be driven.

12.10 Driving the Machinery of Power

Figure 12.1 shows the machinery of power with its five mechanisms of transmitting power as follows:

(1) Creating
(2) Regulating
(3) Enforcing

(4) Reason
(5) Emotion

The model shows only the components of the machinery of power and does not deal with the various ways in which the machine of power may be operated. This depends upon what it is operated to achieve. Metaphorically, it gives a picture of car, without instructions on how to drive it.

Transmitting power via any of these mechanisms requires work to be done and energy to be expended. So these will be rearranged in an economy of effort, as required of an individual, which will be called the order of ease, or the order of laziness. This will be done by asking the question "Why would I bother using any other power tool requiring more effort if this one already gets me what I want?" This results in the following order:

(1) Enforcing
(2) Regulating
(3) Emotion
(4) Reason
(5) Creating

This gives a hierarchy of power mechanisms. It implies that, given a choice and assuming availability of all mechanisms, in the absence of any other reason to act otherwise, an individual is likely to first determine if they have sufficient capacity to enforce or regulate the particular circumstance, then determine whether emotion or reason or is needed or whether they actually have to go to the trouble of creating something. More than one mechanism may be used for good measure, and there is also a loop from the re-arranged 5 back to 1.

The choice of power mechanisms and tools, the 'power use strategy', the chance of breaking out of the order of laziness and choosing the mechanisms and tools most likely to be effective for the task at hand, will be affected by factors such as:

(1) What we perceived worked previously/ in younger life
(2) Attempting to get what was previously desired and denied ('righting' an earlier perceived 'wrong')
(3) Conditioning or habit
(4) Values, beliefs and standard of proof
(5) Awareness and learning, as well as
(6) The mechanisms and tools that are actually available at the time and
(7) One's skill at using them.

Any of these can, and the first four almost certainly will, skew our power use strategy away from choosing mechanisms and tools that are likely to work. The first four can easily draw us into considering only our needs i.e. what will advantage us. So we need a strategy that enables us to get past personal considerations.

An effective change strategy needs to target using mechanisms and tools that will also advantage whoever else is involved in whatever it is we are attempting to achieve or change. So we first have to determine who or what is involved, then understand what their positions are before we can select the power tools that may work on or for them.

The machine of power is driven to compete or achieve or change something. Whether the desired outcome is domination or construction, there will be some form of dissent and resistance. Lukes (2005) states that the liberal, the reformist and the radical all apply 'want regarding' principles, viewing people as "relating their interests to what they want or prefer", with the reformist considering "that not everyone's wants are given equal weight" and the radical considering the system works against some people, and so adding the proviso "were they able to make a choice".

Any person or group in either pro-active and reactive positions will have made or will have to make a choice of tools to progress their cause or purpose. For either group, a way to determine how to drive the machine can be obtained from Lukes (2005). This is enumerated not as separate liberal, reformist and radical views or dimensions, but as an investigative process, expanded slightly with a front and back end added as follows:

(1) Determine the stakeholders
(2) Analyse the decisions made and who they favour
(3) Investigate background values and agendas
(4) Investigate latent conflict and allegiances
(5) Determine the best power mechanisms and tools to effect the desired change
(6) Develop one's skills in their use.

Power can be regarded as a holistic concept, encompassing everything, as everything that exists has some power that forms the basis of its existence. The machinery of power can also be considered to be fractal, making no distinction between groups and individuals down to the level of the tools.

Furthermore, for any circumstance, all available mechanisms must be used or addressed in some way, on the simple basis that ignoring or attempting to exclude any one of them will be akin to pulling a random part out of a machine and still expecting it to function properly.

While it has been stated above that governments must address all of the tools of power categorised under the five mechanisms, there are many life and organisational circumstances where the choice of tools within any particular mechanism will be optional, as will the choice of channels for applying them. Government represents the whole of society within a geographical area and so must deal with all, whereas any particular individual or group does not represent the whole of society, does not have access to all of the mechanisms and tools, and so can only deal in those it has access to. Ignoring any mechanism or tool that an individual or group has access to, is likely to diminish the outcome achieved. In the same way that a government or society must deal with all the mechanisms and all their associated tools within their geographic area, an individual must similarly address all mechanisms and tools within the ambit of their individual lives, something over which we all have individual dominion. This can be further extrapolated to describe 'progress' of societies, and self- development or self-improvement or personal growth of individuals, as increasing skill in using and choosing the various mechanisms and their associated tools of power.

No normative discussion about the exercise of power is entered into here, except insofar as to propose that approaching normative issues using the above model may well result in some disagreements disappearing. Mapping the tools and channels that are possible to use in a particular circumstance and then mapping the tools that are actually being used would enable identification of other options that are not being used, without the need for moralising, proselytising, inquisitions or crusades. It would not presume the existence of any Platonic optimum or 'right' universal answer. Such optimum may not exist at all or there may be only a general optimum varying within a range for any particular circumstance considered. It is also possible that the law of equifinality may apply in some cases i.e. there may well be more than one way that will lead to the same end point.

12.11 Analysis and Conclusion

Following the chosen method has enabled separation of the concepts of power, authority, influence, direction and control and has clearly distinguished between them. Exploring the implications of these definitions has in turn enabled a representation of the machinery of power in Fig. 12.1, extended in Table 12.5 to include categorisation of many terms other than the ones defined. The prior lack of differentiation between key terms may well have previously prevented such a structured approach.

The process followed extended beyond the chosen method, satisfying all four of the Popper (1992) tightness criteria for scientific knowledge; three are covered by the method selected, and the thought experiment and test drive constitute the fourth.

Successful application of the selected method here supports the potential for it to be similarly applied as a means of reducing the number of "radically confused" or "essentially contested" concepts, to use the terminology of Gallie (1956). It is worth noting that an object that physically exists can't be 'essentially contested'; only a concept can be.

It became evident that many of the definitions of power were actually definitions of phrases that contained the word power. Articulating silent qualifiers avoids misunderstanding when using terms across different fields. The same applies to defining of concepts by intension wherever possible, as per the method adopted here, rather than by extension, which leads to unnecessary contest, confusion and consequent waste of productive capacity (power). The same also applies to ensuring content is separated from process by first ensuring the basics of process (simple grammatical rules and the rules developed in Part I of this book) are followed before getting bound up in either the complexities of content or arguments about them.

Adoption and use of the definitions developed in these chapters can contribute to:

- producing power terminology that:
    - removes the confusion between power, authority and influence
    - removes the confusion between power itself and the various types of power
    - separates the process of determining the meaning of a word from the content (types of power), which is where intentionality, morality and ethics – considerations of 'good' versus 'bad' – actually belong.
- removing power from the arena of essentially contested concepts
- moving debate from whether or not a methodology for developing a consistent, generic group of terms should be applied, to whether the derivation:
    - omits any necessary terms from the group
    - omits any fields from consideration
    - contains any flawed reasoning.

This work may present a challenge to any normative work on power which has not distinguished between authority and power. The distinction derived here is difficult to accept and the temptation to use these terms interchangeably is difficult to resist, as this is so entrenched in common usage.

The diagrammatic model of power developed here has built upon previous work by many others in a way that identified gaps and perhaps indicates the dangers of Platonic reasoning without experimentation. However, it has not invalidated any previous theories, but rather shown how they fit together.

This work can assist in identifying and avoiding both under-utilisation and inappropriate use of tools and channels of power, potentially saving organisational time, resources and consequently, money. It could also therefore usefully contribute to resolving or avoiding political or domestic conflict in some circumstances by enumerating the many possible alternative ways of exercising power that participants may not have considered or explored.

There are other terms that have a relationship with the governance and power arenas that are the subject of similar definitional confusion, such as ethics and strategy, together with other terms that overlap with general management, such as stakeholders, responsibility and accountability. These are dealt with in the following chapters in Part II of this book.

Appendix

Table 12.1 Definitions of 'direct'

Dictionary	**Definition of the verb 'direct'** (All sourced on 8/1/2014 ex Macquarie on 24/4/2018)
Business	None
Cambridge	1. going in a straight line towards somewhere or someone without stopping or changing direction 2.without anyone or anything else being involved or between
Collins	verb *(mainly transitive)* 1. to regulate, conduct, or control the affairs of 2. *(also intransitive)* to give commands or orders with authority to (a person or group) 3. to tell or show (someone) the way to a place 4. to aim, point, or cause to move towards a goal 5. to address (a letter, parcel, etc) 6. to address (remarks, words, etc) to someone 7. *(also intransitive)* to provide guidance to (actors, cameramen, etc) in the rehearsal of a play or the filming of a motion picture 8. *(also intransitive)* 1. to conduct (a piece of music or musicians), usually while performing oneself 2. *another word (esp US) for* conduct
Concise Oxford	Address, control, govern the movements of, turn, tell the way, guide, give orders

(continued)

Table 12.1 (continued)

Dictionary	**Definition of the verb 'direct'** (All sourced on 8/1/2014 ex Macquarie on 24/4/2018)
Dictionary.com	*verb (used with object)* 1. to manage or guide by advice, helpful information, instruction, etc 2. to regulate the course of; control 3. to administer; manage; supervise 4. to give authoritative instructions to; command; order or ordain 5. to serve as a director in the production or performance of (a musical work, play, motion picture, etc.). 6. to guide, tell, or show (a person) the way to a place 7. to point, aim, or send toward a place or object 8. to channel or focus toward a given result, object, or end (often followed by *to* or *toward*) 9. to address (words, a speech, a written report, etc.) to a person or persons 10. to address (a letter, package, etc.) to an intended recipient. *verb (used without object)* 11. to act as a guide. 12. to give commands or orders. 13. to serve as the director of a play, film, orchestra, etc
Longman	**1** [transitive always + adverb/preposition] to aim something in a particular direction or at a particular person, group etc **2** [transitive] to be in charge of something or control it **3** [intransitive and transitive] to give the actors in a play, film, or television programme instructions about what they should do **4** [transitive] *formal* to tell someone how to get to a place **5** [transitive] *formal* to tell someone what they should do [= order]
Macmillan	1 going straight to a place and not stopping or changing direction on the way there 2 involving only the two people or things mentioned and with no one or nothing else coming in between 3 exact 4 direct heat or light comes straight at a person or object and is not reflected or reduced in strength 5 saying what you really think in a very clear and honest way 6 related through your parents, grandparents etc and not through other relatives such as uncles or aunts
Macquarie	**1.** to guide with advice; regulate the course of; conduct; manage; control. **2.** to give authoritative instructions to: **3.** to command; order or ordain: **4.** to tell or show (a person) the way to a place, etc. **5.** to organise and supervise the artistic production of (a play or film). **6.** to point or aim towards a place or an object; cause to move, act, or work towards a certain object or end. **7.** to address (words, etc.) to a person. **8.** to mark (a letter, etc.) as intended for or sent to a particular person. *–verb* (*i*) **9.** to act as a guide or director. **10.** to give commands or orders. *–adjective* **11.** proceeding in a straight line or by the shortest course; straight; undeviating; not oblique. **12.** proceeding in an unbroken line of descent; lineal, not collateral. **13.** following the natural order, as in mathematics. **14.** without intervening agency; immediate; personal. **15.** going straight to the point; straightforward; downright.

(continued)

Table 12.1 (continued)

Dictionary	**Definition of the verb 'direct'** (All sourced on 8/1/2014 ex Macquarie on 24/4/2018)
Merriam-Webster	: to cause (someone or something) to turn, move, or point in a particular way : to cause (someone's attention, thoughts, emotions, etc.) to relate to a particular person, thing, goal, etc. : to say (something) to a particular person or group Full Definition of *DIRECT* transitive verb 1 *a obsolete* : to write (a letter) to a person *b* : to mark with the name and address of the intended recipient *c* : to impart orally *d* : to adapt in expression so as to have particular applicability <arguments *directed* at the emotions> 2 *a* : to regulate the activities or course of *b* : to carry out the organizing, energizing, and supervising of <*direct* a project> *c* : to dominate and determine the course of *d* : to train and lead performances of <*direct* a movie> 3: to cause to turn, move, or point undeviatingly or to follow a straight course 4: to point, extend, or project in a specified line or course <*direct* the nozzle down> 5: to request or enjoin with authority <the judge *directed* the jury to acquit> 6: to show or point out the way for <signs *directing* us to the entrance> intransitive verb 1: to point out, prescribe, or determine a course or procedure 2: to act as director
Oxford	1 control the operations of; manage or govern • supervise and control • train or conduct 2 *[with object and adverbial of direction]* aim (something) in a particular direction or at a particular person • tell or show (someone) how to get somewhere • address or give instructions for the delivery of (a letter or parcel • focus (one's thoughts) on or address (one's efforts) towards something. • *archaic* guide or advise in a course or decision
The free dictionary	*v.tr.* 1. To manage or conduct the affairs of; regulate. 2. To have or take charge of; control. 3. To give authoritative instructions to. 4. To cause to move toward a goal; aim. 5. To show or indicate the way for. 6. To cause to move in or follow a straight course 7. To indicate the intended recipient on (a letter, for example). 8. To address or adapt (remarks, for example) to a specific person, audience, or purpose. 9. a. To give guidance and instruction to (actors or musicians, for example) in the rehearsal and performance of a work. b. To supervise the performance of. *v.intr.* 1. To give commands or directions. 2. To conduct a performance or rehearsal.

(continued)

Table 12.1 (continued)

Dictionary	**Definition of the verb 'direct'** (All sourced on 8/1/2014 ex Macquarie on 24/4/2018)
Wiktionary	1. To manage, control, steer. 2. To aim (something) at (something else). 3. To point out or show to (somebody) the right course or way; to guide, as by pointing out the way. 4. To point out to with authority; to instruct as a superior; to order. 5. (*dated*) To put a direction or address upon; to mark with the name and residence of the person to whom anything is sent.

Table 12.2 Definitions of 'control'

Dictionary	**Definition of 'control'** (All sourced on 4/3/2013 ex Macquarie on 24/4/2018)
Business	Manufacturing: Device or mechanism installed or instituted to guide or regulate the activities or operation of an apparatus, machine, person, or system.
Cambridge	to order, limit, or rule something, or someone's actions or behaviour
Collins	1. to command, direct, or rule 2. to check, limit, curb, or regulate; restrain 3. to regulate or operate (a machine) 4. to verify (a scientific experiment) by conducting a parallel experiment in which the variable being investigated is held constant or is compared with a standard 5. 1. to regulate (financial affairs) 2. to examine and verify (financial accounts) 6. to restrict or regulate the authorized supply of (certain substances, such as drugs)
Concise Oxford	Dominate, command; hold in check; check, verify; regulate
Dictionary.com	1. to exercise restraint or direction over; dominate; command. 2. to hold in check; curb. 3. to test or verify (a scientific experiment) by a parallel experiment or other standard of comparison. 4. to eliminate or prevent the flourishing or spread of. 5. *Obsolete* to check or regulate (transactions), originally by means of a duplicate register.
Longman	**1** to have the power to make the decisions about how a country, place, company etc is organized or what it does: **2** to limit the amount or growth of something, especially something that is dangerous: **3** Make somebody/ something do what you want, or make something happen in the way that you want **4** if you control your emotions, your voice, your expression etc, you succeed in behaving calmly and sensibly, even though you feel angry, upset, or excited: **5** to make a machine, process, or system work in a particular way: **6** to make sure that something is done correctly:

(continued)

Table 12.2 (continued)

Dictionary	**Definition of 'control'** (All sourced on 4/3/2013 ex Macquarie on 24/4/2018)
Macmillan	1. power to make decisions 2. power over machine etc 3. law limiting something 4. ability to stop problem 5. ability to remain calm 6. switch on machine 7. in scientific test 8. computer key 9. check rules are applied
Macquarie	*verb* (*t*) **(controlled, controlling)1.** to exercise restraint or direction over; dominate; command. **2.** to hold in check; curb. **3.** to test or verify (a scientific experiment) by a parallel experiment or other standard of comparison. *–noun* **4.** the act or power of controlling; regulation; domination or command. **5.** check or restraint. **6.** something that serves to control; a check; a standard of comparison in scientific experimentation. **7.** a person who acts as a check; a controller. **8.** (*plural*) a coordinated arrangement of devices for regulating and guiding a machine, as a motor, aeroplane, etc. **9.** *Motor Racing, etc.* an appointed place at or from which officials time contestants, check conformity and required conditions, and in general, regulate a race. **10. → control centre.** **11.** (in spiritualism) an agency believed to assist the medium at a seance. **12.** *Philately* an authenticating letter or number printed on the selvage of a sheet of stamps to indicate the plate or cylinder from which the stamps were printed, or the series to which they belong. *–adjective* **13.** characterised by the desire to dominate and exert control:
Merriam-Webster	: to direct the behavior of (a person or animal) : to cause (a person or animal) to do what you want : to have power over (something) : to direct the actions or function of (something) :to cause (something) to act or function in a certain way Full Definition transitive verb 1 *a archaic* **:** to check, test, or verify by evidence or experiments *b* **:** to incorporate suitable controls in 2 *a* **:** to exercise restraining or directing influence over **:** REGULATE *b* **:** to have power over **:** RULE *c* **:** to reduce the incidence or severity of, especially to innocuous levels

(continued)

Table 12.2 (continued)

Dictionary	**Definition of 'control'** (All sourced on 4/3/2013 ex Macquarie on 24/4/2018)
Oxford	1 Determine the behaviour or supervise the running of: 1.1 Maintain influence or authority over: 1.2 Limit the level, intensity, or numbers of: 1.3 Remain calm and reasonable despite provocation: 1.4 Regulate (a mechanical or scientific process):
The free dictionary	1. To exercise authoritative or dominating influence over; direct . 2. To adjust to a requirement; regulate: 3. To hold in restraint; check : 4. To reduce or prevent the spread of: 5. a. To verify or regulate (a scientific experiment) by conducting a parallel experiment or by comparing with another standard. b. To verify (an account, for example) by using a duplicate register for comparison.
Wiktionary	To exercise influence over, to suggest or dictate the behavior of , oversight.

Table 12.3 Definitions of 'regulate'

Dictionary	**Definition of 'regulate'** (All sourced on 4/3/2013 ex Macquarie on 24/4/2018)
Business	None given
Cambridge	to control something, especially by making it work in a particular way
Collins	1. to adjust (the amount of heat, sound, etc., of something) as required; control 2. to adjust (an instrument or appliance) so that it operates correctly 3. to bring into conformity with a rule, principle, or usage
Concise Oxford	Control by rule, subject to restrictions, moderate, adapt to requirements; adjust (machine, clock) so that it may work accurately
Dictionary.com	1. to control or direct by a rule, principle, method, etc. 2. to adjust to some standard or requirement, as amount, degree, etc. 3. to adjust so as to ensure accuracy of operation. 4. to put in good order.
Longman	1 to control an activity or process, especially by rules: 2 to make a machine or your body work at a particular speed, temperature etc.:
Macmillan	1 to control an activity, process, or industry officially by using rules 2 to control a machine so that it works effectively a. to control something so that it produces the results that you want b.to control the way your body works

(continued)

Table 12.3 (continued)

Dictionary	Definition of 'regulate' (All sourced on 4/3/2013 ex Macquarie on 24/4/2018)
Macquarie	**1.** to control or direct by rule, principle, method, etc. **2.** to adjust to some standard or requirement, as amount, degree, etc.: *to regulate the temperature.* **3.** to adjust so as to ensure accuracy of operation: *to regulate a watch.* **4.** to put in good order: *to regulate the digestion.*
Merriam-Webster	: to set or adjust the amount, degree, or rate of (something) : to bring (something) under the control of authority : to make rules or laws that control (something) Full definition 1 *a* : to govern or direct according to rule *b (1)* : to bring under the control of law or constituted authority *(2)* : to make regulations for or concerning : to bring order, method, or uniformity to 3: to fix or adjust the time, amount, degree, or rate of
Oxford	1 Control or maintain the rate or speed of (a machine or process) so that it operates properly 1.1 Control (something, especially a business activity) by means of rules and regulations 1.2 Set (a clock or other apparatus) according to an external standard
The free dictionary	1. To control or direct according to rule, principle, or law. 2. To adjust to a particular specification or requirement: 3. To adjust (a mechanism) for accurate and proper functioning. 4. To put or maintain in order:
Wiktionary	1. To dictate policy. 2. To control or direct according to rule, principle, or law. 3. To adjust to a particular specification or requirement temperature. 4. To adjust (a mechanism) for accurate and proper functioning. 5. To put or maintain in order:

Table 12.4 Definitions of 'regulation'

Dictionary	**Definition of regulation** (All sourced on 4/3/2013 ex Macquarie on 24/4/2018)
Business	Principle or rule (with or without the coercive power of law) employed in controlling, directing, or managing an activity, organization, or system.
Cambridge	An official rule or the act of controlling something
Collins	1. the act or process of regulating 2. a rule, principle, or condition that governs procedure or behaviour 3. a governmental or ministerial order having the force of law
Concise Oxford	Regulating or being regulated; prescribed rule, authoritative direction
Dictionary.com	**1.** a law, rule, or other order prescribed by authority, especially to regulate conduct. **2.** The act of regulating or the state of being regulated. **3.** *Machinery*. The percentage difference in some quantity related to the operation of an apparatus or machine, as the voltage output of a transformer or the speed of a motor, between the value of the quantity at no-load operation and its value at full-load operation.
Longman	1 [countable] an official rule or order: 2 [uncountable] control over something, especially by rules
Macmillan	1[COUNTABLE] an official rule that controls the way that things are done 2[UNCOUNTABLE] control of an activity, process, or industry by official rules
Macquarie	**1.** a rule or order, as for conduct, prescribed by authority; a governing direction or law. **2.** the act of regulating. **3.** the state of being regulated.
Merriam-Webster	: an official rule or law that says how something should be done : the act of regulating something Full definition 1 **:** the act of regulating **:** the state of being regulated 2 *a* **:** an authoritative rule dealing with details or procedure *b* **:** a rule or order issued by an executive authority or regulatory agency of a government and having the force of law 3 *a* **:** the process of redistributing material (as in an embryo) to restore a damaged or lost part independent of new tissue growth *b* **:** the mechanism by which an early embryo maintains normal development
Oxford	1 A rule or directive made and maintained by an authority: 1.1 *[as modifier]* in accordance with regulations; of the correct type: 1.2 *[as modifier]* • *informal* of a familiar or predictable type; formulaic: 2 *[mass noun]* the action or process of regulating or being regulated:
The free dictionary	**1.** The act of regulating or the state of being regulated **2.** A principle, rule, or law designed to control or govern conduct **3.** A governmental order having the force of law.
Wiktionary	1. (*uncountable*) The act of regulating or the condition of being regulated. 2. (*countable*) A law or administrative rule, issued by an organization, used to guide or prescribe the conduct of members of that organization.

Table 12.5 Mechanisms, tools and channels of power

Mechanisms	Tools	Channels
Creating – Constructive action	Initiation	Taking action
		Appointing, engaging, enlisting or securing an agent(s)
		Policy development
		Strategy
		Planning
		Communication
		Finance
		Establishing a new or changing an existing organisation or structure
		Taking over an existing organisation or position
		Leading, taking or accepting responsibility
		Asserting a position on a matter
		Resisting a person or organisation
	Production	Construction or improvement of assets (physical, electronic, intellectual)
		Extraction and use of resources
		Manufacture and supply of products
		Agricultural production and distribution of food or bio-energy
		Provision of services (including sport)
		Team formation, partnerships and marriage
		Contracts
		Finance
	Sustainment	Operation of assets
		Maintenance of assets
		Health care (physical and mental)
		Life growth and amenity care
		Veterinary care
		Environmental care
		Education, learning, training, teaching, coaching, lecturing, mentoring
		Emergency services
		Finance
		Respect, esteem
		Exercise, fitness, strength, mind and body conditioning and training
Regulating	Rule	Organisational governance
	Law	Parliamentary bills – acts and regulations
	Method	Standards
		Prescriptive processes
		Industry methodologies
		'Best practice'

(continued)

Table 12.5 (continued)

Mechanisms	Tools	Channels
	Principle	Values, ethics, morals
		Beliefs
		Intuition
		Self-discipline
	Restriction	Individual codes of conduct
		Parliamentary bills – acts and regulations
		Gravity
		Polarity
	Policy	Deciding and documenting preferred ways of handling circumstances
Enforcing	Compulsion	Military
		Police
		Customs
		Prisons or detention institutions
		Punishment
		Torture (violence)
		Abuse (physical, mental or verbal) (violence)
		Parents
		Organisational management positions
	Restraint	Behaviour review panels, tribunals and mechanisms
		Standards review panels, tribunals and mechanisms
		Licencing
		Parents
		Auditors and auditing
		Withholding desired things
		Setting boundaries
		Disapproving, shaming, embarrassing
	Dispute Resolution or Judgement or Interpretation Of rules	Courts Appeal panels, tribunals and mechanisms Referees, adjudicators, arbitrators, mediators Contract Principal's representatives Selection panels Parents Teachers or coaches of any kind who evaluate students, sports people or performers

(continued)

Table 12.5 (continued)

Mechanisms	Tools	Channels
	Destruction	Taking the life of citizens, including self-defence (violence)
		Killing enemies in war or conflict (violence)
		Dismissing an employee or ending a relationship
		Pest eradication
		Noxious plant eradication
		Demolition
Reason	Advice	Suggesting action, approach or viewpoint
	Information (true and false)	Public relations
		Education
		Deception
		Pay
	Reward	Election promises
Emotion	Love	Relationship(s)
		Sex, intimacy, affection
		Action taken in the best interests of another
	Fun or enjoyment	Relationship(s)
		Infatuation
		Sex, intimacy, affection
		Play, movement and dance
		Sounds – Speech, music
		The arts, beauty, looks, appearances, proportions, form
		Matching energy, pace, rhythm or interests (compatibility)
		Community fellowship or belonging
	Comfort	Religion
		Emotional support
	Assertion	Advertising
		Symbols
	Repetition	Propaganda
		Pestering
		Story telling
		Advertising
	Coercion	Threat or fear
	Obligation	Guilt
	Inducement	Greed

References

Allen, A. (1998). Rethinking power. *Hypatia, 13*(1), 21–40.

Allen, A. (1999). *The power of feminist theory: Domination, resistance, solidarity*. Westview Press.

BusinessDictionary.com. (*Online dictionary* [Online]. Available: http://www.businessdictionary.com [Accessed].

Cambridge. (*Online dictionary* [Online]. Available: http://dictionary.cambridge.org/dictionary/british [Accessed].

Clegg, S. (1989). *Frameworks of power*. Sage.

Collins. (*English dictionary* [Online]. Available: http://www.collinsdictionary.com/dictionary/english [Accessed].

Concise Oxford Dictionary. (1964). *Concise oxford dictionary*. Oxford University Press.

Copi, I. M., & Cohen, C. (1990). *Introduction to logic*. Macmillan.

Dictionary.com. (*Online dictionary* [Online]. Available: http://dictionary.reference.com [Accessed].

Foucault, M. (1978). *The history of sexuality*. Pantheon Books.

French, J. R. P., & Raven, B. (1959). The bases of social power. In D. Cartwright (Ed.), *Studies in social power, Research Center for Group Dynamics*. Institute for Social Research, University of Michigan.

Gallie, W. B. (1956). Essentially contested concepts. *Proceedings of the Aristotelian Society, 56*, 167–198.

Haugaard, M. (2010). Power: A 'family resemblance' concept. *European Journal of Cultural Studies, 13*(4), 419–438.

James, R. (2011). *Juridical, disciplinary and biopolitical power: Basic background on foucault* [online], UNC. Available: https://www.youtube.com/watch?v=X31ayDsG67U [Accessed 20/01/2016].

Longman. (*Dictionary of contemporary English online* [Online]. Available: http://www.ldoceonline.com [Accessed].

Lukes, S. (2005). *Power: A radical view*. Palgrave Macmillan.

Macmillan. (*Dictionary* [Online]. Available: http://www.macmillandictionary.com [Accessed].

Macquarie. (*Dictionary online* [Online], Sydney. Available: http://www.macquarieonline.com.au [Accessed].

McGrath, S. K., & Whitty, S. J. (2015). Redefining governance: From confusion to certainty and clarity. *International Journal of Managing Projects in Business, 8*(4), 755–787.

Merriam-Webster. (*Online dictionary* [Online], Britain. Available: http://www.merriam-webster.com [Accessed].

Nesfield, J. C. (1982). *Outline of english grammar for home and office*. Macmillan.

Nietzsche, F. W., & Kaufmann, W. (1968). *The will to power*. Random Press. [S.l.].

Oxford. (*Dictionaries online* [Online], Oxford. Available: http://oxforddictionaries.com [Accessed].

Pansardi, P. (2012). Power to and power over: Two distinct concepts of power? *Journal of Political Power, 5*(1), 73–89.

Popper, K. R. (1992). *The logic of scientific discovery*. Routledge.

TheFreeDictionary. (*Online dictionary* [Online]. Available: http://www.thefreedictionary.com [Accessed].

Wiktionary. (*Online dictionary* [Online]. Available: http://en.wiktionary.org [Accessed].

Chapter 13
Ethics, Morality, Values, Principles and Beliefs

13.1 Introduction

Definitional confusion has been recognised as a source of difficulty for millennia, dating back to the time of Socrates. Yet the meaning of words can seem so obvious to us in our own thinking that it is difficult to pause long enough to even consider this. Our language treats all words as parts of speech, whether they label uncertain abstract concepts or physical objects about which there is little doubt. The urge to 'just get on with it' when discussing abstract concepts can easily gazump the necessary first step of ensuring we have common understanding of them – a process of agreeing what our words will mean. This step is unnecessary for physical objects, where we can quite simply verify with others the sound we use to signify it by just pointing at it. Conceptual terms can mean different things to different people; and this may be undetected, somewhat contested or even fiercely or essentially contested (Gallie, 1956). This chapter does not deal with labelling according to how fierce or how widely known the contest may be, or whether the confusion has reached the stage of being essentially contested. Rather, it deals with conceptual terms around which there is some amount of contention, which indicates a lack of commonly understood (i.e. agreed) meaning. These are referred to as contested terms.

In defining governance, McGrath and Whitty (2015) (See Chap. 10) clearly distinguished between government, governing, governance, strategy and ethics. They also pointed to the prior intermingling of ethics and governance and the need for a similar definitional exercise to be conducted on the word ethics. The purpose of this chapter is to carry out such an exercise for ethics and a group of related terms, to test their method to see if it can be successfully applied to a different contested subject.

Before proceeding to definition, the literature on ethics and definitional confusion will first be investigated.

S. K. McGrath, *Speaking Management*,
https://doi.org/10.1007/978-981-16-2213-7_13

13.2 Literature Review of Ethics and Definitional Confusion

In writing on utilitarianism, Mill noted that "little progress has been made in the decision of the controversy respecting the criterion of right and wrong… And after more than two thousand years the same discussions continue" (Mill et al., 1987). He indicated the close connection between ethics and morality and says of the intuitive and inductive schools of ethics:

> They recognize also, to a great extent, the same moral laws; but differ as to their evidence, and the source from which they derive their authority. According to the one opinion (intuitive), the principles of morals are evident *a priori*, requiring nothing to command assent, except the meaning of the term to be understood. According to the other doctrine (inductive), right and wrong as well as truth and falsehood, are questions of observation and experience (Mill et al., 1987).

In acknowledging "the tacit influence of a standard not recognized", he noted that "the non-existence of an acknowledged first principle has made ethics not so much a guide as a consecration of men's actual sentiments" (Mill et al., 1987).

A similar sentiment was expressed by Wittgenstein (2007) who noted: "if I contemplate what Ethics really would have to be if there were such a science, this result seems to me quite obvious. It seems to me obvious that nothing we could ever think or say should be the thing".

Ayer (1971) maintained "there is nothing in the nature of philosophy to warrant the existence of conflicting philosophical 'schools'". He held that for Hume's relations of ideas "the a priori propositions of logic and mathematics (are) necessary and certain only because they are analytic… (because) they do not make any assertion about the empirical world, but simply record our determination to use symbols in a certain fashion" (Ayer, 1971). For determining Hume's matters of fact, he proposed

> a modified verification principle. For I require of an empirical hypothesis, not indeed that it should be conclusively verifiable, but that some possible sense-experience should be relevant to the determination of its truth or falsehood. If a putative proposition fails to satisfy this principle, and is not a tautology, then I hold that it is metaphysical, and that, being metaphysical, it is neither true nor false but literally senseless (Ayer, 1971).

More recently, Robinson and Garratt (2013), in asking "Why has ethics become a mess?" noted:

> According to McIntyre, this kind of Greek moral certainty has been eroded by sceptics like Hume and Ayer. Kant made morality a cold and unsympathetic exercise in reason, and the utilitarians reduced it to a set of pseudo-scientific calculations that don't work. All such doctrines, whether 'Enlightenment' or 'Victorian', are also wrong to think that their particular brand of ethics is 'objective', when they are peculiarly 'local' (Robinson & Garratt, 2013).

They then noted "this has led to a society empty of moral values in which people are sometimes utilitarians, sometimes Kantians, sometimes Platonists, and mostly utterly confused" (Robinson & Garratt, 2013).

In proposing a taxonomy of ethical theories, Hare (1997) noted similarly to Mill in saying:

> I am not for a moment denying the importance of using rational argument to decide on substantial moral principles. That is the ambition of all serious moral philosophers. But there is a prior task: that of finding the rules governing the argument. Without these rules, anything goes. ... an ontological dispute like the supposed dispute between realists and anti-realists, if it is a genuine dispute at all, turns fairly rapidly into a dispute which is not ontological but conceptual, and that there is no way of clearly formulating this supposed dispute ... without translating it into a dispute about how moral words get their meaning (Hare, 1997).

In evaluating moral theories, he said "They all reveal different parts of the truth about morality" Hare (1997). This indicates that he does not differentiate between ethics and morality.

This exercise here is not concerned with evaluating Hare's taxonomy, or any ethical theory for that matter. But it is seeking to define terms so that we can all have the same understanding of what it is we are actually talking about when having academic, corporate, political and personal discussions on the subject.

Smith (2014) noted "The definition was an important matter for Plato", "Concern with answering the question "What is so-and-so?" are at the centre of the majority of Plato's dialogues" and "Aristotle himself traces the quest for definitions back to Socrates".

John Locke asked the question:

> And here I desire it may be considered, and carefully examined, whether the greatest part of the disputes in the world are not merely verbal, and about the signification of words; and whether, if the terms they are made in were defined, and reduced in their signification (as they must be where they signify anything) to determined collections of the simple ideas they do or should stand for, those disputes would not end of themselves, and immediately vanish (Locke, 1690).

Copi and Cohen (1990) noted similarly in saying that "definitions, by exposing and eliminating ambiguities, can effectively resolve disputes that are merely verbal". Hobbs also recognised this was not some mere theoretical exercise; he set out the purpose of resolving definitional confusion as follows: "by exact definitions first snuffed, and purged from ambiguity; reason is the pace; increase of science, the way; and the benefit of mankind, the end" (Hobbes, 1996).

In pointing out the need to separate ethics from governance as well as the need to properly define ethics, McGrath and Whitty (2015) highlighted the danger of taking the understanding of a term used by one particular group (auditors) for purposes appropriate to their environment (joint-stock companies), as having general or 'universal' application in other circumstances (e.g. government). This had the effect of promoting the interests of that group while causing confusion for other groups and eventually for the initial beneficiary group itself. The process of ignoring silent or hidden qualifiers, was identified as a major facilitator of that error, along with the failure to separate content (ontology) from process (epistemology).

Variations in meaning can have a confusing effect. While an unconstrained language formation process can have some local utility, it can also produce haphazard and conflicting understandings in different groups. If such inconsistency is identified, it is as well to address this as part of the ongoing language formation process to avoid future confusion and misunderstanding. John Stuart Mill similarly noted:

> In order that we may possess a language perfectly suitable for the investigation and expression of general truths, there are two principal, and several minor, requisites. The first is, that every general name should have a meaning, steadily fixed, and precisely determined. … and the second …, is that we should possess a name wherever one is needed; wherever there is anything to be designated by it, which it is of importance to express (Mill, 1874) (Book IV Chapter IV §1).

He noted that names in common use have often a loose connotation, giving the examples of civilization and gentleman. He continued:

> It would, however, be a complete misunderstanding … to think that because a name has not at present an ascertained connotation, it is competent to anyone to give it such a connotation at his own choice. The meaning of a term actually in use is not an arbitrary quantity to be fixed, but an unknown quantity to be sought.
>
> … To fix the connotation of a concrete name, or the denotation of the corresponding abstract, is to define the name. When this can be done without rendering any received assertions inadmissible, the name can be defined in accordance with its received use, which is vulgarly called defining not the name but the thing. What is meant by the improper expression of defining a thing … is to define the name, subject to the condition that it shall denote those things (Mill, 1874).

The importance of defining such that no received assertions are rendered inadmissible was similarly dealt with by Karl Popper in saying:

> We live in a kind of intellectual prison … formed by the structural rules of our language … it is an odd prison as we are normally unaware of being imprisoned. We may become aware of it through culture clash. But then, this very awareness allows us to break out of the prison. If we try hard enough, we can transcend our prison by studying the new language and by comparing it with our own. Admittedly, the result will be a new prison. But it will be a much larger and wider prison. And again, we will not suffer from it. Or rather, whenever we do suffer from it, we are free to examine it critically, and thus to break out again into a still wider prison. The prisons are the frameworks (Popper & Notturno, 1994).

Finally, it is worth noting that Spinoza et al. (1959) wrote a whole book about ethics without defining it, even though he defined many other terms.

In summary, the literature review suggests the possibility that lack of adequate definition of ethics may have contributed to contention surrounding it. This supports proceeding with the definitional attempt.

13.3 Approach

In their discussion of governance, McGrath and Whitty (2015) demonstrated the pitfalls of defining single intellectual conceptual terms within the bounds of one single field and in isolation from other terms. They developed a method of refining the definitions of contested terms, noting that they only did so because of the absence of a pre-existing method. This chapter will apply that method to the definition of ethics and associated terms, testing its veracity and exploring the outcome.

This approach has objectivist epistemology with a positivist theoretical perspective that seeks to define objective content without claiming that the derived definitions describe anything existential. It simply defines concepts non-normatively, producing definitions which, if agreed and adopted, have the potential to remove unnecessary debate and confusion. It takes the view that, while there may be no absolute truth, to be productive as a society, a discourse that removes confusion is necessary, one that all can participate in, with shared understanding of meaning, removing accidental and undetected differences. This position is therefore midway between (or partly both) realist and post-modernist, as this apparatus (ensuring consistency and universality of terminology), can replace chaos with order.

13.4 Method

The method is fully set out in McGrath and Whitty (2015). The structure followed in the text below reproduces that method, which first considers the group of terms to be defined, before proceeding to define individual terms and concluding with a group consistency check.

Note that for ease of reading, derived definitions and subsequent refined and other contributing definitions are shown in pale grey highlight in the text. Similarly, the main contenders for inclusion in the derived definition are also shown in pale grey highlight in the Tables in the Appendix which survey lexical usage.

Lexical usage is surveyed from the following dictionary sources:

1. A range of dictionaries that have been well known for many years that were available (in 2013/ 14) online (Cambridge, Collins, Longman, Macmillan, Macquarie, Merriam-Webster, Oxford)
2. A range of various online dictionaries (BusinessDictionary.com, Dictionary.com, TheFreeDictionary, Wiktionary) and
3. The Concise Oxford Dictionary (1964) – as a comparator for how these definitions may have changed over the last 50 years.

13.5 Group Rules Pre-definition

Group pre-definition rule 1 – Select the group of terms to be defined

Terms related to ethics requiring inclusion in this group are ethics, principles, values, beliefs and morals. Discussion of these terms inevitably lead to consideration of the terms good and bad, right and wrong. Right and wrong will not be considered as they imply absolute value judgements which the selected method specifically excludes. No separate definitional exercise will be carried out on the terms good and bad as a brief glance at dictionary definitions indicates a multitude of definitions by extension and a dearth of definition by intention. However, Spinoza did define these terms by intention, defining good as "that which we certainly know to be useful to us", and bad as "that which we certainly know will prevent us from partaking any good" (Spinoza et al., 1959). These will be accepted but updated to contemporary wording, defining 'good' as *that which we consider to be useful* and 'bad' as *that which we consider to be a hinderance.*

The group of terms to be selected for definition will therefore be ethics, morals, principles, values and beliefs. The qualification of who or what any particular action may be good or bad for will not be addressed, nor will the degree of personal restraint that may be considered desirable.

Group pre-definition rule 2 – Determine the order of definition

Rule 2 (a) – Identify group term inconsistencies

None present, although usage of several of the terms can overlap.

Rule 2(b) – Compound terms

None present.

Rule 2(c) – Root of Derivative terms

Principle, value, belief and moral will also be defined, but not ethic, which is rarely used in singular form. These will be defined before the plural forms.

Rule 2(d) – Define verb form of term before the noun form

All terms are adjectives or nouns.

Applying these rules is insufficient to provide a full definitional order. Beliefs may be based on principles and so beliefs will be defined after principles but before morals, which can be based on beliefs. To determine the full order, a choice will therefore be made on the basis of non-normativity, which is a feature of the method. The term that has least normative association, namely principles, will be defined first, followed by values, then ethics, then beliefs then morals. This produces an order satisfying the above requirement of defining beliefs after principles but before morals. The order of definition will therefore be principle, principles, value, values, ethics, belief, beliefs, moral and morals.

Group pre-definition rule 3 – Definitional terms requiring prior definition

There are no known terms outside this group that have multiple meanings and are commonly used in defining these terms. Good and bad, which have already been defined above, are normative terms that the method excludes from use.

13.6 Define Principles

Step 1 Define derivative or component terms

Principles are the plural form of principle and both will be defined.

Step 2 Survey lexical usage

Lexical usage is surveyed in Tables 13.1a and 13.1b in the Appendix.

Step 3 Analyse lexical usage

Any reference to values or morals will be avoided as these will be defined below. To remain non-normative, any religious meanings or references to good or bad will not be considered. Truth will also not be selected, as an assumption or a proposition that is untrue can serve as a principle. Source and origin are less specific than other terms and so will not be used. Common terms in Table 13.1a are rule and law. Rule will be selected as it avoids the ambiguity of whether the law referred to is legal or a law of nature. The latter also implies a need for scientific rigour in determining that it is actually a law and principles can exist without scientific rigor. Furthermore, any such scientific laws may just be the best representation or framework available at the time. They may be superseded or found to be incomplete or inaccurate in some circumstances, such as Newtonian mechanics in the face of Einstein's theory of relativity. The other terms used in Table 13.1a will be examined to see if they are as generic as rule.

The term principle has the connotation of providing guidance. The terms source, origin, basic idea, (fundamental) essence, proposition, assumption, essential quality or element all may or may not have such connotations and they are all either less generic or less specific than a rule. A principle can be a basic or guiding belief, theory, idea, maxim, concept, standard, or code but it does not have to be so. An assumption can be a principle and so these terms are less generic and will not be selected. A principle can be a basis for action but providing a basis has an association of being less compelling and is also less specific than the term rule. This exhausts the options in Table 13.1a and so rule will be accepted.

Step 4 Develop a connotative (intensional) conventional definition

Principle can be defined as a rule guiding something. Principles can be defined as a set of rules guiding something. The options from Table 13.1a regarding what is being guided are conduct, behaviour, action, management and prediction. Management is not a term that is commonly used in relation to determining one's actions and is not generic so will not be used. Prediction is one form of action that may be guided by a principle but excludes other types of action and so will not be used. Conduct and behaviour exclude prediction and have an association with value judgement. Both are covered by the term action which is neutral. A principle will therefore be defined as *a rule guiding action.* To avoid confusion, the plural form principles will be defined in terms of the singular definition as a set of rules guiding action. This produces no conflict with the definitions in Table 13.1b.

Step 5 Report academic review of definitions

All EBSCO databases were searched on 15/11/2016 for the terms "principles" and "define" in the title. 82 were found of which 50 were non-identical. None contained any review of definitions. All dealt with defining principles in particular circumstances, rather than with defining the term itself. A similar search was conducted for "definition" and "principles" and 248 were found of which 166 were non-identical. Again, none contained any review of definitions and all dealt with defining principles in particular circumstances, rather than with defining the term itself. One item dealing with the principles of definition is relevant to the general question of definition of all terms. This was by John Stuart Mill and has been mentioned in discussing definitional confusion regarding ethics (Sect. 13.2).

Step 6 Remove unwarranted inclusions

There are no such inclusions remaining.

Step 7 Remove mixed content/process meanings

None present.

Step 8 Reduce divergence/consider additional inclusions

No further checks are necessary beyond what has been covered in Steps 3 and 4.

Step 9 Check against the five rules

The definitions are by genus and difference and satisfy Rules 1 to 5.

Step 10 Report the derived definition

The derived definitions are as follows:

- Principle = (n) *a rule guiding action.*
- Principles = (n) *a set of rules guiding action.*

13.7 Define Values

Step 1 Define derivative or component terms

While the term 'values' is a plural noun derived from the adjective 'value' by adding an s, both can have slightly different meanings and so both will be defined. The verb form to value is not contested and will be ignored.

Step 2 Survey lexical usage

Lexical usage is surveyed in Tables 13.2a and 13.2b in the Appendix.

Step 3 Analyse lexical usage

Any definition specific to any field such as commerce will not be selected. Analysis of Table 13.2a indicates something is of value when it has worth, usefulness (utility), importance, desirability or merit, whether the purpose is (commercial) exchange or not. Quality affects value but is not, on its own, the essence of value itself. Similarly, "the regard that something is held to deserve" well expresses the non-economic aspect of value but does not really accommodate use of the term commercially. The value of something to a particular person may be an individual matter and so any absolute 'value judgement' will be avoided as normative and/ or tautological. This leads to rejecting most of the definitions of the plural term 'values' in Table 13.2b as principles or standards in favour of a definition that simply indicates it is a preference. I may value (prefer) ice cream over protein at a particular time and while there may be a health dimension to these relative values, there is no underlying principle, standard or moral dimension. I may value sport highly at times and relaxation at others; I may also value things that others may perceive as moral or ethical or I may simply not give them quite as high a value as somebody else, without actually devaluing them. So evaluation of subjective individual choices is best handled without the complication of moral judgement hijacking emotions off to some doubtful or contestable conclusion. Arbitrary introduction of 'moral' judgement unnecessarily complicates matters by producing multiple layers of definitions that do not assist in resolving overlap between terms. Any question of morality will therefore be left to the definition of morals below. A definition of values that accommodates preference or importance will therefore be developed.

Step 4 Develop a connotative (intensional) conventional definition

The options not yet ruled out from Table 13.2a are worth, usefulness (utility), importance, desirability or merit. An ornament may have high worth though being emotionally important while also being practically both useless and unimportant. It may be desirable and have great merit, but I may prefer someone else kept it as it may be useless and/or inconvenient to me, even though I may recognise its value. Alternatively, I may consider something to be a work of art and want to invest in it. This short discussion indicates the difficulty of defining value using any of these terms other than worth, which is independent of all the ways in which value can be determined, albeit that worth currently does have a heavier connotation of having a price than value does. Value will therefore be tentatively defined synonymously as *worth*. This is a definition of the uncountable sense of the term.

The plural term 'values' has connotations beyond worth which introduces preferences and actions. Personal and corporate values can include things such as perseverance or discipline. A value such as discipline may not be as important for a creative, artistic person as it may be for a scientist, but this may apply only in those individual's careers and not in other areas of their lives. Values such as diligence, integrity, sustainability, excellence, innovation, open mindedness, learning, growth, creativity and positivity are desirable but secular rather than moral, as are family and work-life balance. Self-interest and making a profit are also values i.e. things that motivate people and organisations to take particular actions. The definition also needs to accommodate the circumstance where we are not conscious of what is really driving us, which may require time, experience, contemplation, awareness, or instruments such as revealed preference surveys to elucidate. Values will therefore be tentatively defined as *preferences guiding the actions of an entity*. The countable singular sense of this term will be taken to mean a particular preference guiding the action of an entity, but as this actually defines a phrase, 'a value', which is generally not used, it will not be listed as a separate definition.

Step 5 Report academic review of definitions

All EBSCO databases were searched on 14/11/2016 for the terms "values" and "define" in the title. 337 were found of which 200 were non-identical and none contained any such review. Many dealt with the defining numerical values of particular variables or with values that define something, rather than with actually defining values. A similar search was conducted for "definition" and "values" and 629 were found of which 409 were non-identical. Most were medical dealing with values of variables used as predictors for various conditions. There was no review of definitions and only four that dealt with the definition of value. These were by Urban, Perry, Sheldon and Sebek, who will be considered in chronological order.

Urban (1907) discussed value from a psychological perspective, seeking to determine the thought process used to determine the worth of an object to a particular subject. He did this by "study of the grammar of worth consciousness (to) find both the nature of the processes through which these funded meanings are acquired and the basis of their classification" (Urban, 1907). He said "Worths are said to be subjective or objective, real or ideal, actual or imputed, intrinsic or instrumental" (Urban, 1907) and proceeded to analyse these. He noted the process of, for any object, "its actual value arising from its capacity to satisfy separate desires" (Urban, 1907). (Note: This is quite close to the academic definition derived below). He noted that "worth judgments express not attributes of objects apart from the subject (even when the value is described as actual and objective) but rather functions of the relation of subject to object" (Urban, 1907). He classified worth objects into three groups; beauty of grace or form; sensory and perceptual activities of consumption; and over-individual (or group) (Urban, 1907).

He discussed whether desire or feeling constitute the worth experience and concluded in favour of feeling rather than desire. "Desire is determined by feeling or feeling dispositions. But we have already seen that worth cannot, in every case be identified with actual desire, but only with the capacity of being desired, desirability" (Urban, 1907).

> The essence of desire is the feeling of lack or want. We '*feel* the need' of something. What further qualifies desire is the kinaesthetic sensations which are irrelevant accompaniments from the standpoint of the essential worth moment... But it is by no means in the same sense true that every worth experience involves explicit desire. We may actually feel the worth of an absent friend without the slightest trace of that qualification of our feeling which we describe as actual desire, although of course a conative disposition is presupposed and may become explicit under suitable conditions. The same is true of aesthetic and mystical states of repose where actual desire is in abeyance. ... In so far, therefore, as our definition is concerned with the desire moment, we must enlarge it to read – an object has worth in so far as it is either desired or has the capacity of calling out desire, has, in other words desirability. This definition includes the mystical and aesthetic states of repose already referred to, for no object can become the object of such feelings which has not been desired and may not under some circumstances be again desired (Urban, 1907).

This purported definition may be a rigorous, meticulous and insightful description of the worth experience and how it arises, but it is an articulation of that process, not a definition of the word 'value'. He also notes "my appreciation of the worth of an object does not necessarily, and in every case, rest upon such explicit judgment of existence, but at most upon a primary undisturbed *presumption* of reality" (Urban, 1907). This reflects the fact that we act on what we think is true, but it may not actually be so.

Our definition does not need to include all of these considerations; that would constitute definition by extension rather than intension. It simply needs to not preclude any of them. All are aspects of the worth experience and are not excluded from the above proposed synonymous definition of value as worth and so this source provides no reason to change either tentative definition.

Perry (1914) did survey definitions and came very close to, but actually stopped short of, giving a complete definition. Nevertheless, he gave sufficient detail for a definition to be constructed from his work. He first despatched the arguments that the term is indefinable, then the view that value consists in *the relation of harmony or fitness* as well as the view that it consists in *the good or best of its kind*. He pointed out that all three views ignore bias or interest and "The belief that this fact, or its characteristic relation, is value has most commonly found expression in the pleasure theory or hedonism" (Perry, 1914). He identified the shortcomings in this ancient view, considering good and evil, pleasure and pain before concluding:

> It is held at the present day with something approaching unanimity that value in the generic sense has to do with a certain constant that we may call bias or interest. We have found that efforts to define value in other terms, and even the argument for its indefinability, point unmistakably to this constant. The justification of this view lies in the fact that bias or interest, with its manifold varieties, conditions, and relations affords the best means of systematically describing that region of our world which the value sciences and the value vocabulary roughly denote. In any case it will doubtless appear that most of our differences of opinion will lie within this view (Perry, 1914).

In addressing definition, he said:

> It is one thing to assert that the fulfilment of interest is essential to value and another thing to say that it constitutes a sufficient definition. In other words it is possible to maintain that satisfaction of interest as such is value, or to maintain that value is a qualified satisfaction of interest (Perry, 1914).

He found inconsistencies in the former and rejected it on grounds including that "The judgment cannot be its own object" (Perry, 1914). He then dealt with the latter and explored the sense of where "a particular liking is not in itself a guarantee of value" (Perry, 1914). However in an attempt to generalise, he went into an unsuccessful attempt to deal with quantification, which lead him into universals and absolutes, clouding the issue and perhaps causing him to not proffer an actual definition, even though he clearly favoured something based upon "a qualified satisfaction of interest" that accommodated the fact that there might be a scale or norm independent of the individual that determines it.

That conundrum will be resolved by drawing upon elements of his earlier discussion of satisfaction of interest concerning having versus getting. I can satisfy an acquisition interest in something by acquiring it (getting it). I can then take pleasure in seeing it or using it (having it), satisfying whatever desire that having it enables me to do. I may find that desire and satisfaction is maintained, increases or even diminishes to the point where I no longer desire it. In that latter case, its emotional and/ or functional value to me diminishes even though it may still have potential interest to others, giving it an economic value to me on a scale judged by others. In circumstances of acquisition, it is therefore the potential to fulfil a future interest (whether it is currently satisfying that interest or not) that gives anything its value to me and therefore is value for me. The thing that no longer satisfies my current interest for now and the future may well fulfil someone else's current interest for now and the future.

Substituting this into the above latter definition of Perry (1914) derives the following definition of value: *the potential satisfaction of interest.* However, this could be considered incomplete in social interactions where some people may be considered to add value in particular circumstances, such as through conversation or performance, and some not. It would not be reasonable to contend that such an experience being enjoyed now does not provide value now because it is being experienced now rather than having the potential to do so. This leads to the definition needing to cover both circumstances, producing a definition of value as *the actual or potential satisfaction of interest.* However, we may then ask whether it is actually necessary to include the two qualifiers. The need to qualify seemed to arise from seeking an external scale to judge against:

> But there is perhaps one fundamental motive after all: the desire, namely, to discover a criterion by which superiority or inferiority shall be assigned to values themselves … It seems to be necessary to provide for a scale or hierarchy in which inclination shall be subordinated to duty, impulse to a 'norm', or enjoyment to an ideal (Perry, 1914).

However, this overlooks the fact that something can be of great value to me that is of little or no value for the same purpose on any objective scale or to anyone else, such as my very comfortable but worn-out old clothes that I may still wear! Omission of the qualifiers avoids the need to specify actual or potential and to thereby rule out interests that may only be imagined. The derived definition is therefore simply *satisfaction of interest.*

This does not constrain the interest to being only that of the individual. It does allow for the interests of others to be a determinant on some external scale. However, it includes no sense of scale. I may consider someone has given me good or poor value, but this is qualified by my understanding of what good means to me in that particular circumstance. Defining exclusive of the silent qualifiers 'good' or 'poor' requires reference to the existence of some sort of scale without actually specifying what that is. So the definition will be modified to be *the degree to which an interest is satisfied.* However, the term degree has other meanings and so would be best replaced with a different word denoting scale.

Quantity, quantum and amount are possible options. Quantity will be selected as quantum has a particular meaning in physics not implied here and amount can imply money. This leaves the derived definition as *the quantity of satisfaction of an interest.*

This chain of reasoning comes full circle to satisfying the desire in Perry (1914) above for a scale qualifying interest, but without accepting universals or absolute judgements.

Sheldon (1914) stated "it seems impossible to give an account of value which has the slightest prospect of general acceptance" and then heads down a similar path to Perry to "treat value as a concrete 'universal' " (Sheldon, 1914). He notes that:

> The objects which are considered valuable, good or bad, worthy of approval or disapproval, are generally acknowledged to belong to at least one of the following six classes: (1) those which "satisfy immediately any fundamental instinctive sense-tendency" of a living organism,7 (2) economic commodities, (3) esthetic or beautiful objects, (4) moral conduct, (5) religious objects, (6) intellectual values. This classification differs from Urban's, though not, I think, disagreeing with it; his analysis being psychological and genetic while ours is of objects rather than psychoses (Sheldon, 1914).

These six classes of objects overlap with each other and do not include things such as scientific discoveries, the discovered bones of ancient creatures, or natural resources. The paper purported to but did not actually define value. It merely gave various allegories such as:

> Do values then exist? Yes, if they are felt; just as much as gravitation, pressure, collisions exist. They may be physical tendencies, or any other kind; so long as they are verifiable as aiding or hindering other tendencies of any kind whatsoever. There is no gulf between value and fact (Sheldon, 1914),

"A perfect value, or a perfect being, consequently, must be actual (and) The fundamental axioms of all knowledge constitute a special case" (Sheldon, 1914). None of these provide anything to add to the definition derived from Perry, albeit that none of them are precluded by it.

Sebek (1973) noted that values "are an important factor in decision-making and selective behaviour". He referred to those with regulative influence as directive and those relating to the quality of objects as gratificational. He surveyed dimensions of values but these all served to sub-classify, requiring more extensions to a definition, rather than revealing the essence of the single word, leaving the proposed definition unchanged.

This review of academic sources has therefore produced a definition of value by genus and difference as *the quantity of satisfaction of an interest.* The synonymous definition derived from analysis of lexical usage was *worth.* A choice needs to be made. Worth has a heavier colloquial connotation of a sum of currency than the term value actually has and so the academic definition is preferable. Defining synonymously also just replaces one difficult to define term with another, rather than actually defining what it actually is. Worth was the best synonym to describe value, but the analysis of academic sources does provide a definition of what it actually is and for that reason will be taken forward as the new tentative definition.

Step 6 Remove unwarranted inclusions

There are no such inclusions remaining.

Step 7 Remove mixed content/process meanings

None present.

Step 8 Reduce divergence/consider additional inclusions

No further checks are required necessary beyond what has been covered in Steps 3 and 4.

Step 9 Check against the five rules

The definition of value is by genus and difference and satisfies the five rules. The definition of values is by genus and difference and satisfies the five rules.

Step 10 Report the derived definition

The derived definitions are as follows:

- Value = (n) the quantity of satisfaction of an interest.
- Values = (n)(pl) preferences guiding the actions of an entity.

13.8 Define Ethics

Step 1 Define derivative or component terms

Although this term has ethic as its stem and is a plural noun formed by addition of an s, the stem is not commonly used and so does not need to be separately defined here. Usage of the term is primarily in the plural form and some dictionaries define both singular and plural forms together and some do not distinguish between them at all. The plural form will be defined here.

Step 2 Survey lexical usage

Lexical usage is surveyed in Table 13.3 in the Appendix. Unless otherwise noted, it is the plural form that the particular dictionary has defined. The references to usage with singular and plural verbs in Dictionary.com and The free dictionary have not been included.

Step 3 Analyse lexical usage

There are two predominating sets of definitions in Table 13.3; one concerned with individual behaviour and the other with the study of it. Only the definitions of individual behaviour have been shaded grey, as the study of it is generally consequential. There is general agreement throughout the definitions in Table 13.3 in referring to principles, rules and standards. Principles are less specific than rules or standards and the nature of many ethical questions is not deterministic, so explicit rules or standards may not exist. When referring colloquially to a 'standard of behaviour', this has a generic intent and implies being a principle anyway.

There are also many references to morals in Table 13.3, however these will not be selected as principles of behaviour can come from sources other than morals. For example, rigour of definition is an important principle and while this may potentially contribute to reducing conflict in the world, and it would be useful if it came to be considered as a standard requirement of ethical discourse, it can hardly be considered to be derived from the conventional sense of morality. It just evolves from seeking functionality, then finding that first accommodating what is good for the whole group enables better outcomes to be achieved more quickly and with less effort.

Avoiding reference to morals also avoids using a term that has not yet been defined.

Step 4 Develop a connotative (intensional) conventional definition

Ethics will therefore be tentatively defined as "principles of behaviour". The question of whether those principles are true or valid or moral will not be addressed.

Step 5 Report academic review of definitions

All EBSCO databases were searched on 31/03/2016 for the terms "ethics" and "define" in the title. 20 were found and none contained any such review. All dealt with defining ethics in particular circumstances rather than with defining the term itself. One actually included the following words in its title "If you ask 20 people you pass in the hall to define ethics or ethical behaviour, you will more than likely get 20 different answers". Similar searches were conducted for "definition" and "ethics" and none were found.

This leaves us to look at other sources. The Oxford On-line dictionary gives the following summary of schools of ethics:

> Schools of ethics in Western philosophy can be divided, very roughly, into three sorts. The first, drawing on the work of Aristotle, holds that the virtues (such as justice, charity, and generosity) are dispositions to act in ways that benefit both the person possessing them and that person's society. The second, defended particularly by Kant, makes the concept of duty central to morality: humans are bound, from a knowledge of their duty as rational beings, to obey the categorical imperative to respect other rational beings. Thirdly, utilitarianism asserts that the guiding principle of conduct should be the greatest happiness or benefit of the greatest number.

McNutt (2010) noted:

> Mandeville's spokesman, Cleomenes (In *Fable of the Bees*), in discussing whether men are naturally good, encapsulates the theme:
>
> Horatio: But are there no Persons in the World that are good by Choice?
>
> Cleomenes: Yes, but then they are directed in that Choice by Reason and Experience, but not by nature, I mean, not by untaught Nature.

This points to the need to learn 'goodness' rather than being innately 'good', and learning can take much time, given the large range of circumstances that present during life. It also points to utility of approaches, rather than to innate or absolute value, as well as indicating cooperation, deferred gratification and wisdom. These elements will be explored below.

Aristotle advocated a middle or mean between excess and deficiency: "temperance and courage, then are destroyed by excess and defect, and are preserved by the mean" (Aristotle & Ross, 1999). Robinson and Garratt (2013) overviewed the field of ethics from Plato to the present time and considered "Aristotle's ideal is essentially a dull middle-aged sensible Athenian male citizen who is calm and rational, avoids extremes and knows how to behave from experience." They also noted:

> Aristotle's views seem strange because nowadays we don't confuse morality with self-fulfillment. ... In a post-Romantic age that celebrates individualism and personal choice, many of us would also reject the idea that 'good citizenship' is the ideal to aim for (Robinson & Garratt, 2013).

McNutt (2010) noted:

> Kant's rule-based ethics is independent of the consequences, his morality is not the same as self-interest and one is acting morally when one performs one's 'duty' and that there are 'moral laws that clearly define what is right and what is wrong'.

Robinson and Garratt (2013) similarly noted that "Morality for Kant is a serious business. It involves choosing duties not wants; motives and not consequences are the central distinguishing feature of a moral action. Morality is not about doing what comes naturally, but resisting what comes naturally". They also noted that "By using our reason and the 'Universability test', we have indirectly discovered a compulsory rule or 'categorical imperative'" (Robinson & Garratt, 2013). They also pointed out:

> Kant's system of compulsory rules seems monolithic and incredible because it doesn't allow for exceptions. It also doesn't help us choose between moral rules. Sometimes it is just not possible to keep a promise and to tell the truth at the same time (Robinson & Garratt, 2013).

Robinson and Garratt (2013) also noted that "In certain rare situations ... utilitarians are allowed to break traditional moral rules if by so doing they produce a balance of happiness over misery." They further noted:

> a moral philosophy that lets you break traditional moral rules 'on occasion' is rather disturbing. Would you like to share a raft with a utilitarian? Furthermore, is it true that Utilitarianism can make ethics 'scientific'? Mill tries to do this by a kind of semantic acrobatics – by declaring that the concept 'good' means the 'greatest happiness of the greatest number.' But what the majority want isn't always good (Robinson & Garratt, 2013).

McNutt (2010) recommended applying Kant's approach within governance, but that approach cannot be satisfactorily applied to the non-corporate behaviour of individuals. It is evident that all three views have difficulties in addressing the question "What should I do in this particular circumstance?" This difficulty arises from which interests are to be served by the possible actions and on what time-scale. However, this is not a question concerning the definition of a word. A better question to ask may perhaps be "What will the best course of action be to give me what I want with minimal adverse consequences to others?"

Interesting as these considerations are, they have no bearing upon the actual definition of the meaning of the single word ethics and so provide no reason to alter the tentative definition.

Step 6 Remove unwarranted inclusions

The adopted method is non-normative and so any reference to good or evil, right or wrong, will be avoided. Consequently, it will not be presumed that ethics must be 'good'. While ethics may be relatively so for particular groups, whether hegemonic or disadvantaged, this will be regarded as not necessarily absolutely or existentially so. This may result in difficulty, due to the colloquial usage of the term 'ethical' as meaning 'good' and 'unethical' meaning 'bad'. However, that difficulty arises when taking language from one field to another without articulating the assumed, silent qualifier, as shown in Chap. 10. In this case, referring to ethics as good will be regarded as just omitting the silent qualifier (good) of a word that is neutral (ethics) to produce something that is satisfactory for colloquial use within a particular community but requiring more specificity when taken outside that community. Interestingly, this also accords with the use of the term ethics as a field of study – which considers all aspects of what might be considered good and bad as well as what works.

Step 7 Remove mixed content/process meanings

Further consideration of 'good' is therefore warranted, particularly concerning its relative versus absolute usage. Bonner (2014) wrote ""We never know what we are talking about," cautioned English philosopher Karl Popper. … But … Wittgenstein had an answer for him: then shut up". This retort, for all its pithy brilliance, was perhaps a little disingenuous as Wittgenstein himself had previously come to a similar conclusion about ethics. He quoted Professor Moore's *Principia Ethica* thus: "Ethics is the general enquiry into what is good" (Wittgenstein, 2007). He then put forward various synonyms including "the enquiry into what is good", "the enquiry into what is valuable", "the enquiry into what is really important", along with several others that are more normative. He noted that all of his suggested expressions are used in an absolute sense: None contain any relativity to a predetermined standard or goal. He pointed out that "the word good in the relative sense simply means coming up to a predetermined standard (and) this is not how ethics uses them (his synonyms)" (Wittgenstein, 2007). He concluded that every statement of relative value is a statement of fact, contending that no statement of fact can ever be a judgement of absolute value. He reminded us of Hamlet's words "Nothing is either good or bad, but thinking makes it so". He then said: "if I contemplate what Ethics really would have to be if there were such a science, this result seems to me quite obvious. It seems to me obvious that nothing we could ever think or say should be the thing" (Wittgenstein, 2007). He claimed that "Ethics, if it is anything, is supernatural and our words will only express facts". He concluded that "Ethics … is no science". Popper (1992), with his scepticism regarding induction and his four tests of scientific knowledge, which none of the ethical schools of thought would pass, would have agreed. The general thrust of Wittgenstein (2007) therefore supports the tentative definition not containing any statement of absolute value, i.e. ethics not necessarily being considered to be only 'good'.

David Hume had a similar view, noting that "belief is nothing but a peculiar feeling, different from the simple conception" (Hume & Mossner, 1969). In a similar vein, Robinson and Garratt (2013) note:

> The one big rule of deductive logic is that no one is allowed to magic extra information from a premises into a conclusion. If you do this then your argument isn't valid. ... You can't prove moral beliefs using logic, which means you can't prove moral propositions by just piling up facts.

Robinson and Garratt (2013) also summarised the similar emotivist argument of A.J. Ayer thus:

> In Ayer's view, all "moral philosophy" had been some kind of linguistic and logical error. There is no such thing as moral "knowledge" or certainty, and there can be no moral experts who can tell us what is right or wrong.

They also pointed out that Ayer's emotivism ignores any idea of community or communal values (Robinson & Garratt, 2013) and that Sartre's existentialist view that every individual is unique "means that moral philosophy cannot be derived from a definition of 'human nature' " (Robinson & Garratt, 2013). In describing the evils of modernism in totalitarian states, they observed that "it was precisely because these societies had a firmly held belief in the **objectivity** of their utopian visions that they were so absolutist and coercive" (Robinson & Garratt, 2013).

The difficulty of the absolute view is further exemplified in the moral conundrum that so troubled Darwin – how a beneficent God could allow such cruelty in the natural world, as exemplified by the female wasp that anaesthetises its prey to keep it alive and fresh while it is being consumed, with "the larvae of ichneumonidae feeding within the live bodies of caterpillars" (Darwin & Beer, 2008). What is good for the ichneumonidae is not good for the caterpillar. There is no absolute 'good' here, unless one makes a value judgement on which entity has the greater value. As he pointed out, "natural selection works solely by and for the good of each being" (Darwin & Beer, 2008). As such, natural selection works on self-interest, not on morality or value judgement.

A similar view emerged from Blackmore (1999) who noted:

> Although the instruction to 'love thy neighbour as thyself' is commonly taken to mean 'love everyone', in the tribal context in which it was first written it may have been meant more literally – in other words love your own tribe, and your own family, but not everybody else (Hartung, 1995). Even the admonition not to kill may originally have applied only to the in-group. Hartung points out that the rabbis of the Talmud used to hold an Israelite guilty of murder if he intentionally killed another Israelite but killing other people did not count.

Belief in absolute 'good' requires full knowledge of content, and acceptance of a precedence or 'pecking order' of the worth of beings, whereas relative 'good' denotes a process of comparing or measuring against something, and so is independent of belief, content, value judgements and prejudice.

Something which is ‘good’ for a particular person or entity is generally associated with bringing them some benefit, which for Wittgenstein (2007) was a statement of fact, as it is a relative measure, gauged against whatever the entity had previously. The word ‘good’ will therefore only be used in its relative sense of ‘good for entity x’, meaning it provides some benefit to x, as accepted in Spinoza’s definitions of good and bad considered in Group Rule 1.

This discussion supports the proposed definition excluding the presumption or implication that ethics must be ‘good’ along with any consideration of absolute ‘good’, correct or moral value.

Step 8 Reduce divergence/consider additional inclusions

Checks (a) Historical usage and (b) Field/speciality usage are the appropriate checks for this term.

Step 8 (a) Historical usage

The Ten Commandments and the list of seven deadly sins have endured for millennia and have provided man with principles of behaviour. They qualify as ethics under the proposed definition.

The reference from Wittgenstein (2007) in Step 7 above to ethics as being supernatural, appears, from his context, to refer to God and religion, which has been the principal custodian of principles of interpersonal conduct. Wittgenstein (2007) went on to say that “Now I want to impress on you that a certain characteristic misuse of our language runs through all ethical and religious expressions. All these expressions seem, prima facie, to be just similes.” Wittgenstein’s view on the history of ethical thought does not conflict with the tentative definition.

Step 8 (b) Field/speciality usage – governance considerations

Ethics and governance are often enmeshed but the governance model presented by McGrath and Whitty (2015) draws a clear distinction between governance and ethics. They do not define ethics, but they do define governance as *the system by which an entity is controlled.* An organisation can make any rules (policies, procedures, codes of conduct etc.) on any subject. These may contain any level of variation between self-interest and the interests of others and strike some balance between competitive and cooperative behaviour. An organisation’s governance arrangements will commonly contain aspects of behaviour that are considered ethical or moral. These arrangements may be evaluated on the basis of whether they contain moral elements or not. But governance arrangements may or may not include measures dealing with ethics and morality; the governance arrangements themselves are simply the vehicle or means or process through which ethics can be expressed, if an organisation chooses to do so. The existence of rules or processes is not the same thing as their content. Where a company develops a code of ethical practice (CoEP) similar to that in the UK Financial Services Authority (FSA) handbook (McNutt, 2010), this would address typical moral conundrums that employees in that particular company are likely to face, providing a deterministic way of dealing with them that suits the rule-based nature of organisational governance arrangements. These simply become a change in or addition to pre-existing organisational governance arrangements.

This indicates no difficulty with the proposed definition.

Step 9 Check against the five rules

This is a definition by genus and difference and satisfies Rules 1 to 5.

Step 10 Report the derived definition

The derived definition is as follows:

- Ethics = *principles of behaviour.*

13.9 Define Beliefs

Step 1 Define derivative or component terms

Beliefs are the plural form of belief and both will be defined.

Step 2 Survey lexical usage

Lexical usage is surveyed in Tables 13.4a and 13.4b in the Appendix.

Step 3 Analyse lexical usage

Most of the dictionaries listed in Table 13.4b did not define the plural form and so by default regarded it as having the same meaning as the singular form. Only one explicitly stated this. The few that did give separate definitions gave definitions that were effectively the same as the singular form. One defined the plural form and not the singular form. Here the commonality of the definitions of singular and plural forms will be accepted and Tables 13.4a and 13.4b will be considered as providing potential definitions of both forms.

Review of these tables indicates that there are three elements of definition required; whatever it is, by whom it is held, and the fact that validity is accepted, with the level of required proof not being specified.

What is it?

Belief may commonly be associated with religion and may involve accepting the existence of some being, phenomenon and/or precepts. But beliefs can be held on matters other than religion and so inclusion of any directly religious terms in definition will be avoided, as will inclusion of related terms such as faith and moral conviction. Similarly, 'good' and 'right' will not be used as some beliefs may not involve these; for example, I may have formed a belief from my knowledge of person x that in a certain circumstance they will do y. A belief can be strongly and passionately held or felt or may be just something believed on the balance of probability. Consequently, the degree of certainty or strength of conviction will be avoided. This leads to rejection of the following terms; mental acceptance, strong, firmly held, certainty, being sure, confidence.

The remaining options from Tables 13.4a and 13.4b regarding what it is are: something, proposition, state or habit of mind, feeling, idea, view, opinion, mental act, condition of, claim, assumption, assertion and conviction. While a belief can be any one of these things, many of them detail the circumstances that a belief can arise from and so would constitute definition by extension. This rules out using idea, claim, assumption, assertion and conviction, leaving something, proposition, feeling, view, opinion, mental act, condition of and state or habit of mind. Mental act and condition of denote state of mind, and a belief can be independent of this. A belief in God would generally not be regarded as a state of mind, rather it would be a conclusion from some process of thinking, as would a belief that was based on some weight of scientific evidence. Feelings/ emotions can arise without being associated with a belief; I may have strong instantaneous feelings for another person without believing or even knowing anything about them at all. Furthermore, non-normative definition is being sought, independent of emotions. A belief may also have no emotion or feeling associated with it at all, such as "I believe $1 + 1 = 2$". The term something is non-normative but does not exclude all non-mental somethings and so is too generic. View is less desirable than opinion as it needs to be used in a phrase such as 'formed a view' to distinguish it from like and dislike as well as from simply viewing or seeing something. This leaves the terms proposition and opinion. Opinion has the connotation of having made a judgement. Use of opinion would provide a single word synonymous definition but religious people could argue that belief is a sub-set of opinion that deals with 'indisputable' propositions. Furthermore, strength of belief and emotion have already been ruled out above. This points to a need for a definition by genus and difference, saying what the term actually means rather than referring to another conceptual term with debatable meaning. It may be useful to consider a contractual analogy, where there must be both offer and acceptance. For a belief to occur, there must have been some proposition coming from somewhere that has been accepted. The term proposition will therefore be selected, and the questions of acceptance and validity will be addressed below.

The definition of belief has to cover a very wide range of circumstances from say, person x loves me, to the sun will come up tomorrow morning or $1 + 1 = 2$. It is not possible for any 'essential substance' to cover the concept of belief across these physical and mental realms, and a definition does not have to satisfy all of everybody's purposes; it just has to be a mental construct not inconsistent with any reasonable usage. Use of the word proposition satisfies these requirements.

Who holds it/where is it held?

Beliefs are individual. Institutions such as a church or a political party may prescribe beliefs for their adherents. Each individual has to decide their level of commitment to the required beliefs. The group will therefore have tenets it declares to be essential for membership, but it is still dependent upon the belief in and collective commitment of its members or adherents to it. So while a group can be said to have a set of beliefs, these are more required of group members than held collectively in some group consciousness. It would therefore seem desirable to limit the term to individuals. However, doing so has an impractical consequence. The mechanics of how particular beliefs or doctrines may wax and wane through percentages of adherents coming to an alternate view is not the province of definition. It is unlikely that anyone would dispute the suitability of a statement of the type "Church x believes y" and so the definition is best to refer to an entity, thus covering both groups and individuals.

Validity and relation to truth

A particular belief may or may not be true. Believing in something that turns out to be non-existent or false does not mean it was not a belief. But the truth of a particular belief is also not the province of definition, ruling out any reference to absolute truth, actuality and reality. Terms that deal with likelihood of truth or reality are; considered to exist or be true, held to be true, likely true, accepted as true or real. However, a person may hold a belief that they find useful even though they may know at the time it isn't true. Self- development affirmations to get to an attainable state is one case in point – "fake it till you make it". Another is acceptance (or belief) that Newtonian mechanics is still useful in day to day application even though it has been expanded by Einstein's theory of relativity. Such beliefs are nevertheless useful/ valuable. Other beliefs could be considered by some to be not valuable because of their consequences, such as various religions' desires of world domination in various ages. This indicates value should be avoided in the definition. Validity accommodates these various circumstances without having to specify them and is a better choice than any phrase indicating acceptance of truth. The remaining options from Tables 13.4a and 13.4b that accommodate proof not being specified are: faith, trust, placing trust or confidence in another, without proof, trust or confidence placed in some person or thing. These all describe ways in which an individual may come to accept a particular belief. They therefore constitute definition by extension and will be rejected in favour of 'considers valid' which is generic and by intension.

Step 4 Develop a connotative (intensional) conventional definition

The definition resulting from the above analysis is therefore *a proposition an entity considers valid.*

Step 5 Report academic review of definitions

All EBSCO databases were searched on 19/12/2016 for the terms "define" and "beliefs" in the title. 6 were found. None contained any such review. All dealt with defining beliefs in particular circumstances rather than with defining the term itself. A similar search was conducted for "definition" and "beliefs" and 63 were found of which 32 were non-identical. Only two actually dealt with an actual definition of the word; by Stephenson (1965) and by Campbell (1967). The remainder dealt with defining beliefs in particular circumstances rather than defining the term itself.

Stephenson considered the definitions of opinion, attitude and belief. He offered a formal definition of opinion as "a *self-referent* statements held … on grounds short of proof" (Stephenson, 1965). He did not actually offer formal definitions of the other two terms but discussed them in relation to opinion. He noted that all three can have unlimited range between momentary and permanent. He quoted McNemer in saying:

> No one has ever seen an attitude; an attitude, however real to its possessor, is an abstraction, the existence of which is inferred from nonverbal overt behaviour, or from verbal or symbolic behaviour. The term opinion is frequently defined as the verbal expression of an attitude (Stephenson, 1965).

He noted that an attitude has "drive value" (Stephenson, 1965) whereas a habit does not. He observed:

> A person with ... a belief must, on occasion, run through his mind all the opinions he holds, as well as others he denies ... What has to be modelled is a large number of opinions, resulting in a few different attitudes, stemming perhaps from only one belief (Stephenson, 1965).

He concluded:

> Opinions are apt to be about trivial matters. Beliefs are based either on evidence or on grounds of faith, dogma, trust, upbringing, authority or the like. In the former case, there is little emotional or ego involvement ... Belief, in our use of the term, has reference to ego-involving conditions ... Attitudes, instead, have references to self (Stephenson, 1965).

Limiting a definition to ego-involving conditions excludes evidence-based beliefs that are held independent of ego. This reflects its author's framework of psychological interest and cannot be accepted for generic definitional purposes. Nevertheless, neither of these two aspects are excluded by the proposed definition. This discussion highlights the need to include definitions of opinion and attitude. As these no longer appear contentious, a full definitional exercise will not be undertaken on them and the Oxford Dictionary definitions will be accepted as follows:

- Opinion = A view or judgement formed about something, not necessarily based on fact or knowledge.

  Note this is essentially the same as Stephenson's definition above.
- Attitude = A settled way of thinking about something.

Campbell (1967) discussed episodic and dispositional, absolute and qualified belief but also did not actually define belief itself. He noted:

> For the practical purposes of everyday life, the ambiguity we have been noting in the ordinary usage of 'belief' is not of great moment. When a man says "I believe X to be the case" even though what he absolutely believes is only that X is very probably the case, his thought and action in relation to X will not as a rule be significantly different from what they would be if he absolutely believed that X *is* the case. It is seldom therefore that his ambiguous language will be seriously misleading. But the ambiguity may be unfortunate if it is imported into philosophical controversy about the nature of belief. Failure to give the double usage of 'belief' explicit recognition can lead to dangerous confusions. Disputants are liable to make confident pronouncements about the nature of belief which they support by examples drawn from *one* usage, while equally confident pronouncements to the contrary are made by those who have taken notice only of the *other* usage.
>
> A distinction in verbal form is obviously desirable to represent the distinction in meaning. In contexts where the use of 'belief' *simplicitor* might occasion misunderstanding, therefore, I shall speak of "absolute belief" where the believer is in no kind of doubt about the truth of the proposition said to be "believed", and of "qualified belief" where believer would admit to at least a measure of doubt (Campbell, 1967).

Note this adds a qualifier to the word belief and so defines two phrases rather than a single word. He then distinguished between strength of belief and emotion.

> It is common usage to talk of some of our beliefs as being stronger than others. ...The notion of "degrees of strength" in belief is meaningless save in respect of qualified belief. ... Some absolute beliefs, admittedly, have livelier emotional accompaniments than others. Where the propositional content of an absolute belief is intimately associated with central human interests – with morals or religion, for example – it naturally tends to carry an especially high emotive charge. There is a "fervour" in the religious man's belief in God that is absent from his belief that 2 plus 2 equals 4. But the difference in strength of these emotional excitements that may attend belief is not to be confused with differences in strength between the beliefs themselves. *Qua* belief, a belief which is absolute is in every case all that a belief *can* be in the way of strength. Obviously it is otherwise with qualified beliefs (Campbell, 1967).

Consideration of the degree of doubt does not alter his definition of the two phrases. He further distinguished judgement from statement, where judgement is internal and mental whereas statement is the public assertion and there may be a discrepancy between the two (Campbell, 1967). Again, this did not alter his definition. He said "whenever one judges p one also believes p" (Campbell, 1967). He then considers the relationship between judging and believing before concluding that a definition "per genus et differentiam seems not to be possible" before proposing:

> Formally stated, our ostensive definition in these terms would read:
> 'Belief, in its basic sense of episodic, absolute belief, is the mental attitude of favour felt by a person *qua* person towards a proposition when and in so far as that proposition is mentally asserted or judged by him to be true' (Campbell, 1967).

This is still a qualified definition of a sub-classification of the word with qualifiers i.e. a phrase, rather than a definition of a single word. In acknowledging the weakness of his definition, he asked "Is the ostensive definition formulated above merely *an* ostensive definition, or is it *the* ostensive definition?" (Campbell, 1967). He concluded: "For to the question 'What other strong candidates are there for the role of 'sufficient condition' for the occurrence of belief?' it seems to me that the correct, if surprising, answer is that there just aren't any" (Campbell, 1967). This is a reasonable question if we are looking to understand how belief occurs, but it is not a valid question regarding the definition of a word, albeit that one way of determining such 'essence' could come through understanding this. It is also proof by induction rather than deduction, which Hume and Popper have shown to be invalid. This is further confirmed by the definitional process used in this chapter having developed a proposed definition above by genus and difference.

He then concluded:

> While emotion is manifestly operative in determining belief, its function is only to *incline*, never to *necessitate*; that even to incline it must function indirectly – 'going round', as were, 'by way of the intellect'. What directly determines a man's belief about p is his appraisal of the evidence about p as he sees it; and appraisal of evidence, whether that evidence is or is not distorted by emotive bias, can be a function only of the intelligence. Despite the superficially strong claims of the emotive life, then, I can find no good reason to deem it capable of providing any ostensive definition of belief. Nor can I find elsewhere a plausible alternative to the ostensive definition in terms of judgement (Campbell, 1967).

The definitional issues Campbell raised have all been addressed in the lexical analysis above. The proposed definition contains all of the elements of Campbell's definition, but refined of unnecessary inclusions and expressed succinctly in a way that does not limit its generality.

A later reference by Haack (2015) located in independent searching includes a section titled "What is belief" which proposes a theory of what believing something involves. It mentions three interlocking elements or dimensions; behavioural, neurophysiological and socio-historical but does not actually provide a definition of the word. However, it does state:

> I would prefer… not to talk of 'beliefs' as 'things' (let alone as 'entities' that should, or should not, be 'admitted into our ontology') but instead to talk about *someone's believing this or that*. Beliefs aren't things a person has, like his car or his pet gerbil, but (complex) states that a person is in (Haack, 2015).

This accords with the distinction between objects and concepts identified in McGrath (2019) (as reported in Part I above) and does not conflict with the proposed definition.

This analysis of academic sources therefore provides no reason to change the proposed definition.

Step 6 Remove unwarranted inclusions

There are no such inclusions remaining.

Step 7 Remove mixed content/process meanings

None present.

Step 8 Reduce divergence/consider additional inclusions

No further checks are necessary beyond what has already been covered in Steps 3 and 4.

Step 9 Check against the five rules

The definitions are by genus and difference and satisfy Rules 1 to 5.

Step 10 Report the derived definition

The derived definitions are as follows:

- Belief = (n) a proposition an entity considers valid.
- Beliefs = (n) propositions an entity considers valid.

Note that this definition does not exclude principles from the ambit of beliefs.

13.10 Define Morals

Step 1 Define derivative or component terms

The term 'morals' is a plural noun derived from the adjective moral by adding an s. Both can have slightly different meanings, so the adjective moral will be defined before the plural noun morals. The singular noun moral, as in the moral of a story, is not contested and will not be analysed.

Step 2 Survey lexical usage

Lexical usage is surveyed in Tables 13.5a and 13.5b in the Appendix.

Step 3 Analyse lexical usage

The singular noun form of moral, as in the moral of a story, is not contested as so will not be considered further. The Oxford Dictionary definition of the singular noun 'moral' as 'a lesson that can be derived from a story or experience' will be accepted. It is the adjective and the plural noun formed from it whose definition overlaps with other words that will be analysed.

Any definitions of morals in terms of ethics will not be selected to avoid such overlap. The most common definitions in Table 13.5a are in terms of good and bad, right and wrong. However, a definition in terms of principles or standards of right and wrong behaviour would immediately lead to the question "What is absolute good?" In religious or international conflict, murder of members of the opposing group becomes moral, requiring a value judgement regarding which side may be entitled to be considered 'good'. This is best avoided and so definitions will be sought that accommodate these terms without actually using them. The quasi-religious connotations of this word noted by the Business Dictionary will be addressed by seeking a secular definition that also covers religious usage, so that it will be consistent with but not dependent upon the set of circumstances and beliefs that may have led to it occurring. The key factor not referred to in Tables 13.5a and 13.5b is that morals tend to be proscriptive rather than prescriptive. Even though they may be expressed in terms such as what one ought to do, this is generally distinct from what one might actually like to do, and so serve as restraint on individual behaviour for a group benefit or greater good or higher purpose. Several definitions in Table 13.5a reference the voluntary aspect of morality rather than legal compulsion and this also needs to be accommodated in the definition. Vague expressions such as "of or concerned with", "founded on" or "relating to" will be ignored.

Step 4 Develop a connotative (intensional) conventional definition

Mutually consistent definitions of these two words that accommodate the above considerations are:

Moral (a): = *in accordance with a belief restraining individual behaviour for a higher purpose.* This definition is equivalent to what an individual may think is right and good, and to what may be considered right and good by most people, without actually using those normative terms. The use of "higher purpose" accommodates personal development, religious belief and benefit to a group that an individual belongs to or considers important. It side-steps the issue of 'absolute' good and of what is good for whom. It also excludes beliefs about matters which induce rather than restrain individual behaviour, such as the believed health benefits of particular diets, foods, chemicals or products.

Morals (n): = *a set of beliefs restraining individual behavioural for a higher purpose.*

Step 5 Report academic review of definitions

All EBSCO databases were searched on 14/11/2016 for the terms "moral" and "define" in the title. 17 were found and none contained any such review. A similar search was conducted for "definition" and "moral". 82 were indicated of which 54 were non-identical items. None contained any such review. Many dealt with moral or other definitions rather than definition of the word moral. Only one actually purported to deal with the definition of morality. Closer examination found that it dealt principally with moral weakness and R.M. Hare's concept of "overridingness" rather than with a definition of morality itself. The only definitional comment in it was "The problem with defining morality is not that of distinguishing the moral from the *immoral* but that of distinguishing the moral from the *non*moral" Frankena (1988). This commented on degrees of not being moral, as distinct from being moral, which by implication is considered 'good'. This does not assist non-normative definition.

It is worth noting that another academic source, located separately, supported not using the term law in the definition of morality. Leslie Green in his introduction to Hart (2012) says "Hart allows that while moral principles are not necessarily a source of law, they could be, provided they were so authorized by things that are a source of law".

A further source located independently that proved useful was Haidt (2012) who noted that "morality differs around the world, and even within societies" (Haidt, 2012). He defined "moral systems" as "interlocking sets of values, virtues, norms, practices, identities, institutions, technologies, and evolved psychological mechanisms that work together to suppress or regulate self-interest and make cooperative societies possible" (Haidt, 2012). This definition describes a phrase rather than a word but does avoid normative considerations. He noted this is a functionalist definition, defining morality by what it does rather than by specifying what content counts as moral. He also noted that "Turiel, in contrast, defined morality as being about "justice, rights, and welfare"" (Haidt, 2012). He also noted that morality binds and blinds (Haidt, 2012) and commented that:

> any effort to define morality by designating a few issues as the truly moral ones and dismissing the rest as "social convention" is bound to be parochial. It's a moral community saying "Here are our central values, and we define morality as being about our central values; to hell with the rest of you." ... Turiel's definition doesn't even apply to all Americans; it's a definition by and for educated and politically liberal Westerners.

> Of course, it is possible that one moral community actually has gotten it right in some sense, and the rest of the world is wrong, which brings us to the second point. Philosophers typically distinguish between descriptive definitions of morality (which simply describe what people happen to think is moral) and normative definitions (which specify what is really and truly right, regardless of what anyone thinks) (Haidt, 2012).

He also noted:

> Turiel discovered that… children recognize that rules about clothing, food, and many other aspects of life are *social conventions*, which are arbitrary and changeable to some extent… (and) that rules that prevent harm are *moral rules*, which Turiel defined as rules related to 'justice, rights, and welfare pertaining to how people ought to relate to each other.' In other words, young children don't treat all rules the same (Haidt, 2012).

His observation of the Azande of Sudan led him to conclude "that groups create supernatural beings not to explain the universe but to order their societies" (Haidt, 2012). His further observations of the Ilongot of the Philippines led him to conclude that morality related to "tension within the group linked to competition between different groups". He also noted the food taboos of the Hua of New Guinea regarding what men and women may eat and the Hebrew Bible's morality involving avoidance of both disease (harm) and disgust (emotion), which led him to consider there must be more to morality than just criteria of harm minimisation. He also observed:

> If Turiel was right that morality is really about harm, then why do most non-Western cultures moralize so many practices that seem to have nothing to do with harm? Why do many Christians and Jews believe that "cleanliness is next to godliness"? And why do so many Westerners, even secular ones, continue to see choices about food and sex as being heavily loaded with moral significance? … There must be something beyond rationalism. (Haidt, 2012).

These considerations led him to analyse morality into what he considered to be six key components; care, liberty, fairness, loyalty, authority and sanctity (Haidt, 2012). He based this on "Durkheim, who said: 'What is moral is everything that is a source of solidarity, everything that forces man to … regulate his actions by something other than … his own egoism' " (Haidt, 2012).

So the conclusion he came to was that what is moral is what restrains the individual for a higher purpose. His list of six things, if taken as a possible definition by extension, affirms the derived definition by intension, as it does not exclude any of them.

This consideration of academic sources therefore provides no reason to alter that definition.

Step 6 Remove unwarranted inclusions

There are no such inclusions remaining.

Step 7 Remove mixed content/process meanings

None present.

Step 8 Reduce divergence/consider additional inclusions

No further such checks required beyond what is included in Step 3.

Step 9 Check against the five rules

The definition of moral is operational rather than by genus and difference and so a check against the 5 rules is not appropriate. Nevertheless, it does actually satisfy them.

The definition of morals is by genus and difference and satisfies Rules 1 to 5.

Step 10 Report the derived definition

The derived definitions are as follows:

- Moral = (a) *in accordance with a belief that restrains individual behaviour for a higher purpose.*
- Morals = (n)(pl) *a set of beliefs restraining individual behavioural for a higher purpose.*

13.11 Group Rules Post Definition

Cross check 1 Consistency within group

There is overlap remaining in the definitions of ethics and morals which needs to be removed. The definitions derived above are:

- Ethics (n) (pl) = *principles of behaviour*
- Moral = (n) *in accordance with a belief that restrains individual behaviour for a higher purpose.*
- Morals (n) (pl) = *a set of beliefs restraining individual behaviour for a higher purpose.*

Both words have the connotation of restraint for the common or greater good, but this is not mentioned in the definition of ethics. The concept of restraint for a higher purpose will therefore be added to the definition of ethics which then becomes *(a set of) principles restraining individual behaviour for a higher purpose.* This brings the definitions into similar format and wording that reflects common usage, however it raises the further issue of how they would be distinguished to avoid overlap? A separate and distinct locus of application therefore needs to be determined for both words.

Morals are more usually associated with matters relating to sexual conduct, however this is not exclusively so. The Ten Commandments command "Thou shalt not kill", so it could be said that morals have more to do with religion than sexual conduct per se. But religion also deals with how we conduct ourselves generally in our interpersonal relationships and our relationship with God rather than with how we conduct ourselves in civic matters. Ethics is used generally in a civic sense whereas morality is used in relation to interpersonal conduct. Interpersonal behaviour is not the sole province of any one religion or even of religion in general as cultural factors also come into play, and referring to interpersonal behaviour accommodates these factors. That then enables a clear distinction between the two. How we conduct some civic matters may well be determined by a minimum standard of how the state should humanely relate to individuals, and so civil ethics may be based upon some minimum moral principles. But although morals may thus drive some ethics, neither definition, thus modified, is actually a subset of the other.

Note also that beliefs may or may not be based on principles, so principles are not a sub-set of beliefs. The definition of ethics refers to principles and the definition of morals refers to beliefs. This is somewhat loose, perhaps resulting from the association of morals with religious beliefs, which was corrected above. So principles will be substituted for beliefs in the definition of morals. This provides full symmetry between the two definitions which now become:

- Ethics = *principles of civic behaviour that restrain individual behaviour for a higher purpose*
- Morals = *principles of interpersonal behaviour that restrain individual behaviour for a higher purpose.*

Cross check 2 Consistency with terms outside the group

There is no known overlap of meaning of any of the above group of terms with any other term outside the group that would prevent the definitions being accepted.

13.12 Summary of Definitions

The accepted definitions are:

- Good = *that which we consider to be useful.*
- Bad = *that which we consider to be a hinderance.*
- Opinion = *a view or judgement formed about something, not necessarily based on fact or knowledge.*
- Attitude = *a settled way of thinking about something.*

The derived definitions are as follows:

- Principle (n) = *a rule guiding action.*
- Principles (n) = *a set of rules guiding action.*
- Value (n) = *the quantity of satisfaction of an interest.*
- Values (n) = *preferences guiding the actions of an entity.*
- Ethics (n) = *principles of civic behaviour that restrain individual behaviour for a higher purpose.*
- Belief (n) = *a proposition an entity considers valid.*
- Beliefs (n) = *propositions an entity considers valid.*
- Moral (a) = *in accordance with a principle of interpersonal behaviour that restrains individual behaviour for a higher purpose.*

- Morals (n) = *principle of interpersonal behaviour that restrain individual behaviour for a higher purpose.*

13.13 Observations on the Refining Method and Its Application

13.13.1 On the Refining Method

Analysis of the method indicated that in Step 10, the word “adopted” should be “derived”. This change corrects what appears to have been a typographical error in the source paper, in which all applications of the method used the word derived.

13.13.2 On the Application of the Refining Method

Application of the chosen McGrath and Whitty (2015) definitional refining method has enabled clear non-normative and non-emotive definitions of the contested English language words ethics, values, morals, principles and beliefs to be developed.

13.13.3 Implications

In essence, these derived definitions state that principles are rules, values are preferences, beliefs are propositions an individual or entity considers valid, and ethics and morals are principles restraining civic and interpersonal behaviour respectively.

Particular morals, principles, ethics and beliefs may be considered true or false and no attempt is made here to judge that. A person could be considered within their own society to be moral yet be judged immoral by another society. For example, the German people before World War II accepted the superiority of the Aryan race, believed in it, and took the consequent, difficult ‘moral’ (for them) action of exterminating Jews, which other societies considered completely immoral. The derived definitions accommodate this and are therefore free of value judgement.

Examination of the implications of these definitions will be useful and this is done in the next chapter.

There is also a lack of transparency in the way we have come to agree the meaning of conceptual terms, as evidenced by the fact that McGrath and Whitty (2015) could not find a pre-existing method for refining the meanings of a group of related terms and so then developed such a method themselves. Lack of transparency in terminology seems to be quite generally, happily tolerated, whereas lack of transparency in organisational governance is not. The wasted effort and monetary loss resulting from the former is hidden or at least opaque. This is an ethical issue of unquantifiable and therefore unknown proportions. As Thomas Hobbes says in Leviathan IV.13 "For the errors of definitions multiply themselves, according as the reckoning proceeds, and lead men into absurdities, which at last they see, but cannot avoid, without reckoning anew from the beginning; in which lies the foundation of their errors" (Hobbes, 1996).

The aspect of restraint in ethics has perhaps tempted confusion with the directing and controlling aspects of governance. But governance (directing and controlling) measures are required to enforce any set of ethics reflecting any standard of morality, whether considered good or bad by external parties. Ethics are an input to governance, not governance itself.

The non-normative definition of ethics derived here also raises the peripheral question of how to fix or interpret normative writing on 'good' ethical strategies. While the presumption of 'good' may often be obvious from the context, explicitly including the previously silent qualifier 'good' is an obvious answer.

13.14 Conclusions

The definitional refining process used in this chapter has developed clear, non-overlapping definitions of the essence of the following words: ethics, values, morals, principles and beliefs. The method used to do this is the same as that used to untangle the terminology surrounding organisational governance, which clearly distinguished between government, governing, governance, strategy and ethics (Chap. 10). This chapter confirms a definition of ethics separate to governance.

Adoption and use of the refined definitions developed in this chapter can provide clarity of meaning, avert development of field specific and differing 'private language' and contribute to avoiding confusion and misunderstanding. This can benefit the community in general and individuals, practitioners and researchers in particular, saving time, resources and money. Furthermore, this chapter has identified the lack of transparency in the way we come to agree the meaning of and use these particular conceptual terms and has highlighted that this is itself an ethical issue.

Successful application of the definitional refining method here also indicates its potential suitability for application to other contested terms.

Appendix

Table 13.1a Definitions of 'principle' (n)

Dictionary	Definition of 'principle' (All sourced on 9/10/2016 ex Macquarie 24/4/2018)
Business	(s) Elementary assumption, concept, doctrine, maxim, or proposition generally held to be fundamental or true for a body of knowledge, conduct, procedure, or system of reasoning, and used as a basis for prediction and action. (pl) Fundamental norms, rules, or values that represent what is desirable and positive for a person, group, organization, or community, and help it in determining the rightfulness or wrongfulness of its actions. Principles are more basic than policy and objectives, and are meant to govern both.
Cambridge	C1 a basic idea or rule that explains or controls how something happens or works: C2 APPROVING a moral rule or standard of good behaviour:
Collins	1. a standard or rule of personal conduct 2. (*often plural*) a set of such moral rules 3. adherence to such a moral code; morality 4. a fundamental or general truth or law 5. the essence of something 6. a source or fundamental cause; origin 7. a rule or law concerning a natural phenomenon or the behaviour of a system 8. an underlying or guiding theory or belief 9. *chemistry* a constituent of a substance that gives the substance its characteristics and behaviour.
Concise Oxford	1. Fundamental source, primary element 2. Fundamental truth as basis for reasoning; General law as a guide to action
Dictionary.com	1. an accepted or professed rule of action or conduct: 2.a fundamental, primary, or general law or truth from which others are derived: 3.a fundamental doctrine or tenet; a distinctive ruling opinion: 4. **principles,** a personal or specific basis of conduct or management: 5. guiding sense of the requirements and obligations of right conduct: 6. an adopted rule or method for application in action: 7. a rule or law exemplified in natural phenomena, the construction or operation of a machine, the working of a system, or the like:
Longman	1. MORAL RULE [countable, uncountable] a moral rule or belief about what is right and wrong, that influences how you behave 2. IDEA BEHIND SOMETHING [countable] the basic idea that a plan or system is based on 3. in principle 4. RULES OF A PROCESS [countable] a rule which explains the way something such as a machine works, or which explains a natural force in the universe.

(continued)

Table 13.1a (continued)

Dictionary	Definition of 'principle' (All sourced on 9/10/2016 ex Macquarie 24/4/2018)
Macmillan	1 [COUNTABLE] a basic belief, theory, or rule that has a major influence on the way in which something is done. [OFTEN PLURAL] one of the major ideas or theories that a system of beliefs is based on, for example in religion or politics 2 [COUNTABLE] [USUALLY PLURAL] a basic rule or belief about what is right and morally good, that influences the way that you behave and the way that you treat other people a. [UNCOUNTABLE] morally correct behaviour 3 [COUNTABLE] a scientific theory or basic natural law that explains the way in which something works
Macquarie	**1.** an accepted or professed rule of action or conduct: **2.** a fundamental, primary, or general truth, on which other truths depend: **3.** a fundamental doctrine or tenet; a distinctive ruling opinion: **4.** (*plural*) right rules of conduct. **5.** guiding sense of the requirements and obligations of right conduct: **6.** fixed rule or adopted method as to action. **7.** a rule or law exemplified in natural phenomena, in the construction or operation of a machine, the working of a system, or the like: **8.** the method of formation, operation, or procedure exhibited in a given case: **9.** a determining characteristic of something; essential quality of character. **10.** an originating or actuating agency or force. **11.** an actuating agency in the mind or character, as an instinct, faculty, or natural tendency. **12.** *Chemistry* a constituent of a substance, especially one giving to it some distinctive quality or effect. **13.** *Obsolete* beginning or commencement.
Merriam-Webster	Simple Definition : a moral rule or belief that helps you know what is right and wrong and that influences your actions : a basic truth or theory: an idea that forms the basis of something : a law or fact of nature that explains how something works or why something happens Full Definition ***1a***: a comprehensive and fundamental law, doctrine, or assumption ***b(1)***: a rule or code of conduct *(2)* ***c***: the laws or facts of nature underlying the working of an artificial device ***2***: a primary source: origin ***3a***: an underlying faculty or endowment ***b***: an ingredient (as a chemical) that exhibits or imparts a characteristic quality

(continued)

Table 13.1a (continued)

Dictionary	Definition of 'principle' (All sourced on 9/10/2016 ex Macquarie 24/4/2018)
Oxford	1. a fundamental truth or proposition that serves as the foundation for a system of belief or behaviour or for a chain of reasoning: **synonyms:** truth proposition concept · idea · theory postulate **1.1** A rule or belief governing one's behaviour. **1.2** *[mass noun]* Morally correct behaviour and attitudes. 2. a general scientific theorem or law that has numerous special applications across a wide field or a natural law forming the basis for the construction or working of a machine: 3. a fundamental source or basis of something:
The free dictionary	**1.** A basic truth, law, or assumption. **2.** **a.** A rule or standard, especially of good behavior. **b.** The collectivity of moral or ethical standards or judgments. **3.** A fixed or predetermined policy or mode of action. **4.** A basic or essential quality or element determining intrinsic nature or characteristic behavior. **5.** A rule or law concerning the functioning of natural phenomena or mechanical processes. **6.** *Chemistry* One of the elements that compose a substance, especially one that gives some special quality or effect. **7.** A basic source.
Wiktionary	1. A fundamental assumption or guiding belief. 2. A rule used to choose among solutions to a problem. 3. (*sometimes pluralized*) Moral rule or aspect. 4. (*physics*) A rule or law of nature of nature, or the basic idea on how the laws of nature are applied. 5. A fundamental essence, particularly one producing a given quality. 6. (*obsolete*) A beginning. 7. A source, or origin; that from which anything proceeds; fundamental substance or energy; primordial substance; ultimate element, or cause. 8. An original faculty or endowment.

Table 13.1b Definitions of 'principles' (n)(pl)

Dictionary	Definition of 'principles' (All sourced on 9/10/2016 ex Macquarie 24/4/2018)
Business	(pl) Fundamental norms, rules, or values that represent what is desirable and positive for a person, group, organization, or community, and help it in determining the rightfulness or wrongfulness of its actions. Principles are more basic than policy and objectives, and are meant to govern both.
Cambridge	No definition.
Collins	(*often plural*) a set of such moral rules
Concise Oxford	No definition.
Dictionary.com	a personal or specific basis of conduct or management:
Longman	No definition.
Macmillan	[OFTEN PLURAL] one of the major ideas or theories that a system of beliefs is based on, for example in religion or politics
Macquarie	No definition.
Merriam-Webster	the laws or facts of nature underlying the working of an artificial device
Oxford	*[mass noun]* Morally correct behaviour and attitudes.
The free dictionary	The collectivity of moral or ethical standards or judgments.
Wiktionary	(*sometimes pluralized*) Moral rule or aspect.

Table 13.2a Definitions of 'value' (n)

Dictionary	Definition of 'value' (All sourced on 9/10/2016 ex Macquarie 24/4/2018)
Business	1. Accounting: The monetary worth of an asset, business entity, good sold, service rendered, or liability or obligation acquired. 2. Economics: The worth of all the benefits and rights arising from ownership. Two types of economic value are (1) the utility of a good or service, and (2) power of a good or service to command other goods, services, or money, in voluntary exchange. 3. Marketing: The extent to which a good or service is perceived by its customer to meet his or her needs or wants, measured by customer's willingness to pay for it. It commonly depends more on the customer's perception of the worth of the product than on its intrinsic value. 4. Mathematics: A magnitude or quantity represented by numbers.
Cambridge	B1 the amount of money that can be received for something: the importance or worth of something for someone: how useful or important something is:

(continued)

Table 13.2a (continued)

Dictionary	Definition of 'value' (All sourced on 9/10/2016 ex Macquarie 24/4/2018)
Collins	1. the desirability of a thing, often in respect of some property such as usefulness or exchangeability; worth, merit, or importance 2. an amount, esp. a material or monetary one, considered to be a fair ex-change in return for a thing; assigned valuation 3. reasonable or equivalent return; satisfaction 4. precise meaning or significance 5. (*plural*) the moral principles and beliefs or accepted standards of a person or social group 6. *mathematics* a. a particular magnitude, number, or amount b. the particular quantity that is the result of applying a function or operation for some given argument 7. *music* short for time value 8. *(in painting, drawing, etc.)* a. a gradation of tone from light to dark or of colour luminosity b. the relation of one of these elements to another or to the whole picture 9. *phonetics* the quality or tone of the speech sound associated with a written character representing it.
Concise Oxford	Worth, desirability, utility, qualities on which these depend; Worth as estimated
Dictionary.com	1. relative worth, merit, or importance: 2. monetary or material worth, as in commerce or trade: 3. the worth of something in terms of the amount of other things for which it can be exchanged or in terms of some medium of exchange. 4. equivalent worth or return in money, material, services, etc.: 5. estimated or assigned worth; valuation: 6. denomination, as of a monetary issue or a postage stamp. 7. *Mathematics.* a. magnitude; quantity; number represented by a figure, symbol, or the like: b. point in the range of a function; a point in the range corresponding to a given point in the domain of a function:
Longman	**1** MONEY [countable, uncountable] the amount of money that something is worth **2** WORTH THE MONEY PAID [countable, uncountable]used to say that something is worth what you pay for it, or not worth what you pay for it **3** IMPORTANCE/USEFULNESS [uncountable] the im-portance or usefulness of something **4** → of value 5 → shock/curiosity/novelty etc. value 6 → values [plural] your ideas about what is right and wrong, or what is important in life **7** AMOUNT [countable] *technical* a mathematical quantity shown by a letter of the alphabet or sign

(continued)

Table 13.2a (continued)

Dictionary	Definition of 'value' (All sourced on 9/10/2016 ex Macquarie 24/4/2018)
Macmillan	1. amount something is worth 2. the degree to which someone or something is important or useful 3. interesting quality 4. values – the principles and beliefs that influence the behaviour and way of life of a particular group or community 5. in mathematics – a mathematical number or amount that is not known and is represented by a letter
Macquarie	**1.** that property of a thing because of which it is esteemed, desirable, or useful, or the degree of this property possessed; worth, merit, or importance: **2.** material or monetary worth, as in traffic or sale: **3.** (*plural*) *Mining* payable quantities of mineral. **4.** the worth of a thing as measured by the amount of other things for which it can be exchanged, or as estimated in terms of a medium of exchange. **5.** equivalent worth or equivalent return:. **6.** estimated or assigned worth; valuation. **7.** force, import, or significance: **8.** *Mathematics* **a.** the magnitude of a quantity or measurement. **b.** (of a function) the number obtained when particular numbers are substituted for the variables. **9.** (*plural*) *Sociology* the things of social life (ideals, customs, institutions, etc.) towards which the people of the group have an affective regard. These values may be positive, as cleanliness, freedom, education, etc., or negative, as cruelty, crime, or blasphemy. **10.** *Ethics* any object or quality desirable as a means or as an end in itself. **11.** *Painting* the property of a colour by which it is distinguished as light or dark. **12.** *Music* the relative length or duration of a note. **13.** *Phonetics* **a.** quality. **b.** the phonetic equivalent of a letter: –*verb* (*t*) **(valued, valuing)** **14.** to estimate the value of; rate at a certain value or price; appraise. **15.** to consider with respect to worth, excellence, usefulness, or importance. **16.** to regard or esteem highly.
Merriam-Webster	Simple Definition : the amount of money that something is worth: the price or cost of something : something that can be bought for a low or fair price : usefulness or importance Full Definition 1: a fair return or equivalent in goods, services, or money for something exchanged 2: the monetary worth of something: market price 3: relative worth, utility, or importance 4: a numerical quantity that is assigned or is determined by calculation or measurement 5: the relative duration of a musical note 6a: relative lightness or darkness of a color: luminosity b: the relation of one part in a picture to another with respect to lightness and darkness 7: something (as a principle or quality) intrinsically valuable or desirable

(continued)

Table 13.2a (continued)

Dictionary	Definition of 'value' (All sourced on 9/10/2016 ex Macquarie 24/4/2018)
Oxford	1 *[mass noun]* The regard that something is held to deserve; the im-portance, worth, or usefulness of something. **1.1** The material or monetary worth of something. **1.2** The worth of something compared to the price paid or asked for it. 2 Principles or standards of behaviour; one's judgement of what is important in life. 3 The numerical amount denoted by an algebraic term; a magnitude, quantity, or number. 4 *Music* The relative duration of the sound signified by a note. 5 *Linguistics* The meaning of a word or other linguistic unit. **5.1** The quality or tone of a spoken sound; the sound represented by a letter. 6 The relative degree of lightness or darkness of a particular colour.
The free dictionary	**1.** An amount, as of goods, services, or money, considered to be a fair and suitable equivalent for something else; a fair price or return. **2.** Monetary or material worth. **3.** Worth in usefulness or importance to the possessor; utility or merit. **4. values** A principle or standard, as of behavior, that is considered important or desirable. **5.** Precise meaning or import, as of a word. **6.** Mathematics A quantity or number expressed by an algebraic term. **7.** Music The relative duration of a tone or rest. **8.** The relative darkness or lightness of a color. **9.** Linguistics The sound quality of a letter or diphthong. **10.** One of a series of specified values.
Wiktionary	1. The quality (positive or negative) that renders something desirable or valuable. 2. (*uncountable*) The degree of importance given to something. 3. That which is valued or highly esteemed, as one's morals, morality, or belief system. 4. The amount (of money or goods or services) that is considered to be a fair equivalent for something else. 5. (*music*) The relative duration of a musical note. 6. (*art*) The relative darkness or lightness of a color in (a specific area of) a painting etc. 7. Numerical quantity measured or assigned or computed. 8. Precise meaning; import. 9. (*in the plural*) The valuable ingredients to be obtained by treating a mass or compound; specifically, the precious metals contained in rock, gravel, etc.

Table 13.2b Definitions of 'values' (n)(pl)

Dictionary	Definition of 'values' (All sourced on 9/10/2016 ex Macquarie 24/4/2018)
Business	No definition given.
Cambridge	B2 the beliefs people have, especially about what is right and wrong and what is most important in life, that control their behaviour:
Collins	The moral principles and beliefs or accepted standards of a person or social group.
Concise Oxford	No definition.
Dictionary.com	No definition.
Longman	Your ideas about what is right and wrong, or what is important in life.
Macmillan	The principles and beliefs that influence the behaviour and way of life of a particular group or community.
Macquarie	No definition.
Merriam-Webster	No definition.
Oxford	Principles or standards of behaviour; one's judgement of what is important in life.
The free dictionary	A principle or standard, as of behavior, that is conside red important or desirable.
Wiktionary	Plural of value.

Table 13.3 Definitions of 'ethics' (n)(pl)

Dictionary	Definition of 'ethics' (All sourced on 11/1/14, checked on 10/10/2016 ex Macquarie 24/4/2018)
Business	The basic concepts and fundamental principles of decent human conduct. It includes study of universal values such as the essential equality of all men and women, human or natural rights, obedience to the law of land, concern for health and safety and, increasingly, also for the natural environment. See also morality.
Cambridge	A system of accepted beliefs that control behaviour, especially such a system based on morals. The study of what is morally right and what is not.
Collins	1. The philosophical study of the moral value of human conduct and of the rules and principles that ought to govern it; moral philosophy. 2. A social, religious, or civil code of behaviour considered correct, esp. that of a particular group, profession, or individual. 3. The moral fitness of a decision, course of action, etc.
Concise Oxford	Moral principles, rules of conduct.
Dictionary.com	1. a system of moral principles. 2. the rules of conduct recognized in respect to a particular class of human actions or a particular group, culture, etc. 3. moral principles, as of an individual 4. that branch of philosophy dealing with values relating to human conduct, with respect to the rightness and wrongness of certain actions and to the goodness and badness of the motives and ends of such actions.

(continued)

Table 13.3 (continued)

Dictionary	Definition of 'ethics' (All sourced on 11/1/14, checked on 10/10/2016 ex Macquarie 24/4/2018)
Longman	[plural] Moral rules or principles of behaviour for deciding what is right and wrong. Ethic [countable] a general idea or belief that influences people's behaviour and attitudes.
Macmillan	1. [plural] A set of principles that people use to decide what is right and what is wrong. a.[uncountable] the study of the principles of right and wrong 2. [SINGULAR] a general principle or belief that affects the way that people behave.
Macquarie	**1.** a system of moral principles, by which human actions and proposals may be judged good or bad or right or wrong. **2.** the rules of conduct recognised in respect of a particular class of human actions: **3.** moral principles, as of an individual.
Merriam-Webster	Simple Definition of ETHIC : Rules of behavior based on ideas about what is morally good and bad **ethics**: an area of study that deals with ideas about what is good and bad behavior: a branch of philosophy dealing with what is morally right or wrong : a belief that something is very important Full Definition 1. *Plural but sing or plural in construction*: The discipline dealing with what is good and bad and with moral duty and obligation 2. a. A set of moral principles: a theory or system of moral values b. Plural but sing or plural in construction: the principles of conduct governing an individual or a group c. c. a guiding philosophy d. a consciousness of moral importance 3. *plural*: a set of moral issues or aspects (as rightness)
Oxford	[usually treated as plural] 1. Moral principles that govern a person's behaviour or the conducting of an activity. 2. [usually treated as singular] The branch of knowledge that deals with moral principles.
The free dictionary	Ethic 1 a. A set of principles of right conduct. b. A theory or a system of moral values. 2 ethics The study of the general nature of morals and of the specific moral choices to be made by a person; moral philosophy. 3 The rules or standards governing the conduct of a person or the members of a profession.
Wiktionary	The standards that govern the conduct of a person, especially a member of a profession.

Table 13.4a Definitions of 'belief' (n)

Dictionary	Definition of 'belief' (All sourced on 10/11/2016 ex Macquarie 24/4/2018)
Business	No separate definition given. Beliefs are defined instead.
Cambridge	The feeling of being certain that something exists or is true: Something that you believe.
Collins	A feeling of certainty that something exists, is true, or is good.
Concise Oxford	Trust or confidence in; Acceptance of any received theology; Acceptance as true or existing; Thing believed, religion, opinion, institution.
Dictionary.com	1. something believed; an opinion or conviction: 2. confidence in the truth or existence of something not immediately susceptible to rigorous proof: 3. confidence; faith; trust: 4. a religious tenet or tenets; religious creed or faith:
Longman	1 the feeling that something is definitely true or definitely exists. 2 the feeling that something is good and can be trusted 3 an idea that you believe to be true, especially one that forms part of a system of ideas.
Macmillan	a Strong feeling that something is true or real a. a strong feeling that something is right or good b. an idea that you are certain is true, especially involving religion or politics
Macquarie	**1.** that which is believed; an accepted opinion. **2.** conviction of the truth or reality of a thing, based upon grounds insufficient to afford positive knowledge: **3.** confidence; faith; trust: **4.** a religious tenet or tenets: *–phrase* **5. beggar belief**, to cause astonishment to the point of disbelief.
Merriam-Webster	Simple Definition : a feeling of being sure that someone or something exists or that something is true : a feeling that something is good, right, or valuable : a feeling of trust in the worth or ability of someone Full Definition 1: a state or habit of mind in which trust or confidence is placed in some person or thing 2: something believed; especially a tenet or body of tenets held by a group. 3: conviction of the truth of some statement or the reality of some being or phenomenon especially when based on examination of evidence

(continued)

Table 13.4a (continued)

Dictionary	Definition of 'belief' (All sourced on 10/11/2016 ex Macquarie 24/4/2018)
Oxford	1 an acceptance that something exists or is true, especially one without proof: 1.1 something one accepts as true or real; a firmly held opinion: 2 trust, faith, or confidence in (someone or something):
The free dictionary	1. The mental act, condition, or habit of placing trust or confidence in another: 2. Mental acceptance of and conviction in the truth, actuality, or validity of something: 3. Something believed or accepted as true, especially a particular tenet or a body of tenets accepted by a group of persons.
Wiktionary	1. Mental acceptance of a claim as likely true. 2. Faith or trust in the reality of something; often based upon one's own reasoning, trust in a claim, desire of actuality, and/or evidence considered. 3. Something believed. 4. The quality or state of believing. 5. Religious faith. 6. One's religious or moral convictions

Table 13.4b Definitions of 'beliefs' (n)(pl)

Dictionary	Definition of 'beliefs' (All sourced on 10/11/2016 ex Macquarie 24/4/2018)
Business	Assumptions and convictions that are held to be true, by an individual or a group, regarding concepts, events, people, and things.
Cambridge	No separate definition given.
Collins	Your views on religious or political matters.
Concise Oxford	No separate definition given.
Dictionary.com	No separate definition given.
Longman	Core values
Macmillan	No separate definition given.
Macquarie	No definition given.
Merriam-Webster	No separate definition given.
Oxford	No separate definition given.
The free dictionary	No separate definition given.
Wiktionary	Plural of belief.

Table 13.5a Definitions of 'moral' (a)

Dictionary	Definition of 'moral' (All sourced on 9/10/2016 ex Macquarie 24/4/2018)
Business	Private conduct based on strict adherence to a sanctioned or accepted code or dogma of what is right or wrong, particularly as proclaimed in a sacred book, or by a non-secular group or sect. Once practically interchangeable with 'ethical,' this term has acquired quasi-religious connotations and has moved closer to 'righteous' following the recent (second half of the twentieth century) schism between private morality and public morality.
Cambridge	B2 relating to the standards of good or bad behaviour, fairness, honesty, etc. that each person believes in, rather than to laws: C1 behaving in ways considered by most people to be correct and honest:
Collins	1. Concerned with or relating to human behaviour, esp. the distinction between good and bad or right and wrong behaviour 2. adhering to conventionally accepted standards of conduct 3. based on a sense of right and wrong according to conscience 4. having psychological rather than tangible effects 5. having the effects but not the appearance of (victory or defeat) 6. having a strong probability 7. *law* (of evidence, etc.) based on a knowledge of the tendencies of human nature.
Concise Oxford	(a) Concerned with character or disposition or with the distinction between right and wrong; Dealing with regulation of conduct; The requirements to which right action must conform
Dictionary.com	1.of, relating to, or concerned with the principles or rules of right conduct or the distinction between right and wrong; ethical: 2. expressing or conveying truths or counsel as to right conduct, as a speaker or a literary work. 3. founded on the fundamental principles of right conduct rather than on: legalities, enactment, or custom 4. capable of conforming to the rules of right conduct: 5. conforming to the rules of right conduct (opposed to immoral): 6. virtuous in sexual matters; chaste. 7. of, relating to, or acting on the mind, feelings, will, or character:
Longman	1 [Only before noun] relating to the principles of what is right and wrong behaviour, and with the difference between good and evil 2 [only before noun] based on your ideas about what is right, rather than on what is legal and practical 3 → moral support 4 → moral victory 5 always behaving in a way that is based on strong principles about what is right and wrong OPP immoral, amoral

(continued)

Table 13.5a (continued)

Dictionary	Definition of 'moral' (All sourced on 9/10/2016 ex Macquarie 24/4/2018)
Macmillan	Relating to right and wrong and the way that people should behave a. based on what you believe is right rather than what law or rules say is right.
Macquarie	**1.** relating to or concerned with right conduct or the distinction between right or wrong: **2.** concerned with the principles or rules of right conduct; ethical: **3.** expressing or conveying truths or counsel as to right conduct, as a speaker, a literary work, etc.; moralising. **4.** founded on the fundamental principles of right conduct rather than on enactment or custom: **5.** capable of conforming to the rules of right conduct. **6.** conforming to the rules of right conduct (opposed to *immoral*): **7.** sexually virtuous; chaste. **8.** of, relating to, or producing an effect upon the mind, feelings, or on results generally: **9.** depending upon what is observed of human nature and actions or of things generally, rather than upon demonstration: **10.** resting upon convincing grounds of probability: *–noun* **11.** the moral teaching or practical lesson contained in a fable, tale, experience, etc.: **12.** the embodiment or type of something. **13.** *Colloquial* a certainty:
Merriam-Webster	Simple Definition : concerning or relating to what is right and wrong in human behavior : based on what you think is right and good : considered right and good by most people: agreeing with a standard of right behavior Full Definition 1a: of or relating to principles of right and wrong in behavior : ethical b: expressing or teaching a conception of right behaviour c: conforming to a standard of right behaviour d: sanctioned by or operative on one's conscience or ethical judgment e: capable of right and wrong action 2: probable though not proved: virtual 3: perceptual or psychological rather than tangible or practical in nature or effect
Oxford	1 Concerned with the principles of right and wrong behaviour. **1.1** Concerned with or derived from the code of behaviour that is considered right or acceptable in a particular society **1.2** *[attributive]* Examining the nature of ethics and the foundations of good and bad character and conduct. 2 Holding or manifesting high principles for proper conduct.

(continued)

Table 13.5a (continued)

Dictionary	Definition of 'moral' (All sourced on 9/10/2016 ex Macquarie 24/4/2018)
The free dictionary	**1.** Of or concerned with the judgment of right or wrong of human action and. character **2.** Teaching or exhibiting goodness or correctness of character and behavior. **3.** Conforming to standards of what is right or just in behavior; virtuous. **4.** Arising from conscience or the sense of right and wrong. **5.** Having psychological rather than physical or tangible effects. **6.** Based on strong likelihood or firm conviction, rather than on the actual evidence.
Wiktionary	1. Of or relating to principles of right and wrong in behaviour, especially for teaching right behaviour. a. Nathaniel Hawthorne 2. She had wandered without rule or guidance in a moral wilderness. 3. Conforming to a standard of right behaviour; sanctioned by or operative on one's conscience or ethical judgment. 4. Capable of right and wrong action. 5. Probable but not proved. 6. Positively affecting the mind, confidence, or will.

Table 13.5b Definitions of 'morals'

Dictionary	Definition of 'morals' (All sourced on 9/10/2016 ex Macquarie 24/4/2018)
Business	No separate definition given.
Cambridge	Standards for good or bad character and behaviour:
Collins	Principles and beliefs concerning right and wrong behaviour.
Concise Oxford	Habits, especially sexual conduct
Dictionary.com	No separate definition given.
Longman	Principles or standards of good behaviour, especially in matters of sex.
Macmillan	Principles of right and wrong behaviour that are generally accepted by a society.
Macquarie	**1.** principles or habits with respect to right or wrong conduct; ethics. **2.** behaviour or habits in sexual matters.
Merriam-Webster	No separate definition given.
Oxford	Standards of behaviour; principles of right and wrong.
The free dictionary	Motivation based on ideas of right and wrong.
Wiktionary	Moral practices or teachings: modes of conduct.

References

Aristotle, & Ross, W. D. (1999). *Nicomachean ethics*. Batoche Books.

Ayer, A. J. (1971). *Language, truth and logic*. Penguin.

Blackmore, S. J. (1999). *The meme machine*. Oxford University Press.

Bonner, W. (2014). *Hormegeddon: How too much of a good thing leads to disaster*. Lioncrest.

BusinessDictionary.com (*Online dictionary*) [Online]. Available: http://www.businessdictionary.com [Accessed].

Cambridge (*Online dictionary*) [Online]. Available: http://dictionary.cambridge.org/dictionary/british [Accessed].

Campbell, C. A. (1967). Towards a definition of belief. *The Philosophical Quarterly, 17*(68), 204–204.

Collins (*English dictionary*) [Online]. Available: http://www.collinsdictionary.com/dictionary/english [Accessed].

Concise Oxford Dictionary. (1964). *Concise oxford dictionary*. Oxford University Press.

Copi, I. M., & Cohen, C. (1990). *Introduction to logic*. Macmillan.

Darwin, C., & Beer, G. (2008). *On the origin of species*. Oxford University Press.

Dictionary.com (*Online dictionary*) [Online]. Available: http://dictionary.reference.com [Accessed].

Frankena, W. (1988). Hare on moral weakness and the definition of morality. *Ethics, 98*(4), 779–792.

Gallie, W. B. (1956). Essentially contested concepts. *Proceedings of the Aristotelian Society, 56*, 167–198.

Haack, S. (2015). Belief in naturalism: An epistemologist's philosophy of mind. In J. Stelmach, B. Brożek, & L. Kwiatek (Eds.), *The normative mind*. Copernicus Center Press.

Haidt, J. (2012). *The righteous mind: Why good people are divided by politics and religion*. Pantheon Books.

Hare, R. M. (1997). *Sorting out ethics* (pp. vii, 1919 p.). Oxford: Clarendon Press.

Hart, H. L. A. (2012). *The concept of law*. Oxford University Press.

Hartnung, J. (1995). Love thy neighbour: The evolution of in-group morality. *Skeptic, 3*(4), 86–89.

Hobbes, T. (1996). *Leviathan*. Oxford University Press.

Hume, D., & Mossner, E. C. (1969). *A treatise of human nature; edited with an introduction by Ernest C. Mossner*. Penguin.

Locke, J. (1690). An essay concerning human understanding. In J. Manis (Ed.), *Electronics classics series*. Hazleton.

Longman (*Dictionary of contemporary English online*) [Online]. Available: http://www.ldoceonline.com [Accessed].

Macmillan (*Dictionary*) [Online]. Available: http://www.macmillandictionary.com [Accessed].

Macquarie (*Dictionary online*) [Online], Sydney. Available: http://www.macquarieonline.com.au [Accessed].

McGrath, S. K. (2019). *What is project governance? Disclosing the source of confusion and revealing the essence of governance*. PhD thesis, University of Southern Queensland.

McGrath, S. K., & Whitty, S. J. (2015). Redefining governance: From confusion to certainty and clarity. *International Journal of Managing Projects in Business, 8*(4), 755–787.

McNutt, P. A. (2010). Edited ethics: Corporate governance and Kant's philosophy. *International Journal of Social Economics, 37*(10), 741–754.

Merriam-Webster (*Online dictionary*) [Online], Britain. Available: http://www.merriam-webster.com [Accessed].

Mill, J. S. (1874). *A system of logic, ratiocinative and inductive*. Harper & Brothers.

Mill, J. S., Bentham, J., & Ryan, A. (1987). *Utilitarianism and other essays*. Penguin.

Oxford (*Dictionaries online*) [Online], Oxford. Available: http://oxforddictionaries.com [Accessed].

Perry, R. B. (1914). The definition of value. *Journal of Philosophy, Psychology and Scientific Methods, 11*, 141–162.

Popper, K. R. (1992). *The logic of scientific discovery*. Routledge.

Popper, K. R., & Notturno, M. A. (1994). *The myth of the framework: In defence of science and rationality*. Routledge.

Robinson, D., & Garratt, C. (2013). *Introducing ethics: A graphic guide*. Icon.

Sebek, M. (1973). To the definition of the concept of value in psychology. *Československá Psychologie: Časopis Pro Psychologickou Teorii a Praxi, 17*(3), 242–258.

Sheldon, W. H. (1914). An empirical definition of value. *Journal of Philosophy, Psychology and Scientific Methods, 11*, 113–124.

Smith, R. (2014). Aristotle's logic. In E. N. Zalta (Ed.), *The Stanford encyclopedia of philosophy (Spring 2014 Edition)*.

Spinoza, B. D., Boyle, A., & Gregory, T. S. (1959). *Spinoza's ethics and de intellectus emendatione*. Dent.

Stephenson, W. (1965). Perspective in psychology: Xxiii. Definition of opinion, attitude and belief. *The Psychological Record, 15*(2), 281–288.

The Free Dictionary (*Online dictionary*) [Online]. Available: http://www.thefreedictionary.com [Accessed].

Urban, W. M. (1907). Definition and analysis of the consciousness of value. *Psychological Review, 14*(1), 1–36.

Wiktionary (*Online dictionary*) [Online]. Available: http://en.wiktionary.org [Accessed].

Wittgenstein, L. (2007). *A lecture on ethics*. Quodlibet.

Chapter 14
Who Are 'Good' Morals/Ethics Good for?

14.1 Introduction

The definitions in Chap. 13 provide the starting point for this chapter. These definitions are independent of any normative considerations and so are free of any religious or transcendental considerations. This differs from conventional views of ethics and morality as being somehow absolute or innate; these definitions can accommodate an action considered acceptable by some being considered unacceptable by others. This raises the question of who a particular ethical or moral view may have benefitted/been good for and what the implications might be for achieving either collaboration or conflict in interpersonal communication. This chapter seeks to provide a basis for answering these two questions.

A first principles approach is adopted, using these rigorous new generic definitions of ethics, morality and related terms in developing a model of the group influences people are subject to when deciding the ethics or morality of a particular action. A model of the communication process between two individuals is then developed that accommodates ethical/moral considerations and that can produce either conflict or collaboration on contested issues. The resulting models are then examined from the perspective of the three well-known schools of ethical thought originating from Bentham, Kant and Aristotle.

14.2 Ethics Chapter Definitions

The definitions from Chap. 13 are pivotal to this chapter and so are repeated below.

Its *accepted* definitions are:

- Good = that which we consider to be useful.

S. K. McGrath, *Speaking Management*,
https://doi.org/10.1007/978-981-16-2213-7_14

- Bad = that which we consider to be a hindrance.

Its *derived* definitions are as follows:

- Principle (n) = a rule guiding action.
- Principles (n) = (pl) a set of rules guiding action.
- Value (n) = the quantity of satisfaction of an interest.
- Values (n) (pl) = preferences guiding the actions of an entity.
- Belief (n) = a proposition an entity considers valid.
- Beliefs (n) (pl) = propositions an entity considers valid.
- Ethics (n) (pl) = principles of civic behaviour that restrain individual behaviour for a higher purpose.
- Morals (n) = principles of interpersonal behaviour that restrain individual behaviour for a higher purpose.
- Moral (n) = in accordance with a principle of interpersonal behaviour that restrains individual behaviour for a higher purpose.

These definitions collectively imply that values are preferences, ethics are principles, and morals are beliefs that may include, but may also be wider than ethics. Ethics tend to be based on known facts rather than on beliefs. Morals and ethics both address the question "What should I do?" with one being guided by secular principles of accepted practice and one being guided by beliefs. Both principles and beliefs may be true or false and no attempt is made here to judge that. This leads to the conclusion that a person could be considered within their own society to be moral yet be judged immoral by another society. The German people accepted the superiority of the Aryan race and took the consequent difficult 'moral' (for them) action of exterminating Jews, which other societies considered completely immoral. These definitions can accommodate this and are therefore free of value judgement.

14.3 Literature Review

Chapter 14 conducted a literature review of ethics, ethical theories and definitional confusion and that will not be repeated here. Rather, the three well-known schools of ethical thought will be very briefly summarised. All three provide guidance on deciding "what should I do" in particular circumstances by prescribing use of a particular moral principle – virtue for Aristotle, rational duty for Kant and maximising utility/happiness for Bentham.

Further insight on ethical positions can be gained by looking at the field of moral psychology in which Haidt offers the view that there are six moral foundations. Comparing this with the three schools of ethical thought, none of them align particularly well. The six moral foundations which Haidt (2012) identified are care, liberty, fairness, loyalty, authority and sanctity. Virtue could be loosely aligned with fairness (and perhaps loyalty and authority), rational duty with authority (and perhaps loyalty) and utility with care. But even these extrapolated equivalences still leave liberty and sanctity untouched. This indicates a narrowness in all three well-known approaches, providing a reason why none have been fully adequate. None deal adequately with the reason versus emotion issue and Haidt presents three such models of this. These are Plato's view that reason should be the master of the passions, Hume's opposite view that reason is the servant of the passions, and Jefferson's view that reason and emotion were co-rulers, with reason controlling those matters that don't involve people (Haidt, 2012). He opts in favour of Hume.

This chapter will explore from first principles and while the starting point for this chapter of clear, non-overlapping, non-normative, naturalist definitions is new, the activities of communication and its consequences of collaboration or conflict are not new and so the literature concerning collaboration, interaction and communication will be reviewed to see what models or representations may have previously been proposed.

14.3.1 Collaboration Models

Nowak and Highfield (2011) noted:

> If you are a co-operator, you will find yourself surrounded by other co-operators so that what you reap is what you sow … to succeed in life, you need to work together – pursuing the snuggle for existence, if you like – just as much as you strive to win the struggle for existence. … Cooperation – not competition – underpins innovation. … Cooperation is the architect of creativity throughout evolution, from cells to multi-cellular creatures, from anthills to villages and cities. Without cooperation there can be neither construction nor complexity in evolution.

They pointed out that:

> Previously there were only two basic principles of evolution – mutation and selection … to understand the creative aspects of evolution, we must now accept that cooperation is the third principle (and that) Many problems that challenge us today can be traced back to a profound tension between what is good and desirable for society as a whole and what is good and desirable for an individual" (Nowak and Highfield, 2011).

They set out ways in which "cooperation can evolve and how it is woven into the very fabric of the cosmos. In all there are five mechanisms that lead to cooperation" (Nowak & Highfield, 2011); these are "tit for tat", indirect reciprocity, spatial games, group selection and kin selection. They noted that "We can draw on all the mechanisms of cooperation … thanks in large part to our dazzling powers of language and communication" (Nowak & Highfield, 2011).

A search of all EBSCO databases for "collaboration model" in the titles of peer reviewed journals on 27 August 2018 found 13 items. EBSCO was selected as it is an 'aggregator' searching multiple databases. All 13 items were examined and were found to be concerned with things such as innovation hubs, setting up partnerships, funding, sharing resources, technology, career development and collaboration models established in various companies including IBM and GEC. However, none dealt with the interpersonal aspects of collaboration and none provided any model of the thought and emotional processes involved in personal interactions.

A similar search for "model for collaboration" was conducted locating 14 items. This identified classroom interventions WOWW (Working with what works) and SFBT (Solution focused group therapy), research collaboration and the C5 model of a cell's influence, but there were only three papers that actually detailed some form of collaboration model.

Lebrón and Tabak (2018) presented a power-based student-centred (PSCM) collaboration model for faculty staff, student and student organisation leaders to operationalize legitimate, coercive, expert, reward and informational power in sharing resources. This comprised four steps of initial discussion, form team, develop structure & processes, then do an experiential learning assignment.

Janssens and Brett (2006) developed a fusion model of collaboration which focused on fusing cross-cultural aspects/elements in contrast to models of collaboration based on principles of the dominant coalition and of integration and/or identity. It was concerned with addressing unequal power relations among team members. They note that a dominant coalition may comprise a majority of the team, but may also be a minority group, or even an individual.

Butterfield et al. (2004) investigated why stakeholder groups form collaborative alliances when dealing with a target organization, what leaders of stakeholder organizations actually think about when collaborating to deal with the target organization, and what outcomes result from the collaboration process. They drew on stakeholder theory as well as on research in interorganizational collaboration and used an inductive, interview-based methodology to build a descriptive model of collaboration among non-profit stakeholder groups. The model comprised six major themes: motivating factors, formation factors, formation moderators, operating factors, outcomes, and outcome moderators.

The above sources are all based on understanding or facilitating or mediating the conflict process or strategizing about it. All had an intervention/control/intervention perspective/paradigm, and none provided any model of first principles, basic personal interactions. While ethics and morality (or lack thereof) may govern communication and can lead to conflict, it is not dispute or conflict resolution that is the focus of this chapter; it is rather the process of communication which may result in either conflict or harmony. This chapter seeks to provide a model to assist individual understanding rather than a tool for an external party to use in attempting to bring about resolution. It is concerned with internal individual processes rather than external intervention. Consequently, the fields of negotiation, facilitation and dispute/conflict resolution were not reviewed. The searches conducted were not field specific and so should have picked up any such models from these fields anyway.

14.3.2 *Interaction Models*

Various other searches were then conducted on various models and processes. A search of all EBSCO databases for "interaction model" in the titles and communication in the abstract of peer reviewed journals was conducted on 29 August 2018 and found 14 items. These were examined and were found to be concerned with things such as pedagogy, intercultural interaction, medical, sport, marketing and fashion. Only one addressed interpersonal communication. This was by Bornstein et al. (2017) who addressed communication between romantic couples. Their investigation was limited to exploring communication about conflict and it found that self-control was associated with better relationship outcomes in terms of less avoidance and demand/withdraw behaviour. It did not provide any model of the interaction process.

A similar search for "model of interaction" in the titles and "communication" in the abstract found 4 items, none of which presented any model of human interaction. A similar search for "conflict process" in the titles of peer reviewed journals was conducted on 29 August 2018 and found 12 items, none of which offered a first principles model of the conflict process. A similar search for "happiness process" located no items and for "satisfaction process" located 10, none of which offered a first principles generic model. A further search for "satisfaction model" in the title and communication in all text located 16 items, none of which offered a first principles generic model.

14.3.3 *Communications Models*

A search of all EBSCO databases for "model of communication" in the title of peer reviewed journals was conducted on 4 October 2018 and found 274 items of which 139 were non-duplicates. All abstracts were examined. Most were case studies of how particular issues had been communicated or marketed or were studies of communication styles or of how electronic communication had been achieved. There were some that modelled particular communication processes using various techniques/bases/circumstances (e.g. based on signs, networks, games, etc.) but none used the individual modelling basis proposed here. Their focus was on theories concerning how communication can be improved, rather than on simply modelling the basics of what actually happens generically when two people communicate.

A further search of all EBSCO databases for "communication model" in the title of peer reviewed journals was also conducted on 4 October 2018 and found 394 items of which 197 were non-duplicates. All abstracts were examined. Most were case studies of communication for particular purposes, many of which were electronic. None used the individual modelling basis proposed here.

While these searches do not prove that no model has previously been developed on similar basis to that proposed here, it indicates there is a high probability this may be the case and so there is value in proceeding.

14.4 Approach

The definitional approach adopted in this chapter follows on from McGrath and Whitty (2015). This directly contradicts the family resemblance concept developed by Wittgenstein and Anscombe (1958), which has received widespread acceptance, such as by Seidl (2007) and Haugaard (2010). However, the difficulties with that concept have recently been identified by McGrath (2019), as reported in Sect. 7.1 of Part I.

This approach has objectivist epistemology with a positivist theoretical perspective that seeks to define objective content without claiming that the derived definitions describe anything existential. It simply defines concepts non-normatively, producing definitions which, if agreed and adopted, have the potential to remove unnecessary debate and confusion. It takes the view that, while there may be no absolute truth, to be productive as a society, a discourse that removes confusion is necessary, one that all can participate in, with shared understanding of meaning, removing accidental and undetected differences. This position is therefore midway between (or partly both) realist and post-modernist, as this apparatus (ensuring consistency and universality of terminology), can replace chaos with order.

The questions posed in the introduction are too broad for a universal answer to be possible and what will be developed here is just a framework for answering them that is independent of any subject matter or content. Any normative factors influencing determination of validity, 'good' and 'bad' will be recognised only insofar as they serve identification of process. No absolute moral/value judgements will be made, and an antithetical, relative approach is taken based upon understanding the process through which both influence and communication occurs.

The analysis will be approached from first principles by considering an individual person as the base unit of analysis. The new definitions will be considered within the context of how communicative interaction occurs between individuals giving rise to behaviour that may be regarded as ethical or not. This takes place within the context of group interactions and allegiances. The specific approaches to developing each of the three key figures in this chapter are outlined below.

14.4.1 Definitional Space

This chapter was prompted by the new definitions developed in the ethics chapter and so these will be adopted and considered within the context of evaluating action to be taken in developing a representation of the definitional space.

14.4.2 Group Allegiances

Mathematical work on game theory has indicated that "the more sets (groups) there are, the better it is for cooperation" (Nowak and Highfield, 2011). To answer the question posed by the title of this chapter, ethics needs to be placed within the context of individuals within society and so consideration of the groups surrounding an individual is necessary. This needs to consider the balance between the governance society exerts over an individual and the exercise of individual freedom i.e. it needs to consider mechanisms of both encouragement and restraint.

Haidt has extensively researched the area of moral psychology in relation to group behaviour and observed that "our 'higher nature' allows us to be profoundly altruistic, but that altruism is mostly aimed at members of our own groups" (Haidt, 2012). He noted that "As Darwin said long ago, the most cohesive and cooperative groups generally beat the groups of selfish individualists" (ibid) and he considered religion to be "an evolutionary adaptation for binding groups together and helping them to create communities with a shared morality" (Haidt, 2012). He further considered that:

> If you think about religion as a set of beliefs about supernatural agents, you're bound to misunderstand it. You'll see those beliefs as foolish delusions, perhaps even as parasites that exploit our brains for their own benefit. But if you take a Durkheimian approach to religion (focusing on belonging) and a Darwinian approach to morality (involving multilevel selection), you get a very different picture. You see that religious practices have been binding our ancestors into groups for tens of thousands of years. That binding usually involves some blinding—once any person, book, or principle is declared sacred, then devotees can no longer question it or think clearly about it (Haidt, 2012).

He also noted that:

> Our ability to believe in supernatural agents may well have begun as an accidental by-product of a hypersensitive agency detection device, but once early humans began believing

> in such agents, the groups that used them to construct moral communities were the ones that lasted and prospered… they used their gods to elicit sacrifice and commitment from members… their gods helped them to suppress cheating and increase trustworthiness. Only groups that can elicit commitment and suppress free riding can grow (ibid).

He concluded that "We humans have an extraordinary ability to care about things beyond ourselves, to circle around those things with other people, and in the process to bind ourselves into teams that can pursue larger projects" (ibid). He also noted that "We need groups, we love groups, and we develop our virtues in groups, even though those groups necessarily exclude non-members. If you destroy all groups and dissolve all internal structure, you destroy your moral capital" (Haidt, 2012). He also noted that "Anything that binds people together into dense networks of trust makes people less selfish". (ibid).

His cross-group study of 360 people conducted in Porto Alegre, Recife and Philadelphia also showed conclusively that "The moral domain varied across nations and social classes" (Haidt, 2012). This indicates that morality is relative to context and is not universal. Haidt favours what he calls "Durkheimian utilitarianism", which takes the lead from Adam Smith in focusing people at the local level where they have understanding and abilities. He considered this to be "utilitarianism done by somebody who understands human groupishness" (Haidt, 2012). He also noted that:

> The idea of opposites as yin and yang comes from ancient China, a culture that valued harmony. But in the Middle East, where monotheism first took root, the metaphor of war was more common than the metaphor of balance. The third century Persian prophet Mani preached that the visible world is the battleground between the forces of light (absolute goodness) and the forces of darkness (absolute evil)… Mani's preaching developed into Manichaeism, a religion that spread throughout the Middle East and influenced Western thinking. If you think about politics in a Manichaean way, then compromise is a sin. God and the devil don't issue many bipartisan proclamations (Haidt, 2012).

He concluded that:

> We all get sucked into tribal moral communities. We circle around sacred values and then share post hoc arguments about why we are so right and they are so wrong. We think the other side is blind to truth, reason, science and common sense, but in fact everyone goes blind when talking about their sacred objects" (Haidt, 2012).

Nevertheless, he also concluded after spending some time in India that happiness, as well as coming from within, also "comes from between. It comes from getting the right relationships between yourself and others, yourself and your work, and yourself and something larger than yourself" (Haidt, 2012).

Given the significance of group allegiances as indicated by the research mentioned above, these will be depicted to provide the necessary context.

14.4.3 Individual Communication Process

George Bernard Shaw said: "The single biggest problem in communication is the illusion that it has taken place" (BrainyQuote, 2018). McGrath (2019) said "Communication isn't what you think you meant. It's what the other person thinks you meant. What you think you meant is just talking or writing". There are obviously challenges in communicating effectively. The concept of autopoiesis can potentially assist with this challenge through connecting language, biology and behaviour, and its use aligns with the approach being taken here of going back to basics to explore the implications of the new definitions.

The Oxford (Dictionary defines autopoiesis as "The self-maintenance of an organized entity through its own internal processes". According to Luhmann (2005), "The term 'autopoiesis' has been invented to define life". Maturana and Varela (1980) invented the term as "a word without a history, a word that could directly mean what takes place in the dynamics of the autonomy proper to living systems". Their epistemology was, in part, that "*objective knowledge* must always be created by the listener: the listener understands, and *objective knowledge* appears transferred, only if he is prepared to understand" (Maturana and Varela, 1980).

Maturana and Varela (1980) considered "that language is connotative and not denotative and that its function is to orient the orientee within his cognitive domain, and not to point to independent entities". They noted this has no regard for the cognitive domain of the orienter i.e. there is no transmission of information or thought through language. The listener just "creates information by reducing his uncertainty through his interactions in his cognitive domain. Consensus arises only through cooperative interactions in which the resulting behaviour of each organism becomes subservient to the maintenance of both". We can only talk about transmission of information "because the speaker tacitly assumes the listener to be identical with him and hence as having the same cognitive domain which he has (which never is the case), marvelling when a 'misunderstanding' arises (Maturana and Varela, 1980).

In considering the cognitive function, they note that "Although many nerve cells may change continuously, their mode of operation and their past history can explain to the observer how their present mode of operation was reached, but not how it is realized now, or what their present participation in the determination of behaviour is" (Maturana & Varela, 1980). Past history in relation to group membership has been addressed in the previous section and the interactive and recursive processes that determine the reaction/behaviour between any two individuals in the present will now be considered.

Luhmann took the concept Maturana developed in biology and applied it to organisations, accepting his definition of autopoietic systems as being:

> systems that are defined as unities, as networks of productions of components, that recursively, through their interactions, generate and realize the network that produces them and constitute, in the space in which they exist, the boundaries of the network as components that participate in the realization of the network (Luhmann, 2005).

He then says "Social systems use communication as their particular mode of autopoietic reproduction. Their elements are communications which are recursively produced and reproduced by a network of communications and which cannot exist outside of such a network" (Luhmann, 2005). This implies that:

> Communications are not 'living' units, they are not 'conscious' units, they are not 'actions'. Their unity requires a synthesis of three selections: namely, information, utterance and understanding (including misunderstanding). This synthesis is produced by the network of communication, not by some inherent power of consciousness, or by the inherent quality of the information. Also – this goes against all kinds of 'structuralism' – communication is not produced by language… It is the network of events which reproduces itself, and the structures are required for the reproduction of events by events (Luhmann, 2005).

He further considers that:

> The synthesis of information, utterance and understanding cannot be programmed by language. It also has to be recreated from situation to situation by referring to previous communications and to possibilities of further communications which are to be restricted by the actual event. This operation requires self-reference. It can in no way use the environment (Luhmann, 2005).

He notes that communication includes understanding as a necessary part of the unity of its operation and does not include acceptance of its content. He also notes it is not the function of communication to produce a consensus as the favoured state of mind.

> Communication always results in an open situation of either acceptance or rejection… the selection of further communication is either an acceptance or rejection of previous communication or a visible avoidance or adjournment of the issues (Luhmann, 2005).

This implies acceptance or resistance, with resistance producing one of acceptance by the other party, compromise or conflict.

The autopoietic process of communication between two individuals will be depicted in Fig. 14.3, taking its basic structure from Fig. 14.1.

14.5 Method

Graphical representations (diagrams and flowchart) will be used to facilitate visualization and conceptualization, as was done by McGrath and Whitty (2015) in mapping the concept of governance, and as has also been done in the power Chap. 12 above, as well as in the stakeholders Chap. 17 below.

The following depictions will be developed:

1. A map of ethical terminology depicting the concept of ethics and associated terms and the relationships between them relative to action that adopting a particular position or communicating particular attitudes will produce, and the impacts this will have.
2. A diagram of allegiances or environmental influences, allowing consideration of context and who particular actions may be good for. This will be done for two individuals interacting.
3. A flow diagram of the communication process depicting a single interaction between two entities from first principles, showing both possible outcomes of collaboration and conflict that may arise between A and B.

The resulting diagrams, which will be referred to as ethical models, will then be evaluated.

14.6 The Ethical Models

The three models are developed below.

14.6.1 *Ethical Cycle – A Map of Terminology*

The first model to be developed by this method is simply a map of the definitional terms defined in the ethics chapter – principles, beliefs, ethics, values and morals. This is shown in Fig. 14.1 below.

This is a bland, non-normative representation of the ethical definitional space. It is quite important because usage of these terms exerts silent governance over the outcomes of ethical discussions. This map facilitates reaching a common understanding of the terms used. It simply categorizes the terms defined in the ethics chapter (principles, beliefs, ethics, values and morals) and arranges them in their logical sequence of occurrence. Organising these terms in this way makes it evident that there is a progression in them with a feedback loop that results from their application.

The second model extends beyond terminology and considers the allegiances of individuals to themselves, others and various groups. It depicts what is good for me,

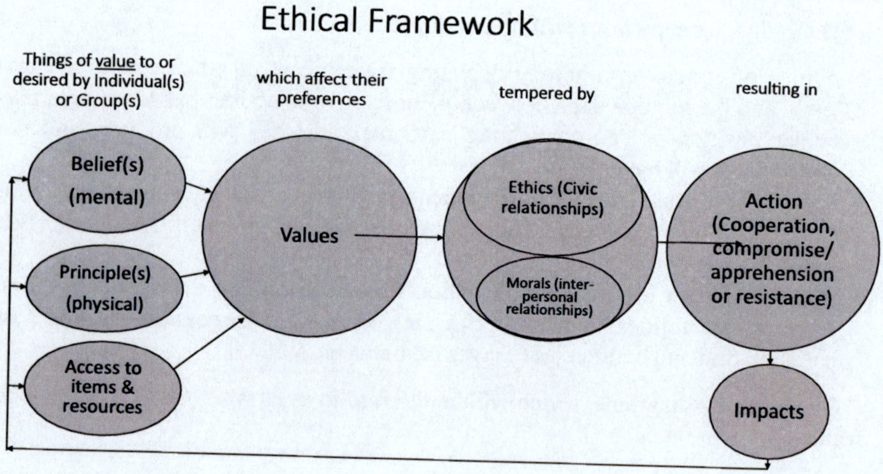

Fig. 14.1 Ethical cycle – a map of terminology

my group(s), you and your group(s), and brings in the potential for competition. It is shown below in Fig. 14.2.

14.6.2 *Ethical Eye – A Map of Allegiances*

The next model developed is the map of allegiances.

Notes on Fig. 14.2:

1. Either competition or cooperation occurs whenever individuals or groups interact, as well as whenever an individual or group line inside the eye diagram is crossed.
2. Competition may arise from seeking things such as water, food, sex, money, objects, land, resources, affection, attention, recognition, acceptance, status, power or glory.
3. Competition may be motivated by desire for survival, comfort/convenience, pleasure, entertainment, pride, dominance or revenge.

Representing the group allegiances of individuals in this way shows how these both constrain behaviour and encourage exercise of personal freedom. It also shows that what may be good for my group, may not be good for yours, or for me, or vice versa. It also exposes universal morality as an impossibility. I may regard as 'good' those things that benefit me or my group, and I may regard as 'bad' those that dis-benefit me or my group, regardless of whether they are 'good' or

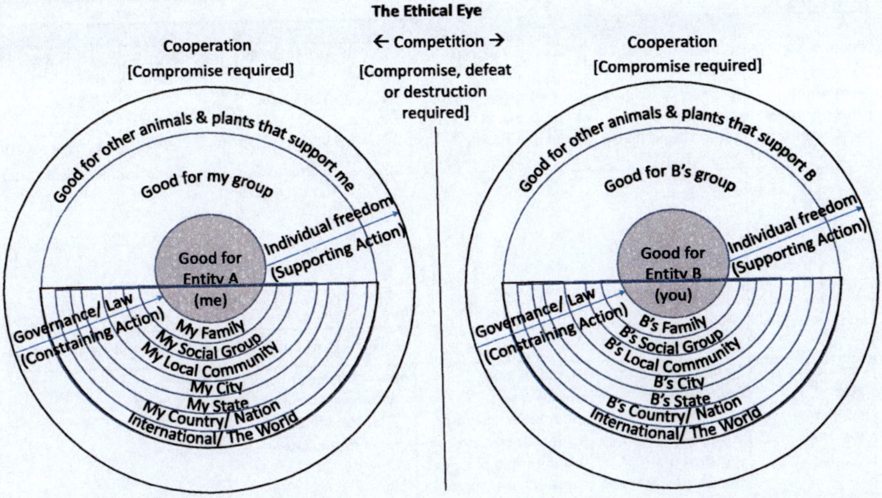

Fig. 14.2 The ethical eye – a map of allegiances

'bad' for you or your group. Furthermore, we also have perceptions and belief filters about what is 'true', 'right' and/or 'good', and what we think 'right' or 'good' for us may not actually be so, and what we might think 'good' for a particular group also may not actually be so. There is also the further matter of timescale, where the short-term effects may be 'good' but the long-term effects may be 'bad'.

All these considerations around Fig. 14.2 indicate that human interactions are very complex; they are relative to (affected by) many circumstances. Failing to specify the necessary qualifiers regarding who a particular moral/ethical position may be good for, and in what circumstances, will unnecessarily increase complexity and confusion, and invite over-simplified, deterministic and erroneous judgement. As John von Neumann said "If people do not believe that mathematics is simple, it is only because they do not realize how complicated life is" (Nowak and Highfield, 2011).

14.6.3 Communication Process

The third model applies the Fig. 14.1 cycle to the two entities of Fig. 14.2, producing Fig. 14.3 which maps the communication that occurs from the perspective of the participants' happiness with the progress and the outcome of their interaction. Note that Figure 14.3:

A's Action	B's Orientation			B's Response	
	Impact - B likes or accepts it		>	>	>
Event occurs - A does or says something (intentionally or accidentally)	**Impact** - B dislikes it/ feels hurt/ frustrated/ doesn't understand/ comprehend how A can do that	This may trigger a **sense making** process in B who may attempt to understand before judging A's motives	B may **consider** possible **responses** based on B's interpretation of A's motives	B **chooses response**	B enacts the chosen response, creating a new event for A to deal with
			n = Number of times to either repeat and escalate, or to		
Contextual factors/ possible responses	B's disposition, expectations, perceptions, principles, beliefs, standard of proof, core values, state of mind (upset), health issues or sleep deprivation	B's disposition, knowledge, experience, maturity, ability to resist pre-programmed amygdala survival fight/ flight behaviour &/ or pride/ ego-driven competitive desire to be right	> don't respond > withdraw attention > attempt persuasion > react immediately with words, actions or force > delay response > plan revenge		
Misperceptions may arise from	Difference in understanding of concepts Difference in self awareness and the impact of actions on others Difference in principles, beliefs, and values				

Fig. 14.3 Communication process model

1. Has an escape mechanism where happy means happy enough = satisfied under the circumstances i.e. euphoria is not required.
2. Models the communication <u>process</u>, not the <u>content</u> of any communication/ agreement/dispute.
3. Is <u>not</u> a conflict resolution process for external third-party application/ intervention.
4. Adopts the usual project control traffic light dashboard approach, where green means proceed, red means stop, and amber mean some change is coming.
5. Can be applied to individuals or groups.

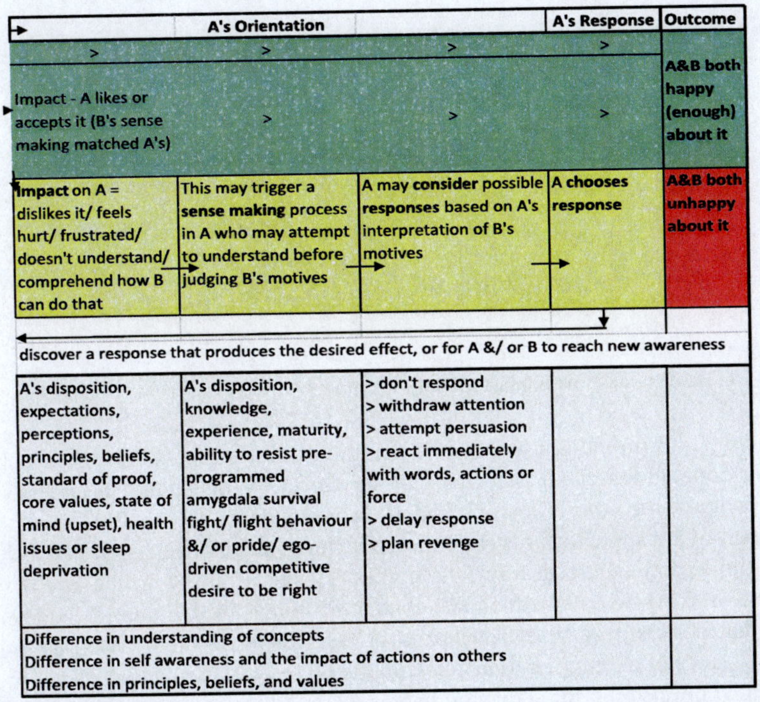

Fig. 14.3 (continued)

Features of Fig. 14.3 bearing upon the accepted schools of ethical thought are as follows:

- It is a binary model with only two outcomes while communication about a contested subject continues – joint happiness or joint unhappiness.
- It does not maximise overall happiness in Bentham's utilitarian sense, although understanding/using it could facilitate that. Either both are happy, or both are not, unless/until the conflict is resolved by one winning or giving in, then one is happy, and one is not and further communication is terminated.
- It is not a deterministic Kantian rule-based approach based on a set of coded beliefs or pre-determined moral code, although it does accommodate the categorical imperative of respect for other rational beings.
- It is not an Aristotelian virtue-based approach, although it is perhaps closest to Aristotle in pointing towards basic underlying human values or virtue, rather than duty to any group.

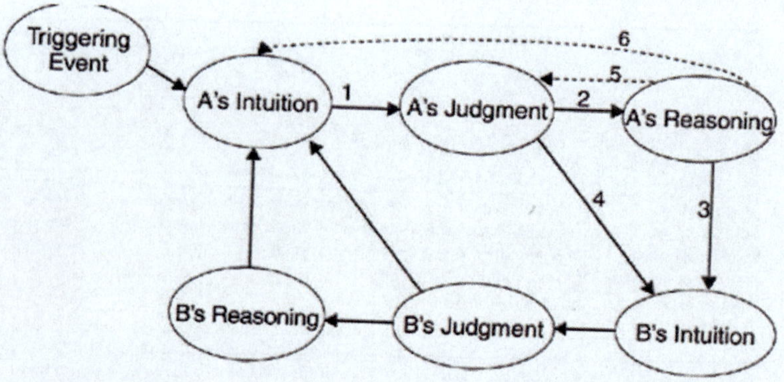

Fig. 14.4 Haidt's Social Intuitionist Model

Figure 14.3 provides a map of the communication process through which conflict or cooperation can arise. This may be useful for disputants in understanding their own and the other's position and as a consequence, may facilitate progressing their part of a dispute towards resolution. However, it is not designed as a technique for a third party to use in resolving conflict. It deals only with the key basics of process, making no comment on any content/dispute subject matter. It lists perspectives that parties may have overlooked or been unaware of. It proposes only the simple basics of attempting to understand the other's position and does not propose any grand philosophy for achieving happiness.

It is immediately evident from Figs. 14.3 and 14.2 that there are a large number of variables affecting whether a particular action or behaviour is 'moral' or 'ethical' in particular circumstances and that ignoring these variables cannot help but produce conflict. It is therefore evident that the unitary criteria proposed by the three schools of ethical thought according to Aristotle, Bentham or Kant are too simplistic to accommodate the complex circumstances of human communication.

It is worth noting that Haidt developed a model from a completely different perspective which arrived at a depiction which looks quite different to, but actually has parallels with Fig. 14.3. He labelled it the "social intuitionist model" and it is presented as Fig. 2.4 in Haidt (2012) and is shown here as Fig. 14.4.

Haidt developed Fig. 14.4 through the lens of moral philosophy, whereas Fig. 14.3 was developed through the lens of definition and motivation, seeking understanding of how we do things. The basic processes in the two figures are similar. Figure 14.3 includes motivation and is a more detailed process than Fig. 14.4. Figure 14.3 is based on ensuring we all know we are talking about the same thing, and that we know some detail about what the processes are that are independent of content, the evaluation of which is left to others.

Given the existence of a similar model, it is useful to briefly outline its author's approach to ethics. Haidt aligns himself with Hume's view of emotions controlling reason, rather than with Jefferson or Plato. He said that Plato believed reason could and should be the master whereas Jefferson believed that the two processes were equal partners (head and heart) ruling a divided empire. Hume believed that reason was (and was only fit to be) the servant of the passions (Haidt, 2012). He considered intuitions come before reasoning which is usually produced to influence other people after a judgment is made. He says:

> We make our first judgments rapidly, and we are dreadful at seeking out evidence that might disconfirm those initial judgments. Yet friends can do for us what we cannot do for ourselves: they can challenge us, giving us reasons and arguments (link 3 (in Fig. 14.4)) that sometimes trigger new intuitions, thereby making it possible for us to change our minds… For most of us, it's not every day or even every month that we change our mind about a moral issue without any prompting from anyone else… Many of us believe that we follow an inner moral compass, but the history of social psychology richly demonstrates that other people exert a powerful force, able to make cruelty seem acceptable and altruism seem embarrassing, without giving us any reasons or arguments (Haidt, 2012).

Figure 14.3 is independent of Haidt's six moral foundations. It is also independent of any presumption that happiness is related to life satisfaction or to the alternative view of Kahneman (2013) that it is related to the well-being of the experiencing self.

14.7 Observations

The following observations of Figs. 14.1 to 14.3 can now be made.

14.7.1 User Requirements

For anyone to derive benefit from Fig. 14.3, they would need to accept the meanings of the terms as defined and recognise that their personal development as well as the passage of time and scientific discoveries may have rendered some of their current beliefs and/or practices obsolete. Furthermore, any one of us has a collection of attitudes and beliefs acquired from multiple sources – parents, teachers, friends, clergy, governments, organisations we become members of etc. The chances that all of their frameworks of belief being mutually consistent is pretty low, leaving us with connundrums to reconcile as we grow older and start to realise some of the conflicts and inconsistencies. Anyone using Fig. 14.3 would also need to be open to considering the standard of proof they deem to be sufficient to justify particular beliefs they may hold. For Fig. 14.3 to contribute to resolving conflict, both (all) participants would need to apply it to themselves. The number of conflicts that can be resolved with a one-sided effort is unlikely to be high and its use could not replace externally directed intervention in some dispute situations, but equally, external intervention cannot be regarded as a universal necessity.

14.7.2 Adherence to Principles

A significant difficulty in achieving collaboration occurs when participants stick rigidly to fixed positions on principle. This characteristic may even be lauded/admired, but again, the universality of such admiration bears questioning. The feedback loop in Fig. 14.3 shows that it is not universally admirable. Sticking 'ethically' to principle can sometimes equate to deterministic/absolutism and pig-headedness, refusing to acknowledge the reality others may have. Following the flow of the model makes it obvious that dogmatically sticking to principles can have quite limited success in resolving conflict. It is much more likely to lead to escalation and possibly, to war.

14.7.3 Universal Morality

The view that emerges from this work is that there is no universal morality; there is only resolution of competing interests (conflict resolution), and there can be only three outcomes for an entity; win, lose or compromise. The only way morality can be regarded as absolute is if all the circumstances, history and boundary conditions surrounding the situation are fully specified before a value judgement is made. This will be likely to produce a range of situations so limited that it will be practically useless.

14.7.4 Standard of Proof

The amount of time required to 'prove' any position is so great that it can rarely be achieved, and it may not even be possible. We do not have time to do a PhD thesis on every single question we have to resolve in life. So, it is practically impossible to make decisions based upon what is actually true; we can generally only make decisions based upon what we think is true. For the mere practicality of functioning, we have to keep making decisions based on what we think is right or best at the time, based upon whatever information we have at that time. So, the question of what standard of proof we require for different types of decisions then becomes a significant issue. I may accept only observation, or hard scientific data, or I may choose just what I feel like at the time. I may also come to believe all teachings of one particular creed or person in one particular book that may serve as an external, objective source of reference for me. But that begs the question of why that particular creed, person or book would be right and others wrong, and whether it/they are literally correct on every single matter. There is also the question as to who else will accept its/their word or opinion. Others, either not following that book or following a different book, may not be quite so impressed and may not accept it as a standard of proof. Standard of proof for an opinion or belief is therefore an important issue.

14.7.5 Normativity and Religion

There is also difficulty with using the statements of spiritual books as 'proof', particularly when they deal with matters that depend upon faith alone that cannot be proven. The work done in this chapter indicates that adopting a non-normative approach in removing arbitrary value judgement does allow clarity to come into definition and consequently into communication. The approach taken here has been simply to recognize any religious moral judgements as being normative and therefore requiring exclusion. They may contain wisdom that science hasn't uncovered yet, but they are unprovable now, and so must be parked to avoid the extra-dimensional 'firewall' of attempting to communicate with different beings that we can't see. For now, we just need to get on with attempting to make sense of what we can, with the people who are in front of us, in the four dimensions we have ready access to.

14.7.6 Religious Texts

We may then reflect on any non-normative conclusions we may reach to see if they coincide with a religious view. One such case is immediately obvious and that is withholding judgement = leaving the judgement to God = not pretending to be God i.e. blaspheming. In this case, the non-normative, secular reasoning demonstrated in this chapter reaches the same conclusion as the Bible's ban on judgement and blasphemy, just by specifying the qualifying words.

It would not be unreasonable to expect that application of advice in religious texts would be supportive of sustaining human life. This accords with the view of religious texts as containing timeless wisdom for the benefit of mankind.

However, the statements of such texts on past territorial matters and family/group/race/non-believer conflicts/world domination actually reflect preferences and/or prejudices from past times that perpetuate rather than assist present-day communication. Such matters would best be consigned to the historical record rather than continuing to fuel current conflict.

14.7.7 Reification

Reification of traditions and beliefs inherited from times past from any source, be it religion, culture, parents, habit, propaganda or whatever, can mask or hide clarity around motivations for actions. Non-normativity excludes this.

14.7.8 Proscriptive Rules

Proscriptive rules are much simpler than prescriptive rules governing morality. The principal Western 'thou shalt not's of the Ten Commandments have survived since Hebrew times, with minor variations over the millennia. It is much easier and quicker to state what should not be done than to foresee all possible circumstances and state what should be done. There is a parallel with the definitional issues in Part I, with proscriptive rules being intensional and just setting boundaries, whereas prescriptive rules deal with extensions, running the risk of ommision.

14.7.9 Truth in Language

There is a problem in seeking truth in language, as the words we use to describe concepts are constituted only of sounds agreed by – we often don't know who. This suggests the following guidelines:

1. First ensure we agree about exactly what our words signify
2. Find out what the surrounding circumstances and boundary conditions are
3. Describe just what we know to have happened
4. Qualify any generalisations or speculations to these circumstances.

It is pointless to search for meaning through words that can only represent something that may or may not have been agreed. This is a fundamental problem that generates needless moral conundrum and debate, as outlined in McGrath (2019) and in Part I above.

14.7.10 *Happiness Versus Reality*

The outcome of the Fig. 14.3 communication process is not necessarily happiness. Some unfortunate measures may become necessary to achieve a sustainable outcome. For example, the manufacture of weapons may well be necessary for 'my group' to have a chance of surviving and reproducing to reach its universally peaceful utopia, if it is threatened by an aggressive, destructive, armed party or ideology, such as occurred in World War II.

14.8 Implications for Ethical Schools of Thought

Extending the definitions into the models in Figs. 14.1 to 14.3 identified the difficulties, noted in earlier sections above, with the positions of the various ethical schools that do not accommodate the complexity of circumstances that can arise. Their rules presume that universal morality exists, which the above discussion has shown to be false.

For Aristotle's virtue or Kant's duty, intuition is also a problem. Aristotle regarded intuition as infallible but, as Popper points out, this is not so:

> For somebody else may have just as strong an intuition that the same theory is false… Francis Bacon, for example, sneered at those who denied the self-evident truth that the sun and the stars rotated around the earth, which was obviously at rest (Popper, 1995).

Popper suggested an alternative approach to ethics that avoids idealisation and grand narratives by simply focusing on what seems to be wrong. He said:

> I proposed that, in the main, happiness should be, and that it can only be, left to private initiative, while the alleviation of avoidable suffering is a problem of public policy. Of course, I never suggested that the minimization of suffering should be made the highest moral principle. In fact, I do not believe in the existence of such a thing as a single highest universally valid moral principle. On the contrary, I suggested that in matters of public policy we have to constantly reconsider our priorities, and that in drawing up a list of priorities avoidable suffering rather than happiness should be our main guide. Perhaps not forever: there may come a time when the alleviation of avoidable suffering will be less important than it is today (Popper, 2002).

This view is compatible with the models presented in the above figures.

The nearest to a 'highest moral principle' emerging from Figs. 14.1 to 14.3 is "whatever is best in the particular circumstances for the individual/group's long-term survival" with minimisation of suffering being a sub-set of, and a limiting exception to, that. This could be expressed as 'utility' but is not the same as Bentham's maximising happiness (for now in making a decision that must be taken now). He said "Nature has placed mankind under the governance of two sovereign masters, pain and pleasure. It is for them alone to point out what we ought to do" (Mill et al., 1987).

The 'utility' referred to in the previous paragraph may happen to coincide with an average for the group over all circumstances, now and into the unknowable future, with exceptions or limits to the suffering of individuals that may be necessary to bring this about. This revised approximation of the highest moral principle is not incompatible with the more traditional understanding of the words 'morals' and 'ethics', but leaves out any ethereal or *a priori* notion, thereby avoiding the confusion of dual simultaneous understandings of essence (and some other words) where the ethereal meaning randomly but consistently gazumps the secular meaning, as identified in McGrath (2019) and in Part I above.

The 'good for x' approach of Fig. 14.2 is also compatible with Darwin's principle that natural selection works solely by and for the good of each being (Darwin and Beer, 2008). Herd and flock cooperative behaviour has evolved and as Nowak and Highfield (2011) point out, evolution discovers cooperation in certain circumstances. This is evident for the internal workings of our bodies as well as for flocks, groups or species. But the natural order is to compete for advantage, and once that competition has produced an organism that preys upon others, there can be no overt cooperation between predator and prey – at least not without conscious intent and experience bringing knowledge of the consequences of over-predation. So there are natural cycles that can bring balance. If we can, with our superior brains, comprehend a longer time-scale and recognise this, we can potentially avert or mitigate the cycles, even though the outcomes of the grand social experiments to date with Socialism and Nazism do not inspire much confidence in mankind's ability to successfully engineer such an outcome.

The figures developed in this chapter provide an explanation of Mill's noting that "little progress has been made in the decision of the controversy respecting the criterion of right and wrong… And after more than two thousand years the same discussions continue" (Mill et al., 1987). He also noted:

> When it has become our habit to group things in wrong classes… and when, in the belief that these badly made classes are those sanctioned by nature, we refuse to exchange them for others or will not make up our general conceptions from any other elements… all the evils which Bacon ascribes to his 'notiones temere abstractae' really occur. This was what the ancients did in physics, and what the world in general does in morals and politics to the present day (Mill, 1874).

Edmonds and Eidinow (2001) noted in chronicling the conflict between Popper and Wittgenstein that there are things Wittgenstein would have loved to be able to grapple with, like morality, which he thought philosophy incapable of responding to. Figure 14.2 supports Wittgenstein's view, at least for determining universal *a priori* morality; while it may not be impossible to determine absolute morality within a given group and set of circumstances, there can be no universal singular morality. It simply devolves to whether co-operation is advantageous to the group being considered and what self-sacrifice is required from whom to bring that advantage. Consequently, consideration has to be given to who or what a particular action, is good for.

14.9 Conclusions

Figure 14.1 provides a map of the ethical definitional space for the terms derived in the ethics chapter, namely ethics, values, morals, principles and beliefs.

Figure 14.2 provides an understanding of competing group influences/allegiances that bear upon the ethics/morality of actions taken and provides an understanding of what is good for whom.

Figure 14.3 provides a tool for understanding of the communication process in which individual beliefs and motivations contribute to producing either conflict or collaboration. It does so independent of any normative ideology or philosophy.

All three figures provide tools that individuals and groups can use that avoid the inconsistencies of attempting to determine universal moral value. They indicate that individual restraint that advantages whatever group is being considered in the circumstances is the determinant of ethics and morals rather than any ethereal or *a priori* considerations.

Ten observations were then made suggesting alternatives to commonly accepted approaches to ethics.

General acceptance of the definitions proposed in the introduction coming from the previous chapter and use of the figures developed in this chapter can provide clarity of meaning and contribute to avoiding confusion and misunderstanding, potentially benefitting community wellbeing and saving time, resources and money.

References

Bornstein, J. X., van Dellen, M. R., & Shaffer, A. (2017). Examining trait self-control and communication patterns in romantic couples using the actor-partner interaction model. *Personality and Individual Differences, 106*, 222–225.

BrainyQuote (2018). *BrainyQuote* [Online].. Available: https://www.brainyquote.com/quotes/george_bernard_shaw_385438 [Accessed 25 Sept 2018].

Butterfield, K. D., Reed, R., & Lemak, D. J. (2004). An Inductive model of collaboration from the Stakeholder's perspective. *Business & Society, 43*(2), 162–195.

Darwin, C., & Beer, G. (2008). *On the origin of species*. Oxford University Press.

Edmonds, D., & Eidinow, J. (2001). *Wittgenstein's poker: The story of a ten-minute argument between two great philosophers*. Faber.

Haidt, J. (2012). *The righteous mind: why good people are divided by politics and religion*. Pantheon Books.

Haugaard, M. (2010). Power: A 'family resemblance' concept. *European Journal of Cultural Studies, 13*(4), 419–438.

Janssens, M., & Brett, J. M. (2006). Cultural intelligence in global teams: A fusion model of collaboration. *Group & Organization Management, 31*(1), 124–153.

Kahneman, D. (2013). *Thinking, fast and slow*, Farrar, .

Lebrón, M. J., & Tabak, F. (2018). Leading in the real world: Operationalizing a power-based model of collaboration for leadership experiential learning. *Organization Management Journal (Routledge), 15*(3), 110–129.

Luhmann, N. (2005). The autopoiesis of social systems. In D. Seidl & K. Becker (Eds.), *Niklas Luhmann and organization studies*. CBS Press.

Maturana, H. R., & Varela, F. J. (1980). *Autopoiesis and cognition: the realization of the living*. Reidel.

McGrath, S. K. (2019). *What is project governance? Disclosing the source of confusion and revealing the essence of governance*, PhD Thesis, University of Southern Queensland.

McGrath, S. K., & Whitty, S. J. (2015). Redefining governance: From confusion to certainty and clarity. *International Journal of Managing Projects in Business, 8*(4), 755–787.

Mill, J. S. (1874). *A system of logic, ratiocinative and inductive*. Harper & Brothers.

Mill, J. S., Bentham, J., & Ryan, A. (1987). *Utilitarianism and other essays*. Penguin.

Nowak, M. A., & Highfield, R. (2011). *Super cooperators: Evolution, altruism and huamn behaviour or why we need each other to succeed*. Canongate.

Oxford. (*Dictionaries online* [Online], Oxford. Available: http://oxforddictionaries.com [Accessed].

Popper, K. R. (1995). *The open society and its enemies: Volume 2 Hegel and Marx*. Routledge.

Popper, K. R. (2002). *Conjectures and refutations: The growth of scientific knowledge*. Routledge.

Seidl, D. (2007). General strategy concepts and the ecology of strategy discourses: A systemic-discursive perspective. *Organization Studies, 28*(2), 197–218.

Wittgenstein, L., & Anscombe, G. E. M. (1958). *Philosophical investigations*. Basil Blackwell.

Chapter 15
Leadership and Strategic Management

15.1 Introduction

The concepts of leadership, strategy, management and strategic management are inter-related and have been somewhat entangled, lacking clear, non-overlapping definitions; Leadership has long been associated with management and was subsumed within it until around the 1980s (Rost, 1991; Borgelt, 2014) and Borgelt (2014) noted the terms still entangled; McGrath and Whitty (2015) noted the confusion among governance, leadership and strategy; and Ronda-Pupo and Guerras-Martin (2012) documented lack of agreement on the concept of strategy.

If academics are confused over the definitions of these terms, there seems little chance of practitioners or the general public having separately and independently arrived at clear definitions. This can only cause waste of time and money and adversely impact productivity within both the practitioner and research communities.

These individual concepts are explored here in detail using a definitional refining method developed especially for groups of related conceptual terms. 'Refined' is taken to mean "with unnecessary elements removed" - an abbreviation of the Oxford Dictionary definition of removing impurities or unwanted elements. The method used is non-normative, i.e. it avoids making moral or value judgements. It is also non-behavioural and non-institutional. Each term is approached from a purely definitional viewpoint, without entering into any debate concerning the merits or otherwise of any other aspect of the subject terms or their associated areas of study; this work simply develops non-overlapping definitions with a view to removing confusion, thereby potentially achieving improved organizational, individual and research outcomes.

Consequently, this paper develops a refined definition of the essence of the contested English language terms leadership, strategy, management and strategic management. It also clearly distinguishes between a strategy and a plan, removes problematic field-specific extensions from the definitions of leadership and

S. K. McGrath, *Speaking Management*,
https://doi.org/10.1007/978-981-16-2213-7_15

management and proposes a resolution of long-standing contest around the meaning of the term strategic management.

15.2 Definitional Confusion Regarding Leadership, Strategy and Management Terminology

Lack of clarity of definition cannot possibly assist productivity in any human activity dealing with physical things, whether considered from the perspective of practitioners, academics or the general public. However, it is very difficult to get hard evidence enabling this to be quantified. If definitional confusion or overlap is even recognised at all, it is potentially corporately embarrassing to acknowledge, let alone to admit its cost. In the instances the author is aware of, the wasted costs were unquantifiable, except for one failed project whose cost at abandonment was approximately $10 M. It is also very difficult to measure an 'after' state occurring after agreement and implementation of clear definitions - as any costing of savings must rely on estimates of money not wasted, which can only be speculation. This chapter therefore proceeds with the notion that it must save something and therefore must be worthwhile doing.

Definition of terms has been recognised as a significant issue by many including Socrates, Plato, Aristotle, Hobbes, Locke and Wittgenstein. This has been documented by McGrath and Whitty (2015), who also separated strategy from governance and pointed to the need to properly define strategy (see Chap. 10).

Before proceeding to definition, it is worthwile briefly reviewing the literature on each of these terms to be sure that definitional confusion actually exists around them.

15.2.1 Strategy

The lack of agreement on a definition of strategy has been noted by many authors. Steiner and Miner (1982) observe that "Unfortunately, there is no consensus about the meaning of the word…strategy." Dietrich and Lehtonen (2005) note that "the concept of strategy itself is rather ambiguous and rather abstract in nature." Ronda-Pupo and Guerras-Martin (2012) comment that "To understand the essence of any concept, it first must have a clear definition…Unfortunately, the absence of a broad, comprehensible, and shared vocabulary is an obstacle that this field has still not managed to overcome." They document many other authors having come to the same conclusion.

15.2.2 Leadership and Management

In spite of the efforts of Rost (1991) in surveying and defining leadership, Borgelt (2014) still found it necessary in her PhD thesis to survey usage to distinguish between the terms, indicating some degree of ongoing confusion.

15.2.3 Strategic Management

In the absence of agreement on the definition of strategy as mentioned above, there can be no doubt that there must also be contention over its compound term strategic management. Many different understandings of the concept of strategic management are documented in the section dealing with it below.

15.3 Approach

McGrath and Whitty (2015) demonstrated the pitfalls of defining single intellectual conceptual terms within the bounds of one single field and in isolation from other terms. See Chap. 10. Their approach will be used here. It has objectivist epistemology with a positivist theoretical perspective that seeks to define objective content without claiming that the derived definitions describe anything existential. It simply defines concepts non-normatively, that is without allowing any value judgements to intrude into any definition, producing definitions which, if agreed and adopted, have the potential to remove unnecessary debate and confusion. It takes the view that while there may be no absolute truth, to be productive as a society, a discourse that removes confusion is necessary, one that all can participate in, with shared understanding of meaning, removing accidental and undetected differences. This position is therefore midway between (or partly both) realist and post-modernist, as this apparatus (ensuring consistency and universality of terminology), can replace chaos with order.

This paper is, in effect a further test of the application of their method to see if it can remove confusion from the group of terms dealing with leadership, strategy and management.

15.4 Method

The McGrath and Whitty (2015) definitional refining method is set out below: Lexical usage is surveyed from the following dictionary sources:

1. A range of dictionaries that have been well known for many years that were available (in 2013/ 14) online (Cambridge, Collins, Longman, Macmillan, Macquarie, Merriam-Webster, Oxford)
2. A range of various online dictionaries (BusinessDictionary.com, Dictionary.com, TheFreeDictionary, Wiktionary) and
3. The Concise Oxford Dictionary (1964) – as a comparator for how these definitions may have changed over the last 50 years.

Group rules pre-definition:

1. Select the group of terms to be defined.
2. Determine the order of definition as follows:

(a) Identify any inconsistencies within the group that may require one term to be defined before another.
(b) Where a compound term is to be defined, define the component terms first.
(c) Where a derivative term is to be defined, define the root term first.
(d) Where a term has a noun and a verb form, define the verb first.

3. Consider any terms that are likely to be used in definition that may themselves require prior definition.

Steps to determine a connotative (intensional) conventional definition of each term:

1. Define derivative or component terms using the root or component definitions that have previously been defined by this process or are clear and accepted in their meaning. (This obviates the need to proceed through the remaining definitional steps unless there is other reason to do so, such as confusion in the meaning of the compound or derivative term itself).
2. Survey lexical usage (This and the following two steps may be omitted if there is a known comprehensive academic review of definitions of the term).
3. Analyse this to determine the main contenders for inclusion in the definition (and show these in pale grey highlight).
4. Develop a connotative (intensional) conventional definition. (This may be synonymous, operational or by genus and difference).
5. Report and analyse any known academic review of definitions of the term
6. Remove unwarranted inclusions.
7. Remove divergence of meaning resulting from mixing content and process by removing any reference to content (for generic conceptual terms).
8. Remove any remaining divergence of meaning and for operational definitions, consider the need for additional inclusions, by checking against the following, as appropriate to the particular term:

   (a) Historical usage
   (b) Field/specialty usage - the definition most generic to as many fields as possible will be selected
   (c) Practitioner usage (via practitioner literature, considering the influence of opinion and marketing)
   (d) Competing concepts and frameworks (considering the influence of opinion and marketing)

9. Check any resulting definitions by genus and difference against the Copi and Cohen (1990) five rules and discard any which do not satisfy them.
10. Report the ~~adopted~~ derived definition. (Note; this change corrects what appears to have been a typographical error in the source paper, in which all applications of the method used the word 'derived')

Group rules post definition:

1. Cross-check terms defined in this group for any inconsistency and resolve.
2. Cross-check any terms defined in this group known to be used interchangeably with other terms outside the group and resolve any inconsistency.

The five rules for checking a definition by genus and difference, sourced from Copi and Cohen (1990) are as follows:

1. States the essential attributes of the species
2. Avoids circularity
3. Neither too broad nor too narrow
4. Avoids ambiguous, obscure or figurative language
5. Affirmative rather than negative.

Lexical usage will be sourced from the following dictionary sources:

1. A range of dictionaries that have been well known for many years that were available (in 2013/14) online (Cambridge, Collins, Longman, Macmillan, Macquarie, Merriam-Webster, Oxford)
2. A range of various online dictionaries (BusinessDictionary.com, Dictionary.com, TheFreeDictionary, Wiktionary) and
3. The Concise Oxford Dictionary (1964) - as a comparator for how these definitions may have changed over the last 50 years.

Tables surveying lexical usage for all terms appear in the Appendix.

15.5 Group Rules Pre-definition

15.5.1 Group Pre-definition Rule 1 – Select the Group of Terms to Be Defined

McGrath and Whitty (2015) indicated that governance is related to strategy, ethics and power, which are also the subject of similar definitional confusion. These all impinge on leadership and management. However, the definitions of leadership, strategy and management are not dependent on these other terms, and so those terms are not included in the group to be defined here. They have, of course, now been so defined in the Chap. 13.

McGrath and Whitty (2015) also found that leadership and strategy had been incorrectly included under the ambit of governance. The boundary between management and leadership is another common confusion. So the group of terms to be selected for definition will be leadership, strategy and management. This will then allow strategic management to be defined.

15.5.2 Group Pre-definition Rule 2 – Determine the Order of Definition

Rule 2 (a) – Identify group term inconsistencies

None present.

Rule 2(b) - Compound terms

The only compound term in the group is strategic management and so both component terms will be defined first.

Rule 2(c) – Root of Derivative terms

The root terms of the derivative words in this group are lead(er) and manage, and while none of these appear contentious, defining lead, leader and manage may potentially assist in removing confusion and so these three will be defined ahead of their respective derivative.

Rule 2(d) - Define verb form of term before the noun form

As per 2(c), lead and manage will be defined ahead of leader, leadership and management.

General

Leadership is the most general and will be defined first, followed by strategy, which is the province of leadership, followed by the more procedural management. This will then allow definition of strategic management.

The order of definition will therefore be as follows: leadership, strategy, management, strategic management.

15.5.3 Group Pre-definition Rule 3 – Definitional Terms Requiring Prior Definition

There are no other terms outside this group that have multiple meanings and are commonly used in defining these terms. While the term plan is sometimes confused with strategy, the term plan itself is not contested and so the Oxford dictionary definition will be adopted: a detailed proposal for doing or achieving something.

15.6 Define 'Leadership'

Step 1 Define derivative or component terms

Leadership is a derivative of the word leader, which is, in turn, a derivative of the word lead. Lead will therefore be defined first followed by leader, then leadership.

Step 2 Survey lexical usage

Lexical usage is surveyed in Tables 15.1a, 15.1b and 15.1c, which show the key parts of the dictionary definitions.

Step 3 Analyse lexical usage

In Table 15.1a, the most commonly used definition of the word lead is to "show the way". To "guide" is the next most commonly used and several use to "go in front" and one uses "cause to go with". Show the way is the most generic, includes the others and is therefore the most suitable for use in the tentative definition.

In Table 15.1b, the most commonly used definition of the word leader is one who leads, with directs or controls also being mentioned. Direct and control are implied by the term leading anyway and so this simple definition as one who leads refers back to its root term, which accords with the selected method and is acceptable for use in the tentative definition.

In Table 15.1c, there is general consensus around two definitions of leadership, the position of leader and the capacity or ability to lead. The former describes a role rather than the function, and this is not contentious. However, such usage generally occurs prefixed with article 'a' or 'the', qualifying it as unique. It is unqualified essence being sought here, not unique instantiation and so the former definition will be ignored. The second definition deals with that unqualified essence and will be accepted.

Step 4 Develop a connotative (intensional) conventional definition

The tentative definitions are therefore as follows:

Lead = to show the way
Leader = one who shows the way
Leadership = the ability to show the way

Step 5 Report academic review of definitions

A comprehensive review of both dictionary and academic definitions of leadership was carried out by Rost (1991), who then proposed the following definition: "an influence relationship among leaders and followers who intend real changes that reflect their mutual purposes". He considered this definition contained the "four essential elements that must be present if leadership exists or is occurring" (Rost, 1991). A more recent review was done by Borgelt (2014) who settled on the Rost (1991) definition.

Rost (1991) had conducted an extensive survey of dictionary definitions and his review of preceding academic sources was also extensive, indicating 500 academic, dictionary and practitioner sources (Rost, 1991). He also separated the concept of leadership completely from management, which he also defined. He noted that the previous "industrial paradigm of leadership" had "conceptualised leadership as good management" (Rost, 1991). In developing his definition, he stated he wished to avoid the pitfalls of "one discipline scholars" defining the word with an adjective in front of it, such as business, educational or political (Rost, 1991). His objectives were to "critique the efforts of leadership scholars and practitioners in the twentieth century to understand leadership based on the values and cultural norms of the industrial paradigm" and "to move our understanding of leadership forward, towards the post-industrial paradigm that will take hold in the twenty-first century" (Rost, 1991). He also set out to redress his finding that:

> Most of the research on leadership has emphasised the same two items – the peripheral aspects and the content of leadership – and almost none has been aimed at understanding the essential nature of what leadership is, the process whereby leaders and followers relate to one another and achieve a purpose (Rost, 1991).

Over two decades later, Borgelt (2014) noted:

> Rost's definition … is relevant to any discipline and, arguably, applicable to any era. It establishes what leadership is and untangles the confusion between leadership and leader, so that leadership processes and applications become much more transparent. Therefore this definition can be used as a benchmark against which to determine how well, and by what means, leaders create mutual purposes, effect change and influence relationships.

However subsequent work has indicated some difficulty with his resulting definition. His definition initially appears to be by intension but is actually limited by value judgements to one particular extension. That extension is a socially inclusive, moral, non-coercive influence process. There are other circumstances where leadership occurs, as Burns alluded to at the end of his Foreword to (Rost, 1991) "the role of great conflict in great leadership; Rost leans toward … consensus procedures and goals that I believe erode such leadership". Rost (1991) states categorically that "A relationship in which the pattern of behaviours is classified as predominantly coercive and authoritarian is not leadership." This is problematic as it would exclude much military and police leadership as well as ship captains who must have command and authority. His discussion of this also raises the difficult question of degree; what proportion of authoritarian behaviour would be needed before the behaviour one was witnessing became something other than leadership. It is not just through influence that power is exercised. It is also exercised through authority and force, and all these means of exercise cannot not occur without a leader. Leaders may have influenced their followers to the point where they will obey commands without thinking too much and this may be absolutely necessary in difficult or crisis situations. However, the restriction to the single extension of influence makes the definition deterministic and static, fixed to the time at which influence is occurring and not accommodating changing circumstances over time.

However there is nothing in the Rost (1991) definition that conflicts with the derived definition and this discussion does not challenge his definition of what might be termed "democratic leadership" or "leadership through influence". However his definition is limited to that type of leadership and so cannot be accepted as a generic, essential definition of the term.

This discussion makes no comment on leadership methods, characteristics, styles, desirable qualities, outcome or performance achievement, or cross-cultural factors or impacts. These can be normative or strategic matters and are covered by other work such as the Global Leadership and Organizational Behavior Effectiveness (GLOBE) study which has been researching cross-cultural factors in leadership over several decades. (Hoppe, 2007).

Step 6 Remove unwarranted inclusions

There are no unwarranted inclusions in the proposed definition.

Step 7 Remove mixed content/process meanings

None present.

Step 8 Reduce divergence/consider additional inclusions

The Rost definition captured the relationship aspect of leadership but had the problems mentioned above and unacceptably (recursively) used the term "leaders" in its own definition. However, the tentative definitions omit any requirement for anyone to follow. If a person shows the way and no one follows i.e. the leadership attempt was unsuccessful, does the action then become not leadership? Should success be integral to the definition i.e. if it does not produce any followers, is or was it actually leadership?

Introducing such a requirement is really introducing a differentiation between 'good' and 'bad' leadership, and it is the unqualified essence of the base term that is being defined, not a phrase with a silent qualifier. Success is undoubtedly a criterion for how good the leadership is, but it is irrelevant to the definition of what it is. In dance, a man can lead, but if the woman resists or does not follow, the attempted leadership will be unsuccessful. But he has still led, and they are both still dancing; they are just not dancing together very well. His lead just didn't work; which means one or both parties had insufficient knowledge or skill and one or the other may terminate the arrangement. Similarly, if a military commander gives an order to storm out of the trenches and no one obeys, he is still a military leader, but an ineffective one – one who has been unable to induce his troops to follow his order. Accolades will follow 'good' leadership and not 'bad', but 'bad' leadership does not become 'not leadership'.

Consequently, no change will be made to the tentative definitions of lead and leader. However, a slight addition to the definition of leadership is perhaps warranted to make it clear that leadership is not only about showing the way but also inducing others to follow. So that definition can be revised to "the ability to show the way and to induce others to follow". This makes it clear that leadership is judged on two criteria, without falling into the trap of attempting to introduce the silent qualifier 'good'. The word induce has been used rather than persuade as it better covers the various means that may be used - influence, authority or force (See Chaps. 11 and 12 dealing with power).

Step 9 Check against the five rules

The definitions by genus and difference satisfy Rules 1 to 5.

Step 10 Report the derived definition

The derived definition are therefore as follows:

- Lead = to show the way
- Leader = one who shows the way
- Leadership = the ability to show the way and to induce others to follow

15.7 Define 'Strategy'

Step 1 Define derivative or component terms

This is not a derivative or compound term.

Step 2 Survey lexical usage

Lexical usage is surveyed in Table 15.2, which shows only the key parts of the dictionary definitions.

Step 3 Analyse lexical usage

Any definitions referring to any particular area or type of organization or position (e.g. military general, board, CEO, general manager, business, politics etc.) will be rejected so that a generic definition is produced. As strategy is a term that is often linked in colloquial organizational use with leadership, management and sometimes governance, any reference to these will be rejected. However, it is noteworthy that Table 15.2 contains no such references, other than indirectly to leadership via the term generalship. The word plan is the most commonly used definition in Table 15.2, with method and series of actions also being mentioned, along with achieving a goal, a desired future, or something over the long term.

Step 4 Develop a connotative (intensional) conventional definition

Use of any of the Table 15.2 definitions that include 'plan' with 'goal' or 'future achievement' has several difficulties; the future time scale, differentiating strategy from planning (or from a plan), and exclusion of circumstances where there was no planning - where actions occur and the strategy can only be deduced afterwards (e.g. evolution or circumstances where we act automatically on inherited, instinctive or habitual rules or guiding principles without necessarily being aware of what our strategy actually is). Strategy in a game of Chess will have a completely different timescale to that in an infrastructure plan. A strategy is broad whereas a plan is associated with detail, so it is best not to include the word 'plan' directly in the definition. Furthermore, strategy may not be evident from looking at a plan. For example, a strategy for an infrastructure plan may be simply to do as much as can be done with the money made available, or to do particular things in particular electorates to win an election, or to provide a key missing piece of infrastructure to achieve another objective (such as economic stimulus or providing something out of reach of private enterprise). Strategy behind government regulation may be to resolve conflict, to advantage a particular group, or to establish a new market. These may or may not be stated in the legislation.

The following tentative definition of strategy can therefore be derived: "A series of actions that achieve a goal". This accepts the key elements in Table 15.2 but removes the dependency on the word 'plan', resolves the time scale concerning the future and accommodates circumstances where there was no design or planning but still some unconscious strategy. However, this definition could equally well define a plan, whose meaning is not contested and for which the Oxford definition as a detailed proposal for doing or achieving something has already been accepted. To overcome this difficulty, the order will be reversed, and strategy tentatively defined as "The goal achieved by/contained in a series of actions". However, the word 'goal' is also problematic, as strategy is more an approach to achieving a goal than the goal itself. So the definition will be modified to "The approach contained in a series of actions".

Step 5 Report academic review of definitions

The academic distinction between methodology and method is similar to the distinction between strategy and plan. Crotty (1998) referred to methods as techniques or procedures, and to methodology as "The strategy, plan of action, process or design lying behind the choice and use of particular methods and linking the choice and use of methods to desired outcomes." This lacks distinction between strategy and plan and is too verbose for our purposes, but its essence is contained in Mintzberg (1978) which defined strategy as "a pattern in a stream of decisions" which "enables us to consider both sides of the strategy formation coin: strategies as intended, a priori guidelines as well as strategies as evolved". This is very similar to the proposed definition.

Events or actions that are random have no pattern and therefore, by the Mintzberg definition, no strategy. Where a pattern can be found then there can be said to have been a strategy. Analysis of natural or historical events is the province of scientists and historians, who might work out why things happened or where a sequence of events may have been heading. These would normally be referred to as scientific discoveries or societal trends rather than as strategy, as there is no human determination of natural laws, and the trend of historical events is often not obvious when they are occurring (e.g. the battle may be lost but the war won). However, these scientific and historical interpretations would not be excluded by the Mintzberg definition or by that derived above from Table 15.2.

Back analysis of past events contains no element of the future sense of strategy. However, people may interpret events that happen to them from a spiritual or personal growth perspective, seeking God in them or a pattern in their own behaviour that they may not have been previously aware of. These would normally be referred to as faith, personal growth or changing habits, but could also be referred to as life strategies, which neither definition excludes.

So a combined definition would be "The approach/a pattern in a series/stream of actions/decisions".

Some choices therefore need to be made. The easiest one is between series and stream. Stream implies a continuous flow that may not necessarily be present and so series will be used. While strategy is carried out for future action, past strategy can also be identified and it is no less strategy because it was in the past. So pattern is more general than approach as it better covers back-analysis as well as circumstances where no pre-planning or approach was consciously known in making the decision to take the particular action. Actions will be preferred to decisions as any action requires a prior decision anyway and it is the action that others will notice rather than the decision to take it, whether that action is physical, written or verbal.

So the derived definition is "a pattern in a series of actions".

This clearly distinguishes a plan from a strategy. A plan with timing for a particular sequence of steps may achieve a number of strategic objectives, such as sequencing projects to achieve a realistic expenditure flow, balancing available resources, ensuring continuity of employment, and/or ensuring a network operates effectively by scheduling dependent works after their precedents have been completed. These latter comprise the strategy. Of course, this does not preclude any particular document from including both a plan and a strategy, but it would suggest they be appropriately labelled as such.

Strategizing done in present time is about the future. But this does not mean that strategy should be defined as referring to the future. If we look at a series of past events and attempt to determine what the strategy was, we are not at liberty to influence it. So timescale must be omitted. The proposed definition accommodates usage of the term in past, present or future tense. We can say "the strategy was" or "the strategy is" or "the strategy will be".

Step 6 Remove unwarranted inclusions

None remain.

Step 7 Remove mixed content/process meanings

None present.

Step 8 Reduce divergence/consider additional inclusions

Historical check (a) and field/specialty usage (b) are the appropriate checks for this term.

Step 8(a) Consider historical usage

Strategy has historically derived from the Greek word for "generalship", as noted in the Business Dictionary definition in Table 15.2. This also concurs with the fifth century BC Chinese author Sun Tzu's famous work. He refers thus to the silence and lack of obvious sign of strategy: "All men can see the tactics whereby I conquer, but what none can see is the strategy out of which victory is evolved" (Sun & Cleary, 1988) and "in war the victorious strategist only seeks battle after the victory has been won" (Sun & Cleary, 1988). This does not conflict with the derived definition.

Step 8 (b) Field/speciality usage

Chandler (1962) considered "Strategy can be defined as the determination of the basic long-term goals and objectives of an enterprise, and the adoption of courses of action and the allocation of resources necessary for carrying out these goals." This definition refers to how strategic management might be done rather than what strategy actually is.

Quinn (1980) said "A strategy is the pattern or plan that integrates an organization's major goals, policies and action sequences into a cohesive whole". This is compatible with derived definition but it includes reference to a plan and elements of strategic management that do not need to be included in a definition of strategy.

Feurer and Chaharbaghi (1995) open with their interpretation of early definitions as "strategy is a rational decision-making process by which the organization's resources are matched with opportunities arising from the competitive environment." They observed that regardless of whether strategy is environmental or resource driven "all these frameworks have one thing in common which is that they all aim at maximizing the performance of an organization by improving its position in relation to the other organizations operating in the same competitive environment" (Feurer & Chaharbaghi, 1995). They also mention other definitions as "Strategy is the primary means of reaching the focal objective" and "the direction and scope of an organization over the long term" (Feurer & Chaharbaghi, 1995). The first of these three definitions describes an approach to strategic management, the second is vague and the third includes considerations that have been discussed in reaching the derived definition.

Artto and Dietrich (2004) observed:

> Early theories of organizational strategy saw 'strategy as an action of intentionally and rationally combining selected courses of action with the allocation of resources in order to carry out organizational goals and objectives in order to achieve strategic fit and thereby obtain competitive advantage (Hatch 1997)'.

This does not conflict with the derived definition but it adds much about the how and why, which is not essential in a definition of what it is.

Morris and Jamieson (2005) considered "Corporate strategy is a means of thinking through and articulating how an organization's corporate goals and objectives will be achieved." This is vague, referring to a means of thinking, rather than to what it actually is.

Milosevic and Srivannaboon (2006) noted that "Though the definitions of business strategy vary, these - in general - do focus on how to better deal with the competitive environment (Tse & Olsen 1999)". This is also vague and gives the purpose of strategic management rather than defining what strategy actually is.

Ensign (2008) noted that "While it is correct to view strategy as a prescriptive or normative statement of goals, strategy also involves behaviour" and "There is a making or shaping of strategy (formulation) and the act of using strategy implementation" (Ensign, 2008). He then proposed the following definition: "Strategy is a systematic series of actions directed to some ends that seek to maintain or optimize a firm's position, plan, pattern or perspective" (Ensign, 2008). The key elements of this definition are compatible with the derived definition; the remainder are specific to strategic management and so cannot be included as an essential feature of strategy. The normative determination of goals, the impact on behaviour and the way strategy is formulated and implemented are not excluded but do not need to be included as they are all about how it might be done rather than what it actually is. He also pointed out that "strategy can be dichotomized as intended or emergent" (Ensign, 2008). This is accommodated in the derived definition, as mentioned in Step 4.

Nichols et al. (2008) said "Strategy, then, is not about delivering step-by-step instructions for achieving a goal. When people approach it that way, reality always gets its way. Instead strategy is more about preparing people to act appropriately in the face of the unexpected." This could equally well define risk management and is vague.

Meskendahl (2010) noted that "Business strategy describes the way in which a firm decides to compete in the market compared to its competitors (Varadarajan & Clark, 1994; Walker & Ruekert, 1987)." This describes style and doesn't say what strategy actually is.

Aggerholm et al. (2012) considered:

> Strategy here is defined as a 'situated, socially accomplished activity, while strategizing comprises those actions, interactions and negotiations of multiple actors and the situated practices that they draw upon (Jarzabkowski, 2005; Jarzabkowski & Spee, 2009; Johnson et al., 2007)'.

This description of strategizing includes much about how it is done, while the definition of strategy itself is vague.

McKeown (2012) said "Strategy is about shaping the future. That's the reason we're interested. And that's the best definition I can offer you." This describes a desired outcome of ogranisational strategic planning but is not actually a definition of the word strategy. It also excludes evolved strategy but is not incompatible with the derived definition.

Wiesner and Millett (2012), in considering definitions noted:

> Van Gelderen, Frese and Thurik (2000) define strategies at the individual level as plans for actions that influence how people are doing things. The working definition of 'strategy' employed in our study is consistent with the definition offered by Gibcus and Kemp (2003). They define strategy as as "a mechanism to focus the efforts of a company".

Neither of these two definitions distinguishes plan from strategy.

Ronda-Pupo and Guerras-Martin (2012) reviewed 91 definitions between 1962 and 2008 before concluding that "the essence of the strategy concept is the dynamics of the firm's relation with its environment for which the necessary actions are taken to achieve its goals and/or to increase performance by means of the rational use of resources." Again, this is vague and does not specify what strategy actually is. This is more of an understanding of the elements of strategic management than a definition of the single word strategy. It is evident that they regarded strategy and strategic management almost synonymously. Their co-factor analysis of nouns and verbs was relative to their involvement in strategic management rather than about definition of the word strategy. It was, in effect, an attempt to define two words rather than one, using a form of voting process. This method can only produce definition by extension, not intension.

Many of the above definitions focused on the content of strategic management rather than on the process of the English language definition of a word. This lead to competing definitions by extension rather than to definition by intension, which enables the essential meaning to be determined.

This discussion finds no reason to change the derived definition.

Step 9 Check against the five rules

This is a definition by genus and difference and satisfies Rules 1 to 5.

Step 10 Report the derived definition

The derived refined definition is as follows:

- Strategy = the pattern in a series of actions.

15.8 Define 'Management'

Step 1 Define derivative or component terms

Management is a derivative of the word manage, which will be defined first.

Step 2 Survey lexical usage

Lexical usage is surveyed in Tables 15.3a and 15.3b, which show only the key parts of the dictionary definitions.

Step 3 Analyse lexical usage

In Table 15.3a, the most commonly used words are control, deal with, in (or take) charge of, handle, direct, organise and supervise. The most general is to take charge of, which covers both organising and supervising. To deal with and to handle are both vague terms that can mean other things as well as management, such as punishing or debating. Control and direct have been separately defined as part of a group of power related terms (See Chap. 12), using the above method, as:

- Control = to ensure that actions occur in a particular way.
- Direct (v) = to give orders, commands or instructions.

McGrath and Whitty (2015) have defined governing as directing and controlling (See Chap. 10). Managing the ongoing operation of an organization is generally much broader than the governance structures and processes it is directed and controlled by, and taking charge captures that essence. The sense of succeeding that is present in some definitions implies managing well and, to avoid value judgement, this will not be considered.

In Table 15.3b, the most commonly used words are the act, art, manner, practice and process of managing/controlling/organising/coordinating/dealing with. Act is the most generic of the genus terms and includes practice and process. The words art and manner are more descriptive of style than of the activity. The alternatives for the difference term 'managing' were also found in Table 15.3a, with the exception of coordinating. Two sources listed organising and controlling (Cambridge and Longman). One listed organization and coordination (Business). By including two descriptors, both sets of words include the sense of both organising something and then monitoring operations and taking corrective action. However, it could also be argued that organising involves coordinating anyway, and furthermore, both aspects are covered by taking charge. If there is someone taking charge of an activity, then it is being managed, whether it is in the organization or operations phases.

Step 4 Develop a connotative (intensional) conventional definition

Manage will be tentatively defined as to take charge, and management will be tentatively defined as the act of managing (taking charge).

Step 5 Report academic review of definitions

Borgelt (2014) surveyed definitions of both leadership and management. She found definitions of management congregated around two main schools, typified by Rost and Mullins, and she was principally concerned with avoiding overlap between leadership and management within the organizational context. Borgelt (2014) first considered "Management is an authority relationship between at least one manager and one subordinate who coordinate their activity to produce and sell particular goods and/or services. (Rost, 1991)." She noted this definition included extraneous items (production, sales, goods and services) and excluded self-management and particular circumstances where no authority exists. This led her to prefer the definition of the other school "[M]anagement takes place within a structured organizational setting and with prescribed roles; is directed towards the (set) aims and objectives; is achieved through efforts of other people (or self); and uses systems and procedures (Mullins, 1989)" (Borgelt, 2014). She noted that this "contains no reference to selling and allows for self-management". However, while this is the case, and this definition does facilitate the distinction between leadership and management within the organizational context, there are other contexts within which the term management is used which this definition does not readily cover, such as a family situation, where household finances are managed.

The Mullins (1989) definition could be considered either a precising definition or a definition by extension. It is also very specific to the organizational context and cannot readily be reduced to essential concepts. However the Rost (1991) definition can be reduced to a satisfactory definition by intension if its specifics of authority, relationship and subordinate are omitted and a more generic description of purpose (rather than the very specific production and selling of goods and services) is adopted. This produces a definition of management as "coordination of activity to produce an outcome". This definition satisfies Borgelt's requirements regarding selling, self-management and keeping separate the concepts of management and leadership.

Step 3 concluded that taking charge was more generic than coordination, and so this will be replaced to give "taking charge of activity to produce an outcome". The question then remains as to whether the qualification "to produce an outcome" is essential. There would be little point taking charge of something if there was no purpose. That purpose could range from doing something for the good of the managed entity to doing something for the good of the manager. Either way, there is still an outcome desired. In the interest of avoiding tautology, qualification will be considered unnecessary and removed, leaving the definition proposed in Step 4 unchanged.

Step 6 Remove unwarranted inclusions

There are no such inclusions remaining.

Step 7 Remove mixed content/process meanings

None present.

Step 8 Reduce divergence/consider additional inclusions

Only check (a) is necessary.

Step 8(a) Consider historical usage.

The early management work of Fayol (1949) published in English 24 years after his death, and 33 years after its original publication in French in 1916, set out the five primary functions of management as being to forecast and plan, organise, command or direct, coordinate and control (which in the French sense of the word also included monitoring). The proposed definition above is silent on forecasting and planning but does not preclude them. The same can also be said for the Rost (1991) and Mullins (1989) definitions. This presents no problem for a definition by intension. The remaining four Fayol primary functions and in fact all five, for that matter, can be seen as extensions of the type of activity necessary to coordinate activity to produce an outcome. So the Step 4 definition is consistent with the early meaning of the term 'management' as outlined within an organizational context while not limiting its meaning to that context.

Step 9 Check against the five rules

The definition of manage is operational. The definition of management is by genus and difference and does satisfy Rules 1 to 5.

Step 10 Report the derived definition

The derived definition is as follows:

- Manage = to take charge.
- Management = the act of managing (taking charge).

15.9 Define 'Strategic Management'

Step 1 Define derivative or component terms

Management is a derivative of the words strategy and management which have been defined above, removing the need for Steps 2 and 3.

Step 4 Develop a connotative (intensional) conventional definition

Combining the two terms that have already been defined above produces the following definition: the act of taking charge of the pattern in a series of actions. This is generic and can be applied on an individual as well as an organizational basis. It is silent on means of implementation, allocation of resources etc.

Step 5 Report academic review of definitions

This has been addressed in defining strategy.

Step 6 Remove unwarranted inclusions

There is one such inclusion regarding timescale that results from simply combining the definitions of these two words. Carrying out the activity of strategy development in the present time requires dealing with future activity. Strategic analysis of past actions determines what the strategy actually was. Note that in the preceding two sentences, qualifiers are used around the word strategy to denote time. Strategic management cannot be done as a back-analysis. A set of past actions will have been strategically managed by someone else already, whether intentionally or not and those activities are no longer available to be strategically managed. Strategic management has future intent. The definition of strategy must be neutral on timescale to allow for past, present and future, but this is inappropriate when combining these two words together into a new term. The definition will therefore be modified to the act of taking charge of the pattern in a series of future actions.

Step 7 Remove mixed content/process meanings

None present.

Step 8 Reduce divergence/consider additional inclusions

None present or required.

Step 9 Check against the five rules

The definition satisfies Rules 1 to 5.

Step 10 Report the derived definition

The derived definition is as follows:

- Strategic management = the act of taking charge of the pattern in a series of future actions.

15.10 Group Rules Post Definition

Cross check 1 Consistency within group

The definitional method has not resulted in any inconsistency between terms in this group.

Cross check 2 Consistency with terms outside the group

There is no known overlap of meaning of any of the above group of terms with any other term outside the group that would prevent the definitions being accepted.

15.11 Summary of Definitions

The accepted Oxford Dictionary definition is as follows:

- Plan: a detailed proposal for doing or achieving something

Other accepted definitions derived using the McGrath and Whitty (2015) method in Chap. 12 are as follows:

- Control: to ensure that actions occur in a particular way
- Direct: to give orders, commands or instructions

The definitions derived in this paper are as follows:

- Lead: to show the way
- Leader: one who shows the way
- Leadership: the ability to show the way and to induce others to follow
- Strategy: the pattern in a series of actions
- Manage: to take charge
- Management: the act of managing (taking charge).
- Strategic management: the act of taking charge of the pattern in a series of future actions

15.12 Observations and Refinements on the Method and Its Application

15.12.1 *On the Method*

Analysis of the method indicated that in Step 10, the word "adopted" should be "derived". This change corrects what appears to have been a typographical error in the source paper, in which all applications of the method used the word derived.

Definitional Step 2 of the method indicates lexical usage can be omitted if there is a known, comprehensive academic review of definitions of the term. Such reviews existed for leadership and management. The extensive reviews conducted by two academic sources two decades apart, who both settled on the same definition of leadership, had tempted acceptance. However closer examination revealed that although it was an intensional definition, it was actually of one particular extension of the word. It was therefore necessary in both cases to do the lexical analysis anyway. In both cases, the academic definitions had focused on a particular extension, resulting in unwarranted exclusions. The allowed omission in Step 2 of the adopted method should therefore have an additional qualification "that has produced a definition by intension, not specific to any extension". This finding has been included in the process given in Chap. 10.

15.12.2 *On the Application of the Method*

Application of the chosen method has enabled clear non-normative definitions of the essence of the contested English language words strategy, leadership and management, as well as the compound term strategic management.

The definitions derived from lexical analysis was unchanged by the academic analysis for management and leadership. For strategy, logical analysis of the lexical input produced a definition that had little resemblance to any of the starting definitions, and the subsequent analysis of academic definitions modified this only slightly.

15.12.3 *Implications*

The analysis highlighted the veracity of defining by intension rather than by extension whenever possible, as well as the advisability of articulating any silent or assumed qualifiers to avoid defining a phrase rather than a word, which can result in difficulties when using a term across different fields.

A common factor in the definitions of strategy and leadership was confusion between the subject of the (English grammatical) rules and the rules themselves, or to put it another way, between the use of the tool (or rule or artefact) and the tool itself, or to put it yet another way, between the English language process of defining a word and the content it signifies. McGrath and Whitty (2015) also found this to be the case for governance. In the case of strategy, this had resulted in attempts to find a common essence of a series of phrases, the futility of which is evident from the fact that the qualifying words are actually needed to describe something that is actually different.

Defining strategy highlighted definitional confusion between strategy and strategic management, similar to what McGrath and Whitty (2015) found between governance and corporate governance. The problem of treating and defining a general term within the boundary of a particular field appears to occur when authors in that field do not recognize their preoccupation with that field. This seems to lead to overlooking the grammatical rules of the English language game and creation of private language, specific to that particular field. This causes a problem when subsequent attempts are made to apply it generically outside that field. As Haidt (2012) said, "people who devote their lives to studying something often come to believe that the object of their fascination is the key to understanding everything". In rushing to understand/generalise without recognising boundaries/context, we can become the victims of our own pattern seeking and good intentions, creating Hamartia.

Another trend observed was the tendency for simplicity of understanding and expression to become lost in confused complexity over time, such as occurred in strategic management where the 1978 definition of strategy was found to be closer to the essential meaning than any subsequent one.

Unnecessary confusion can occur when the meanings of particular words are not universally accepted. The process used in this paper can be likened to a pastry mangle, which takes a variety of inputs and produces a smooth uniform output. The starting blobs of inputs consist of the ways people use and interchange terms. The process applied here analyses these and resolves this to sort out the mess of conflicting meanings that people using the words are often unaware of. (This paper led to the process in Chap. 10 being referred to as 'the Mangle').

The approach taken here also satisfies Popper's requirements for objective knowledge (Popper & Notturno, 1994). He points out that the scientific method can only falsify and that any theory is contestable and should provide a means by which it can be tested. The means of testing here is clear; if anyone can find a valid circumstance that the definition does not allow for, then it requires re-working to accommodate all the previous circumstances considered as well as the new circumstance identified.

15.13 Conclusions

This paper has developed clear definitions of the essence of several contested English language terms, namely leadership, strategy, management and strategic management. It has also resolved clearly the distinction between a strategy and a plan, removed problematic specific extensions from the definitions of leadership and management and proposed a resolution to long standing contest around the meaning of the term strategic management.

Adoption and use of these refined definitions can provide clarity of meaning, avert development of field specific and differing "private language" and contribute to avoiding confusion and misunderstanding. This can benefit the community in general and practitioners and researchers in particular, saving time, resources and money. While it is not possible without speculation to estimate the savings that can result from widespread adoption of these definitions, continuation of the confusion around these concepts cannot possibly enhance productivity or reduce conflict. Successful application of the definitional refining method here indicates its potential suitability for application to other contested terms.

A key feature of the method used is its differentiation between the definitional process and the content (the material dealt with), facilitated through its non-normative and non-emotive approach to determining essence.

Two minor changes to the method are indicated as follows:

1. Step 2 should have an additional qualification at the end, stating "that has produced a definition by intension, not specific to any extension."
2. Step 10 of the method should read "Report the ~~adopted~~ derived definition".

Appendix

Table 15.1a Definitions of 'lead' (vt)

Dictionary	Definition of lead (All sourced on 9/6/2016 ex Macquarie 3/4/2018)
Business	Not defined
Cambridge	To show the way.
Collins	1. to show the way to (an individual or a group) by going with or ahead 2. to guide or be guided by
Concise Oxford	1. Conduct, guide, esp. by going in front
Dictionary.com	1. to go before or with to show the way; conduct or escort: 2. to conduct by holding and guiding: 3. to influence or induce; cause:
Longman	1. Take somebody somewhere by going in front of them 2. Go in front
Macmillan	to show someone the way to a place by going there with them
Macquarie	1. to take or conduct on the way; go before or with to show the way.
Merriam-Webster	*1 a* : to guide on a way especially by going in advance
Oxford	1. cause (a person or animal) to go with one
The free dictionary	1. To show the way to by going in advance: 2. To guide or direct in a course:
Wiktionary	Not defined

Table 15.1b Definitions of 'leader'

Dictionary	Definition of leader (All sourced on 9/6/2016 ex Macquarie 3/4/2018)
Business	A person or thing that holds a dominant or superior position within its field, and is able to exercise a high degree of control or influence over others.
Cambridge	A person in control
Collins	1. a person who rules, guides or inspires others;
Concise Oxford	Counsel who leads in case
Dictionary.com	1. a person or thing that leads.
Longman	**1** the person who directs or controls
Macmillan	1. someone who is responsible for or in control of
Macquarie	1. someone or something that leads.
Merriam-Webster	*1* : something that leads:
Oxford	1. The person who leads or commands
The free dictionary	1. One that leads or guides. 2. One who is in charge or in command of others.
Wiktionary	Any person that leads or directs

Table 15.1c Definitions of 'leadership'

Dictionary	Definition of leadership (All sourced on 9/06/2016 ex Macquarie 3/4/2018)
Business	2. The activity of leading a group… or the ability to do this.
Cambridge	The position or fact of being a leader: The person or people in charge:
Collins	1. the position or function of a leader: 3. the ability to lead 4. the leaders as a group:
Concise Oxford	Not defined
Dictionary.com	1. the position or function of a leader, a person who guides or directs a group: 2. ability to lead:
Longman	1 the position of being the leader 4 the position of being in front of others in an activity or competition:
Macmillan	1. the position of being the leader or being in charge
Macquarie	1. the position, function, or guidance of a leader.
Merriam-Webster	*1* : the office or position of a leader *2* : capacity to lead
Oxford	1. The action of leading a group… or the ability to do this:
The free dictionary	1. The position or office of a leader: 2. Capacity or ability to lead: 3. A group of leaders: 4. Guidance; direction:
Wiktionary	1. the capacity of someone to lead

Table 15.2 Definitions of 'strategy'

Dictionary	Definition of strategy (All sourced on 12/1/14 ex Macquarie 3/4/2018)
Business	1. A method or plan chosen to bring about a desired future, such as achievement of a goal or solution to a problem. 2. The art and science of planning and marshalling resources
Cambridge	a detailed plan for achieving success
Collins	2. a particular long-term plan for success
Concise Oxford	Generalship
Dictionary.com	4. a plan, method, or series of manoeuvres or stratagems for obtaining a specific goal or result
Longman	1 a planned series of actions for achieving something
Macmillan	1 a plan or method for achieving something, especially over a long period of time
Macquarie	1. a plan which is devised to achieve a particular outcome.
Merriam-Webster	: a careful plan or method for achieving a particular goal
Oxford	1a plan of action designed to achieve a long-term or overall aim
The free dictionary	2. A plan of action resulting from strategy or intended to accomplish a specific goal.
Wiktionary	2 A plan of action intended to accomplish a specific goal.

Table 15.3a Definitions of 'manage'

Dictionary	Definition of manage (All sourced on 13/06/2016 ex Macquarie 3/4/2018)
Business	1. To control
Cambridge	dealing with something, especially something difficult
Collins	1. to be in charge (of); 4. to exercise control or domination over
Concise Oxford	Handle, wield; conduct (undertaking); control (household, institution, State); take charge of
Dictionary.com	2. to take charge or care of: 4. to handle, direct, govern, or control in action or use:
Longman	**1** to direct or control
Macmillan	3 organize and control
Macquarie	Not available
Merriam-Webster	• to have control of (something • to take care of and make decisions about • to handle or direct
Oxford	1 Be in charge of; run: 1.4 Maintain control over
The free dictionary	a. To have charge of; direct or administer: b. To exert control over; regulate or limit toward a desired end: c. To direct or supervise (employees or other staff):
Wiktionary	1. To direct or be in charge of. 2. To handle or control

Table 15.3b Definitions of 'management'

Dictionary	Definition of management (All sourced on 13/06/2016 ex Macquarie 3/4/2018)
Business	The organization and coordination… to achieve defined objectives.
Cambridge	The control and organization of something:
Collins	3. the technique, practice, or science of managing, controlling or dealing with
Concise Oxford	governing body, board of directors, etc.
Dictionary.com	1. the act or manner of managing; handling, direction, or control.
Longman	**1** the activity of controlling and organizing the work
Macmillan	1 the control and operation of A) the people who control and operate 2 the process of controlling or managing something
Macquarie	Not available
Merriam-Webster	*1* : the act or art of managing : the conducting or supervising of
Oxford	1 The process of dealing with or controlling things or people:
The free dictionary	1. The act, manner, or practice of managing; handling, supervision, or control:
Wiktionary	1. Administration; the process or practice of managing.

References

Aggerholm, H. K., Asmuß, B. & Thomsen, C. (2012). The role of recontextualization in the multi-vocal, ambiguous process of strategizing. *Journal of Management Inquiry.*

Artto, K. A. & Dietrich, P. H. (2004). Strategic business management through multiple projects. *The Wiley guide to managing projects,* Vol. No. pp. 144–176.

Borgelt, K. (2014). *First and second order leaders and leadership: A new model for understanding the roles and interactions between leaders and managers working in contemporary australian-based organisations undergoing change,*. PhD, Charles Darwin.

BusinessDictionary.com. (*Online dictionary* [Online]. Available: http://www.businessdictionary.com [Accessed].

Cambridge. (*Online dictionary* [Online]. Available: http://dictionary.cambridge.org/dictionary/british [Accessed].

Chandler, A. D. (1962). *Strategy and structure: Chapters in the history of the american industrial enterprise*. Beardbooks.

Collins. (*English dictionary* [Online]. Available: http://www.collinsdictionary.com/dictionary/english [Accessed].

Concise Oxford Dictionary. (1964). *Concise oxford dictionary*. Oxford University Press.

Copi, I. M., & Cohen, C. (1990). *Introduction to logic*. Macmillan.

Crotty, M. (1998). *The foundations of social research: Meaning and perspective in the research process*. Sage Publications.

Dictionary.com. (*Online dictionary* [Online]. Available: http://dictionary.reference.com [Accessed].

Dietrich, P., & Lehtonen, P. (2005). Successful management of strategic intentions through multiple projects–reflections from empirical study. *International Journal of Project Management, 23*(5), 386–391.

Ensign, P. C. (2008). Small business strategy as a dynamic process: Concepts, controversies, and implications. *Journal of Business and Entrepreneurship, 20*(2), 25.

Fayol, H. (1949). *General and industrial management.* Isaac Pitman and Sons Ltd., [S.l.].

Feurer, R., & Chaharbaghi, K. (1995). Strategy development: Past, present and future. *Management Decision, 33*(6), 11–21.

Haidt, J. (2012). *The righteous mind: Why good people are divided by politics and religion.* Pantheon Books.

Hoppe, M. H. (2007). *Culture and leader effectiveness: The globe study* [Online]. Available: http://www.inspireimagineinnovate.com/PDF/GLOBEsummary-by-Michael-H-Hoppe.pdf. [Accessed 23 March 2016 2014].

Longman. (*Dictionary of contemporary English online* [Online]. Available: http://www.ldoceonline.com [Accessed].

Macmillan. (*Dictionary* [Online]. Available: http://www.macmillandictionary.com [Accessed].

Macquarie. (*Dictionary online* [Online], Sydney. Available: http://www.macquarieonline.com.au [Accessed].

McGrath, S. K., & Whitty, S. J. (2015). Redefining governance: From confusion to certainty and clarity. *International Journal of Managing Projects in Business, 8*(4), 755–787.

McKeown, M. (2012). *The strategy book.* Pearson.

Merriam-Webster. (*Online dictionary* [Online], Britain. Available: http://www.merriam-webster.com [Accessed].

Meskendahl, S. (2010). The influence of business strategy on project portfolio management and its success—a conceptual framework. *International Journal of Project Management, 28*(8), 807–817.

Milosevic, D., & Srivannaboon, S. (2006). A theoretical framework for aligning project management with business strategy. *Project Management Journal, 37*(3), 98–110.

Mintzberg, H. (1978). Patterns in strategy formation. *Management Science, 24*(9), 934–948.

Morris, P., & Jamieson, A. (2005). Moving from corporate strategy to project strategy. *Project Management Journal, 36*(4), 5–18.

Mullins, L. J. (1989). *Management and organisational behaviour.* Pitman.

Nichols, R., Bodla, R. & Mark, C. (2008). Agile strategy execution—Creating strategic alignment. *From Strategy to Execution.* Springer.

Oxford. (*Dictionaries online* [Online], Oxford. Available: http://oxforddictionaries.com [Accessed].

Popper, K. R., & Notturno, M. A. (1994). *The myth of the framework: In defence of science and rationality.* Routledge.

Quinn, J. B. (1980). In R. D. Irwin (Ed.), *Strategies for change: Logical incrementalism.* Homewood.

Ronda-Pupo, G. A., & Guerras-Martin, L. Á. (2012). Dynamics of the evolution of the strategy concept 1962–2008: A co-word analysis. *Strategic Management Journal, 33*(2), 162–188.

Rost, J. C. (1991). *Leadership for the twenty-first century.* Praeger.

Steiner, G. A., & Miner, J. B. (1982). *Management policy and strategy.* Macmillan/Collier Macmillan.

Sun, T. & Cleary, T. F. (1988), *"The art of war"*, Shambhala, .

TheFreeDictionary. (*Online dictionary* [Online]. Available: http://www.thefreedictionary.com [Accessed].

Wiesner, R., & Millett, B. (2012). Strategic approaches in australian smes: Deliberate or emergent? *Journal of Management & Organisation, 18*(1), 98–122.

Wiktionary. (*Online dictionary* [Online]. Available: http://en.wiktionary.org [Accessed].

Chapter 16
Accountability and Responsibility

This chapter summarises McGrath and Whitty (2018) which applied the Mangle of Chap. 10 to accountability and responsibility, producing clear, non-overlapping definitions. This chapter paraphrases and/or reproduces selected portions of that paper, which found that the concepts of accountability and responsibility are often confused, and many dictionaries define one in terms of the other.

The paper noted that definitional clarity around the terms accountability and responsibility is important for management in defining roles and responsibilities and position descriptions. However, the distinction between the two terms was found to have attracted little academic interest - apart from Ieraci (2007) and Cornock (2011). It was not the purpose of the paper to survey all the different ways in which accountability (and responsibility) are implemented; it was simply to determine what they actually are.

16.1 Application of the Definitional Refining Method

The terms selected for definition, in order, were responsibility, responsible, accountability and accountable i.e. the nouns were defined before the adjectives. This was done because accountability is a 'thing', albeit a concept, whereas 'accountable' describes a person, position or organisation. So the 'thing' is best described first, before ascribing it to an entity, so that we may first know what it is we are ascribing. Apart from that, the application of the method given in Chap. 10 was straightforward. However, issues relating to practitioner usage were identified.

S. K. McGrath, *Speaking Management*,
https://doi.org/10.1007/978-981-16-2213-7_16

16.2 Practitioner Usage Issues/Considerations

Two common means of ensuring accountability are Responsibility Assignment Matrices (RAMs) and Position Descriptions (PDs).

There are many coding conventions currently in practitioner use for RAMs, with acronyms such as ARCI, CAIRO, DACI, PACSI, PARIS, RACI, RAPID, RATSI (Wikipedia, 2017). Some use Accountability while others use Agree, Authority or Approve. Several are variations of the RACI code such as RASCI which includes Support. One has a driver at a higher level, separate from an approver (DACI). One RACI alternative dispenses with any form of accountability synonym, denoting A as 'assists', having been specifically designed to "avoid potential confusion of the terms accountable and responsible" (Wikipedia, 2017). This indicated a need for the exercise carried out in this paper and shed no light on the definitional question itself.

A sample of PDs was also reviewed. Five were selected describing senior roles in four different public sector organisations, as advertised on the Queensland Government 'Smart jobs' and South-East Queensland local government websites, the applications for which closed between October 2016 and April 2017. Some listed responsibilities and included accountabilities. Others listed accountabilities and included responsibilities. Accountabilities were generally referred to by words such as lead and/or manage with broad outputs or outcomes being nominated. One listed generic "outcomes" (which were accountabilities) separately to other responsibilities, with all listed under the heading "Key Responsibilities". This was the only one that attempted to separate these two concepts. This again indicates practitioner confusion regarding definition, further demonstrating the need for this definitional exercise.

A significant problem in the commonly used RACI code was identified via an undocumented example of an unsuccessful attempt to apply it that the authors were aware of. This example also highlighted that accountability may come from multiple sources, including legislative and organisational. It was an attempt to allocate "universal" accountabilities using the RACI code across all management levels of one large Government department.

The attempt started unsurprisingly from the perspective of the controlling legislation. However, once legislative accountability was determined, the question of managerial and business unit accountability immediately arose. If a particular position is nominated to be legislatively accountable for everything, who does the person holding that position hold to account? Once the A for accountability using the RACI code is allocated, how are formal delegations of authority denoted? And how is organisational accountability shown to accommodate managers at each level holding their staff accountable? For every task of any nature one can look for who is actually doing the work and who is responsible for ensuring it is done properly. Sometimes this may be the same person, sometimes not.

These difficulties resulted in a hiatus in that organisational development project which depended upon this mapping, with senior executives being confounded and unable to complete the accountability tables assigned to them. The issue was only resolved after many months by one person retrieving the task, substituting "Accountable" with the word "Approve" and completing the table on their behalf.

16.3 Summary of Definitions

The following definitions were produced:

- Account: a report or description of an event or experience
- Responsibility: an obligation to satisfactorily perform a task
- Responsible: accepting responsibility = accepting an obligation to satisfactorily perform a task
- Accountability: liability for ensuring a task is satisfactorily done.
- Accountable: having accountability = having liability for ensuring a task is satisfactorily done.

16.4 Implications of these Definitions

The confusion between responsibility and accountability can be characterised as a failure to separate the obligation to satisfactorily perform a task (responsibility) from the liability to ensure that it is satisfactorily done (accountability). Making this distinction clear:

- Accommodated the various sources of liability/accountability, such as legislative, organisational and informal.
- Provided an understanding of how these can cascade down through an organisation, transitioning across organisational levels, with a role's accountabilities being converted into their staff members' responsibilities for which they can then be held accountable.
- Enabled identification of the accountability errors in the commonly used RACI code.

16.5 Sources of Liability/Accountability

Accountability may come from legislative or organisational sources. While accountability arising from any of these sources cannot be delegated whereas responsibility can be, managers at any level will make their staff accountable under some organisational or contractual arrangement for the tasks those staff are allocated responsibility for. So, in going down one organisational level, responsibilities are converted into organisational and/or contractual accountabilities, and one transitions into the other between levels. It then follows that any attempt to allocate "universal" accountabilities across multiple levels of an organisation in a single table will not work. Accountability may be a universal concept but determining any particular accountability can only be done relative to a particular task. The transition between legislative and organisational accountabilities is the highest-level transition point within a government organisation and there are other management level transitions below that. Furthermore, it is also possible for the source of accountability to be neither legal nor contractual. There can be consequences in social groups, both inside and outside the law, for breaking unwritten codes of conduct to which members will be held accountable by being corrected, ostracised or worse.

So recognition of the existence of multiple sources of accountability (legislative, organisational, employment contract or unwritten code), as well as recognising that responsibility and accountability transition between organisational levels, is accommodated by the derived definitions.

16.6 Responsibility Assignment Matrices (RAMs) and Position Descriptions (PDs)

Both RAMs and PDs include similar information presented in different levels of detail and in formats appropriate for different circumstances. The duties they contain should correspond, but the timescales they are designed for are different. Differences between them develop over time, requiring periodic alignment.

The PD format is used for recruitment and so is updated only sporadically, when somebody leaves and is replaced, or the organisation undergoes a review or some structural change.

The RAM format is more detailed and suitable for use as an ongoing management tool at any level to determine who will do what on various tasks. It provides a means of ensuring all resources and all aspects of tasks are addressed and lends itself to updating as circumstances change and new tasks arise.

A well-maintained RAM is therefore a useful tool to have in updating PDs.

16.7 A RAM Is a Responsibility, Not an Accountability Assignment Matrix

A RAM without some code for responsibility isn't a RAM - it is something else, some matrix of some other sort, even if its format is the same. We could similarly have an accountability assignment matrix, an AAM, but that would again be a different thing to a RAM, albeit having the same format. It would be a small matrix, as once accountability is allocated, that's it; it can't be delegated. Combining these two types of matrices into one is definitionally incorrect and invites confusion, whatever codes are used. Use of the RACI code using A for accountability is therefore best abandoned.

16.8 RAM Coding Conventions and Task Specification

The main logical problem is the allocation of A for accountability within a RAM. This can be resolved quite simply by having the A denote something else. The obvious candidate is approval, the means used to resolve the problem on the undocumented example mentioned above. If a person is accountable for something, they will have the say on how it is done and the authority to approve all the necessary arrangements, as noted in Cornock (2011), within the scope of organisational policy constraints. Accountability means ensuring all necessary tasks are determined and allocated (which proper use of a RAM can accomplish) and then ensuring satisfactory completion (which approval by the accountable person can accomplish). So, completing a RAM using a code A for approval satisfies both accountability requirements – it identifies an aspect of a task that needs to be done and provides the means for ensuring accountability, without confusing the two concepts. This implies that any RAM should include A and R. Without an R, it's not a RAM. And without an A (for some equivalent code) for approval, it does not serve the purposes of accountability.

In the limited circumstance where a RAM has an A denoting accountability and does not cross organisational levels and multiple sources of accountability do not come into play, then the looseness of definition will not become evident or pose a serious problem. However making a universal generalisation from these quite limited circumstances is simply a mistake, producing unnecessary and avoidable difficulty. Use of A for approval rather than accountability in the RACI set of RAM codes clears up definitional confusion around both the terminology and the purpose of a RAM.

An important aspect of doing this is that the nature of the task needs to be carefully and appropriately specified as e.g. a project manager or director on a large project in the public service may have the authority to approve all the delivery arrangements for that project, but will still have an expenditure delegation limit and not have authority to submit directly to Cabinet for higher expenditure or changed budgetary allocation. If the senior person does not have the authority to approve the task, then they are not the accountable person and the task needs to be expressed in terms over which that person does have control. So in the circumstance just mentioned, the project manager or director would have the authority to have the cabinet submission prepared and to approve its technical content for submission, but not to actually submit it, as it may have implications for areas that the project manager or director does not control. That requires a separate activity by another person who does have the authority to do that. This again highlights the dangers in seeking 'universal' application of various interpretations of the term accountability (or any term for that matter) compared to simply seeking a universal definition of its essence. The former is seeking universality of labelling rather than of meaning and will just result in confusion. Universal definition of terms can produce clarity whereas universal application of different understandings of a term cannot.

So if the A in the RACI code is taken to mean approve, as occurred in the undocumented example mentioned above, the concept of accountability is converted into a responsibility, suitable for allocation within RAM, which is, after all, is a responsibility assignment matrix - a functional tool for allocating responsibility, not a tool for philosophically debating the concept of accountability or for using it just because it sounds so much more impressive than responsibility. Some tasks cannot be regarded as complete until whoever is responsible for doing it has completed it and the person with the necessary authority has approved it. This satisfies one of the important uses of a RAM – to ensure nothing is overlooked. If it risks confusion over various aspects or sources of accountability, then it is not achieving one of its purposes. This also acknowledges that approval requires time and needs to be allowed for in any time schedule. The remaining codes C = consult and I = inform are not contentious and are useful for tasks impacting others, require time which can affect completion date and so similarly contribute to the outcome of ensuring nothing is overlooked.

This work also found no reason why these four codes could not be supplemented on an as-needs basis with codes such as S where others may need to support or assist, Q where product quality is measurable and needs to be certified, or V for verifier on particularly large contracts. This highlights the need for any reference to responsibility matrices to be to a RAM rather than to RACI matrix or to any other commercially promoted set of codes. These just limit the flexibility of the practitioner to use appropriate RAM codes and can accidentally lead to the irreconcilable error mentioned above.

16.9 Blurring of Boundaries

The concept of blurring was raised by Etzkowitz and Leydesdorff (1998) in developing their Triple Helix model of innovation. While this concept could be regarded as referring to definition, it actually does not. It is related to blurring boundaries between industry, government and academia in innovation, or between industry groupings where one group supplies another. Blurring of these boundaries is a means of overcoming organisational silos, generating inclusion and progressing innovative ideas. It is a deliberate networking technique, not a means of definition. Nevertheless, it illustrates a more general difficulty with definition.

Concepts that are clearly and uniquely defined can overlap in application, creating an illusion of what could be called blurriness. Consider the terms global and international, as mentioned by Archibugi and Lammarino (2002). Anything global is also international but not everything international is global. According to the Oxford Dictionary, global means "relating to the whole world; worldwide" whereas international means "existing, occurring, or carried on between nations". A term such as global warming refers to the whole of the earth and so the usage of the term global in that phrase is clearly valid. But if we look at a company whose products appear in many countries, does this mean that if we can find one country where its products are not sold that the company is not global? To avoid this difficulty we might, for example, agree that a company could be classified as global if its products are sold on every continent. However, in doing so, we would be defining a phrase such as "commercially global", rather than the single word global. This would be legitimately qualifying the usage of a term within a particular environment. However if we subsequently take it outside that environment, forget that we have qualified it and attempt to equate the meaning of a single word (global) with that of a phrase (commercially global), its usage can easily be considered blurred. There is no confusion about what global means whereas there can be contention regarding what 'commercially global' might mean. Omitting the assumed or silent qualifiers of a word can result in confusion that could be called blurriness. But this is not the same sort of blurriness as mentioned in Etzkowitz and Leydesdorff (1998); it is blurriness born of omission rather than desire for inclusion.

16.10 Observations and Conclusions

The previous confusion between responsibility and accountability arose from failing to separate the obligation to satisfactorily perform a task (responsibility) from the liability to ensure that the task is satisfactorily done (accountability).

The commonly accepted statement, that accountability cannot be delegated while responsibility can be, was confirmed, with the proviso that this specifically refers to only one managerial level or one piece of legislation or a single employment contract.

The McGrath and Whitty (2015) definitional refining method did produce essential and non-overlapping definitions for all four terms, suitable for use across multiple fields.

Universal definition of a term according to its essence did produce clarity, whereas universal allocation of a term as a label for differing understandings of it did not.

Through providing greater clarity of both definition and application, the findings of this definitional refining exercise can potentially benefit recruitment, selection and induction process, providing a clearer basis for motivating and rewarding employees and even assisting with staff termination processes. Clarity around both the definition and the way RAMs can be used will hopefully assist in increasing usage of the RAM, facilitating the updating of PDs. This can also result in greater clarity in contracts, potentially reducing disputes during and after project delivery, leading to improved project and organisational delivery performance.

References

Archibugi, D., & Lammarino, S. (2002). The globalization of technological innovation: Definition and evidence. *Review of International Political Economy, 9*(1), 98–122.

Cornock, M. (2011). Legal definitions of responsibility, accountability and liability. *Nursing Children & Young People, 23*(3), 25–26.

Etzkowitz, H., & Leydesdorff, L. (1998). The triple helix as a model for innovation studies. *Science and Public Policy, 25*(3), 195–203.

Ieraci, S. (2007). Responsibility versus accountability in a risk-averse culture. *Emergency Medicine Australiasia, 19*, 63–64.

McGrath, S. K., & Whitty, S. J. (2015). Redefining governance: From confusion to certainty and clarity. *International Journal of Managing Projects in Business, 8*(4), 755–787.

McGrath, S. K., & Whitty, S. J. (2018). Accountability and responsibility defined. *International Journal of Managing Projects in Business, 11*(3), 687–707.

Wikipedia. (2017). *Responsibility assignment matrix* [Online].. Available: https://en.wikipedia.org/wiki/Responsibility_assignment_matrix.. Accessed 1 May 2017.

Chapter 17
Stakeholders

This chapter summarises McGrath and Whitty (2017) and paraphrases and/or reproduces selected portions of it. The aim of that paper was to remove definitional confusion surrounding use of the term stakeholder from the general and project management arenas.

The paper noted that stakeholder management has provided a linkage between ethics and management since Freeman (1984) broadened its remit (beyond its previous confines of company shareholders) to include customers, employees, suppliers, governments, competitors, consumer advocates, environmentalists, special interest groups and the media. Fassin (2009) noted the increasing usage of the concept of stakeholders since that time.

The paper also noted considerable contention over what the term actually means (Miles, 2012; Mainardes et al., 2011, Eskerod and Huemann, 2013, Littau et al., 2010). Miles (2012) even concluded that stakeholder is an essentially contested concept as defined by Gallie (1956) and also noted "Miles (2011) analysis of 435 different definitions from 493 articles: a new definition every 1.13 articles published".

The paper this chapter summarises took a purely definitional approach that had not previously been used, applying the Mangle of Chap. 10 to stakeholders and its associated terms. It proposed and answered the following research questions:

1. What is the essence of the term stakeholder that can define its meaning across all fields of study and without restriction to an organisational ambit?
2. How does this definition affect categorisations of stakeholders?

S. K. McGrath, *Speaking Management*,
https://doi.org/10.1007/978-981-16-2213-7_17

17.1 Application of the Definitional Refining Method

Application of the Mangle as described in Chap. 10 was straightforward, albeit lengthy, and is not reproduced here other than to report its key definitional considerations.

17.2 Key Definitional Considerations

The paper made no comment on any stakeholder management techniques, but noted that, in practical project management terms, competitors, terrorists, blackmailers, fraudsters and thieves, all of whom could be said to have an interest, and are therefore included in the proposed definition, would typically be introduced to consideration via risk management, which is where the Office of Government Commerce (2009) would place them, rather than being elevated to stakeholder status under the Project Management Institute (2008) elements of stakeholder management, or communications. However, the differing categorisation of stakeholders in both these documents, as identified in Eskerod and Huemann (2013), does not conflict with the proposed definition; the documents simply provide added specification by extension. The derived definition is robust and neither precludes nor proscribes any method of classifying or dealing with stakeholders.

Academic definitional difficulty seems to have arisen from the variety of types and/or categories of stakeholders producing conflicting definitions by extension, rather than defining by intension, which focuses on the essential meaning of an English language word. The fact that different types or categories can be defined differently is unsurprising as they are effectively definitions of a phrase containing the word stakeholder rather than definitions of a single word. The different qualifying words are needed to convey a different meaning, otherwise the qualification would be unnecessary. The mistake is either in not recognising, or inadvertently omitting, the qualifying word(s) in the phrase, and seeking supremacy for the accepted usage of the word in one field, or part of it.

Practically all the academic definitions had the word interest or some equivalent, and so, amongst the apparent disagreement, agreement on the meaning of the single word was actually quite strong and also accorded with the lexical sources.

17.3 Summary of Definitions

The following definitions resulted from application of the derived method:

- Stake: an interest
- Stakeholder: an entity with a stake (interest) in the subject activity

17.3.1 Impact on and Relationship with Previous Stakeholder Categorisations

The impact of these seemingly innocuous definitions on previous stakeholder categorisations was explored by mapping the stakeholder space into what was labelled as a locus of interest.

17.4 The Stakeholder Locus of Interest

Previously considered competing definitions and categorisations can all be seen as dealing with some particular interest - relating to a particular type of activity or content area, or to a particular type of relationship to the activity, as noted by Miles (2012) in saying “Different stakeholder definitions highlight core themes and give weighting to components that are relevant to the context and situation in which they are developing or using the construct”.

A depiction of categories of stakeholder interest was developed relative to a single generic activity. The space was initially drawn by arranging terms associated with the word into logical groupings. This was then iterated to remove inconsistencies until there was no contradiction remaining in the words used, and the depiction accommodated individual, government and commercial activities. Figure 17.1 is the result. It distinguishes only between categories of stakeholders, <u>not</u> categories of stakeholder <u>management techniques</u>. The paper clarifies the former and excludes

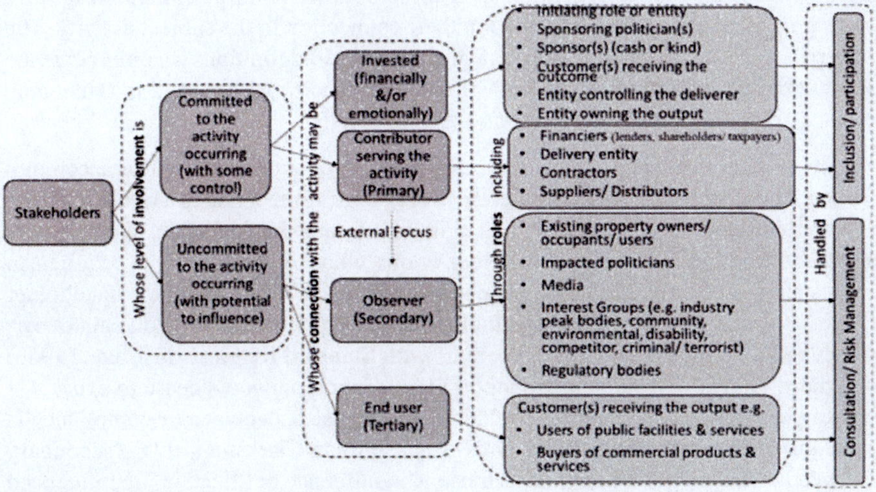

Fig. 17.1 Stakeholder Locus of Interest

the latter. Note that Fig. 17.1 below adds "(lenders, shareholders/taxpayers)" after Financiers to Fig. 17.1 of the original paper to provide additional clarity.

Note that the particular activity may be a task, a project, a program, an undertaking of a corporation or government entity or even a particular instance of a person's behaviour. In the latter case, not all of the roles come into play, but the diagram has been drawn to accommodate stakeholder circumstances for the most complex activities, for otherwise, the diagram would be incomplete.

The key to the diagram is the identification and separation of both the level of involvement and the type of connection that various stakeholders may have. It shows two levels of involvement (committed and uncommitted to the activity occurring) and then two types of connection with the activity for each of these. Note that the terms primary and secondary come from the literature while the depiction itself suggests the tertiary category, which is sub-labelled as such. The time scale is different for each level of connection; the contributor or primary roles are affected immediately, observer or secondary roles may be affected immediately or once the activity is completed and tertiary end users are impacted by the completed activity (aside from any adverse impacts during activity implementation, which are covered under existing users in the secondary category). Also, a particular person may find themselves in more than one role and others may transition between roles over time, from top to bottom e.g. from affected landholder or occupant or contributor to user. So the diagram depicts roles rather than persons; it also covers an extended timescale and relates only to a single activity or a single aggregation of activities.

17.5 New Stakeholder Category Definitions

Definitions of the four categories of stakeholders shown in third column of Fig. 17.1 were proposed. These were based upon their connection to the subject activity. The paper also demonstrated that these categories and their definitions accommodate the most common definitions given by Miles (2012), and those reported in (Huemann et al., 2016). The category definitions are as follows:

- An invested stakeholder is one who has some control of the activity. This accommodates the Clarkson (1994) view that they "bear some form of risk as a result of having invested some sort of capital, human or financial, something of value, in a firm".
- A contributing (primary) stakeholder is one whose participation is required to sustain the activity. This is based upon Clarkson (1995) "A primary stakeholder group is one without whose continuing participation the corporation cannot survive as a going concern". It also aligns with Stanford Research Institute. (1963) "those groups without whose support the organization would cease to exist".
- An observer (secondary) stakeholder is one whose acceptance or compliance is required to sustain the activity. This is based upon Clarkson (1995) "secondary stakeholder groups are defined as those who influence or affect, or are influenced or affected by, the corporation, but they are not engaged in transactions with the

corporation and are not essential for its survival. ...however such groups can cause significant damage to a corporation". "Acceptance or compliance" has the connotation of both influence and being affected by; it does not mean agreement and avoids the need to include reference to damage.

- A tertiary stakeholder is one who uses the output of the activity.

17.6 Interpretation and Relationship to Previous Classifications

Some of the definitions in Miles (2012) were based upon Freeman's 1984 definition as "any group or individual who can **affect or is affected** by the achievement of the organization's objectives" (Freeman, 1984). The stated restriction to an organisation, and the unstated further restriction to one with a joint-stock company structure (as further detailed below), both unnecessarily limit the ambit of the base term and invite conclusions to be drawn that may not be generic to other circumstances. However, the key "affects and is affected by" element is generic and can be applied to all four categories defined above; it is just not as succinct as the definition derived above. If one has an interest in an activity, then one may be affected by it, or seek to have an effect upon it.

(Miles, 2012) also asked whether **terrorists** are a stakeholder group. The definitions above allow for this without precluding the handling of supportive and antagonistic observer stakeholders in completely different ways. The activity used for the depiction in Fig. 17.1 is generic and so can apply to law enforcement, which does not have a joint-stock company organisational structure. Law enforcement activities are directly affected by criminals and terrorists who fall into the observer (secondary) category, and not into the invested category; it is the community that receives the beneficial outcome of offenders being locked up, and it is the victims of their activities that are the (unwilling) end users or output customers. However if we consider one individual criminal act by a person, that person is invested and will receive an outcome from it, whereas the police and courts are observer stakeholders and the victim is again the (unwilling) output customer, receiving the detrimental output in whatever nefarious form it takes.

Figure 17.1 categorises in terms of connection rather than influence, thereby avoiding the issues associated with **power imbalance and moral consequences** mentioned by Miles (2012) and Kaler (2002). The moral duties owed by a business to claimants are covered under primary, secondary and tertiary categories, which cover various aspects of liability. Normativity in addressing any definitional question was avoided because of its potential to distort, confuse and polarize.

Miles (2012) noted one classification based upon power to influence, legitimacy and urgency (Mitchell et al., 1997). This was more a classification than a definition, as they actually stated. Figure 17.1 is for definitional purposes and accommodates the power to influence as well as legitimacy but does not accommodate urgency.

Urgency may be important in determining the necessary speed of resolution of a stakeholder issue, but this is activity dependant and has no bearing upon which of the above four categories a particular stakeholder happens to be in. The classification Myles referred to was actually depicted in Mitchell et al. (1997) and shows eight classifications, but these incorporate aspects of stakeholder management, beyond simply defining, and are not just restricted to the connection with the activity as outlined in Fig. 17.1. They were concerned with classifying both who and what really counts, as stated in their publication title. Urgency does not relate to who; it relates to what might need to be done and how quickly. We are concerned only with defining who. Their classifications of dangerous, definitive, dependent and demanding stakeholders all fit within our secondary stakeholder category and many of the roles shown in Fig. 17.1 can at times require urgent attention.

A similar issue arose in Clarkson (1995) who developed a classification of **management strategies** that he refers to as a RDAP Scale, meaning reactive, defensive, accommodative or proactive (Clarkson, 1995). All of these are ways of managing various categories of stakeholder and Fig. 17.1 categorised on a completely different basis, which is silent on and therefore accommodates any method of management, none of which relates to defining categories of stakeholders.

Huemann et al. (2016) listed examples of stakeholder definitions in the literature. Some of these have been mentioned above and there is a group of six definitions mentioned, five of which are accommodated under the invested or contributing (primary) categories. The one remaining definition regarding those whose lives, environment, or business are affected is accommodated in the observer (secondary) and end user (tertiary) stakeholder categories.

Miles (2011) listed all the terms that had been used in all 563 definitions and found there were 36; these included interest as well as 12 others that were considered and excluded. The remaining 23 terms were reviewed and none were considered suitable candidates for expressing the generic essence of the term, as they related to either particular types of interest or to normative matters.

McGrath and Whitty (2017) therefore produced a classification of stakeholders that accommodates all these previous views but side-steps their limitations.

17.7 Primary, Secondary & Tertiary Stakeholders

If it were not for the previous usage of Clarkson (1995), primary stakeholders could have been labelled as contributing stakeholders and the remaining two categories of observer and end user as primary and secondary rather than secondary and tertiary. This could have been justified in project management terms where stakeholder management is mainly concerned with what we have here labelled as observer stakeholders and there are formal organisational processes and prescribed roles for contributing or primary stakeholders.

However, it could equally be argued that those financially and emotionally invested are the primary stakeholders and should be labelled as such. But this would leave those that project management is principally concerned with managing through stakeholder management as tertiary stakeholders, with end users being quaternary stakeholders. This would take us one step further away from the whole purpose of determining who the observer stakeholders are. In any activity, it is usually relatively easy to identify who is actually carrying out the activity whereas it may be quite difficult to determine who may affect, or be affected by the activity, which is the whole purpose of the theory. Consequently, both these options were rejected and the primary/secondary/tertiary classification was accepted as the most practical. It reflects power to influence the initiators of the activity. It also addresses the circumstance of managements not considering their staff and suppliers as stakeholders.

The alternative would be to drop any such attempted numbering, referring only to two categories within each of committed and uncommitted stakeholders. This is what was proposed in the paper, even though both were shown in the definitions and in the depiction in Fig. 17.1 because of the labelling simplicity of the numbered alternative. This enables the proposed nomenclature to not contradict or attempt to alter any existing usage or definition (of primary and secondary) with the exception of the position of the customer and government/regulatory bodies, which receives special consideration below.

Consideration was also given to whether the observer or secondary category should be split. But the deliberate decision was made not to do this as it would have required normative considerations before being able to categorise them, such as having to determine whether a particular stakeholder is for or against, "dangerous" (Mitchell et al., 1997), or a "grumbler" (Jepsen and Eskerod, 2009). This is impractical as some impacted stakeholders may be either for or against, depending upon their circumstances and their view of the potential financial accommodation that may be made. This is confirmed by comments of the project managers of the four sample projects in Jepsen and Eskerod (2009) who:

> pointed out that it is not possible to make a detailed front end stakeholder analysis. They did not have the cognitive capacity to consider all stakeholders in detail, nor did they find such a detailed analysis worthwhile. Firstly, it is impossible to foresee interactions with stakeholders in the distant future. Secondly, the contributions needed from each stakeholder may vary in different stages in the course of the project and due to unforeseeable events in the project.
>
> Further, the project managers spent quite a long time conducting the stakeholder analysis mainly because they had difficulty in getting access to important stakeholders. In some cases, the result was that they had to decide on and implement a stakeholder management strategy without having the proper information to do so because the project needed to get in motion. (Jepsen and Eskerod, 2009).

One further issue that needs to be addressed concerns the definition of contributor or primary stakeholder given above. While it has been based on Clarkson (1995), following his definition he went on to say "Primary stakeholder groups typically are comprised of shareholders and investors, employees, customers, and suppliers, together with what is defined as the public stakeholder group" (Clarkson, 1995).

However, Fig. 17.1 excludes customers from the contributor or primary category. This is a difference to previous practice that requires special consideration which is given below.

17.8 Stakeholder Theory – A Company or an Activity Base?

Recent stakeholder theory has been based upon the joint-stock company model. This is evidenced by Freeman's original depictions (Freeman, 1984) which show the company at the centre of the diagram. Fassin also included similar depictions and even explicitly presented a "Stake model of the firm" which has company management at the centre (Fassin, 2009). He also showed customers as internal rather than external stakeholders. While Freeman was aware of its wider application, he said "I shall concentrate on the applications of the stakeholder concept to corporations, and in particular, for profit corporations" (Freeman, 1984). 33 years later he said "In stakeholder theory, we need more cases of real companies and real stakeholders interacting with each other" (Freeman, 2017). However, stakeholder theory is now being applied widely to other entities, organisational forms and fields, such as individuals, projects, government departments and politics (Miles, 2011). So while Freeman's initial break from shareholder theory allowed other interests to be accommodated, its development within the joint-stock company environment used terminology generic to that field which was not applicable outside it, and so stakeholder theory has to be broadened further. Implementing an activity base produced the stakeholder locus and revised definitions which enable the theory to become truly generic, accommodating other forms of entity and organisation.

Factors supporting change to an activity base are:

1. If a company's activities change, some of its stakeholders will change. This means the activity is more fundamental than the company.
2. Representing stakeholder theory in terms of a company centric view of the world invites an absolute answer for the question of who stakeholders might be, which is unattainable and bound to fail as activities change.
3. The whole imprecision of ignoring minor definitional issues and the niggling little question regarding how this applies exactly to government or projects, and whether the translation is fully valid or not, is avoided.
4. It can be applied to activities that produce some result or output from the effort expended which is not a product or service. Examples include a parents' stake in their children's behaviour, or activities such as exercise or training which produce an output of a better functioning and or more skilled body, that may or may not have end users interested in the competitive result.
5. There are niggling inconsistencies in the application to companies anyway because of the inclusion of customers within both Clarkson's primary and Fassin's internal stakeholder groups.

The following section addresses the last factor given above and highlights duality of terminology in relation to use of the term customer.

17.9 What Type of Stakeholders Are Customers?

In Fig. 17.1, the term customer is used in two different places; one where the person is committed to the activity occurring, and one where the person is not. The former has a stake in the activity of producing a product or service and the latter has a stake simply in using or consuming the product or service that the activity produces. Both are customers and from a producing company perspective, both are of primary commercial importance and so could be legitimately labelled as primary. However Fig. 17.1 is drawn from an activity perspective, which facilitates recognising that there are two different roles here, requiring one at the top and one at the bottom of the activity based diagram; one type of customer is an invested stakeholder and the other is an end user or tertiary stakeholder. There are different roles played by these two different types of customer and these have been shown in Fig. 17.1 as output and outcome customers. Depicting Fig. 17.1 using an activity base highlighted this issue and also highlighted potential confusion in terminology among invested stakeholders regarding which one to label as the customer.

Support for identifying these various interests comes from Winch (2007) in noting: "the interests of financiers, clients, and sponsors may be divergent". We will further illustrate the need for identifying these through giving examples of complex activities the author has had experience with as follows:

1. **Government reform programs or programs to improve social welfare or some aspect of indigenous life**: These may be initiated from outside government, by politicians or by a government entity. Funding will come from government. The entity receiving the outcome (outcome customer) is the person or group within government who will have to administer or deal with the developed system and live with the consequences if the measures introduced do not achieve the outcome desired. This may be a different entity to that controlling the deliverer. The output customers are those using the facility or service provided.
2. **Providing channel markers to a particular destination**. This may be done for a local initiating agitator, developer or politician, and the local community receives the outcome of increased safety and marine traffic but it may be funded and most likely owned (and therefore maintained) by the maritime authority with jurisdiction of those waters. So while the facility provided is actually used by local residents and their suppliers who are the output customers, the entity providing the money is not necessarily the customer of the (non-financial) outcome.
3. **Design and construction of the above channel markers**: This is going down to a more detailed activity level. In this case, requirements will be set by the maritime authority on the basis of end users or output customers being vessels of varying sizes rather than people. The authority will either directly let the construction contracts or will have functional requirements it can impose upon the local authority or developer that may arrange its construction. Whoever lets the contracts, the maritime authority with jurisdiction over the waters will be an outcome customer irrespective of who pays.

4. **Parents buying a drum-set or violin on request from their child**: The child plays the initiating role and will be the end user (output customer). The parents will be the sponsors in both cash and kind (providing practice space). They will also be the recipients of the outcome; the initially dreadful noise and the satisfaction of seeing the personal development of their child. The neighbours affected by the practice noise are observer stakeholders who may exert an influence.
5. **Purchase or use of a product or service that generates dependence**: Uncommitted (output) customers may become dependent and subsequently committed to the ongoing (and different) activity of continued production of the product, but this will still only mean they will then fit into two categories; observer as well as end user, for that later activity.

Again, it is important to remember that the right-hand side of Fig. 17.1 details roles and not individuals. Individuals may play multiple roles. In some of the above examples, the person or entity funding the activity is not the outcome customer. Similarly, a well-intentioned group with influence can impose impractical arrangements on other areas of government, through the government agency being influenced not realising the need for this internal governance distinction between who pays and who is lumbered with the outcome. The conclusion from this is that a truly generic stakeholder governance model cannot be based on financial arrangements, even though it must, of course, accommodate them.

The reasoning for choosing the customer labelling shown in Fig. 17.1 will now be given.

17.10 Rationale for Customer Labelling

The term customer has been used rather than client, as a client generally pays (Winch, 2007) whereas a customer may or may not. The latter can occur in government.

The means of labelling customers in a way that did not lead to contradiction was to separate the output from the outcome. Two other options were considered and rejected. Distinguishing between contracted and un-contracted does not accommodate the circumstance where the person receiving the outcome has no money or authority to undertake the activity and so there is no contract, except possibly for some vague "social contract". It also does not accommodate the circumstance where organisational authority or rank prevails, or where the activity gets its authority from some accepted organisational practice for which there is either no contract or some general clause in an employment contract. This approach would lead in some vague direction to further hair-splitting, getting further from the genericity being sought. The other option considered was to distinguish between internal and external (relative to producing the activity). This avoids these contractual difficulties but still does not accommodate the circumstance that can occur within government where the person or group receiving the outcome has no money or authority to undertake the activity and may be external to it. So both these options lead to other unnecessary debates and were rejected in favour of demarcation in terms of output and outcome.

Reliance on the joint-stock company model also presumes there will be a monetary price for the product or service. This leads to the conclusion that a customer is always one who pays. As mentioned above, this is not necessarily the case for government. Government has many people using its services, both willingly and unwillingly and many of these do not make a monetary payment for the service and some, in fact, receive money. These are all (output) customers of government; There is some sort of service provided to the public, so what else can the people who use those services be called that might be non-normative? Consequently, any definition of a customer that requires there to be a monetary payment is inappropriate for government. Government services provide some sort of value to somebody and so there is some sort of value exchange; one that is more complex than the simple exchange of a product for monetary consideration. So it is preferable to make the concept generic by defining a customer in terms of the value exchange rather than restricting it to a user of a product or service who happens to pay for it. This can be done quite simply by describing a conventional (output) customer as one who receives the product or service.

17.11 Customer Terminology

The above discussion leads us to develop customer terminology that accommodates both government and the joint-stock company model as follows:

- A customer is one who receives some value from an activity
- An output customer is one who receives the output of an activity.
- An outcome customer is one who receives the outcome of an activity.

The joint-stock company customer who pays for the product or service that the activity produces is simply a sub-set of the term which we have qualified as an output customer, namely one who pays, or a paying customer or client. These definitions also accommodate government usage, in which it is possible that either category of customer may not pay. This allows government to effectively use the theory that developed within the private sector environment without becoming confused by the different organisational structure, or appearing disingenuous when labelling those who are hostage to it as customers.

17.12 Veracity Check

Consideration of the application of the definitions and locus to two further and quite different complex activities will serve to check its veracity:

1. **Operating a driver licencing system**. Potential young drivers desiring a licence are the output customers of the activity, but they are also captive to the system for which the government has a monopoly. The rest of us are the outcome customers, invested in driving on the roads, who may receive whatever safety and insurance premium outcomes that may result. So, the value that learner drivers get from being captive to such a system is their own safety. In this case, the output customer also pays for the piece of paper or card they receive. Of course, the circumstance can occur where a private company effectively has a similar monopoly over a particular product or service, in which case its customers are also effectively captive. So, whether the customer is captive or not makes no difference to the fact that they are a customer.
2. **A fraudster appearing to offer a service to customers and those customers being taken in**: There is still a value exchange here; the value to the customer becomes negative as the flow of money goes in a direction opposite to their intentions. It makes little sense to refer to a positive or negative customer. However, it does make sense to refer to the value they receive as positive, zero or negative. The fact that they received zero or negative value does not mean they are not a customer. They just happened to end up with an additional descriptor of victim. There has still been a value exchange.

Given that the examples above have not invalidated Fig. 17.1, and that it accommodates circumstances that current stakeholder theory does not, this figure is proposed as an updated representation of stakeholder theory. As John Stuart Mill said:

> It would, however, be a complete misunderstanding … to think that because a name has not at present an ascertained connotation, it is competent to anyone to give it such a connotation at his own choice. The meaning of a term actually in use is not an arbitrary quantity to be fixed, but an unknown quantity to be sought. … To fix the connotation of a concrete name, or the denotation of the corresponding abstract, is to define the name. When this can be done without rendering any received assertions inadmissible, the name can be defined in accordance with its received use (Mill, 1874).

Previous stakeholder theory unjustifiably arrogated the term to the joint-stock company and Fig. 17.1 provides the means to remove the terminology from that capture.

17.13 Summary of all Definitions

- Stake: an interest
- Stakeholder: an entity with a stake (interest) in the subject activity
- An invested stakeholder is one who has some control of the activity.
- A contributing (= primary) stakeholder is one whose participation is required to sustain the activity.
- An observer (= secondary) stakeholder is one whose acceptance or compliance is required to sustain the activity.
- An end user (= tertiary stakeholder) is one who uses the output of the activity.

- A customer is one who receives some value from an activity
- An output customer is one who receives the output of an activity.
- An outcome customer is one who receives the outcome of an activity.

There were a further two terms used in this paper for which definitions were effectively given but not explicitly listed. These are:

- A committed stakeholder is one who is committed to the activity occurring (with some ability to control it).
- An uncommitted stakeholder is one who is not committed to the activity occurring (with potential to influence it).

17.14 Observations

Definitional Step 2 of the method had previously allowed omission of lexical usage analysis when there was a known, comprehensive academic review of definitions of the term. Such reviews existed for stakeholders, but lexical usage was nevertheless analysed. The surprising result was that it produced more clarity of definition than the debate within the academic literature; that had focused on particular types of stakeholders, i.e. on particular extensions, resulting in unwarranted exclusions. The omission allowed in Step 2 of the mangle was therefore modified (and included in Chap. 10) by adding the qualification "that has produced a definition by intension, not specific to any extension."

Analysing stakeholders as an essentially contested concept (Miles, 2012) lead to a dead end that did not produce clarity, whereas using a definitional refining and mapping process did. This has implications for the future of essential contestability.

Previous stakeholder theory was found to have been based on assumptions and terminology that were generic within the confines of the joint-stock company model but not outside it. It had not adequately separated process from content. By considering output customers as primary stakeholders, it had mixed the (joint-stock company model) content with the definitional process causing confusion for other entities and organisational forms.

The definition of stakeholder and the categories and roles contained in Fig. 17.1 remove confusion and inconsistency without invalidating any prior usage of the term stakeholder, including its application to the joint-stock company. This showed that no previous usage was sufficient for generic use and that definitional sufficiency can be achieved by:

1. adding the missing qualifying words, namely the category (one of the above four – invested, contributor, observer or end user)
2. specifying the field or area to which the particular labels or findings apply (such as project management, corporate management, accounting, psychology, law enforcement etc.)
3. specifying whether the customer is for the output or the outcome of the activity.

So, for example, within project management, we may state that when we abbreviate and use the term stakeholder, we really mean observer or secondary stakeholder. We may also then refer to tertiary stakeholders not as stakeholders but as end users and accommodate invested and primary stakeholders in our normal organisational and governance roles. This excludes them from the external focus that project stakeholder management generally assumes and focuses stakeholder management in the area within project management where its power lies and its impact is greatest. Asset and strategic management considerations normally address the needs of the end user and the focus during a project is to locate and deal with the observer stakeholders. General acceptance of this could potentially remove confusion in usage of the term within the project management field, requiring minimal change of existing usage.

Figure 17.1 also has implications for project governance arrangements, methodologies and models that do not separate the various invested stakeholder roles for the particular activities being undertaken. For many projects, the (outcome) customer, sponsor, owner and entity controlling the deliverer are the same person or organisation. However, where different people or organisations hold these roles, differentiation in governance arrangements is necessary to enable their differing interests to be accommodated.

The refined definitions and consequent category and role definitions easily accommodate current trends in stakeholder management thinking as they are independent of any stakeholder management techniques.

17.15 Conclusions

McGrath and Whitty (2017) used the definitional refining method (the mangle) of Chap. 10 to produce definitions of stake and stakeholder in terms of interest and activity. This provided a means of avoiding all extensions of meaning resulting from defining particular types of stakeholders and/or their degrees of impact; direct or indirect, primary or secondary, legitimate or derivative and so on.

These definitions were carried forward into a mapping of the stakeholder locus of interest, Fig. 17.1, which adopted an activity rather than a company base. This enabled a generic categorisation of stakeholders to be proposed for use in both private and public sectors. These were labelled as invested, contributor, observer and end user stakeholders.

A governance difficulty with the term customer was recognised. This was resolved by relating the term to value exchange and identifying two types of customer; output and outcome. This released the term from dependence upon financial consideration for the product or service provided, enabling their use by projects and government organisations. It consequently freed stakeholder theory from capture by the joint-stock company model, correcting the accidental exclusion that had required awkward adaptations.

Figure 17.1 enables much current terminology usage to continue, provided its location within the stakeholder locus of interest is identified. Adding suitable qualifiers and equivalences to glossaries of terms can avoid confusion for readers outside those fields. It can also avoid pointless competition for exclusive use of particular terms.

This paper effectively removed stakeholder from the list of essentially contested concepts and fundamentally challenges the existence of essential contestability.

Adoption and use of the definitions developed in this paper can provide clarity of meaning, avert development of field specific and differing "private language" and contribute to avoiding confusion and misunderstanding. This can benefit practitioners and researchers in particular, as well as the community in general, by saving time, resources and money.

This application of the McGrath and Whitty (2015) method found two minor changes required to the method as follows:

1. Step 2 should have an additional qualification at the end stating "that has produced a definition by intension, not specific to any extension."
2. Step 10 should read "Report the ~~adopted~~ derived definition".

These have been included in Chap. 10.

References

Clarkson, M. B. E. (1995). A stakeholder framework for analyzing and evaluating corporate social performance. *The Academy of Management Review, 20*(1), 92–117.

Clarkson, M. E. (1994). A risk based model of stakeholder theory. In *Second Toronto Conference on Stakeholders 1994*, Toronto

Eskerod, P., & Huemann, M. (2013). Sustainable development and project stakeholder management: What standards say. *International Journal of Managing Projects in Business, 6*(1), 36–50.

Fassin, Y. (2009). The stakeholder model refined. *Journal of Business Ethics, 84*(1), 113–135.

Freeman, R. E. (1984), *Strategic management: A stakeholder approach,* Pitman, Boston [Mass.]; London.

Freeman, R. E. (2017). *Differentiating stakeholders* [Online].. Available: http://redwardfreeman.com/stakeholder-management/.. Accessed 19 May 2017.

Huemann, M., Eskerod, P. & Ringhofer, C. (2016). Rethink project stakeholder management. Project Management Institute, Newton Square, Pennsylvania.

Jepsen, A. L., & Eskerod, P. (2009). Stakeholder analysis in projects: Challenges in using current guidelines in the real world. *International Journal of Project Management, 27*(4), 335–343.

Kaler, J. (2002). Morality and strategy in stakeholder identification. *Journal of Business Ethics, 39*(1), 91–100.

Littau, P., Jujagiri, N. J., & Adlbrecht, G. (2010). 25 years of stakeholder theory in project management literature (1984–2009). *Project Management Journal, 41*(4), 17–29.

Mainardes, E. W., Alves, H., & Raposo, M. (2011). Stakeholder theory: Issues to resolve. *Management Decision, 49*(2), 226–252.

McGrath, S. K., & Whitty, S. J. (2015). Redefining governance: From confusion to certainty and clarity. *International Journal of Managing Projects in Business, 8*(4), 755–787.

McGrath, S. K., & Whitty, S. J. (2017). Stakeholder defined. *International Journal of Managing Projects in Business, 10*(4), 721–748.

Miles, S. (2011). Stakeholder definitions: Profusion and confusion. *The EIASM 1st interdisciplinary conference on stakeholder, resources and value creation 2011*, Barcelona, IESE Business School, University of Navarra, Barcelona.

Miles, S. (2012). Stakeholder: Essentially contested or just confused? *Journal of Business Ethics, 108*(3), 285–298.

Mill, J. S. (1874). *A system of logic, ratiocinative and inductive*. Harper & Brothers.

Mitchell, R. K., Agle, B. R., & Wood, D. J. (1997). Toward a theory of stakeholder identification and salience: Defining the principle of who and what really counts. *The Academy of Management Review, 22*(4), 853–886.

Project Management Institute. (2008). *Guide to the project management body of knowledge (PMBOK guide)*. Project Management Institute.

Stanford Research Institute. (1963). Internal memo (unpublished). *Stanford Research Institute, Menlo Park.*

Winch, G. M. (2007). Managing project stakeholders. In P. W. G. Morris & J. K. Pinto (Eds.), *The Wiley Guide to Managing Projects*. Wiley.

Part III
How to Speak Management and Know What We Are All Talking About

Chapter 18
How to Speak Management

Part I of this book has demonstrated the confusion in management terminology caused by a combination of generally accepted linguistic practices (the ten traps). It has proposed ways of avoiding them that are independent of any normative value system and then applied this in Part II to a wide range of commonly used conceptual terms, providing an open and transparent basis for avoiding confusion. But this will produce little if these confusion-inducing practices are not recognised and definitions are not agreed and widely accepted, to the point where they supplant existing usage. This is well beyond the control of any individual, posing the question of how to achieve this.

This Part is an attempt to facilitate reaching that agreement. The previous Parts have been carefully reasoned and academically justified, dealing with the logic of the arguments. It is the less straightforward normative work that remains – informing and influencing opinion. The former was analytically complicated but has now been done. What remains is complex because it depends upon many human interactions occurring. This Part therefore extends beyond the academic domain, into the practitioner domain, drawing upon the author's experience and observations.

This Part is written to show how to use the previous Parts without necessarily having to read them all. It is intended to serve as a 'dummies' or 'idiots' guide and contains some unreferenced material derived from the authors experience.

18.1 Context

Management is a strange field; it has such a mishmash of relative and absolute matters – from the how much money do we have left right now, to who would we prefer to favour with selection for a position. It is therefore a sitting duck in the crosshairs of the whole group of linguistic issues identified earlier.

If you are a medico or an engineer or other professional, engrossed in and preoccupied with your speciality, you will likely ignore management theory until it starts

S. K. McGrath, *Speaking Management*,
https://doi.org/10.1007/978-981-16-2213-7_18

to become important for your ego and/or financial and/or career progression. You may well then assume that somebody else has rigorously figured out all the theory and that the frameworks that you are presented with are all consistent with each other and mesh neatly together. Oh, dear!

Unfortunately, framework marketing success does not equate with the realisation of universal truth. Some inconsistencies may slowly become obvious and grate mildly with you, but you are likely be too busy to take too much notice of that, let alone take the time or trouble to research it, or go against supposed 'proven' truth and its associated peer-pressure and organisational propaganda. So you will very likely, unwittingly play your part in perpetuating myths in the practitioner community. If this goes on for long enough and remains outside the realms of academic checking, it will eventually come to be accepted as fact by later-generation academics dependent upon industry for funding their research. The chances of recognising the inconsistencies reduce as blind belief in the practices (indeed 'best practice') becomes more entrenched and the 10 steps to grand disaster (McGrath & Whitty, 2020) (see Sect. 18.10) are well underway.

This Part is written from the perspective of a long-suffering cynic, no longer constrained to appear to believe the corporate speak necessary to curry favour with, or at least avoid offending, any sensitive more senior/powerful ego whose propaganda departments (PR & HR) have duly hoisted their petard to some dubious invented framework or some pithy and supposedly deeply meaningful slogan. This Part gives circumstances, guidance and examples based upon the academic work in the preceding Parts, laced with some acerbic commentary on basic human nature.

Contested and confused concepts are presented here within their group of associated terminology, commencing with the old chestnut of accountability and proceeding through governance, power, stakeholders, leadership and ethics before looking at the meaning of meaning, soul, essence and truth as a group. For each of these, key distinguishing features are given; what it is and what it isn't, what it looks like when you have it and when you don't, and whether you are dealing with it or not. Circumstances, contexts and qualifiers are clarified before identifying the traps that previous understandings and definitions of the terms have fallen into.

18.2 Re-ordering of Rule Numbers

The derivation of definitional issues and rules in Part I produced 10 of each, but their numbers were allocated as they were developed and so rule numbers did not correspond with trap/issue numbers. For simplicity of reference and ease of usage in this Part, the rules need to be re-ordered. Issues 2 and 7 did not lend themselves to direct antidote rules whereas the other eight did, and there were two rules that did not directly correspond to those Issues but were not incompatible with them. Consequently, the issue/trap numbers have remained the same as developed in Part I, but the rule numbers have been slightly rearranged and new lower-case Roman numerals assigned to them in the third column of Table 18.1 as follows, while retaining reference to the original Arabic rule number.

18.3 Accountability and Responsibility

Table 18.2 outlines are the key features of these concepts.

The real questions about accountability are for what and to whom. Accountability can be to an individual entity (a person, a company or a government) or to a group. If you work for an entity that acts for a group, your accountability is to the entity and its authorised representatives, not to the group. It is the head of that entity that is accountable to the group. Making decisions regarding what is best for the group is therefore their accountability, not yours, even though you may well have a view on that, and some influence.

When an organisation and its leaders expect the good of the group to be the basis of employee recommendations, then alignment of values can occur. This become complex when the basis for recommendations and consequent decisions tends towards the good of a particular individual (or their beliefs). Decisions may then be based on retention or maximisation of their power so that their interest or view can be advanced. While some may take a dim view of this, it makes no difference to the

Table 18.1 Traps and rule numbering

Issue = Trap		Rules	
#	Description	#	Description
1	Fact v opinion (attitudes)	(i)	1: Exclude attitudes from definition
2	Meaning v representation	(ii)	6: Use the Mangle to resolve contention for conceptual terms
3	Word v phrase meanings	(iii)	2: Identify any silent or assumed qualifiers
4	Dogma v human framework	(iv)	3: Exclude beliefs from definition
5	Secular v ethereal essence (beliefs)	(v)	4: Exclude ethereal significations from the definition of unqualified terms with dual simultaneous meanings such as 'essence' by adding the qualifiers 'ethereal' or 'secular' to them
6	Intension v extension	(vi)	5: Define by intension rather than by extension where-ever possible
7	Objects v concepts	(vii)	8: In defining a system, recognize the connections between its parts
8	Detail v overview	(viii)	7: Use precision only to the point where clarity is reached
9	Process v content	(ix)	9: Consider process and content separately
10	Set v sub-set	(x)	10: Identify the context within which the term is being defined and refrain from making any generalisations that have not been tested outside that context

Table 18.2 Key features of accountability and responsibility

Term	What it is	What it isn't	Features
Accountability	Liability for ensuring a task is satisfactorily done.	Doing the work	Can't be delegated
Responsibility	Obligation to satisfactorily perform a task.	Signing off on acceptance	Can be delegated
Accountable	Having liability for ensuring a task is satisfactorily done.		
Responsible	Accepting an obligation to satisfactorily perform a task.		
Account	A report or description of an event or experience.		

accountability situation. See Rules (i) and (iv) which exclude normative matters from consideration in definition.

If you don't have authority to sign off for your organisation on acceptance (of the report, final product, work quality, project scope, spending or whatever), you may well be responsible for doing something, but you are not accountable to the organisation for it; you may be accountable to your boss for performing according to your duty statement, but that is a different accountability. Failing to make this distinction drops you into Trap 3 (word vs phrase meanings) and breaks Rule (iii)(2) (identify any silent or assumed qualifiers).

A Responsibility Assignment Matrix (RAM) is about responsibility, not accountability. It lists only tasks. This would seem rather obvious, but the popular RACI code which attempts to allocate accountability within a responsibility matrix gets this completely confused. The difficulty and confusion caused by including accountability in a RAM can be avoided by including approval as a task for which someone is responsible. That allows it to be time scheduled and by default, denotes where accountability lies without causing confusion. Accountability sounds so much more important than responsibility but attempting to puff up responsibility by labelling it as accountability is just window-dressing to impress and can serve to avoid and confound true accountability.

Sources of accountability can be legislative, organisational, contractual or informal. These can control matters such as financial dealings and payments, procurement and staff recruitment. These are likely to be subject to different delegations. It is necessary to be specific regarding which accountability is being referred to. Vague references to general accountability serve little effective purpose.

You may delegate responsibility for tasks to staff and then hold them accountable to you for the quality of their work. They may, in effect, 'sign off' on the quality of their work that is presented to you, but they cannot sign off on behalf of the organisation. You can require them to fix it or do something different i.e. you can convert a responsibility of yours into an accountability for somebody else to you if you have the authority to do so i.e. responsibility can get converted to a new accountability, but it is to a different person. You cannot delegate any accountability that is delegated to you.

These definitions of accountability and responsibility were resolved by applying the mangle Rule (ii)(6) and:

- avoiding normative considerations (value judgements) – Trap 1/Rule (i)(1) attitudes, Trap 4/Rule (iv)(3) beliefs and Trap 4/Rule (v)(4) human frameworks.
- avoiding unnecessarily detailed inclusions (Trap 8/Rule (viii)(7)).

18.4 Governance

Table 18.3 addresses the key (essential) features of this concept.

Implementing this table results in:

- exclusion of some items that have been purloined into existing definitions of governance, notably strategy and ethics
- relegation to organisational governance arrangements of some items that have been seen by some as part of governance, thereby separating process from content
- exclusion of accountability from the definition of governance and inclusion of accountability in the definition of organisational governance.

The terms developed are generic and are applicable across the whole governance ambit – national and international, private and governmental as well as political power structures of whatever nature – democratic, autocratic, monarchical, dictatorial, communist or other form.

The terms 'corporate governance' and 'board' sound awfully important. Power is intoxicating to be around, provided you don't get on the wrong side of it. Governance-speak is impressive. It is important for career progression to appear to know what it is. It can be even more important to be heard dropping governance words liberally, whether they make any sense or not, as there's a fair chance that whoever you are dropping them in front of won't know either.

If you are playing this game, then you are inflating the importance of your own words to impress others and/or increase your influence. Attempting to influence or impress is fine but doing it in this way can confuse others and is for your benefit only, not theirs. So why do it? Consider exercising the restraint required for this as undergoing an adolescent tribal initiation ceremony, demonstrating to the group that you can suffer pain for the greater good and so be trusted and accepted. If conceptual words have greater long-term impact than guns, then there's serious damage (diminished productivity, unnecessary wastage of scarce resources or time) you can do to wider groups you are a member of if you don't get this sorted. It can also usefully be regarded as basic hygiene/toilet training, which is for everybody's benefit: it stops the spread of dangerous viral notions.

Governance is a very important sounding idea that has been hijacked by various interests to gain advantage and influence. Understanding and removing this influence using the Table 18.3 will be uncomfortable for some, but can lead to clarity for many, resulting in the avoidance of confusion and misunderstanding, avoiding their

Table 18.3 Key features of governance terms

Term	What it is	What it isn't	Features
Govern	To direct and control.		
Governance	The system by which an entity is directed and controlled.	Accountability, Corporate Governance (that's governance of a particular type of entity – a joint-stock company)	A dictator is unaccountable but will still have effective or 'good' governance.
Organisational governance	The system by which an organisation is directed, controlled and held to account.	Strategy, ethics, PR, management, leadership, decision-making, coordinating, rationalising or relationships.	Accountability is necessary when more than one person governs i.e. authority is shared. You need more than one person to have an organisation.
Decision-making		Governance	However, allocating the authority to make decisions is part of organisational governance arrangements.
Corporate governance	Governance of one type of organisation – a corporation, which is based on the joint-stock company model.	Governance of a government organisation	Any usage referring to government is a misnomer.
Project governance	Governance of a project.		
Public governance	Governance of one type of organisation – a publicly controlled or government organisation.	Governance of a joint-stock company or private sector organisation	Any use referring to joint-stock companies is inappropriate.
Organisational governance arrangements	The component parts of organisational governance – an entity's structure, positions, rules, decision making processes and reporting arrangements.	Governance or organisational governance	The qualifiers are necessary for sense to be made and internal consistency of definition to be maintained.

consequent waste of time, resources and money. This can benefit organisations both public and private as well as their taxpayers, shareholders and the general public.

Previous definitions have:

- fallen into Trap 3 (word vs phrase meanings), confusing governance with corporate governance and breaking Rule (iii)(2) (identify any silent or assumed qualifiers)
- not abided by Rule (vii)(8) requiring the system or connections between parts to be recognised

- fallen into Trap 8 (including too much detail), much of which was unwarranted and led to breaking Rule (viii)(7) (inclusion of strategy and ethics) and
- fallen into Trap 9, not separating process from content (governance from governance arrangements), thereby breaking Rule (ix)(9).

18.5 Power

Table 18.4 addresses the key features of power terms.

These definitions contain no evaluation of social or political theory. They accommodate biological, political, social or mechanical power. They dispel the definitional disdain in our linguistic usage promoted by Wittgenstein's family resemblance concept of meaning. The arrangement of non-contested terms and the machinery of power diagram in Chap. 12 give an internally consistent set of terms and a pictorial representation that shows the locus of previous theories of power. Power is a simple word that needs definition; it is not its means of exercise, nor techniques for harnessing it, important as those things may be.

Table 18.4 Key features of power terms

Term	What it is	What it isn't	Features
Legitimate (a)	Condoned by those with authority and accepted by the group affected.	Authority	Both elements are necessary.
Legitimacy (n)	The quality of being legitimate, or the quality of being condoned by those with authority and accepted by the group affected.	Authority	Both elements are necessary.
Authority (n)	The right to make decisions, give orders and enforce obedience.	Power	It enables the exercise of power.
Power (n)	The capacity to act (whether exercised through authority, force or influence).	Authority, Power to, over or with, or anything to do with how it is exercised.	This defines the unqualified term. Power may or may not rely on authority.
Influence (v)	To affect the thoughts or actions of an entity and (n) the effect of one entity upon another.	Power generically	It's one form of power.
Direct (v)	To give orders, commands or instructions.		
Direction (n)	An order, command or instruction.		
Control (v)	To ensure that actions occur in a particular way.		
Regulate (v)	Control by rule, principle, law, restriction, policy or method.		
Regulation (n)	A rule, law or method as well as the act or process of regulating.		

The issues that had to be resolved in applying the mangle (Rule (ii)(6) to defining power were:

- identifying and removing presumed qualifiers, allowing definition of the word rather than a phrase containing it (Trap 3, Rule (iii)(2)) (the will to power and power to/over/with, expert/referent power, episodic/dispositional/facilitative etc. etc.)
- defining by intension rather than extension (Trap 6/Rule (vi)(5)) as defining by extension tempts omission, as well as all the other errors listed here
- removing confusing and unnecessary detail (Trap 8/Rule (viii)(7)) (such as legal, political, governmental, religious or supernatural, familial, astrological, mathematical)
- separating process from content (Trap 9/Rule (ix)(9)) (such as power to/over/with)
- identifying contexts and removing any impingement upon definition that resulted in them defining non generic sub-sets (Trap 10/Rule (x)(10)) (such as legal, political, governmental, religious or supernatural, familial, astrological, mathematical)
- removing normative considerations Trap 1/Rule (i)(1) attitudes and Trap 4/Rule (v)(4) human frameworks, Trap 5/Rule (iv)(3) beliefs as well as Trap 4 concerning dogma (such as political, governmental, religious or supernatural, familial, astrological)
- removing unnecessary detail, Trap 8, Rule (viii)(7), which is introduced by all the above.

Previous definitions of power have previously fallen into every trap and broken every rule except (vii)(8). Some of these had triggers extending like tripwires into other traps.

While in theory, all the issues/traps are quite different, in practice, some cases can involve combinations of them such that it may be difficult to determine which is the most critical or causative one.

18.6 Stakeholders and Customers

Table 18.5 addresses the key features of these concepts.

Note that specifying stakeholder type explicitly specifies the silent or assumed qualifier of Issue 3 as per Rule (iii)(2) and avoids the conflict of fighting over exclusive use of the base term.

Note also that the particular activity referred to may be a task, a project, a program, an undertaking of a corporation or government entity or even a particular instance of a person's behaviour.

There are many things of great importance in determining **how** stakeholders should be managed that are completely irrelevant to determining **what** they are i.e. whether they are a stakeholder or not. Examples of such irrelevancies include:

Table 18.5 Key features of stakeholder terms

Term	What it is	What it isn't	Features
Stake	An interest.		
Stakeholder	An entity with a stake (interest) in the subject activity.	Any particular type of stakeholder.	Based on an activity, not a joint stock company model. Accommodates all types of organisations as well as individual behaviour.
Invested stakeholder	One who has some control of the activity.	An end-user who strongly opposes the activity.	Does not need to be treated in the same way as secondary and tertiary stakeholders.
Committed stakeholder	One who is committed to the activity occurring (with some control).		
Uncommitted stakeholder	One who is un-committed to the activity occurring (with potential to influence).		
Contributing or primary stakeholder	One whose participation is required to sustain the activity.		
Observer or secondary stakeholder	One whose acceptance or compliance is required to sustain the activity.		
End user or tertiary stakeholder	One who uses the output of the activity.		
Customer	One who receives some value from an activity.		There are two types of customers who may or may not be the same person/entity.
Output customer	One who receives the output of an activity.	Universally who pays.	It's who receives the output. In some government programs, the output customer may pay for the service or may pay a negative price i.e. receive a benefit payment.
Outcome customer	One who receives the outcome of an activity.		The intended beneficiary who makes use of the output.

- the degree of risk they pose
- their power or legitimacy
- the urgency of their issue
- whether they are claimant or influencer, normative or derivative, dangerous or dormant, competitors, activists, terrorists, or the media
- the sustainability of the activity
- the ethics of the organisation undertaking the activity
- the difficulty of identifying who individual stakeholders and stakeholder groups are.

Including in definition (the 'what') items determining how stakeholders will be managed (the 'how') introduces Issue 9, breaking Rule (ix)(9) which requires process and content to be separated.

Early stakeholder theory considered only joint-stock company shareholders as stakeholders. Freeman's stakeholder theory was a big step forward in removing that restriction, but it failed to see or remove the company restriction i.e. it ignored or omitted that qualifier, thus falling into Trap 3 and breaking Rule (iii)(2). Leaving in the unnecessary (company) detail also introduced Trap 8, breaking Rule (viii)(7) requiring precision to be used to the point where clarity is reached. It also introduced Trap 10, considering a sub-set to be the full set, thereby breaking Rule (x)(10) requiring the context to be identified before generalising. This all created difficulty for individual and government use, especially around law enforcement and customers.

Once evidence has been found indicating that any of the 10 rules of linguistic usage have been broken in a field's usage of a term, the field needs to go back to first principles and start again, developing consistent terminology that follows all the rules before moving forward.

18.7 Leadership

Table 18.6 addresses the key features of these concepts.

While some people may have an aura of leadership and/or authority which may assist in inducing other people to follow, we know that leadership can be taught and so it is not something genetic that a person either possesses or not. It is also not something that can be exercised continuously. For example, we generally lead our children, but they will at times lead us i.e. show us the way that we will agree to follow, whether we like it or not. And that is much more likely to be due to circumstances that arise where their will is stronger than ours, rather than our innate leadership qualities having been genetically passed on. So leadership is not an ethereal thing and is independent of relative physical size or age. Giving a lead becomes effective when somebody follows. The reason for their agreeing to follow does not matter. It may be free choice, or fear of the consequences from a military commander or a dictator, or anything in between, such as obligation. The definitions are independent of all these things.

If my lead is not accepted, then I have no choice but to abandon leading and shift into managing.

The issues that had to be resolved in applying the mangle to these leadership and management terms were:

- identifying and removing presumed qualifiers (the word 'good' in this case), allowing definition of the word rather than a phrase containing it (Trap 3, Rule (ii)(2))
- defining by intension rather than extension (Trap 6/Rule (vi)(5)) (by rejecting the extensions of the Rost (1991) definition given in Chap. 15).

Table 18.6 Key features of leadership terms

Term	What it is	What it isn't	Features
Plan	A detailed proposal for doing or achieving something.	Strategy	Contains detailed actions that may be based on some strategy.
Control	To ensure that actions occur in a particular way.		
Direct	To give orders, commands or instructions.		
Lead	To show the way.	Manage	Constitutes an invitation to follow.
Leader	One who shows the way.	Manager	Although a manager may also lead.
Leadership	The ability to show the way and to induce others to follow.	Management	
Strategy	The pattern in a series of actions.	A plan	It is broad, short and doesn't include a plan, although it may append or refer to one (an implementation plan).
Manage	To take charge.	Leading	Although a leader may also manage.
Management	The act of taking charge (managing).	Leadership	
Strategic management	The act of taking charge of the pattern in a series of future actions.		

- removing confusing and unnecessary detail (Trap 8/Rule (viii)(7)) (again by removing the unnecessary specifics of the Rost (1991) definition).
- separating process from content (Trap 9/Rule (ix)(9)) on confusion between the subject of the (English grammatical) rules and the rules themselves, or between the use of the tool (or rule or artefact) and the tool itself (again by removing references to the particular content area of inspirational leadership).
- identifying contexts and removing any impingement upon definition that resulted in them defining non-generic sub-sets (Trap 10/Rule (x)(10)) (again by removing the context of inspirational leadership).
- removing normative considerations (Trap 1/Rule (i)(1) attitudes and Trap 4/Rule (v)(4) human frameworks, Trap 5/Rule (iv)(3) beliefs (all achieved by removing association with the word 'good').

As with power, previous definitions of leadership have previously fallen into every trap and broken every rule except (vii)(8).

The problem of treating and defining a general term within the boundary of a particular field (mistaking a sub-set for the full set) appears to occur when authors in that field do not recognize their preoccupation with that field. This seems to lead to overlooking the grammatical rules of the English language game and creation of private language, specific to that particular field. This causes a problem when subsequent attempts are made to apply it generically outside that field.

Another trend observed was the tendency for simplicity of understanding and expression to become lost in confused complexity over time, such as occurred in strategic management where the 1978 definition of strategy was found to be closer to the essential meaning than any subsequent one.

18.8 Ethics

Table 18.7 addresses the key features of ethics.

These derived definitions essentially state that principles are rules, values are preferences, beliefs are propositions that an individual or entity considers valid, and ethics and morals are principles restraining individual behaviour in the civic and individual areas respectively.

The term ethics is often used assuming it means good ethics, and ethics regarded as bad are often considered to be not ethics at all. This causes confusion. Particular morals, principles, ethics and beliefs may be considered true or false and these definitions do not judge that. A person could be considered within their own society to be moral yet be judged immoral by another society. For example, the German people before World War II accepted the superiority of the Aryan race, believed in it, and took the consequent, difficult 'moral' (for them) action of exterminating Jews,

Table 18.7 Key features of ethics terms

Term	What it is	What it isn't	Features
Good	That which we consider to be useful.		Contains no value judgement.
Bad	That which we consider to be a hinderance.		Contains no value judgement.
Opinion	A view or judgement formed about something, not necessarily based on fact or knowledge.		
Attitude	A settled way of thinking about something.		
Ethics	Principles of civic behaviour that restrain individual behaviour for a higher purpose.	Good or bad	Contains no value judgement.
Principle	A rule guiding action.		
Principles	A set of rules guiding action.		
Value	The quantity of satisfaction of an interest.		
Values	Preferences guiding the actions of an entity.		Contains no value judgement.
Belief	A proposition an entity considers valid.		
Beliefs	Propositions an entity considers valid.		
Moral (n)	In accordance with a principle of interpersonal behaviour that restrains individual behaviour for a higher purpose.		Contains no value judgement.
Morals (n)	Principles of interpersonal behaviour that restrain individual behaviour for a higher purpose.		Contains no value judgement.

which other societies considered completely immoral. The derived definitions accommodate this and are therefore free of value judgement. The serious error in the German starting position is a separate matter which can be adequately described without introducing unnecessary definitional confusion.

The principal feature of all these definitions is the absence of value judgement. This avoids Traps 1 Fact vs Opinion, 4 Dogma vs human framework (c.f. reification in Chap. 14) and 5 Secular vs ethereal essence. The derived definitions follow Rule (i)(1) excluding attitudes, Rule (iv)(3) excluding beliefs, and Rule (v)(4) excluding ethereal significations. Excluding all such normative considerations was the key to making secular sense of all these terms.

Deriving these definitions also required addressing denotation. We can sense things without being able to necessarily express them exactly in words. Using the framework or tool we call language is just one way of representing what we experience. Tonality, volume, gestures and body language are others. This is Trap 2 – distinguishing meaning from representation or seeking meaning in the words themselves rather than in what they denote or signify.

The view that emerges from this work is that there is no universal morality; there is only resolution of competing interests (conflict resolution), and there can be only three outcomes for an entity; win, lose or compromise (see Chap. 14).

18.9 Meaning, Soul, Essence and Truth

Table 18.8 addresses the key features of these concepts.

A most important distinction here is between definition and meaning. Definition applies only to labels or noises that we call words. Meaning applies to more than words e.g. feelings and the other senses.

Soul is effectively defined as a physical thing that can be felt but not seen by humans. It (life force = some form of electro-magnetic energy) can be observed (converted into something we can see) through Kirlian photography. This is similar to sound waves that we cannot see being converted by an ultrasound machine into pictures that we can see. Soul therefore cannot exist purely in an ethereal dimension. The definition does not preclude it having such ethereal existence, it simply does not rely on that. This begs the question of whether we have historically just reified something we cannot see such that we have attributed it with an ethereal existence that it does not have. That would seem highly likely, with significant implications for religion in general, but this is not further explored here.

Note that the definitions here imply that the phrase 'meaning of life' makes no sense, whereas the phrase 'purpose of life' does.

While there may be no absolute truth in definition, to be productive as a society, a discourse that removes confusion is necessary so that all can participate with shared understanding of meaning, removing accidental and undetected differences, so that we may have order rather than chaos. This requires agreeing on definitions and then, and only then, regarding them as if they were absolute. The measure of

Table 18.8 Key features of Meaning, soul, essence and truth

Term	What it is	What it isn't	Features
Concept	An abstract idea (Oxford).	A physical object	It can't be seen.
Term	A word or phrase used to describe a thing or to express a concept (Oxford).		
Define	To state what is signified by a term.		
Definition	A statement of what is signified by a term.	The thing itself	
Mean	Intend to convey.		
Meaning	What is intended to be conveyed.	Purpose	
Normative	Including an opinion	Objective	
Process	A series of actions or steps taken in order to achieve a particular end (Oxford).	The content it is applied to.	
Purpose	The reason for which something is done or created or for which something exists.	Meaning	
Soul	Life-force.		An unseen physical thing
Essence	A property or group of properties of something without which it would not be what it is.	How it is handled or managed.	
Essential definition	A definition in terms of essence only.	It is not the how, when, where or why.	It is the what only.
Content [mass noun]	The material or subject matter dealt with in or by a process, form or style.	Process	
Truth	The quality of being in accordance with the facts.		

truth is then that it is "in accordance with the fact" of agreement having been reached on its definition.

As in ethics above, these definitions are independent of value judgement. This avoids Issues (Traps) 1 Fact vs Opinion, 4 Dogma vs human framework (c.f. reification in good for paper) and 5 Secular vs ethereal essence. The definition of soul also avoids Issue 7 as it is a concept, not an object, so has no physical existence that can be seen. We may be able to feel or sense it in some other way. Its physical existence is limited to the electromagnetic and other impulses in our bodies and brains.

The derived definitions avoid Traps 1, 5 and 9 by following Rule (i)(1) excluding attitudes, Rule (v)(4) excluding ethereal significations and Rule (ix)(9) separating process from content.

18.10 Avoiding the Disaster Cycle

The McGrath and Whitty (2020) ten steps to grand disaster were mentioned in Sect. 18.1. This shows how a conceptual error can progress to mature solidity and grand disaster as follows:

1. Someone has an idea with some merit in some context
2. The idea spreads within that context
3. Wishful thinking occurs about its applicability to everyone/everything else
4. The originator or early converts write a text/book and/or keep asserting its genericity
5. The idea becomes reified, attracting acolytes and commercial interest
6. Zealous, evangelistic marketing occurs, and niggling difficulties are ignored
7. 'Thinking people', keeping up with modern trends, accept it as fact
8. It becomes a fad and people's livelihoods come to depend upon it
9. General delusion occurs and 'group think' suppresses any questioning
10. A paradigm/quantum shift is then necessary to dislodge it.

By the time phase 7 is reached, outcomes (reputations, positions and profits) are locked in. The consequences of the disaster for the recipients is unaffected by whether the proponents are attempting to do 'good' or 'bad'. As the proverb (of unknown source) says: "The road to hell is paved with good intentions".

Two examples can serve to demonstrate this. One is Wittgenstein's family resemblance concept. As discussed comprehensively in Part I, it has permeated much of western philosophical thinking since his time. It must have seemed like a good and convincing idea at the time, but it has reached Phase 10, generated much philosophical confusion, and now needs to be dislodged, as demonstrated earlier.

The other is creating a society modelled on Plato's republic, which could have been considered a noble task. Rigid belief in and adherence to it, together with some legitimate as well as some dubious extensions of it, were labelled National Socialism and subsequently Nazism. It passed through Phase 4 with publication of *Mein Kampf* and reached Phase 10 in Germany. It required a World War to dislodge it, costing 5.5 million lives. Too bad that the city-state ideology of Plato's Republic, which Hitler and others throughout history were inspired by, had been rendered obsolete by Alexander the Great's conquests when Plato's ink was barely dry. Although 'National Socialism' was somewhat of a misnomer, socialism itself has not fared well either, with its implementations labelled communism repeatedly descending into totalitarianism with great loss of life.

This general cycle can therefore have dire consequences across a wide range of human endeavour.

Our tendency to generalise from our experience can be insightful, but it can also be dangerous if that knowledge has boundary limitations we are unaware of. It can become even more dangerous if we start dogmatically implementing and enforcing it without adequately responding to difficulties with it, particularly when that involves taking hold of the reins of government.

We would perhaps be well served by regarding 'ism's, e.g. political parties and religions, as places where people with all the same ideas can get together and find out how they really don't work! But what do they do when they find that something about it doesn't work and their careers, reputations, followings, egos and family livelihoods have been built around them?

There is no simple answer to this question once the problem has been created and reached Phase 10. However, recognising what is happening is a good start which can make a contribution to stopping the accidental generation of such future problems. It shines sunlight on their source, potentially catching them at Phase 3, enabling the rest of the disaster cycle and its consequences to be avoided.

References

McGrath, S. K., & Whitty, S. J. (2020). The suitability of PRINCE2 for engineering infrastructure. *The Journal of Modern Project Management, 7(4)*(22), 312–347.

Rost, J. C. (1991). *Leadership for the twenty-first century*. Praeger.

Chapter 19
Observations and Conclusions

19.1 Observations

The times when we might start to fight each other are:

1. When we don't like something about the other person
2. When we don't understand what they were talking about or some words they used
3. When we have a genuine conflict, i.e. when we are actually competing for something we value.

This book provides tools that can assist with 1 but primarily deals with 2 and does not deal with 3. It contains the theoretical basis for what can be labelled '**conflict dissolution**' – alignment of understandings of key concepts that removes conceptual misunderstanding as a source of conflict. It therefore deals with a precursor to conflict resolution, rather than with conflict resolution per se. It removes unnecessary conflict where the parties do not realize they actually agree – simply because of their differing understandings of conceptual words. This may seem an unlikely occurrence but is actually quite common, as the case studies presented in this book demonstrate.

This book also highlights a general human tendency to look for **patterns** and generalise from them without adequately checking their applicability to other circumstances/boundaries/contexts. The Chapters of Part II demonstrate how easy and common it is for experienced practitioners to become victims of their own pattern seeking – the 'practitioners trap'; as Haidt (2012) said "people who devote their lives to studying something often come to believe that the object of their fascination is the key to understanding everything".

An extension of this occurs when we assume that, because we have advanced so far materially since the industrial revolution, we can now **control** everything and have anything we want, at a time of our choosing, whether it is material (i.e. absolute) or relative (dependent upon other people). This lacks specification of

S. K. McGrath, *Speaking Management*,
https://doi.org/10.1007/978-981-16-2213-7_19

appropriate context and stops one level of diarrhesis short, pretending that people can be regarded as objects or machines. Physical things are absolute and prototypes/gadgets either work or they don't. But matters of interactions between people are relative and much less predictable and context dependent. Our ability to develop rules of thumb in those relative matters can lead us to draw conclusions that omit consideration of all the necessary circumstances, qualifications and boundary conditions. This assumption of control over everything can perhaps be described as the hubris of our age. It drops straight into the abovementioned disaster cycle.

A further extension also not previously mentioned here is that **exaggeration for dramatic effect (influence) does not equal truth or fact** but can easily be mistaken for such when it transitions into mythology and dogma-when others take our words literally or we start to believe our own propaganda.

All of these tendencies are counter-productive when seeking clarity of definition and can be mitigated by being specific about what it is we are actually talking about, using the techniques developed in this book. As noted in Chap. 13, lack of transparency of definition is a significant governance issue that is not tolerated in other areas of governance in western democracies.

We use the tool we call language for all sorts of purposes other than to exactly specify fact. We use it to persuade, soothe, entertain, trick, exaggerate, self-promote etc. etc. It is these latter activities that give life its spice. Why would we want to not use language in those ways? But when is it that we really need to become pedantic about our language use? It is when we need to prove, understand or report something. It is then that dropping our environmental manipulation tricks that serve our individual competitive survival/welfare/convenience becomes useful.

We seek patterns to make sense of the world and once we find one, we can then so easily jump to the conclusion that it is universally true without adequately considering its circumstances and boundary conditions. The standard of proof we apply is so often deficient.

So we have to regain control of this language tool that our ancestors invented. We need to recognise that we have overlooked reaching agreement on the meaning of some very important conceptual words and do something about it by using the agreement generation device, namely the Mangle as detailed in Chap. 10 of Part II.

19.2 Conclusion

This book has demonstrated the importance of making sure we all have the same understanding of the conceptual words we use before focusing our energy on changing the opinions or behaviours of others about those concepts, or before we start fighting over them. Achieving this would require a shift from what can be labelled as a 'disagree first, define later' paradigm to an alternative one of 'define first, disagree later'. This should not be so difficult to bring about; the means of doing so are under all of our individual control and involve simply becoming aware of linguistic traps so we can avoid them. This does not require introduction of or belief in any grand social system intended to maximize happiness. It does not require any cathartic mystical experience. It just requires firstly a little knowledge of linguistic traps and then a little self-discipline in avoiding them that few people currently realise is necessary. The potential for reducing the amount of conflict in our personal and organisational lives is surely worth it.

Reference

Haidt, J. (2012). *The righteous mind: Why good people are divided by politics and religion*. Pantheon Books.

Appendix – Lexicon of Contested and Associated Terms

Table A.1 lists in in alphabetical order all 70 terms defined in Parts I and II (Table A.1).

Table A.1 Definitions from Parts I and II

Term	Definition
Account	A report or description of an event or experience.
Accountability	Liability for ensuring a task is satisfactorily done.
Accountable	Having liability for ensuring a task is satisfactorily done.
Attitude	A settled way of thinking about something.
Authority (n)	The right to make decisions, give orders and enforce obedience.
Bad	That which we consider to be a hinderance.
Belief	A proposition an entity considers valid.
Beliefs	Propositions an entity considers valid.
Committed stakeholder	One who is committed to the activity occurring (with some ability to control it).
Concept	An abstract idea (Oxford).
Content [mass noun]	The material or subject matter dealt with in or by a process, form or style.
Contributing or primary stakeholder	One whose participation is required to sustain the activity.
Control (v)	To ensure that actions occur in a particular way.
Corporate governance	Organisational governance of a corporation = the system by which a corporation is directed and controlled and held to account.
Customer	One who receives some value from an activity.
Define	To state what is signified by a term.
Definition	A statement of what is signified by a term.
Direct (v)	To give orders.
Direction (n)	An order.
End user or tertiary stakeholder	One who uses the output of the activity.

(continued)

S. K. McGrath, *Speaking Management*,
https://doi.org/10.1007/978-981-16-2213-7

Table A.1 (continued)

Term	Definition
Essence	A property or group of properties of something without which it would not be what it is.
Essential definition	A definition in terms of essence only.
Ethics	Principles of civic behaviour that restrain individual behaviour for a higher purpose.
Good	That which we consider to be useful.
Govern	To direct and control.
Governance	The system by which an entity is directed and controlled.
Government	An entity that controls a geographic area
Influence (v)	To affect the thoughts or actions of an entity and (n) the effect of one entity upon another.
Invested stakeholder	One who has some control of the activity.
Lead	To show the way.
Leader	One who shows the way.
Leadership	The ability to show the way and to induce others to follow.
Legitimate (a)	Condoned by those with authority in the particular circumstance.
Legitimacy (n)	The quality of being legitimate, or the quality of being condoned by those with authority in the particular circumstance.
Manage	To take charge.
Management	The act of taking charge (managing).
Mean	Intend to convey.
Meaning	What is intended to be conveyed.
Meaning of life	Nil. The purpose of life is a separate question that does make grammatical sense.
Moral (a)	In accordance with a principle of interpersonal behaviour that restrains individual behaviour for a higher purpose.
Morals (n)	Principles of interpersonal behaviour that restrain individual behaviour for a higher purpose.
Normative	Including an opinion
Observer or secondary stakeholder	One whose acceptance or compliance is required to sustain the activity.
Opinion	A view or judgement formed about something, not necessarily based on fact or knowledge.
Organisational governance	The system by which an organisation is directed, controlled and held to account.
Organisational governance arrangements	The component parts of organisational governance – an entity's structure, positions, rules, decision making processes and reporting arrangements.
Outcome customer	One who receives the outcome of an activity.
Output customer	One who receives the output of an activity.
Plan	A detailed proposal for doing or achieving something.
Power (n)	The capacity to act (whether exercised through authority, force or influence).

(continued)

Table A.1 (continued)

Term	Definition
Principle	A rule guiding action.
Principles	A set of rules guiding action.
Process	A series of actions or steps taken in order to achieve a particular end (Oxford).
Purpose	The reason for which something is done or created or for which something exists.
Project governance	Governance of a project.
Public governance	Organisational governance of a publicly owned (i.e. government) entity. = the system by which a publicly owned (i.e. government) entity is directed, controlled and held to account.
Regulate (v)	Control by rule, principle, law, restriction, policy or method.
Regulation (n)	A rule, law or method (countable) and the act or process of regulating (uncountable).
Responsibility	Obligation to satisfactorily perform a task.
Responsible	Accepting an obligation to satisfactorily perform a task.
Soul	Life-force.
Stake	An interest.
Stakeholder	An entity with a stake (interest) in the subject activity.
Strategy	The pattern in a series of actions.
Strategic management	The act of taking charge of the pattern in a series of future actions.
Term	A word or phrase used to describe a thing or to express a concept (Oxford).
Truth	The quality of being in accordance with the facts.
Uncommitted stakeholder	One who is not committed to the activity occurring (with potential to influence it).
Value	The quantity of satisfaction of an interest.
Values	Preferences guiding the actions of an entity.

There is another group of terms relating specifically to project management that have been the subject of similar definitional exercises. These were published in international journal papers which developed 18 definitions of terms dealing with or associated with projects, programs and portfolios as well as with project management methodology (McGrath and Whitty, 2019, 2020). These are of more specialist project management nature and so chapters on them have not been included in this book. However, the definitions produced are potentially of broader interest due to the relationship they have with general management. These definitions have therefore been included in a separate Table A.2, which is also arranged in alphabetical order. This means that this Appendix contains definitions of all 88 terms defined to date using the Mangle approach.

Table A.2 Project management definitions

Term	Definition
Component project	Part of a larger project that cannot independently produce a required outcome.
Implementation	Initiating establishment if necessary (i.e. if not already existing), controlling through directing and setting timelines, giving approvals, monitoring, initiating corrective action where necessary, reviewing to determine future action and closing where necessary, all subject to any higher-level approvals that may be required.
Method	A procedure for approaching a task.
Methodology	A system of methods.
Operations	Ongoing activity enabled by completion of a project.
Organizational portfolio	A collection of an organization's activities that may include ongoing organizational operations, program(me)s of projects, individual projects not part of any program(me), and other works.
Organizational portfolio management	The activity of deciding and implementing parameters including objectives, strategy, funding, rules and selection criteria = business management.
Organizational portfolio management of projects	The activity of deciding and implementing program and project parameters including objectives, strategy, funding, rules and selection criteria.
Organizational program	A group of related projects.
Organizational program management	The activity of selecting and implementing projects including evaluating project inclusion and determining sequencing and delivery methods.
Organizational project	A sustained effort to change a situation.
Organizational project management	The activity of deciding and implementing work methods.
Portfolio	A diverse collection of things – such as items or activities.
Program(me)	A planned series of related things.
Project	An endeavour to create something.
Project Management Methodology (PMM)	A system of methods used in project management = an organization's process for managing the full lifecycle of its projects.
Schedule	A list of things – such as items or planned activities.
Sub-project	Part of a larger project that can independently produce a required outcome.

References

McGrath, S. K., & Whitty, S. J. (2019). What is a program: An examination of terminology in practitioner reference documents. *Journal of Modern Project Management, 6(3)*(18), 6–27.

McGrath, S. K., & Whitty, S. J. (2020). Practitioner views on project management methodology (PMM) effectiveness. *Journal of Modern Project management, 8(1)*(23), 188–215.